Empirical Research and Normative Theory

Empirical Research and Normative Theory

—

Transdisciplinary Perspectives on Two Methodical
Traditions Between Separation and Interdependence

Edited by
Alexander Max Bauer and Malte Ingo Meyerhuber

DE GRUYTER

ISBN 978-3-11-077707-9
e-ISBN (PDF) 978-3-11-061379-7
e-ISBN (EPUB) 978-3-11-061214-1

Library of Congress Control Number: 2020931456

Bibliographic information published by the Deutsche Nationalbibliothek
The Deutsche Nationalbibliothek lists this publication in the Deutsche Nationalbibliografie;
detailed bibliographic data are available on the Internet at http://dnb.dnb.de.

© 2021 Walter de Gruyter GmbH, Berlin/Boston
This volume is text- and page-identical with the hardback published in 2020.
Cover image: M.C. Escher's "Hand with Reflecting Sphere" © 2018 The M.C. Escher Company,
The Netherlands. All rights reserved. www.mcescher.com
Printing and binding: CPI books GmbH, Leck

www.degruyter.com

Foreword

There has long been an active and highly sophisticated debate, cutting across multiple disciplines, about the relationship between empirical science and normative theory. In recent years, however, this discussion has taken on a special urgency that it did not previously have. The key change has not arisen primarily from any shift in our understanding at a more abstract level of the relationship between the two fields. Rather, the change has come, at least in the first instance, from recent advances in our understanding of specific concrete issues in the empirical sciences themselves.

Back when I first entered academia, much of the work on the relationship between empirical science and normative theory had a more hypothetical or metaphilosophical character. Often, a paper would begin by asking the reader to imagine that scientists of the future find an answer to some question of normative importance. "Suppose scientists of the future uncover the factors that determine how happy a person feels". "Suppose scientists figure out precisely what is happening in people's minds when they make moral judgments". "Suppose scientists are able to remove your brain, place it in a vat, and stimulate it in such a way that you have precisely the experiences you would have if you were leading a deeply satisfying and rewarding life". The inquiry would then be concerned with what we should conclude within normative theory if empirical science ever did advance to this point.

As even a brief glance at the chapters included in this volume will show, work on these issues has taken a very different turn over the past few decades. We have seen truly remarkable strides within empirical science on exactly the sorts of questions that seem most directly relevant to normative theory and, as a direct result, the emergence of serious research programmes devoted to exploring in detail the implications of those findings. In short, work on these questions is no longer merely hypothetical or metaphilosophical; it is genuinely normative. The questions we face these days are mostly not of the form "Suppose scientists of the future..." but rather of the form "Given that empirical science actually has discovered..., what should we now conclude about how human beings ought to live?"

One of the most striking aspects of this new form of inquiry is its conspicuous interdisciplinarity. If we are to explore in any serious way the relationship between empirical research and normative theory, we will need to rely on insights from an enormous variety of different disciplines: philosophy, sure, but also psychology, sociology, political science, economics, and many others besides. The present volume therefore offers precisely what is needed – not simply a conversation among different researchers in the same discipline but a more far-reaching discussion that cuts across disciplines that were, at least at one time, far more insulated from one another. This is the discussion we need to be having, and one that I hope this volume will help to develop and further encourage.

New Haven, Connecticut, September 2019   Joshua Knobe

Preface

This volume sheds some light on the wide field of tension that opens up between is and ought. With the contributions gathered in it, we hope to provide you, the reader, with some interesting insights into the controversial debates surrounding the relationship between is and ought as well as between empirical research and normative theory. We invite you to join us and our authors in reflecting critically on this area of tension and wish you stimulating reading, just as we had a stimulating time compiling the volume. – It goes back to an international summer school on this topic, which took place from October 28 to 29, 2017. The event was organised by the editors as part of the "Oldenburg School for the Social Sciences and the Humanities" and featured contributions by Max Agostini, Martijn Boot, Maarten Derksen, Niklas Dworazik, Carlos A. de Matos Fernandes, Andrea Klonschinski, Jannis Kreienkamp, Marvin Kunz, Albert W. Musschenga, Elsa Romfeld, Hanno Sauer, Sebastian Schleidgen, Mark Schweda, and Lars Schwettmann, as well as two public lectures by Stefan Müller-Doohm and Philipp Hübl.

We would like to take this opportunity to thank all of them once again, as well as the Graduate School for Social Sciences and the Humanities (3GO) – especially its coordinator Rea Kodalle and our assistants Lukas Brüggen, Philipp Kochan, and Isabel Sturm – under whose roof the event took place. It was also made possible by the support of the Foundation and Innovation Centre, the General Student Committee (AStA), the Institute of Philosophy, as well as the Faculties II and IV of the Carl von Ossietzky University of Oldenburg, the Research Training Group "Self-Making – Practices of Subjectivation" of the German Research Foundation (DFG), and the doctoral programmes "Cultures of Participation" and "Border Formations in Migration Societies".

For both of us the present and the German volume *Philosophie zwischen Sein und Sollen – Normative Theorie und empirische Forschung im Spannungsfeld* were the first projects of this kind. Fortunately, we were able to fall back on the experience of others. Theory and practice, however, are two different pairs of shoes. And that's probably how it stands with experiences as well: You can hear or read about them; but making them yourself is something completely different. Christoph Schirmer and Tim Vogel of Walter de Gruyter, in particular, supported us in collecting these experiences and were always patient and helpful. Moreover, we thank Oliver Schoenbeck for important insights, Mark Siebel for his valuable support, as well as Oda Siqveland and Paloma Hammond of Springer for making James Konow's reprint possible. We also collected our experiences together with our authors, with whom it was a great pleasure to work together: Without Max Agostini, Kurt Beyertz, Daniel Füger, Carlos A. de Matos Fernandes, Guillermina

Jasso, James Konow, Jannis Kreienkamp, Marvin Kunz, Marcel Mertz, Sylke Meyerhuber, David Miller, Albert W. Musschenga, Norbert Paulo, Philip Penew, Elsa Romfeld, Sebastian Schleidgen, Reinhard Schulz, Mark Schweda, Lars Schwettmann, Widukind Andreas Schweiberer, Stephen J. Sullivan, and Peter Wiersbinski the present and the German volume wouldn't be what they are. Furthermore, we are grateful for the copy-editing by Gisella Vorderobermeier and Konrad Vorderobermeier. All remaining errors, of course, are our own. We would also like to thank Margareth Verbakel of the M.C. Escher Company for the opportunity to use Escher's "Hand with Reflecting Sphere" as a cover image.

Moreover, we have to thank our friends. Many thanks go to Wolfgang Altmann, Tobias Horst Bocklage, Ann-Christin Gerber, Emily Dora Heitmann, Kai Henke, Jonas Ferdinand Hilgefort, Hauke Kolweyh, Gerrit Kolweyh, Felix Mitrovics, Tibor Mitrovics, Anna Nitzsche, Ulrieke Offermann, Linda Tezlow, and the whole Zomer family. Lena Marie Zomer proved to be particularly patient. Not to forget Jessica Allermann, Jan Romann, Xenia Sharon Wolfgramm, and Marco Zieger. Thanks are also due to our parents. Marion and Manfred Bauer as well as Ursel and Udo Meyerhuber have once again proven to be extremely patient.

Bremen, November 2018

Alexander Max Bauer
and Malte Ingo Meyerhuber

Table of Contents

Foreword — V

Preface — VII

List of Abbreviations — XI

Alexander Max Bauer and Malte Ingo Meyerhuber
Introduction — 1

Alexander Max Bauer and Malte Ingo Meyerhuber
Two Worlds on the Brink of Colliding
   On the Relationship Between Empirical Research and Normative Theory — 11

Sylke Meyerhuber
Normative Theories and Their Influence on Empirical Research
   Theoretical Expositions and Practical Examples from a Qualitative Researcher in Applied Social Psychology — 35

Jannis Kreienkamp, Maximilian Agostini, Marvin Kunz, Malte Ingo Meyerhuber, and Carlos A. de Matos Fernandes
Normative Influences in Science and Their Impact on (Objective) Empirical Research — 75

Guillermina Jasso
Is and Ought
   From Ideas to Theory to Empirics — 105

Albert W. Musschenga
Empirically Informed Moral Intuitionism — 129

Norbert Paulo
A Principle of Psychological Realism for Moral Epistemology — 151

Stephen J. Sullivan
Moral Epistemology Naturalised
  Theory Justification in Ethics and Science —— 169

Marcel Mertz
Empirical Incursions
  Or How Empirical Information May Influence the Validity of a Moral Norm —— 189

James Konow
Is Fairness in the Eye of the Beholder?
  An Impartial Spectator Analysis of Justice —— 237

David Miller
Needs-Based Justice
  Theory and Evidence —— 273

Lars Schwettmann
A Simple Vote Won't Do It
  Empirical Social Choice and the Fair Allocation of Health Care Resources —— 295

Peter Wiersbinski
Conceiving the Anthropological Difference as a Categorical Divide
  Is There Any Room Left for Empirical Research? —— 317

Alexander Max Bauer and Malte Ingo Meyerhuber
Epilogue
  On Doxa and Aletheia —— 337

List of Contributors —— 343

Index of Names —— 347

Index of Subjects —— 349

List of Abbreviations

CEC	Clinical Ethics Consultation
CFO	Chief Financial Officer
DS	Deep Structure
ELSI	Ethical, Legal, and Social Issues
EPA	Environmental Protection Agency
ESC	Empirical Social Choice
HTA	Health Technology Assessment
ISO	Impartial and Sympathetic Observer
JEF	Justice Evaluation Function
MLD	Mean Log Deviation
NA	Norm Addressee
NAT	Norm Authority
NB	Norm Beneficiary
NK	Norm Kind
NUT	New Unified Theory
OLS	Ordinary Least Squares
PIR	Purely Individual Risk Preferences
PMPR	Principle of Minimal Psychological Realism
PRDP	Principle of Minimal Psychological Realism for Moral Epistemic Decision Procedures
PSO	Primordial Sociobehavioural Outcome
PTA	Post-Trial Access
QRP	Questionable Research Practice
RCT	Randomised Controlled Trial
REC	Research Ethics Committee
RVS	Rokeach Value Survey
SS	Surface Structure
SVS	Schwartz Value Survey
SWF	Social Welfare Function
VOI	Veil of Ignorance
WEIRD	Western, Educated, Industrialized, Rich, and Democratic

Alexander Max Bauer and Malte Ingo Meyerhuber
Introduction

1 A Glimpse of the Field Ahead[1]

Two questions often shape our view of the world: On the one hand, we ask ourselves what there is and, on the other, we ask what ought to be. These two perspectives reveal a whole series of dualisms that have become characteristic of our thinking: Besides "facts" and "values" there are, e.g., "descriptive" and "normative", "rational" and "emotional", "objective" and "subjective", "causes" and "reasons", "is" and "ought", "science" and "ethics" – or "empirical research" and "normative theory". These contrasts already indicate that work in the scientific realm may often touch on both of these types of questions, potentially leading to conflicts (e.g., of morality) for everyone involved. This can occur, e.g., when the need for regulation arises as a result of new technical developments (Lenk 2001). Here, Albert Einstein may come to mind, who warned in a 1939 letter to Franklin Roosevelt, then President of the United States, of the possible consequences should the National Socialists succeed in developing a functioning nuclear weapon. This judgement was clearly a contributing factor to the establishment of the Manhatten Project. Only after the devastating atomic bombings of Hiroshima and Nagasaki did Einstein and others become aware of the consequences of these endeavours, which led to the establishment of the Committee for the Prevention of Nuclear War (Green 2015). The Göttingen Eighteen may also come to mind; an association of 18 prominent physicists from the Federal Republic of Germany who published a declaration in 1957 against the efforts to arm the Bundeswehr – the unified armed forces of Germany – with nuclear weapons (Wetzel 2004).

Recently, a debate about such a need for regulation has emerged from a psychological perspective. In 2017, Lance Dodes and Joseph Schachter wrote a public letter to the *New York Times*, signed by 33 colleagues, which contains speculations about the mental health of Donald Trump, the president of the United States. Both Donald Trump's speech and action would reveal an inability to tolerate views other than his own, leading to rage reactions, and indicating an inability to empathise with others. The authors conclude by saying that the severe emotional instability shown in Donald Trump's speech and action makes him in-

---
[1] This part of the introduction is also published slightly altered in German in Bauer and Meyerhuber (2019a).

capable of serving as president (Dodes and Schachter 2017). With *The Dangerous Case of Donald Trump* (Lee 2017), 27 scientists have also published their diagnoses as a book. Therewith, they are deliberately breaking the so-called "Goldwater Rule" (American Psychiatry Association 2013): In 1973, the American Psychiatric Association proclaimed that it would be unethical to diagnose someone from afar and make such a diagnosis public, reacting to a controversy on the publication of psychiatric diagnoses on then presidential candidate Barry Goldwater. "We fear that too much is at stake to be silent any longer", Dodes and Schachter (2013, par. 2) write.

Those examples demonstrate that empirical scientific work also has consequences for the world itself, thereby carrying severe normative implications (e.g., regarding ethical guidelines). However, many scientific fields seem to seldom reflect on the relation of their empirical work to normative questions, and vice versa. Most explicitly discussed was this relation, one may argue, in philosophy: Philosophy, it might be said, has always been situated between those perspectives when it tries both to understand and to order the world in which we live. It brought forth the dualisms introduced above, arranged around the spheres of "is" and "ought". Here, David Hume may come to mind: He famously addresses the gap between is and ought with an argument that came to be known as *Hume's Law*. In his *Treatise on Human Nature* he writes:

> In every system of morality, which I have hitherto met with, I have always remark'd, that the author proceeds for some time in the ordinary way of reasoning, and establishes the being of a God, or makes observations concerning human affairs; when of a sudden I am surpriz'd to find, that instead of the usual copulations of propositions, *is*, and *is not*, I meet with no proposition that is not connected with an *ought*, or an *ought not*. This change is imperceptible; but is, however, of the last consequence. For as this *ought*, or ought *not*, expresses some new relation or affirmation, 'tis necessary that it shou'd be observ'd and explain'd; and at the same time that a reason should be given, for what seems altogether inconceivable, how this new relation can be a deduction from others, which are entirely different from it (Hume 1960, p. 469).

Hume confidently adds that he is "persuaded, that this small attention wou'd subvert all the vulgar systems of morality, and let us see, that the distinction of vice and virtue is not founded merely on the relations of objects, nor is perceiv'd by reason" (Hume 1960, p. 469 f.). In general, his "law" has been interpreted as the formulation of a logical fallacy, according to which it is not logically allowed to derive prescriptive conclusions from descriptive premises alone, since there is a fundamental difference between propositions describing what is and propositions describing what ought to be (Hudson 1969). Subsequently, attempts have been made to rely on normative premises for the foundation of ethical theories that are as consensusable as possible. Thereby, the role of additional empirical premises may have come out of view, although they are by no means categorically excluded by Hume (Eckensberger and Gähde 1993a).

Not only did he strongly influence ethical debates, Hume also had an effect from a broader epistemological perspective. Here he found advocates in Bertrand Arthur William Russell, Alfred Jules Ayer, or Charles Leslie Stevenson for whom nothing remains objective outside the natural sciences (Marchetti and Marchetti 2017a). Amongst others, Rudolf Carnap's (1959) *The Elimination of Metaphysics Through Logical Analysis of Language* may come to mind, as well as Bertrand Russell's (1935) *Religion and Science*, or Max Weber, who in *Science as a Vocation* goes back to Tolstoy to give an answer to the question of what the meaning of science is: "Science is meaningless", he writes, "because it has no answer to the only questions that matter to us: 'What should we do? How shall we live?'" (Weber 2014, p. 17). With regard to such questions, science can only achieve a certain clarity, Weber argues:

> Always assuming that clarity is something we ourselves possess. Insofar as we do, we can make clear to you that in practice we can adopt this or that attitude toward the value problem at issue – I would ask you for simplicity's sake to take examples from social phenomena. *If* you take up this or that attitude, the lessons of science are that you must apply such and such *means* in order to convert your beliefs into a reality. These means may well turn out to be of a kind that you feel compelled to reject. [...] This brings us to the last contribution that science can make in the service of clarity, and at the same time we reach it's limits. We can and should tell you that the *meaning* of this or that practical stance can be inferred consistently, and hence also honestly, from this or that ultimate fundamental ideological position. It may be deducible from one position or from a number – but there are other quite specific philosophies from which it cannot be inferred. [...] The discipline of philosophy and the discussion of what are ultimately the philosophical bases of the individual disciplines all attempt to achieve this (Weber 2004, p. 26).

Despite a frequently claimed separation between empirical research and normative theory, attempts at mutual methodological rapprochement can currently be observed both from the individual sciences as well as from philosophy, e.g., when individual sciences devote themselves to the subject of morality – in the field of psychology research is carried out on the influence of emotions and intuitions on ethical theory formation, behavioural economics investigates the influence of morality on rational decision making, anthropology attempts to reconstruct the historical origins of moral traits, primate research looks for basic building blocks of human morality in primates (Christen et al. 2014), and social sciences investigate preferences on questions of distributive justice – or when empirically informed ethics or experimental philosophy attempt to make the methods or results of empirical research fruitful for their own objects and questions. Moreover, the dichotomy itself was problematised by prominent voices, such as Donald Davidson, Philippa Foot, John McDowell, Iris Murdoch, Hilary Putnam, Ruth Putnam, or Richard Rorty (Marchetti and Marchetti 2017a).

This may give a fleeting glimpse of the field ahead. The tension underlying it has promoted some works that are outstanding in our eyes; such as, amongst many others, the volume *Facts and Values – The Ethics and Metaphysics of Normativity* edited by Giancarlo Marchetti and Sarin Marchetti (2017b) and the volume *Empirically Informed Ethics – Morality Between Facts and Norms* edited by Markus Christen, Carel van Schaik, Johannes Fischer, Markus Huppenbauer, and Carmen Tanner (2014b). Nonetheless, the topic still seems to struggle to get the attention that we think it deserves. We want to invite you, the curious reader, to delve into this divisive debate, to strive for answers together, and to contemplate on questions such as whether and to what extent the normative discourse has to be related to empirical facts, how our thinking about facts is guided by norms, or where the two spheres meet and how their relationship is to be determined there.

Flipping through the pages of this volume as well as of our German volume (Bauer and Meyerhuber 2019b), the interested reader will notice that some of the contributions take quite conflicting stances. We deliberately do not want to present a coherent, unified body of knowledge in which the arguments of each contribution go hand in hand or mesh like cogwheels. Instead, we want to invite you to step out into the agora with us where a controversial debate is ongoing, wrestling for the truth. Straggling around this agora, we will come about reflections on such manifold topics as the role of intuitions both in philosophy and psychology; the relation between is and ought questions from the perspective of social sciences; the role of normative influences in empirical social science research both from a quantitative and a qualitative perspective; as well as arguments that evolve around morals and norms themselves. Herewith we hope to make a small contribution to foster further interest in this socially as well as scientifically and philosophically important field.

2 On the Contributions in This Volume

First, we (chapter 1) open up perspectives on the historical background of the question at hand. Many people today may regard empirical research and normative theorising as two distinct fields that either have little to no relation to each other, or which, if they do, seem to be at tension constantly. The conflict both areas experience today, we argue, can be traced back to certain historical developments, such as the advent of modern sciences. Against this background, some exemplary historical arguments, debates, and developments are highlighted. After that, two positions regarding this relation are elaborated upon more deeply. Lastly, some possible systemic interdependencies between the two fields are illustrated, and the potential influences between empirical research and normative theory are explored.

Sylke Meyerhuber (chapter 2) invites the reader from the perspective of a social psychologist into an exploration of the normative system underpinning her work as a scientist. From the viewpoint of qualitative research and in favour of issues concerning social sustainability in organisations, she first delineates general normative frameworks that influence her empirical work. Furthermore, she reflects in which respect paradigms and methods provide parts of the normative theory influencing the work of research; foremost by example of the not yet internationally introduced "Core-Sentence Method" which operationalises research ideals in the tradition of symbolic interactionism. Overall, Meyerhuber perceives several "layers of normative theories" – rooted in personality, field of expertise, further professional and research paradigms, and concrete methods – culminating in a guiding compass for scientific professionalism and identity.

That research is – though not always consciously – conducted on several levels of normative assumptions, paradigms, and theorems is a view that Jannis Kreienkamp, Max Agostini, Malte Ingo Meyerhuber, Marvin Kunz, and Carlos A. de Matos Fernandes (chapter 3) pick up on. They discuss the role of normative influences in empirical social science research from the perspective of young researchers. Empirical research, they say, aspires to inform us about some kind of "objectively true" state of the world. This ambition especially holds for the natural sciences, but also extends to the social sciences. In the context of recent developments and theoretical discussions, the authors discuss the influence of normative assumptions on the different stages of empirical research. To do so, they analyse normative influences within the six conceptual steps of the empirical research process: idea generation, research funding, research planning, data collection, data analysis, and scientific output. They close with a summary of current directions that may help move to a more reflective, nuanced, and transparent scientific process.

Next, Guillermina Jasso (chapter 4) investigates the relation between is and ought questions and their relation to theory and empirics from the view of sociology. Against this background, she presents two approaches that investigate the constituents of happiness, framed as justice, status, and power. Theories on all three of those carriers of happiness have been integrated into a new unified theory. Jasso examines postulates and predictions from this new unified theory and its component theories. Thereafter, she traces the path from ideas to theory to empirics. Along the way she notes the classical sources for the ideas, the special tools such as probability distributions for theory and factorial surveys for empirics, and the major embedded is and ought questions. This chapter also introduces a new kind of question – is-about-ought – which represents the scientific search for knowledge about the normative views to which persons subscribe.

Thematically situated between ethics, philosophy, and psychology, Albert W. Musschenga (chapter 5) elaborates on the role of intuitions both in philosophy and psychology. He considers psychological intuitionism, the claim that many human judgements result from unconscious, automatic processes, and relates this to moral judgements to investigate whether the model of an empirically informed theory is also useful for connecting philosophical and psychological moral intuitionism. This exploration takes place in successive steps. First, Musschenga presents the philosophical view on (moral) intuitions. He then offers an account of (moral) psychological intuitions as the product of unconscious and automatic processes, before discussing how psychological moral intuitions relate to philosophical moral intuitions. Thereafter, he turns to the relation between the justification of intuitions and their reliability, and discusses whether we need reasons to trust our intuitions. Finally, he concludes with some thoughts about sense and feasibility of an empirically informed moral intuitionism.

Thereafter, Norbert Paulo (chapter 6) examines whether the principle of psychological realism, which demands of moral theories to consist of behaviours people are actually able to do, may not only apply to the content of moral claims (i.e., first-order morality), but also to those decision procedures which are used to determine the "proper" contents of these claims (i.e., second-order morality). To do so, he starts with Owen Flanagan's "Principle of Minimal Psychological Realism" for first-order moral theory. Paulo argues that a similar principle of psychological realism also applies to (second-order) moral epistemic decision procedures which are used to determine the proper contents of first-order morality. He calls it the "Principle of Minimal Psychological Realism for Moral Epistemic Decision Procedures", stating: "Make sure when constructing a moral epistemic decision procedure that the character and decision processing prescribed are possible, or are perceived to be possible, for creatures like us".

Stephen J. Sullivan (chapter 7) continues with theory justification in ethics. He presents the "methodological naturalist" thesis that the justification of normative ethical theories employs roughly the same empirical method as the justification of scientific theories. Sullivan argues that ethical inquiry into the nature of moral properties such as rightness and wrongness, goodness and badness closely parallels scientific inquiry into the nature of the natural kinds studied in the natural sciences. He illustrates this in analogy to the H_2O theory of water: A corollary that becomes apparent, he argues, is that ethical theories can be subjected to observational testing in much the same way as their scientific counterparts. Also, the limits of this parallel and some objections to the thesis are addressed.

Marcel Mertz (chapter 8) reflects on moral norms as an essential part of both lived morality and ethical reflection, and examines how empirical evidence may play a crucial role in considerations of their validity. On the basis of the assumption that moral norms are central both to lived morality and professional ethical reflection, he aims to identify empirical incursions into normative theory by showing how empirical information from social scientific research in particular may influence various dimensions of the validity of moral norms. To do so, he first provides a definition and analysis of the structure of a moral norm, then establishes a number of dimensions of the validity of moral norms that correspond to specific elements of this structure (including philosophical or social justification and legitimacy, applicability to specific situations, social implementation, and the effects of norms), while also discussing how these dimensions may be influenced by empirical information. Mertz concludes with a critical consideration of the significance of these dimensions of validity and the empirical influences on them for different ways of "doing ethics".

Turning towards questions of impartiality, James Konow (chapter 9) deals in this reprint from *Social Choice and Welfare* with the popular sentiment that fairness is inexorably subjective and incapable of being determined by objective standards. The study presented by him seeks to establish evidence on unbiased justice and to propose and demonstrate a general approach for measuring impartial views empirically. Most normative justice theories associate impartiality with limited information and consensus. In both the normative and empirical literature, information is usually seen as the raw material for self-serving bias and disagreement. In contrast, this chapter proposes a type of impartiality that is associated with a high level of information and that results in consensus. The crucial distinction here is the emphasis on the views of impartial spectators, rather than implicated stakeholders. Konow describes the quasi-spectator method, i.e., an empirical means to approximate the views of impartial spectators. Results of a questionnaire provide evidence on quasi-spectator views and support this approach as a means to elicit moral preferences. By establishing a relationship between consensus and impartiality, this chapter helps lay an empirical foundation for welfare analysis, social choice theory, and practical policy applications.

Thereafter, David Miller (chapter 10) takes a closer look at philosophical analysis and empirical evidence for claims of need in distributive justice. He aims to use both philosophical analysis and empirical evidence to map the way in which claims of need feature in our thinking about distributive justice. The first question is whether a clear line can be drawn between needs and other demands that can be described as interests or preferences, and if so, how? Where can needs be identified and what role do they play in decisions over resource allocation? In particular, does justice require that those whose needs are greatest should always have first claim on the resources available, or should resources be distributed more widely and evenly, for example in proportion to relative degrees of need? Might there even be cases in which triage is considered to be a just practice, with priority given to those whose needs can be fulfilled with least expenditure of resources? What difference, if any, does it make if recipients are responsible for having unsatisfied needs as a result of their past behaviour? Does this diminish their claim to be helped, or maybe eliminate it entirely? By reviewing experimental and other work on relevant aspects of justice, the author explores how far philosophical theories of needs-based justice capture the role that needs play in lay thinking about just distributions.

The potential interdependence between empirical and normative research in the context of allocating scarce health care resources is then considered by Lars Schwettmann (chapter 11). He discusses relevant aspects with respect to an approach known as empirical social choice, which intends to provide empirical evidence on the tenability of axioms characterising different arbitration schemes. Schwettmann distinguishes different roles for empirical work. Scholars in the field of empirical social choice claim that their studies reveal ethical judgements and, thereby, provide input to an interpersonal reflective equilibrium. Furthermore, it is argued that the roles ascribed determine answers on four central methodological question: First, should studies utilise hypothetical or real distribution problems? Second, who should be asked? Third, which perspective should be taken? Fourth, should quantitative or qualitative approaches be used?

Thereafter, Peter Wiersbinski (chapter 12) elaborates on the role of empirical research for the idea of an anthropological categorical difference – a basic, categorical divide between humans and animals. Reviving the ancient doctrine that human beings are set apart from other animals by a categorical divide rather than a difference of degree, contemporary accounts of the anthropological difference appear to conflict with the fact that human rationality is investigated in empirical psychology. According to these accounts, the idea of human rationality is part of a conceptual nexus that is known a priori and can be investigated through philosophical reflection. Thus, it might seem that empirical methods cannot have any say in the matter. Against this, the author makes room for the idea that the investigation of a priori concepts is dependent on experience by using an analogy between a priori concepts and thick moral concepts, which appear to be subject to moral experience and continual learning.

Closing, we (epilogue) take a look back at the long-standing line of thought in Western philosophy that the mere *doxa*, the opinion, of people is of little relevance for the pursuit of *aletheia*, the truth. Alfred North Whitehead famously noted that the "safest general characterization of the European philosophical tradition is that it consists of a series of footnotes to Plato". It might thus be worthwhile taking a look at Plato to discover where this strand of thought might origin from. Indeed, Plato is well known for the separation between doxa and aletheia. The question remains: How did he come to hold his views on this topic? Hannah Arendt formulated a thesis that seeks to answer this question looking at Plato's relationship to Socrates and his inability to cope with the death sentence the latter received.

The contributions in this volume, of course, do not aim to be exhaustive; the questions that arise from the dichotomy between is and ought are far too diverse. With these contributions we merely hope to shed some light on a few of the interesting debates that take place in the wide field of tension that lies between is and ought. We invite you to join us and our authors in reflecting critically on this area of tension and wish you stimulating reading, just as we had a stimulating time compiling the volume.

Bibliography

American Psychiatric Association (ed.) (2013): *The Principles of Medical Ethics. With Annotations Especially Applicable to Psychiatry*. Arlington: American Psychiatric Association.

Bauer, Alexander Max and Meyerhuber, Malte Ingo (2019a): "Einleitung". In: id. (eds.): *Philosophie zwischen Sein und Sollen. Normative Theorie und empirische Forschung im Spannungsfeld*. Berlin and Boston: Walter de Gruyter, pp. 1–11.

Bauer, Alexander Max and Meyerhuber, Malte Ingo (eds.) (2019b): *Philosophie zwischen Sein und Sollen. Normative Theorie und empirische Forschung im Spannungsfeld*. Berlin and Boston: Walter de Gruyter.

Carnap, Rudolf (1959): "The Elimination of Metaphysics Through Logical Analysis of Language". In: Ayer, Alfred Jules: *Logical Positivism*. Glencoe and London: Allen & Unwin, pp. 60–81.

Christen, Markus; van Schaik, Carel; Fischer, Johannes; Huppenbauer, Markus, and Tanner, Carmen (2014a): "Introduction. Bridging the Is-Ought-Dichotomy". In: id. (eds.): *Empirically Informed Ethics. Morality Between Facts and Norms*. Cham: Springer, pp. IX–X.

Christen, Markus; van Schaik, Carel; Fischer, Johannes; Huppenbauer, Markus, and Tanner, Carmen (eds.) (2014b): *Empirically Informed Ethics. Morality Between Facts and Norms*. Cham: Springer.

Dewey, John (1939): "Theory of Valuation". In: Boydston, Jo Ann (ed.): *The Later Works of John Dewey 1925–1953. Vol. 13. 1938–1939. Experience and Education, Freedom and Culture, Theory of Valuation, and Essays*. Carbondale: Southern Illinois University Press, pp. 203–228.

Dodes, Lance and Schachter, Joseph (2017): "A Mental Health Warning on Trump". In: *The New York Times*. https://www.nytimes.com/2017/02/13/opinion/mental-health-professionals-warn-about-trump.html, retrieved on November 19, 2018.

Eckensberger, Lutz and Gähde, Ulrich (1993a): "Einleitung". In: id. (eds.): *Ethische Norm und empirische Hypothese*. Frankfurt am Main: Suhrkamp, pp. 7–19.

Eckensberger, Lutz and Gähde, Ulrich (eds.) (1993b): *Ethische Norm und empirische Hypothese*. Frankfurt am Main: Suhrkamp.

Green, Jim (2015): "Albert Einstein on Nuclear Weapons". In: *Nuclear Monitor* 802 (4466), pp. 7–8.

Hudson, Donald (ed.) (1969): *The Is-Ought Question. A Collection of Papers on the Central Problems in Moral Philosophy*. London: Macmillan.

Hume, David (1960): *A Treatise of Human Nature*. Oxford: Clarendon Press.

Kant, Immanuel (2003): *Groundwork of the Metaphysics of Morals*. Cambridge: Cambridge University Press.

Lee, Bandy (2017): *The Dangerous Case of Donald Trump. 27 Psychiatrists and Mental Health Experts Assess a President*. New York: St. Martin's Press.

Lenk, Hans (2001): *Wissenschaft und Ethik*. Stuttgart: Reclam.

Marchetti, Giancarlo and Marchetti, Sarin (eds.) (2017): *Facts and Values. The Ethics and Metaphysics of Normativity*. New York and London: Routledge.

Russell, Bertrand (1935): *Religion and Science*. Oxford: Oxford University Press.

Ruß, Hans Günther (2002): *Empirisches Wissen und Moralkonstruktion. Eine Untersuchung zur Möglichkeit und Reichweite von Brückenprinzipien in der Natur- und Bioethik*. Frankfurt am Main and New York: Hänsel-Hohenhausen.

Weber, Max (2004): "Science as a Vocation". In: id.: *The Vocation Lectures*. Indianapolis and Cambridge: Hackett, pp. 1–31.

Wetzel, Manfred (2004): *Praktisch-politische Philosophie. Vol. 1. Allgemeine Grundlagen*. Würzburg: Königshausen & Neumann.

Alexander Max Bauer and Malte Ingo Meyerhuber
Two Worlds on the Brink of Colliding[1]

On the Relationship Between Empirical Research and Normative Theory

Abstract: Many people today may see empirical research (say, e. g., empirical social sciences) and normative theory (say, e. g., ethics) as two distinct fields that either have little to no relation to each other, or which, if they do, seem to be at tension constantly. The conflict both areas experience today, it is argued, can be traced back to certain historical developments, such as the advent of modern sciences. Against this background, some exemplary historical arguments, debates, and developments are highlighted. After that, two positions regarding this relation are elaborated upon more deeply. Lastly, some systemic interdependencies between the two fields are illustrated and potential influences between empirical research and normative theory are explored.

It is a long-standing assumption, both within and without the domain of science, that science itself is free of values (see, e. g., Lacey 1999). Galileo (1957, p. 270, as quoted by Lacey 1999, p. 2) already stated that science investigates "the facts of Nature [sic], which remains deaf and inexorable to our wishes". Corresponding views are still frequently expressed, take, e. g., a *New York Times* opinion article by Gregory Mankiw (2011, par. 17), former chair of the economics department at Harvard University, who stated that he does not "view the study of economics as laden with ideology", referring to Keynes, who said: "The theory of economics does not furnish a body of settled conclusions immediately applicable to policy. It is a method rather than a doctrine, an apparatus of the mind, a technique for thinking, which helps the possessor to draw correct conclusions" (Keynes 1922, p. V).

One may also argue, however (and rightfully so, as we will see), that science itself is not always free of normative influences in its search for truth. Even the

---

[1] A slightly modified version of this chapter has been published in German as Bauer and Meyerhuber (2019).

"purest" science, mathematics, may reveal this: Through an aesthetic of the formulaic, normativity can here find its way into the research process. A proof, e.g., can be considered elegant or "beautiful" if it is based on as few additional assumptions or preceding results as possible or if it is particularly concise. A first mathematical proof found may not be considered the best against this background. E.g., there are by now hundreds of known proofs for the Pythagorean theorem (Loomis 1972). In the field of mathematics, however, such considerations may not yet seem very questionable. But also in theoretical physics – especially when advancing into areas for which few or no empirical data is available yet – one is inclined to orient theory construction towards such a notion of "beauty"; having consequences for what comes into the focus of research as well as its limited resources in the first place (Hossenfelder 2018). Against this background, the principle of parsimony, Ockham's razor, may also come to mind (Mole 2003), which has unfolded its effect since scholasticism and continues to influence modern theory and practice of science (Glymour 1980, Harman 1965, Kelly 2007).

In such cases, one may indeed speak of a more or less *desired* normative influence; one needs a guideline that can be used in dealing with theories when – or as long as – there is no empirical data. Such a normative influence on science, though, is not always intended, e.g., when the *Zeitgeist* colours the results of research. Prehistoric gender studies, to name one example, investigate the social orders of our early ancestors, which sometimes depend on attributions owed to the socialisation of researchers themselves. At a burial of a man and a woman in a tomb with a wagon and many other burial objects, the literature speaks of a prince who was buried with his wife, even though it could also have been a female ruler with her chauffeur (Selg 2016, par. 22). In the more recent – but not less controversially interpreted – past lies the time of the Vikings: Fighting Viking women were long dismissed as a myth. Though only recently, DNA analyses of bones from a prototypical tomb of a believed male Viking warrior have shown that he is not a man, but a woman (Hedenstierna-Jonson et al. 2017). Such an influence of social norms can also be problematised for biology: Joan Roughgarden (2004) criticises Darwin's theory of sexual selection in her book *Evolution's Rainbow*, in which she argues that Darwin simply negated animals showing queer behaviours and that he, therefore, falsely attributed heteronormativity to animals. As seen above, such influences can determine what is being researched in the first place. Dahl illustrates this in her attempt to find out which proportion of girls bleeds after their first sexual contact. This should be something fairly easy to explore, she says. But, according to her, gynaecologists do not think this is important because it does not affect any disease; ignoring the fact that there is another social reason – besides physical health – to clarify this question (Bracher 2018, par. 24).

Now, what do all these examples have in common? They represent a – sometimes more, sometimes less explicit – combination of is and ought. These two concepts form one of the great dualisms of our efforts to gain knowledge, of our scientific practice, and of our language. Both describe complex concepts that can be interpreted in very different ways. Since the present volume combines diverse perspectives from various schools of thought and disciplines, we would like to limit ourselves to the greatest common denominator, which *might* be identified on the semantic level: There, a distinction is made between descriptive, explicative, prescriptive, and evaluative statements (e.g., Opp 1972, Hare 1991). This linguistically constructed framework contains implications which, of course, extend far beyond language. E.g., questions of an epistemic difference are connected to this semantic differentiation: If one wants to fathom the truthfulness of such statements, this can presuppose a different methodology, given that these statements are also associated with an ontic difference. The question arises: Of what kind of nature are the objects of knowledge to which these types of statements refer? And how are they investigated? It is often assumed that empirical research tends to use descriptive and explicative statements when making conclusions about reality through methods such as surveys, observations, and other measurements. On the contrary, it might be said that normative theory primarily adopts prescriptive and evaluative statements to open up a value-based view of how the world or a particular issue ought to be (Velasquez 2008); and what ought to be is primarily sought after by reflection (e.g., Kant 2015) or discourse (e.g., Apel 1988, Habermas 1990), with a few exceptions.[2]

That these two spheres can hardly be separated that strictly may already be seen from what has been foretold. In the following – after a brief historical roundabout – we will, therefore, examine the question of what positions there are with regard to an integration of these two before finally attempting to show briefly some crucial interdependencies between these spheres.

---

[2] Here theories of ethical or moral naturalism come into view, in which it is assumed that ethical qualities can be reduced to non-ethical qualities (e.g., Carrier 2011, Harris 2010). For a critical view, see, e.g., Hunter and Nedelisky (2018).

1 The Question's Historical Background

Many people today may see empirical research and normative theory as two distinct fields that either have little to no relation to each other, or which, if they do, seem to be at tension constantly. This perspective, however, can be seen as the result of a long historical development. Before we start trying to define possible relationships between the two, it thus may be useful to have a look at past perspectives on the topic first (e. g., Kreuzer 2004, Ritter 1971). Such a look can, of course, only be a very shortened and selective one within this narrow framework.[3] Nevertheless, it reveals: Normative theory and empirical research have gone hand in hand for a long time under the veil of philosophy. This close relationship becomes clear when we look into the history of thought: In early times and classical understandings of the field, philosophy appears to be somewhat universal (e. g., Aristotle 1966, Cassiodorus 2004). Such universality is reflected in the early modern period by Descartes (1983), who expressed his famous metaphor of philosophy being a tree, with metaphysics as its roots, physics as its trunk, and all other sciences as its branches. – Although there will not be a universal consensus about what philosophy is, neither intertemporal nor amongst the intellectuals of a given time, and although contrary conceptions can be found, it seems clear nonetheless that such a methodical and contentual holistic perspective is a central and recurring conception of (classical understandings of) philosophy.

The relationship between normative and empirical considerations may have experienced first tensions with the advent of modern sciences, which Dilthey (1991) situates at the end of the middle ages. It seems since then that the two entered an occasionally difficult and not always easily definable relationship. This general tension becomes apparent in various philosophical or meta-ethical arguments, in the development of different epistemic schools of thought, or in controversies about the theory of science. Two prominent methodological disputes, mainly in the German-speaking realm of sociology, also took up and discussed the problem around this relationship. Protagonists such as Max Weber, Werner Sombart, Gustav Schmoller, or Rudolf Goldscheid addressed in their dispute about value judgements (*Werturteilsstreit*) in the late 19th and early 20th century the potential role of social sciences in formulating normative guidance for political action (e. g., Albert 1972). Similarly, in the positivism dispute (*Positivismusstreit*) in the 60's, advocates of critical rationalism, such as Karl Popper or Hans Albert, and advocates of the Frankfurt School, such as Theodor Adorno

---

[3] Moreover, it is Eurocentric and male-dominated (Elberfeld 2012).

or Jürgen Habermas, debated the socio-critical role of science and the importance of value judgements for scientific theory building (e.g., Adorno et al. 1976, Dahms 1994).

Today, some scholars explicitly recognise the separation of empirical and normative work within their scientific domain. Miller (1992), e.g., notes that the fields of political theory, including normative theories of justice, and of empirical research on people's justice beliefs seem to regard each other's work as irrelevant for their own, while being in theory closely intertwined. This is also the case within economics, as exemplified by Schwettmann (2015, p. 8):

> On the one hand, behavioural or positive economics applies descriptive strategies and regards what "is". In particular results of monetarily incentivised experiments have stimulated descriptive theories of social preferences, which inter alia include fairness concerns as well as related moral preferences, such as unconditional altruism or reciprocity which occasionally have also been labelled as fairness. On the other hand, normative economics uses prescriptive analyses and concerns what "ought to be" (for comparisons, see Konow 2003, Konow and Schwettmann 2015, Gächter and Riedl 2006, Herrero, Moreno-Ternero, and Ponti 2010).

Such statements certainly lead back to old questions: Are these spheres really that distinct from each other? Does a connection between them promise to be fruitful? Which influences of normativity or normative theory are at work in the empirical world or in empirical research? Which influences of the empirical world or of empirical research are at work in normative judgements or theories? Moreover, which normative aspects should empirical research and which empirical findings should normative theory take into account? The possible arguments here are just as manifold as the questions themselves. In order to illustrate this diversity, we will consider the cons (section 2) and pros (section 3) of integrating the results of empirical research into a specific normative theory formation next.

2 Critical Arguments Concerning the Integration of Empirical Research in Normative Theory

The potential perspectives of integrating the results of empirical research into normative theory formation, in this case for ethics, may be simplified into two conflicting positions, a critical perspective which we will denote as *Platonic* and an affirmative perspective which we will denote as *Aristotelian* (in line with Miller 1994, p. 178, Schwettmann 2009, p. 20 f.).⁴ Critical arguments concerning an integration of normative theorising and empirical research have been made throughout the last centuries by many well-known voices. A famous example may be the *is-ought dichotomy*, formulated by David Hume (1960), who argued that one could not derive an ought-statement from is-statements alone. Or consider George Edward Moore's (1993) concept of the *naturalistic fallacy*, stating that it is a fallacy to define the predicate "good" based on natural properties. Max Weber (2004) acknowledged in a similar fashion that science cannot tell us what we should do or how we should live, but that it would rather help us gain some clarity by structuring our potential opinions about moral problems, side effects of reaching certain goals, and which positions to derive from different ideological standpoints.⁵

Such notions carry a sceptical tone. This reflects the typical theoretical approach in classical normative theorising, which can be characterised by a paradigm that constitutes critical reflection and thorough assessment of arguments as the central elements of its theory building. Following this line of thought, empirical research only plays a neglectable role in the epistemic process, especially when the opinion of laypeople is involved. Miller (1994) notes the similarities between this perspective and the elitist position of Plato, who had developed a strong aversion against the *doxa* – the common belief or popular opinion – and who subsequently developed a model of truth which he strongly differentiated from common opinions (see also Arendt 1990). Only with a unique method of thinking, which philosophers possess, "true knowledge" (Miller 1994, p. 178) can be obtained, so the assumption. Along with this perspective comes a sharp devaluation and sometimes outright rejection of public opinion, often also linked to a dismissal of any relevance of empirical research concerned with such opinions. Such an "armchair traditionalism" tends to deny "the relevance of empirical data to normative justification" (Christen and Alfano 2014, p. 4), since laypersons – whose intuitions are often the focus of such research – would run the risk of being wrong, confused, or imprecise in their conceptions, because they do not operate with the appropriate tools for gaining knowledge, such as, e. g., a priori reflection or conceptual analyses (Kauppinen 2007, p. 96).

Regarding the presumed irrelevance of gathering laypersons' intuitions for advancing philosophy in general or for moral theory specifically, Knobe and

---

4 Kauppinen (2014, p. 280 f.) alternatively speaks of "Armchair Traditionalism" and "Ethical Empiricism".
5 This might resemble the notion of *nonoverlapping magisteria*, which describes the view that religion does not come into conflict with science as both areas of inquiry would be distinct from each other, as proposed by Gould (1997) and Whitehead (1925).

Nichols (2008) list some common arguments. One of these states that every other scientific inquiry relies on trained and skilled experts rather than laypersons, questioning why this should be any other in the field of philosophy or morals, since it "would be absurd for physicists or biologists to conduct surveys on folk intuitions about physics or biology" (Knobe and Nichols 2008, p. 8). One might object that many philosophical problems arise from common-sense intuitions in the first place, thus giving the research on such intuitions a different relevance. Granting this might, nonetheless, lead to another objection: Even if common-sense concepts were relevant for philosophical inquiries, philosophers are the ones trained to handle them with precision, while laypersons might struggle to apply them correctly. Moreover, philosophy cannot settle for observing existing opinions or asking how people think: "Rather, when we are truly philosophising, we need to subject people's intuitions to criticism, looking at arguments that might show that people's intuitions are actually mistaken in certain cases" (Knobe and Nichols 2008, p. 10). Lastly, empirical research might show us what people think or which psychological processes ground specific outcomes, but, it is argued, it cannot give us criteria that allow to distinguish whether or not these processes are reliable or whether the intuitions are correct. Valuation thus seems to be grounded in other things than empirical investigation.

Such arguments for a separation of normative theory and empirical research have proven to be very effective in the debate. Nevertheless, positions have also emerged which argue against such an "armchair philosophy", as will be shown below.

3 Affirmative Arguments Concerning the Integration of Empirical Research in Normative Theory

Contrasting those views, according to Miller (1994), are Aristotelian positions, which have recently gained traction.[6] Terminologically leaned upon Aristotle's methodological use of "common sense" (e.g., Aristotle 2013),[7] it is assumed that normative theorising (or its critique) can benefit strongly from empirical

---

[6] Consider, e.g., Putnam (2002) or the notion of "thick concepts" (e.g., Williams 1985, pp. 143 ff., Roberts 2013).

[7] It could be argued that especially for representatives of a common-sense philosophy, for example in the tradition of the Scottish School, it can be important to empirically find out what this "common sense" actually is.

data; even from that which reflects laypeople's opinions. While one may argue from a Platonic perspective that only the intuitions of experts are relevant, as they can free themselves from those cultural, socioeconomic, and other biases that laypersons cannot free themselves from, the Aristotelian perspective *somewhat* diminishes the relevance of such experts.

Here, once again, the arguments are manifold. Schwettmann (2015, p. 1), e. g., concludes that empirical work "could be used to investigate the acceptance of normative ideas by laypeople, to identify researchers' biases, to discover new normative questions or to complement theoretical approaches". Others have described it as a process of self-correction: While a philosopher's theorising is typically guided by her intuitions (and maybe those of her correspondence partners), empirical research could extend the sample size of introspections (Bar-Hillel and Yaari 1993). Moreover, one can turn the theoretician herself into a research object and thus seek to explore the conditions for the emergence of normative theory contained in the human factor. This may concern, e. g., the development of intuitions that are commonly used as justifiers[8] and raises questions about the nature of intuitions, such as whether they are interculturally and interepochally valid. In an empirical study, Vaesen, Peterson, and van Bezooijen (2013) have shown that intuitions of philosophical experts concerning an epistemological question are systematically different along linguistic affiliations, although subjects belong to a culturally and academically relatively homogeneous group[9] (differences in that regard also were found for experts' cultural, socialeconomic, and educational backgrounds; see, e. g., Nichols, Stich, and Weinberg 2003, Weinberg et al. 2010, Machery et al. 2004, 2013).

An overview of attempts to empirically inform normative theories can be found in Appiah (2008), Knobe and Nichols (2008), as well as in Alfano and Loeb (2017). In this regard, Knobe and Nichols (2008, p. 12) state: "We think that the patterns to be found in people's intuitions point to important truths about how the mind works, and these truths – truths about people's minds, not about metaphysics – have great significance for traditional philosophical questions".

Another possible contribution, as seen above, may be to identify previously unrecognised moral problems or practical dilemmas that may, moreover, point to

---

8 And this also outside of philosophy, e. g., by Elster and Harsanyi, who explain that their concepts follow from common sense (Schwettmann 2009, p. 21).
9 They state: "[...] contrary to what is commonly assumed by armchair philosophers, the epistemic intuitions of trained philosophers are susceptible to a linguistic background effect" (Vaesen, Peterson, and van Bezooijen 2013, p. 560). For the resulting doxastic diversification and the problem it may pose for moral realism, see Doris et al. (2017).

deficits in already formulated normative theories (Braddock 1994, de Vries and Gordijn 2009). Such an "identification of morally relevant problems" (Salloch et al. 2015, p. 6) can be observed, e.g., in the field of biology and medicine: One needs a concept of the "stem cell" in order to be able to recognise and reflect on the moral problems associated with it first and foremost. The term itself appears with Ernst Haeckel in the second half of the 19th century (Ramalho-Santos and Willenbring 2007); only the access by cell research – an empirical science – opens the concept and with it the technical-medical potential, against whose background the currently debated ethical controversies could first unfold.

Empirical research can also serve to falsify empirical assumptions in existing normative theories or provide empirical facts for further normative theorising (Salloch et al. 2015, p. 6). Representing this line of thought, von Kutschera (1988) stated that if the conception of man being required by certain ethical theories could no longer be maintained in the light of empirical findings, these theories should be revised. Assumptions which were taken at face value in the past and the questions related to them, may thus be subjectable to newer empirical methods. One example of the efforts to test assumptions of ethical theories can be found concerning John Rawls' (2005) *Theory of Justice*, which proposes certain assumptions about human judgement and behaviour in specific situations. It was tried to establish aspects of those situations, the position behind a "veil of ignorance", in laboratory situations, to study its actual effects on human beings and to compare the results with the theoretical speculations. There it was tried to "induce aspects of impartial reasoning among groups of subjects and hence gain information regarding preferences over principles of distributive justice" (Frohlich and Oppenheimer 2002, p. 29).[10] Other investigations deal, e.g., with justice, examining laypersons' justice evaluations and their role for informed normative theories (Cappelen et al. 2007, 2013, Deutsch 1975, Konow 2003, 2009, Miller 1992, Swift 2003, Traub et al. 2005). Empirical research can help to investigate the validity of assumptions in theories across all kinds of domains, such as done by Kahneman and colleagues (1986) in the field of economics, who used dictator games to "refute the income maximisation assumption of economics textbooks" (Engel 2011, p. 26) or in political science, where the factual truth-tracking potential of political deliberation can be investigated (Habermas 2006, Chambers 2005).

Moreover, there is a series of pragmatic considerations regarding the use of empirical data for normative theorising: If one assumes that a normative theory,

---

[10] Rawls was, of course, keen to present his theory as independent of such considerations (Rawls 1974–1975, also see Brickman 1977).

especially in ethics, is built to be implemented at some point (Bossert 1998, Schokkaert 1999), then the theorist also has to find acceptance and support for her theory. The results of empirical research can help to shed light on possible difficulties or misunderstandings in public (see, e. g., Williams 1985) by investigating the relationship between theory and existing moral norms to come to conclusions regarding its feasibility or its psychological acceptance (de Vries and Gordijn 2009). Besides this ex-ante perspective, there is, of course, also an ex-post perspective: If measures are implemented to foster certain behaviours in light of a specific moral background, e. g., by politics, then the success of such means can also be evaluated afterwards (Sugarman and Sulmasy 2001, Salloch et al. 2015).

In accordance with such considerations, new developments take place at the intersection of empirical research and normative theory, which aim at a synthesis of the two, e. g., with the emergence of experimental philosophy or empirically informed ethics. The former, experimental philosophy, understands itself as a new interdisciplinary approach, utilising methods that are common, e. g., in the domain of empirical social research, to shed light on philosophical questions, which are otherwise examined primarily by reflection or methods such as conceptual analyses (but that nonetheless frequently contain empirical claims). Experimental philosophy often aims at collecting laypeople's intuitions about such problems, hoping to gain insights that can promote the theoretical reflections about them (for a methodological overview, see Sytsma and Livengood 2015). Certain authors argue that this approach is less of a revolutionary new way (Appiah 2007, Lackman 2006) and more of a somewhat consequent continuation of the historical unity of empirical research and philosophical theorising (Knobe et al. 2012).

Assuming that intuitions play an important role for philosophical reflections and are often regarded as an important source of evidence (Knobe et al. 2012, p. 82), it may seem only logical also to include the intuitions of laypeople into one's reflections. This seems especially important – as already mentioned above – if there are indications that the intuitions of experts are not fundamentally superior to those of laypeople. Moreover, some assumptions about intuitions made in theoretical works can – to a certain extent – be tested in controlled experiments. Experimental philosophers, therefore, assume that it is not beneficial to maintain a strict separation, e. g., between philosophy and psychology (Knobe et al. 2012, p. 82). A broad range of philosophical problems is – as Knobe and colleagues (2012) point out – already being empirically investigated, including the objectivity of moral propositions (Beebe and Buckwalter 2010, Brink 1989, Goodwin and Darley 2008, Mackie 1977, Nichols 2004a, Shafer-Landau 2003, Smith 1994), free will and its relationship to deterministic concepts

(Nichols and Knobe 2007, Weigel 2011, Feltz and Cokely 2009, Nahmias, Coates, and Kvaran 2007, Nahmias and Murray 2010), knowledge (Machery et al. 2017, Mukerji 2016, Weinberg, Nichols, and Stich 2001, Swain, Alexander, and Weinberg 2008, Nagel, Juan, and Mar 2013, Kim and Yuan 2015), coherence (Koscholke and Jekel 2016, Schippers and Koscholke 2020), consciousness (Gray, Gray, and Wegner 2007, Gray and Wegner 2009, 2010, Johnson 2003, Knobe 2011, Knobe and Prinz 2008, Sytsma and Machery 2009), natural kinds (Pinder 2017), or distributive justice (Weiß, Bauer, and Traub 2017). Moreover, new methodological concepts, such as experimental explication (Schupbach 2017), also emerge against the background of these movements.

The latter, empirically informed ethics (Lütge, Rusch, and Uhl 2014), might be understood in part as a reaction to a recent increase in scientific publications on morality, which has been evaluated quite differently by different ethicists. Those who embrace the empirical results argue that – since "morality may indeed be located *between* facts and norms" (Christen et al. 2014, p. X) – empirical investigations of morality may lead to valuable insights that are of some relevance for ethical thinking itself. The empirical material, they argue, may be used in a variety of ways, e. g., regarding the foundation of normative theories themselves (Nichols 2004b), to undermine the normative importance of intuitions (Singer 2005), or to improve the context-sensitivity of ethical theories (Musschenga 2005). It has furthermore been argued that empirical research about morality could also benefit from an interchange with the domain of ethics about the insights gained there, as empiricists also require an in-depth understanding and concept of their object (see, e. g., Fischer and Gruden 2010).

Fischer and Gruden (2010) thus already presage that not only empirical findings can influence the theory construction and evaluation of, e. g., ethics. Moreover, normative theory can, of course, have an influence on empirical research. In the following, we will thus take a closer look at some possible interdependencies.

4 On the Relationship Between Is and Ought as well as Empirical Research and Normative Theory

A closer look reveals a number of interdependencies between is and ought as well as between empirical research and normative theory, which are to be listed,

predominantly in *modus potentialis*, simplified and without claiming to be exhaustive, as twelve theses, corresponding to figure 1,[11] below:
- "Ought" can be related to "is".
- "Empirical research" can investigate "ought" in terms of empirically present judgements.
- "Is" can contain empirically present judgements about "ought".
- "Empirical research" can enter "normative theory".
- "Normative theory" can investigate "ought". It is at the same time part of "ought".
- "Ought" can influence "normative theory".
- "Normative theory" can be related to "is". It is at the same time part of "is".
- "Is" can influence "normative theory".
- "Empirical research" can investigate "is". It is at the same time part of "is".
- "Ought" can influence "empirical research".
- "Is" can be the object of "empirical research".
- "Normative theory" can influence "empirical research".

This should serve as a first, very rough approximation of the field ahead. "Is" might be the widest category in this context. It may also incorporate what is in the world as empirical research and as normative theory. Whether there are "normative facts", on the other hand, is debatable (e.g., Ayer 1936, Stevenson 1937).

"Ought" often refers to the empirical world (1). This can be illustrated with the example of morals. They only become necessary through empirical conditions and, in turn, aim at influencing those very conditions. Morals are located in a social context; between actions, judgements, negotiations, and other interactions between social beings. Normative influences guide people's thoughts, emotions, deliberations, and actions, and thus exert an impact on the empirical world (Christen and Alfano 2014). Moral questions usually are conceptually related to this empirical reality; they operate with facts and concepts that make moral problems articulable in the first place.[12] In a more general, nonmoral sense – and in the spirit of teleology –, one can argue that both normativity and the empirical world are connected even in the most fundamental way:

---

[11] Given that the borders of the categories depicted and their interrelations seem to be fluid, another representation might be more suitable, e.g., utilising a form of set diagram.

[12] It thus can be tried to trace value questions back to factual questions (Christen and Alfano 2014). It may be, however, that normative assumptions hide within those seemingly factual questions. In this regard, one can also consider Hans Albert's (1965) notion of crypto-normative, implicit value judgements.

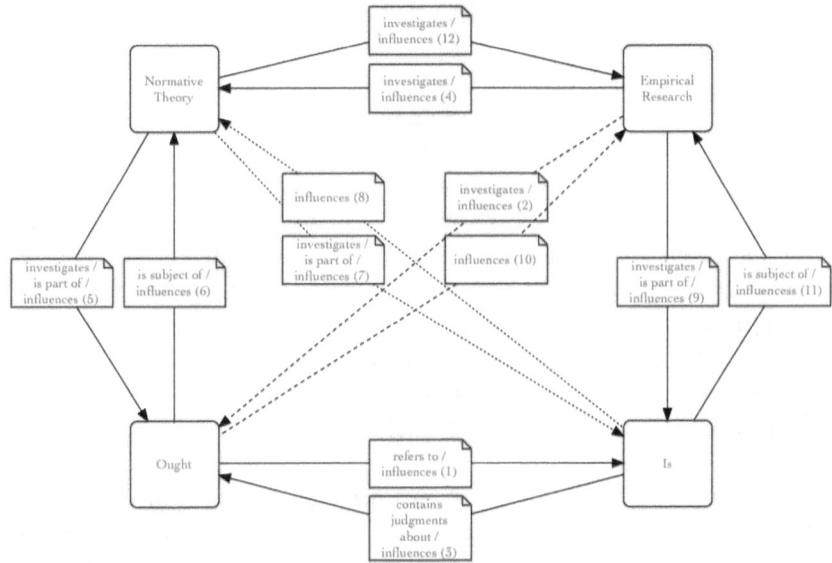

Figure 1: Some possible interdependencies between empirical research and normative theory as well as between is and ought

> Normativity is woven into the most basic structures of life: all life-forms (including even plants, fungi, protozoa, and bacteria) have built-in "desired states" or "goal states" with respect to basic needs and threats, sensors to detect them, and actors to seek or avoid them (Christen and Alfano 2014, p. 7).

In recent times, normativity has often become the subject of empirical research (2). E.g., moral judgements are not seen as an independent property, but as dependent on certain conditions, such as historical or psychological ones (3). If one assumes that normative theory is embedded in history (e.g., Ellmers and Elbe 2011), historical research about this background may help to shed light on the historical conditionality of normative theories (4). In this context, one can understand normative theories as children of their time, with their development being closely linked to the empirical reality of the theorists.[13]

"Normative theory" examines and determines what ought to be (5); its development is itself subject to normative assumptions about what good normative theories are (6). Here, one may consider demands such as that of a theory's in-

---

[13] Whether such an endeavour is of philosophical (e.g., Nietzsche 1998) or empirical nature, one's efforts of deciphering the development of human morals will also always be influenced by one's pre-conceptions (Christen 2010).

ternal consistency. Normative theories also may trigger the development of new normative approaches, e.g., to criticise or further develop a former theory. They are, as is the realm of "ought" in general, related to the realm of "being" (7). Against this background, it can also incorporate the results of empirical research (4). Formulating normative theory can also have to deal with similar methodological problems as empirical research (8); here, too, a theorist may be subject to certain cognitive distortions if she makes use of methods such as introspection or conceptual analysis or uses her intuitions as a moment of justification. As with empirical research, the *Zeitgeist* can also have an influence on the formulation of a theory. And besides that, normative theories can also spark new empirical research (12). This may be the case to, e.g., evaluate the societal acceptance of specific theories or to investigate the validity of a theory's underlying assumptions, such as those concerning human nature.

"Empirical research", in turn, investigates being things (9). Such research projects tend to be influenced by normative assumptions (10), unconscious ones as well as such about what constitutes proper research, which methodologies one should use, and what kind of research questions and methods are deemed acceptable (12); think, e.g., of Kuhn's (1962) concept of research paradigms. The *Zeitgeist*, again, can also influence empirical research through norms (11). Empirical research also entails further empirical research, e.g., to replicate prior results or because new research questions arise from prior work. In addition, the research process itself can become the object of empirical research (11).

Lastly, empirical research may also lead to new normative debates (4), as becomes clear with the following historical example: In 1939, Albert Einstein wrote a highly impactful letter to the then president of the United States, Franklin Roosevelt, in which he urgently warned of the consequences should Nazi Germany develop nuclear weapons. This letter, in combination with the solicitation of Einstein and other members of the scientific community to preempt the Germans in the development of a nuclear weapon, ultimately led to the founding of the Manhattan Project. Robert Oppenheimer, one of the heads of the project, is said to have quoted the Hindu writing *Bhagavadgita* with the words "Now I have become Death, destroyer of worlds" (Hijiya 2000) after witnessing a test-detonation of a nuclear bomb. After the horrors of Hiroshima and Nagasaki, Einstein and many others realised the consequences of their endeavours, and Einstein, together with other scientists, founded the Emergency Committee of Atomic Scientists (Green 2015). Similarly, famous German physicists such as Carl Friedrich von Weizsäcker and Werner Heisenberg came forth with a plea to the public in the 60's, in which they urged not to use research results from nuclear physics for purposes of military armament (Wetzel 2004, also see Heisenberg 1971, Lorenz 2011).

The question whether (and to which degree) there is obligation in expertise can also further be illustrated from the field of psychology: The *American Psychiatric Association* decided in the 70's, in reaction to a controversy regarding the publication of psychiatric diagnoses for the then presidential candidate Barry Goldwater, that it is unethical to diagnose someone from a distance and make the diagnosis publicly available. Until today, this so-called *Goldwater Rule* is in place in the association's *Principles of Medical Ethics* (American Psychiatry Association 2013). Nonetheless, it occasionally is violated: E.g., in February 2017 experts wrote a public letter about the mental health of the contemporary president of the United States, Donald Trump, to the *New York Times* (Dodes und Schachter 2017). 27 psychiatrists and mental health experts have also published their judgements concerning the same question in the book *The Dangerous Case of Donald Trump* (Lee 2017). The assumption behind publishing such pieces may have been that possessing expert knowledge means one also carries responsibility for society.

Although the borders of those categories and their interrelations are fluid, this reveals a first glimpse at the complex interdependencies between is and ought as well as empirical research and normative theory. Against this background, the questions posed at the beginning unfold a new weight: Are these spheres really that distinct from each other? Does a connection between them promise to be fruitful? Which influences of normativity or normative theory are at work in the empirical world or in empirical research? Which influences of the empirical world or of empirical research are at work in normative judgements or theories? Moreover, which normative aspects should empirical research and which empirical findings should normative theory take into account? The contributions in this volume take up some of these questions.

Acknowledgements

This chapter has profited much from the critical comments both from Allard Tamminga and Mark Siebel. Many thanks are also due to the discussants at talks given at the 10th Doctoral Symposium of the Austrian Society for Philosophy (ÖGP) at the Alpen Adria University of Klagenfurt, at a workshop of the doctoral students of the research group "Need-Based Justice and Distribution Procedures" of the German Research Foundation (DFG) at the University of Bremen, at the 3rd Conference of the German Society for Positive Psychological Research

(DGPPF) at the Ruhr University Bochum, and at a talk given at the Karl Jaspers Society in Oldenburg.

Bibliography

Adorno, Theodor; Albert, Hans; Dahrendorf, Ralf; Habermas, Jürgen; Pilot, Harald, and Popper, Karl (1976): *The Positivist Dispute in German Sociology*. London: Heinemann.

Albert, Hans (1965): "Wertfreiheit als methodisches Prinzip. Zur Frage der Notwendigkeit einer normativen Sozialwissenschaft". In: Topitsch, Ernst (ed.): *Logik der Sozialwissenschaften*. Cologne: Kiepenheuer & Witsch, pp. 181–210.

Albert, Hans (1972): *Ökonomische Ideologie und politische Theorie*. Göttingen: Otto Schwartz.

Alfano, Mark and Loeb, Don (2017): "Experimental Moral Philosophy". In: Zalta, Edward (ed.): *The Stanford Encyclopedia of Philosophy*. https://plato.stanford.edu/archives/fall2017/entries/experimental-moral/, retrieved on November 26, 2018.

American Psychiatric Association (ed.) (2013): *The Principles of Medical Ethics. With Annotations Especially Applicable to Psychiatry*. Arlington: American Psychiatric Association.

Apel, Karl-Otto (1988): *Diskurs und Verantwortung. Das Problem des Übergangs zur postkonventionellen Moral*. Frankfurt am Main: Suhrkamp.

Appiah, Kwame (2007): "The New New Philosophy". In: *The New York Times*. https://www.nytimes.com/2007/12/09/magazine/09wwln-idealab-t.html, retrieved on November 5, 2018.

Appiah, Kwame (2008): *Experiments in Ethics*. Cambridge: Harvard University Press.

Arendt, Hannah (1990): "Philosophy and Politics". In: *Social Research* 57 (1), pp. 73–103.

Aristotle (1966): *Aristotle's Metaphysics*. Bloomington: Indiana University Press.

Aristotle (2013): *Aristotle's Politics*. Chicago: The University of Chicago Press.

Ayer, Alfred (1936): *Language, Truth and Logic*. London: Victor Gollancz.

Bar-Hillel, Maya and Yaari, Menahem (1993): "Judgments of Distributive Justice". In: Mellers, Barbara and Baron, Jonathan (eds.): *Psychological Perspectives on Justice. Theory and Applications*. Cambridge: Cambridge University Press, pp. 55–84.

Bauer, Alexander Max and Meyerhuber, Malte Ingo (2019): "Zwei Welten am Rande der Kollision. Zum Verhältnis von empirischer Forschung und normativer Theorie, insbesondere vor dem Hintergrund der Ethik". In: id. (eds.): *Philosophie zwischen Sein und Sollen. Normative Theorie und empirische Forschung im Spannungsfeld*. Berlin and Boston: Walter de Gruyter, pp. 13–37.

Beebe, James and Buckwalter, Wesley (2010): "The Epistemic Side-Effect Effect". In: *Mind & Language* 25 (4), pp. 474–498.

Bossert, Walter (1998): "Comments on 'The Empirical Acceptance of Compensation Axioms'". In: Laslier, Jean-François; Fleurbaey, Marc; Gravel, Nicolas, and Trannoy, Alain (eds.): Freedom in Economics. London: Routledge, pp. 282–284.

Bracher, Katharina (2018): "Diese beiden Frauen verhelfen Ihnen zu besserem Sex". In: *NZZ am Sonntag*. https://nzzas.nzz.ch/gesellschaft/diese-beiden-frauen-verhelfen-ihnen-zu-besserem-sex-ld.1359722/, retrieved on November 5, 2018.

Braddock, Clarence (1994): "The Role of Empirical Research in Medical Ethics. Asking Questions or Answering Them?". In: *The Journal of Clinical Ethics* 5 (2), pp. 144–147.
Brickmann, Philp (1977): "Preference for Inequality". In: *Sociometry* 40 (4), pp. 303–310.
Brink, David (1989): *Moral Realism and the Foundations of Ethics*. Cambridge: Cambridge University Press.
Cappelen, Alexander; Hole, Astri; Sørensen, Erik, and Tungodden, Bertil (2007): "The Pluralism of Fairness Ideals. An Experimental Approach". In: *American Economic Review* 97 (3), pp. 818–827.
Cappelen, Alexander; Moene, Karl; Sørensen, Erik, and Tungodden, Bertil (2013): "Needs Versus Entitlements. An International Fairness Experiment". In: *Journal of the European Economic Association* 11 (3), pp. 574–598.
Carrier, Richard (2011): "Moral Facts Naturally Exist (and Science Could Find Them)". In: Loftus, John (ed.): *The End of Christianity*. Amherst: Prometheus, pp. 333–364.
Cassiodorus (2004): *Institutions of Divine and Secular Learning. On the Soul*. Liverpool: Liverpool University Press.
Chambers, Simone (2005): "Measuring Publicity's Effect. Reconciling Empirical Research and Normative Theory". In: *Acta Politica* 40 (2), pp. 255–266.
Christen, Markus (2010): "Naturalisierung von Moral? Einschätzung des Beitrags der Neurowissenschaft zum Verständnis moralischer Orientierung". In: Fischer, Johannes and Gruden, Stefan (eds.): *Die Struktur der moralischen Orientierung. Interdisziplinäre Perspektiven*. Berlin: Lit-Verlag, pp. 49–123.
Christen, Markus and Alfano, Mark (2014): "Outlining the Field. A Research Program for Empirically Informed Ethics". In: Christen, Markus; van Schaik, Carel; Fischer, Johannes; Huppenbauer, Markus, and Tanner, Carmen (eds.): *Empirically Informed Ethics. Morality Between Facts and Norms*. Cham: Springer, pp. 3–27.
Christen, Markus; van Schaik, Carel; Fischer, Johannes; Huppenbauer, Markus, and Tanner, Carmen (2014): "Introduction. Bridging the Is-Ought-Dichotomy". In: id. (eds.): *Empirically Informed Ethics. Morality Between Facts and Norms*. Cham: Springer, pp. IX–X.
Dahms, Hans-Joachim (1994): *Positivismusstreit. Die Auseinandersetzungen der Frankfurter Schule mit dem logischen Positivismus, dem amerikanischen Pragmatismus und dem kritischen Rationalismus*. Frankfurt am Main: Suhrkamp.
de Vries, Ron and Gordijn, Bert (2009): "Empirical Ethics and Its Alleged Meta-Ethical Fallacies". In: *Bioethics* 23 (4), pp. 193–201.
Descartes, René (1983): *Principia Philosophiae. Principles of Philosophy*. Dordrecht: Reidel.
Deutsch, Morton (1975): "Equity, Equality and Need. What Determines Which Value Will Be Used as the Basis of Distributive Justice?". In: *Journal of Social Issues* 31 (3), pp. 137–149.
Dilthey, Wilhelm (1991): *Selected Works. Vol. 1. Introduction to the Human Sciences*. Princeton: Princeton University Press.
Dodes, Lance and Schachter, Joseph (2017): "A Mental Health Warning on Trump". In: *The New York Times*. https://www.nytimes.com/2017/02/13/opinion/mental-health-professionals-warn-about-trump.html, retrieved on November 23, 2018.

Doris, John; Stich, Stephen; Phillips, Jonathan, and Walmsley, Lachlan (2017): "Moral Psychology. Empirical Approaches". In: Zalta, Edward (ed.): *The Stanford Encyclopedia of Philosophy*.
https://plato.stanford.edu/entries/moral-psych-emp/, retrieved on November 7, 2018.

Elberfeld, Rolf (2012): "Einleitung". In: id. (ed.): *Was ist Philosophie? Programmatische Texte von Platon bis Derrida*. Stuttgart: Reclam, pp. 13–15.

Ellmers, Sven and Elbe, Ingo (2011): "Vorwort". In: id. (eds.): *Die Moral in der Kritik. Ethik als Grundlage und Gegenstand kritischer Gesellschaftstheorie*. Würzburg: Königshausen & Neumann, pp. 7–10.

Engel, Christoph (2011): "Dictator Games. A Meta Study". In: *Experimental Economics* 14 (4), pp. 583–610.

Feltz, Adam and Cokely, Edward (2009): "Do Judgments About Freedom and Responsibility Depend on Who You Are? Personality Differences in Intuitions About Compatibilism and Incompatibilism". In: *Consciousness and Cognition* 18 (1), pp. 342–350.

Fischer, Johannes and Gruden, Stefan (eds.) (2010): *Die Struktur der moralischen Orientierung. Interdisziplinäre Perspektiven*. Münster: Lit-Verlag.

Frohlich, Norman and Oppenheimer, Joe (2002): "Empirical Approaches to Normative Theory". In: *Political Economy of the Good Society* 11 (2), pp. 27–32.

Gächter, Simon and Riedl, Arno (2006): "Dividing Justly in Bargaining Problems with Claims. Normative Judgments and Actual Negotiations". In: *Social Choice and Welfare* 27 (3), pp. 571–594.

Galilei, Galileo (1957): "The Assayer. A Letter to the Illustrious and Very Reverend Don Virginio Cesarini". In: Drake, Stillman (ed.): *Discoveries and Opinions of Galileo*. Garden City: Doubleday, pp. 231–280.

Glymour, Clark (1980): *Theory and Evidence*. Princeton: Princeton University Press.

Goodwin, Geoffrey and Darley, John (2008): "The Psychology of Meta-Ethics. Exploring Objectivism". In: *Cognition* 106 (3), pp. 1339–1366.

Gould, Stephen (1997): "Nonoverlapping magisteria". In: *Natural History* 106 (2), pp. 16–22.

Gray, Heather; Gray, Kurt, and Wegner, Daniel (2007): "Dimensions of Mind Perception". In: *Science* 315 (5812), p. 619.

Gray, Kurt and Wegner, Daniel (2009): "Moral Typecasting. Divergent Perceptions of Moral Agents and Moral Patients". In: *Journal of Personality and Social Psychology* 96 (3), pp. 505–520.

Gray, Kurt and Wegner, Daniel (2010): "Blaming God for Our Pain. Human Suffering and the Divine Mind". In: *Personality and Social Psychology Review* 14 (1), pp. 7–16.

Green, Jim (2015): "Albert Einstein on Nuclear Weapons". In: *Nuclear Monitor* 802 (4466), pp. 7–8.

Habermas, Jürgen (1990): *Moral Consciousness and Communicative Action*. Cambridge: MIT Press.

Habermas, Jürgen (2006): "Political Communication in Media Society. Does Democracy Still Enjoy an Epistemic Dimension? The Impact of Normative Theory on Empirical Research". In: *Communication Theory* 16 (4), pp. 411–426.

Hare, Richard (1991): *The Language of Morals*. Oxford: Oxford University Press.

Harman, Gilbert (1965): "The Inference to the Best Explanation". In: *Philosophical Review* 74 (1), pp. 88–95.

Harris, Sam (2010): *The Moral Landscape. How Science Can Determine Human Values*. New York: Free Press.
Hedenstierna-Jonson, Charlotte; Kjellström, Anna; Zachrisson, Torun; Krzewińska, Maja; Sobrado, Veronica; Price, Neil; Günther, Torsten; Jakobsson, Mattias; Götherström, Anders, and Storå, Jan (2017): "A Female Viking Warrior Confirmed by Genomics". In: *American Journal of Physical Anthropology* 164 (4), pp. 853–860.
Heisenberg, Werner (1971): *Physics and Beyond. Encounters and Conversations*. New York: Harper Collins.
Herrero, Carmen; Moreno-Ternero, Juan, and Ponti, Giovanni (2010): "On the Adjudication of Conflicting Claims. An Experimental Study". In: *Social Choice and Welfare* 34 (1), pp. 145–179.
Hijiya, James (2000): "The 'Gita' of J. Robert Oppenheimer". In: *Proceedings of the American Philosophical Society* 144 (2), pp. 123–167.
Hossenfelder, Sabine (2018): *Lost in Math. How Beauty Leads Physics Astray*. New York: Basic Books.
Hume, David (1960): *A Treatise of Human Nature*. Oxford: Clarendon Press.
Hunter, James and Nedelisky, Paul (2018): *Science and the Good. The Tragic Quest for the Foundations of Morality*. New Haven and London: Yale University Press.
Johnson, Susan (2003): "Detecting Agents". In: *Philosophical Transactions of the Royal Society of London B, Biological Sciences* 358 (1431), pp. 549–559.
Kahneman, Daniel; Knetsch, Jack, and Thaler, Richard (1986): "Fairness and the Assumptions of Economics". In: *Journal of Business* 59 (4), pp. 285–300.
Kant, Immanuel (2015): *Critique of Practical Reason*. Cambridge: Cambridge University Press.
Kauppinen, Antti (2007): "The Rise and Fall of Experimental Philosophy". In: *Philosophical Explorations* 10 (2), pp. 95–118.
Kauppinen, Antti (2014): "Ethics and Empirical Psychology. Critical Remarks to Empirically Informed Ethics". In: Christen, Markus; van Schaik, Carel; Fischer, Johannes; Huppenbauer, Markus, and Tanner, Carmen (eds.): *Empirically Informed Ethics. Morality Between Facts and Norms*. Cham: Springer, pp. 279–305.
Kelly, Kevin (2007): "A New Solution to the Puzzle of Simplicity". In: *Philosophy of Science* 74 (5), pp. 561–573.
Keynes, John (1922): "Introduction to the Series". In: Robertson, Dennis Holme (ed.): *Cambridge Economic Handbooks. Vol. 2. Money*. Cambridge: Cambridge University Press, pp. V–VI.
Kim, Minsun and Yuan, Yuan (2015): "No Cross-Cultural Differences in the Gettier Car Case Intuition. A Replication Study of Weinberg et al. 2001". In: *Episteme* 12 (3), pp. 355–361.
Knobe, Joshua (2011): "Finding the Mind in the Body". In: Brockman, Max (ed.): *Future Science. Essays from the Cutting Edge*. New York: Vintage, pp. 184–196.
Knobe, Joshua; Buckwalter, Wesley; Nichols, Shaun; Robbins, Phillip; Sarkissian, Hagop, and Sommers, Tamler (2012): "Experimental Philosophy". In: *Annual Review of Psychology* 63 (1), pp. 81–99.
Knobe, Joshua and Nichols, Shaun (2008): *Experimental Philosophy*. New York: Oxford University Press.
Knobe, Joshua and Prinz, Jesse (2008): "Intuitions About Consciousness. Experimental Studies". In: *Phenomenology and the Cognitive Sciences* 7 (1), pp. 67–83.

Konow, James (2003): "Which Is the Fairest One of All? A Positive Analysis of Justice Theories". In: *Journal of Economic Literature* 41 (4), pp. 1188–1239.
Konow, James (2009): "Is Fairness in the Eye of the Beholder? An Impartial Spectator Analysis of Justice". In: *Social Choice and Welfare* 33 (1), pp. 101–127.
Konow, James and Schwettmann, Lars (2015): "The Economics of Justice". In: Sabbagh, Clara and Schmitt, Manfred (eds.): *Handbook of Social Justice Theory and Research*. New York: Springer, pp. 83–106.
Koscholke, Jakob and Jekel, Marc (2017): "Probabilistic Coherence Measures. A Psychological Study of Coherence Assessment". In: *Synthese* 194 (4), pp. 1303–1322.
Kreuzer, Johann (2004): *Über Philosophiegeschichte*. Oldenburg: BIS-Verlag.
Kuhn, Thomas (1962): *The Structure of Scientific Revolutions*. Chicago: The University of Chicago Press.
Lacey, Hugh (1999): *Is Science Value Free? Values and Scientific Understanding*. London: Routledge.
Lackman, Jon (2006): "The X-Philes. Philosophy Meets the Real World". In: *Slate*. http://www.slate.com/articles/health_and_science/science/2006/03/the_xphiles.html, retrieved on November 3, 2018.
Lee, Bandy (2017): *The Dangerous Case of Donald Trump. 27 Psychiatrists and Mental Health Experts Assess a President*. New York: St. Martin's Press.
Loomis, Elisha (1972): *The Pythagorean Proposition. Its Demonstrations Analyzed and Classified*. Washington: National Council of Teachers of Mathematics.
Lorenz, Robert (2011): *Protest der Physiker. Die "Göttinger Erklärung" von 1957*. Bielefeld: transcript.
Lütge, Christoph; Rusch, Hannes, and Uhl, Matthias (eds.) (2014): *Experimental Ethics. Toward an Empirical Moral Philosophy*. New York: Palgrave Macmillan.
Machery, Edouard; Mallon, Ron; Nichols, Shaun, and Stich, Stephen (2004): "Semantics, Cross-Cultural Style". In: *Cognition* 92 (3), pp. 1–12.
Machery, Edouard; Mallon, Ron; Nichols, Shaun, and Stich, Stephen (2013): "If Folk Intuitions Vary, Then What?". In: *Philosophy and Phenomenological Research* 86 (3), pp. 618–635.
Machery, Edouard; Stich, Stephen; Rose, David; Chatterjee, Amita; Karasawa, Kaori; Struchiner, Noel; Sirker, Smita; Usui, Naoki, and Hashimoto, Takaaki (2017): "Gettier Across Cultures". In: *Noûs* 51 (3), pp. 645–664.
Mackie, John (1977): *Ethics. Inventing Right and Wrong*. Harmondsworth: Penguin.
Mankiw, Gregory (2011): "Know What You're Protesting". In: *The New York Times*. https://www.nytimes.com/2011/12/04/business/know-what-youre-protesting-economic-view.html, retrieved on November 25, 2018.
Miller, David (1992): "Distributive Justice. What the People Think". In: *Ethics* 102 (3), pp. 555–593.
Miller, David (1994): "Review of K. R. Scherer (ed.): Justice. Interdisciplinary Perspectives". *Social Justice Research* 7 (1), pp. 167–188.
Mole, Phil (2003): "Ockham's Razor Cuts Both Ways. The Uses and Abuses of Simplicity in Scientific Theories". In: *Skeptic* 1 (10), pp. 40–47.
Moore, George (1993): *Principia Ethica*. Cambridge: Cambridge University Press.
Mukerji, Nikil (2016): *Einführung in die experimentelle Philosophie*. Paderborn: Wilhelm Fink.
Musschenga, Albert (2005): "Empirical Ethics, Context-Sensitivity, and Contextualism". In: *The Journal of Medicine and Philosophy* 30 (5), pp. 467–490.

Nagel, Jennifer; Juan, Valerie, and Mar, Raymond (2013): "Lay Denial of Knowledge for Justified True Beliefs". In: *Cognition* 129 (3), pp. 652–661.

Nahmias, Eddy; Coates, Justin, and Kvaran, Trevor (2007): "Free Will, Moral Responsibility, and Mechanism. Experiments on Folk Intuitions". In: *Midwest Studies in Philosophy* 31 (1), pp. 214–242.

Nahmias, Eddy and Murray, Dylan (2010): "Experimental Philosophy on Free Will. An Error Theory for Incompatibilist Intuitions". In: Aguilar, Jesús; Buckareff, Andrei, and Frankish, Keith (eds.): *New Waves in Philosophy of Action*. Basingstoke and New York: Palgrave Macmillan, pp. 189–216.

Nichols, Shaun (2004a): "After Objectivity. An Empirical Study of Moral Judgment". In: *Philosophical Psychology* 17 (1), pp. 3–26.

Nichols, Shaun (2004b): *Sentimental Rules. On the Natural Foundations of Moral Judgment*. Oxford: Oxford University Press.

Nichols, Shaun and Knobe, Joshua (2007): "Moral Responsibility and Determinism. The Cognitive Science of Folk Intuitions". *Nous* 41 (4), pp. 663–685.

Nichols, Shaun; Stich, Stephen, and Weinberg, Jonathan (2003): "Metaskepticism. Meditations in Ethno-Epistemology". In: Luper, Steven (ed.): *The Skeptics*. Aldershot: Ashgate, pp. 227–258.

Nietzsche, Friedrich (1998): *Beyond Good and Evil*. Oxford: Oxford University Press.

Opp, Karl-Dieter (1972): *Methodologie der Sozialwissenschaften. Einführung in Probleme ihrer Theoriebildung*. Hamburg: Rowohlt.

Putnam, Hillary (2002): *The Collapse of the Fact/Value Dichotomy and Other Essays*. Cambridge and London: Harvard University Press.

Ramalho-Santos, Miguel and Willenbring, Holger (2007): "On the Origin of the Term 'Stem Cell'". In: *Cell Stem Cell* 1 (1), pp. 35–38.

Rawls, John (1974–1975): "The Independence of Moral Theory". In: *The American Philosophical Association Centennial Series* 48 (5), S. 283–298.

Rawls, John (2005): *A Theory of Justice*. Cambridge: Belknap Press.

Ritter, Joachim (1971): "Vorwort". In: Ritter, Joachim; Gründer, Karlfried, and Eisler, Rudolf (eds.): *Historisches Wörterbuch der Philosophie*. Vol. 1. Basel: Schwabe, pp. V–XI.

Roberts, Debbie (2013): "Thick Concepts". In: *Philosophy Compass* 8 (8), pp. 677–688.

Roughgarden, Joan (2004): *Evolution's Rainbow. Diversity, Gender, and Sexuality in Nature and People*. Berkeley, Los Angeles, and London: University of California Press.

Salloch, Sabine; Vollmann, Jochen; Schildmann, Jan, and Wäscher, Sebastian (2015): "The Normative Background of Empirical-Ethical Research. First Steps Towards a Transparent and Reasoned Approach in the Selection of an Ethical Theory". In: *BMC Medical Ethics* 16 (20), pp. 1–9.

Schippers, Michael and Koscholke, Jakob (2020): *Kohärenz und Wahrscheinlichkeit. Eine Untersuchung probabilistischer Kohärenzmaße*. Berlin and Boston: Walter de Gruyter.

Schokkaert, Erik (1999): "M. Tout-le-monde est 'post-welfariste'. Opinions sur la justice redistributive". In: *Revue Economique* 50 (4), pp. 811–831.

Schupbach, Jonah (2017): "Experimental Explication". In: *Philosophy and Phenomenological Research* 94 (3), pp. 672–710.

Schwettmann, Lars (2009): *Trading off Competing Allocation Principles. Theoretical Approaches and Empirical Investigations*. Frankfurt am Main: Peter Lang.

Schwettmann, Lars (2015): "The (Difficult) Interdependence Between Empirical and Normative Research. Empirical Social Choice and the Fair Distribution of Health Care Resources". In: *Volkswirtschaftliche Diskussionsbeiträge* 78 (1), pp. 1–36.

Selg, Anette (2016): "Forscher entzaubern die Steinzeit-Klischees". In: *Deutschlandfunk Kultur.*
http://www.deutschlandfunkkultur.de/geschlechterrollen-forscher-entzaubern-die-steinzeit.976.de.html?dram:article_id=342902/, retrieved on November 3, 2018.

Shafer-Landau, Russ (2003): *Moral Realism. A Defence.* Oxford: Clarendon Press.

Singer, Peter (2005): "Ethics and Intuitions". In: *The Journal of Ethics* 9 (3–4), pp. 331–352.

Smith, Michael (1994): *The Moral Problem.* Oxford: Blackwell.

Stevenson, Charles (1937): "The Emotive Meaning of Ethical Terms". In: *Mind* 46 (181), pp. 14–31.

Sugarman, Jeremy and Sulmasy, Daniel (2001): *Methods in Medical Ethics.* Washington: Georgetown University Press.

Swain, Stacey; Alexander, Joshua, and Weinberg, Jonathan (2008): "The Instability of Philosophical Intuitions. Running Hot and Cold on Truetemp". In: *Philosophy and Phenomenological Research* 76 (1), pp. 138–155.

Swift, Adam (2003): "Social Justice. Why Does It Matter What the People Think?" In: Bell, Daniel and de-Shalit, Avner (eds.): *Forms of Justice. Critical Perspectives on David Miller's Political Philosophy.* Lanham: Rowman & Littlefield, pp. 13–28.

Sytsma, Justin and Livengood, Jonathan (2015): *The Theory and Practice of Experimental Philosophy.* Peterborough: Broadview Press.

Sytsma, Justin and Machery, Edouard (2009): "How to Study Folk Intuitions About Phenomenal Consciousness". In: *Philosophical Psychology* 22 (1), pp. 21–35.

Traub, Stefan; Seidl, Christian; Schmidt, Ulrich, and Levati, Maria (2005): "Friedman, Harsanyi, Rawls, Boulding – or Somebody Else? An Experimental Investigation of Distributive Justice". In: *Social Choice and Welfare* 24 (2), pp. 283–309.

Vaesen, Krist; Peterson, Martin, and van Bezooijen, Bert (2013): "The Reliability of Armchair Intuitions". In: *Metaphilosophy* 44 (5), pp. 559–578.

Velasquez, Manuel (2008): "Normative Theory Versus Positive Theory". In: Kolb, Robert (ed.): *Encyclopedia of Business Ethics and Society.* Vol. 1. Thousand Oaks: Sage, p. 1524.

von Kutschera, Franz (1988): "Empirische Grundlagen der Ethik". In: Henrich, Dieter and Horstmann, Rolf-Peter (eds.): *Metaphysik nach Kant? Stuttgarter Hegel-Kongreß 1987.* Stuttgart: Klett-Cotta, pp. 659–670.

Weber, Max (2004): "Science as a Vocation". In: id.: *The Vocation Lectures.* Indianapolis and Cambridge: Hackett, pp. 1–31.

Weigel, Chris (2011): "Distance, Anger, Freedom. An Account of the Role of Abstraction in Compatibilist and Incompatibilist Intuitions". In: *Philosophical Psychology* 24 (6), pp. 803–823.

Weinberg, Jonathan; Gonnerman, Chad; Buckner, Cameron, and Alexander, Joshua (2010): "Are Philosophers Expert Intuiters?". In: *Philosophical Psychology* 23 (3), pp. 331–355.

Weinberg, Jonathan; Nichols, Shaun, and Stich, Stepehn (2001): "Normativity and Epistemic Intuitions". In: *Philosophical Topics* 29 (1–2), pp. 429–460.

Weiß, Arne Robert; Bauer, Alexander Max, and Traub, Stefan (2017): "Needs as Reference Points. When Marginal Gains to the Poor Do Not Matter". In: *DFG Research Group 2104, Need-Based Justice and Distribution Procedures, Working Paper 2017-13.*

Wetzel, Manfred (2004): *Praktisch-politische Philosophie. Vol. 1. Allgemeine Grundlagen.* Würzburg: Königshausen & Neumann.
Whitehead, Alfred (1925): "Religion and Science". In: *The Atlantic.* https://www.theatlantic.com/magazine/archive/1925/08/religion-and-science/304220/, retrieved on November 21, 2018.
Williams, Bernard (1985): *Ethics and the Limits of Philosophy.* London: Routledge.

Sylke Meyerhuber
Normative Theories and Their Influence on Empirical Research

Theoretical Expositions and Practical Examples from a Qualitative Researcher in Applied Social Psychology

Abstract: The author is a social psychologist, inviting the reader into an exploration of the normative system underpinning her research work as a scientist. From the viewpoint of qualitative research and in favour of issues concerning social sustainability in organisations, she first delineates general normative theory frameworks that influence her empirical work. Furthermore, the author reflects in which respect paradigms and methods provide parts of the normative theory influencing the work of research; foremost by example of the not yet internationally introduced "Core-Sentence Method" which operationalises research ideals in the tradition of symbolic interactionism. Overall, she perceives several "layers of normative theories" or more simply put, value-and-belief systems – rooted in personality, field of expertise, further professional and research paradigms, and concrete methods –, culminating in a guiding compass for scientific professionalism and identity.

1 Psychology of Normative Theories

> Maxims are to the intelligence what statutes are to conduct; they do not enlighten, but they guide, they direct, and although blind themselves, save us insensibly. They are the thread in the labyrinth, the compass during the night (Joubert 1899, p. 91).[1]

From early on, Philosophy tried to understand the human being, its conscience, ethics and beliefs, its impulses and reasoning as a framework of human action and decision-making. Eventually, this led to the emancipation of psychology as a

---

[1] Joubert was a French moralist and essayist, remembered today largely for his *Pensées* ("Thoughts"), a book published 1899 posthumously. I include in this chapter author's cultural backgrounds because some discourses I think have to be embedded not only temporally but also culturally.

newer branch of the sciences, from its beginning as a stand-alone discipline heavily influenced also by medicine and experimental sciences. All the same, a strong collaboration with philosophy remains, particularly through its questions and knowledge interests. Until today, psychologists have always earned their doctoral degrees as "Dr. phil.", a reminder of the common roots.

The first normative similarity between philosophy and psychology that I will consider is the *demand of logical chains in all their reasoning*, orally and in writing. Whenever I try to explain this requirement to my students, I compare the underlying logic for compiling a text like this: Imagine you have to conduct a mathematical derivation, but with words. Only by actually writing down your thoughts will you discover gaps in your reasoning. Only by trying to state the logical chain of your deduction will you see where you are in need of further explanation, or of a source offering explicit evidence for something you thought of as a given, and so forth.

In both disciplines, courses of study aim to educate future academics in precisely this kind of reasoning while the subject matter varies. I understand that both fields of study are based on the very *demand of explicating their reasoning in logical chains*, which I, therefore, label as a basic normative theory underlying both scientific disciplines.[2]

If one starts thinking about it, normative theories are in many respects part of everyday life. I would however also call them *value-and-belief systems*, since "theories" are more accurately models, approaches, attempts to describe realities, as far as they are capable while formulated in the awareness that one theory will never be able to cover all of reality, and also will never be able to avoid gaps, misconceptions, or misinterpretations. Therefore, I would think that calling such beliefs "theories" in order to give them more seriousness is part of the academic game. In other words, my normative theory about normative theories in the professional context of the sciences is somewhat self-reflexive and questions objectivity. "It could be different", whispers caution in light of this viewpoint, always. That is just another normative theory occupying my thoughts: the belief that *change of perspective* is an essential professional ability as a psychologist, a starting point for gaining access to others, to an understanding of different viewpoints and qualities of experience. For psychotherapy, counselling, and qualitative research, psychologists are trained to be able to flexibly adapt to the logic of

---

[2] In this regard I am well aware that with the advent of modern sciences and development of individual disciplines, philosophy can be seen as a "mother of the sciences" while psychology developed a more specific scope.

others, instead of insisting on being in the right. In and of itself, this is one of the normative theories my thinking as a psychologist is based on.

I state this here explicitly because I assume that other professions evolve other forms of thinking and reasoning (and you may observe that the professionalised thinking reflex explained before is active right now). In light of the above, I consider them not better or worse, but just different. Nevertheless, from other disciplinary viewpoints, this flexible adaptability as part of a professional attitude might be seen as "odd" or even "wrong". On the contrary, in humanistic psychology, it is not.

This brings me to a further normative theory underlying everything – the *conception of man*. Psychologically, the "idea of man" a person harbours in their heart can be understood as part of their overall worldview, since convictions about "how people are" are part of one's view of "how the world is". In social psychology, such subjective theories are seen as part of a person's self-image and view of others. These conceptions are discussed as individual patterns, consisting of core-topics and rim-topics, individually composed by personality and influences from culture and society, of value orientations and subjective answers to fundamental questions of life. Insofar, social psychology sees a person's idea of man as a subjective theory which forms an important part of an individual's everyday life theory.[3] For the person, these conceptions have normative character, being taken into account in private as well as in occupational life. Therefore, in the social sciences a critical view on how far questionnaires or interviews mirror a scientist's own beliefs and conceptions is typical, also in light of a cultural bias in postmodern times. Accordingly, the threat of artefacts in research that are based on such vantage points are to be reflected. Nonetheless, such ideas of man have a cognitive and emotional function, being significant as "guiding principles" for all areas of life.[4]

With social psychologist Hoff (1992), the genesis of individual basic assumptions as subjective interpretation patterns and sense-making patterns can be understood in more detail, which is particularly discussed as the individual's

---

[3] Note, that the psychologist's conception of man is therefore *not* identical to philosophy's discourse on a *condicio humana* as a much more essentialist idea of human nature.

[4] In organisational psychology, these are critically discussed for leadership styles, e.g., in the prominent *Theory X versus Theory Y* by American leadership researcher McGregor (1960), later on more differentiated by social psychologist Lewin's pupil Schein (2010) (rational-economic man, social man, self-actualising man, complex man), and further reflected with their impact on personnel recruitment issues by, e.g., German personnel recruitment specialist Preiser (1992).

"locus of control".⁵ According to the author, the locus of control is a relative constant of an individual's personality, a personal normative theory about where the control lies in one's life, so to say. Following the approach of Hoff, these subjective paradigms can be categorised as foremost internal, external, or interactionistic convictions: "It is about the main inner viewpoints of a person, related to themselves, their environment and their behaviour or action. In these subjective mental ideas, identity is expressed in the sense of the uniqueness and distinctiveness of the individual" (Hoff 1992, p. 55).

According to authors in this line of psychological reasoning, people view the events of life from their general locus of control as a normative theory about themselves within the world: Do I feel responsible for most of what happens around me? Or is everything for sure the fault of everyone but me? Or do I have a sense of what my own share in a given situation is and what aspects are influenced by others alone? These variations express main differences in people's locus of control, leading to very different perceptions and perspectives on even the same social situation (cf. Rotter 1966, Hoff 1992, in more detail about extreme world-views, see, e.g., Perry, Sibley, and Duckitt 2013).

Concluding this small journey into psychology, the non-psychologist might appreciate that normative theories play an important role in the psyche of man, providing orientation and thereby inner stability in an increasingly complex world. The importance of such stabilising elements cannot be stressed enough. In fact, subjective normative theories play a defining role in the everyday life of everyone. Though often not consciously reflected, they are nevertheless the underpinning of life in many respects, guiding a person's perceptions, interpretations and decisions, their actions or omissions, playing a role in organising how people think and what they do (cf. Lewinski, pp. 69–72). Seeing as scientists are, like everyone else, people first and professionals later, they carry their normative theories – biographically formed by personality and experience due to primary and secondary socialisation agencies – into their professions, and as scientists into their research.

Based on this line of thought, the inclined reader might ask: Which values, beliefs, and expectations do I consider building up inside of me as normative theories? And where do they come from? A person cannot avoid influences from their social environment(s). Even while in part unconsciously, people can

---

5 German social psychologist Hoff (1992) develops in his book on work, leisure time, and personality the theory of American psychologist Rotter (1966) on the individual's locus of control further by introducing a third, interactionistic pattern (referring, e.g., to Levenson 1974, Badura 1977, Krampen 1987, and Schallberger 1989). A more elaborated account can be found in Meyerhuber (2001, pp. 48–66).

at least partially reflect on these influences, particularly in adult life, adapting to some by choice and refusing others. Especially occupational choices can be viewed partly in this light to some extent. Overall though, therapy theory states as a rule of thumb that the things that influence a person will be somewhat incorporated, and therefore expressed by them. In this way, the interconnectedness of individual and environment via interaction is empathised.

"The subjective situation can be realised as a cross-point of the present and subjectively reconstructed realisation of the past. Thereby, the basis for a cognitive construction of the future is also laid" (Hoff 1992, p. 51).

It is also important to stress that *structural tensions and incompatibilities of the real world do find their way into a person's psyche*, their inner world. Here, they lead to inner tensions that a person is obliged to deal with, within and in interaction with the outer world (Leithäuser 1988, pp. 81ff.). Issues arising from this structural interconnectedness are very demanding for the psyche – imagine what happens if incorporated normative theories clash within. E.g., by personality, a person might shy away from conflict, but as part of their profession it is required of them to negotiate aggressively. Another typical example, privately a police officer might sympathise with activists protesting nuclear power, but during a demonstration the officer is commanded to act against them with force. Psychologically, internal frictions are to be expected in role- and value-conflicting situations, which over time can lead to depressive or psychosomatic reactions if the person is not able to find a psychologically more balanced solution. I, therefore, conclude that:

(a) People often hold normative beliefs they are not aware of, especially insofar as these remain unquestioned. Particularly in light of irritations, these beliefs become a subject of reflection (e.g., when people do things differently in another team, organisation, or culture, and one finds oneself exposed to these differences), or the difference is rejected as wrong, in order to hold on to one's own normative theories.

(b) If psychoanalytical social psychology is right in assuming that conflicting structural issues lead to inner tensions, it would be prudent to strive for consistency in the normative theories a person incorporates. In other words: If a person's Over-I representatives[6] are cooperative and friendly towards each

---

6 Until today, our understanding of the workings of the psyche depends on the topological model of the psyche by Austrian father of psychoanalysis Freud. In psychoanalysis theory, the Over-I (the British term is used here just as Freud himself did, not the American term Super-Ego, which Freud himself declined; cf. Bettelheim 1984) is considered a part of the structure of the psyche, a concept introduced by Freud (1959, 1969, 1989). It is the inner instance we call conscience, where imperatives, commandments, and rules are instilled, and where guilt and

other and further aspects of a person's inner world, the everyday life of the said person will be much easier or rather more harmonic.

When defining the relation of normative *target-perspective* and actual *action practice*[7] I find it most refreshing to reflect on the underlying assumptions, values, and rules in a given situation. Based on that, the reality of how they gain influence in real-life situations must then be contemplated in order to see if they are just statements of good intentions or really a normative theory of influence in a given situation. To me as a psychologist, the difference between talk and action is a very important one. I also consider this distinction helpful in light of the issue here: What is only talked about importantly, and what actually becomes an *influencing factor in social interactions?*[8] Intellectual talk without actual impact on reality does not count in this respect, since the interest pursued in this chapter is to discuss normative theories and their actual influence on empirical research.

From what has been unfolded so far, I summarise that in a person's mindset normative theories are "normative" if non-deceivable and fundamental, acting as an inner guide for one's actions or omissions, providing a moral ground, and offering a frame of reasoning in favour of a certain inner logic. Interestingly, similar things can be said for *professional standards:* they also provide a framework of "dos" and "don'ts" that cannot be sidestepped without repercussions, taking effect in part implicitly and in other aspects explicitly. Therefore, I conclude that professional standards are also normative theories. And since it has been concluded above that a scientist is a person first and professional role-inhabitant later, they carry their normative theories into their professions and their research. A further look into this entanglement is in order.

---

shame derive from. Psychotherapy is often concerned with a reduction of its influence to reasonable measures in adult life, since a too strong Over-I influence can cause a person great suffering and unhappiness.

[7] In German "Soll(-Perspektive) und Sein" differentiates the "what should be" from the "what is", or psychologically aspects of the I-ideal in relation to the I, if described from the angle of the structural model of the psyche by Freud.

[8] In accordance, recent quantitative psychological studies show that behavioural intentions only predict a relatively small part of people's actual behaviour ($r = 0.38$, meaning that it explains around 15 percent of actual behaviour, also related to the type of behaviour in question), demonstrated, e.g., by Riebl et al. (2015).

2 Layers of Normative Theory as the Framework of a Profession

> Neither love nor friendship, respect nor admiration, gratitude nor devotion, should rob us of our conscience, and our discernment for good and evil. This is a passion that we are forbidden to sell, and for which nothing could repay us (Joubert 1899, p. 99).

In light of the basic thoughts introduced so far, I will now establish and discuss some of the normative theories influencing me on a daily basis in my profession as a social psychologist at the university.[9] This section will provide examples of where the normative theories of influence in the profession as a researcher in psychology come from, and in which respect they may influence research practices.[10]

2.1 Humanistic Psychology

First of all, the paradigm in psychology which influences me most as an "inner compass" is that of humanistic psychology. The humanistic conception of man states that all human beings have an *inherent drive of self-actualisation*, a wish to realise and to express their capabilities and talents. Over the course of their lifetime people aim to become whole, so to say. It is a holistic view on the existence of man, taking all the impulses a person harbours seriously, asking how these can be positively and consciously integrated into the personality as an important part of one's life journey. Therefore, humanistic psychology encourages self-exploration and tries to integrate the different needs of a human being constructively. Applied to therapy, the approach leads to a counselling style in support of letting clients make their own choices. Important pioneers in this field are Carl Rogers (self-actualisation, non-directive talk, client-centred therapy) or for working with groups Ruth Cohn (Theme-Centered Interaction, dynamic balance of I, we, it, and globe). Humanistic psychology encourages a non-pathologising view of man, strengthening the awareness of the healthy and resourceful sides of

---

[9] The author holds a permanent academic position at the University of Bremen (Germany), at the artec Sustainability Research Centre.
[10] Here unfold in light of research, the principles of course influence counselling and lecturing as well.

a client. Seen from the context of postmodernism, similarities to branches of systemic therapy (Virginia Satir) and a resource-oriented health approach as *Salutogenesis* (Aaron Antonovsky) have become apparent.

A profession takes place in a society and therefore must be in harmony with societal and political values up to a point.[11] In the author's democratic home country Germany, the constitution states in its first commandment: "The dignity of men is inviolable", similarly to be found, e.g., in the *Charta of Fundamental Rights* of the European Union. Not only do European and German political values coincide here – for the level of psychological practice, humanistic psychology differentiates in more detail what the "dignity of men" includes (cf. Greening 2006, Aanstoos et al. 2000):

- First, the human being is seen as *no-reducible into components*, being always more than the sum of her or his parts. For my line of work, meaning the application of social psychology to work-related research, that means the awareness that a person stays human at the workplace and cannot be reduced to selling manpower to an employer. A holistic view of people in their work life does not neglect other spheres of their life, their wishes and needs, but reflects interconnectedness and compatibility.
- Humanistic psychology also acknowledges that human beings are *spiritual beings*, in the sense that they exist in a unique context of humanity and also in a cosmic environment. This leads to a deep respect for the belief and awareness of the other, with high regard for the other, their objective realities or even esoteric perceptions. For the research process, this leads to openness not only for logical but also intuitive impulses in the exploration of meaning from a subject's perspective.
- Humanistic psychology empathises on the *awareness* of men. In its light, people are understood as cognizant to be aware, of having a consciousness about themselves in a social and interactive context. In research, I tend to explore this awareness of the self with respect for the other through specifics of real-life situations that my interview partners describe as relevant for them in their field of work.
- The approach also stresses man's ability to *make choices* and the *responsibility* deriving from them. Accordingly, I do not believe in mere helpless subjection to situations but in active choices (nevertheless within situations and their dynamic). By choosing not to act, an individual is to be held as respon-

---

11 E.g., in Germany research is associated with the ministry of education and research, while in America it is controlled by the ministry of defence. One might wonder if this leads to differences in what and how research is conducted and disclosed.

sible as a person who decides to take on something actively. Of course, due to different situations, such choices bare different consequences. E. g., structural and interactionistic forces in organisations have a strong influence on people and their ability to react to them, as research shows (cf., e. g., Leithäuser and Vomerg 1988, Hoff 1992, Meyerhuber 2009, 2012, 2013, 2017, 2019), but my reflex in everyday life as well as in research is to hold people at least co-responsible for their lives and the situations they find themselves in. The dialectic of objective structures and subjective experience and action is therefore of great interest in my research (cf. Meyerhuber 2009), including questions about the structural spheres of and the subjective ability for making own choices or for acting responsibly. The extent to which postmodern organisations weaken this side of humane work is the subject of much debate in my field of study (cf., e. g., Pongratz and Voss 2002, Sennett 1990, 1998, 2002).[12]

- Additionally, humanistic psychology understands men as *intentional* in the sense that they aim for goals and are somewhat aware of future events that they may cause by their actions in the present. In this capacity, people are recognised as seeking meaning and being creative. For my research, I try to support the idea that my interview partners express the meaning something has for them, while holding back with my own thoughts as much as possible. The technique of "active listening" (cf. Rogers 1942, 1951, Meyerhuber 2019)[13] supports such communication positively. I also encourage research partners to express what has value to them and why, exploring their intentions and sense-making in an appreciating manner; a shared process towards a better understanding. Therefore, the research process in particular is experienced as very beneficial to both partners, not just the researcher.

Overall, humanistic psychology provides me with a *viable inner compass* for what an appropriate way of dealing with people and understanding them might be. When conducting research, the humanistic conception of man leads me to methods of qualitative interviews instead of, e. g., quantitative con-

---

[12] This is a very good example where my humanistic beliefs and my attitude based on symbolic interactionism have to be negotiated carefully; since a naive idea neglecting how responsibility is always embedded in complex social and psychological realities would be short-sighted.

[13] "Active listening" is a technique in communication, originally developed by Rogers for non-directive counselling and therapy work. In an appreciative and empathic way, careful listening and mirroring back of what has been understood is conducted, in order to signal keen interest, to deepen what has been said by eliciting further details, and to support the reflection and deepening of what has been said so far.

structs.[14] I understand my interview partners as partners in the research process instead of subjects, and research finds its borders if these partners feel it necessary (cf. example ethically reflected in Meyerhuber 2013).

I believe that the way the basic assumptions of humanistic psychology impact my thinking as a psychologist can be understood as a normative theory, since they provide guidelines for my professional mentalisation and action, and I feel bad if circumstances make it difficult for me to uphold the humanistic principles in my work. In conclusion, I would also say they form a substantial part of my work ethic.

2.2 Ethical Norms of the Psychology Profession

In Germany, a professional ethical code for psychologists is in effect (Berufsverband Deutscher Psychologinnen und Psychologen 2016, pp. 34 ff.). All psychologists are obliged to uphold this code in their profession. Explicitly intended as "ethical" norms, they give further orientation and offer guidance especially in ambiguous situations. Additionally, they are quite compatible with the above-explained cornerstones of humanistic psychology. Altogether, this professional code is a normative guideline of how to act as a psychologist.

In paragraph 1.2 (Berufsverband Deutscher Psychologinnen und Psychologen 2016, p. 7 f.) on ethical and professional attitude, it is pointed out that the dignity of man has to be acknowledged and a person must be respected in their actions, in acceptance of the right of the individual to live based on their own convictions and responsibility. Moreover, psychologists are requested to support self-determined personality development and thus to support basic conditions. Psychologists should promote understanding in social coexistence and respectful interaction and overall act in the general interest of the good and well-being of all people. Furthermore, they should act in favour of the natural, social-economic, and cultural living conditions of individuals and communities, in support of upright togetherness by their own example. They should also increase knowledge about the human being through research and by teaching, based on scientifically substantiated knowledge. They eventually are encouraged to look after their own psychological and physiological health as a prudent basis for their own occupational activities, and to acknowledge the disparity in the distribution of power in occupational relationships. And so on. Even this *exemplary*

---

[14] While the humanistic approach itself offers a positive idea of men, but it does not deliver a clear enough methodology to conduct research based on it alone (cf. Hutterer 1998).

presented catalogue reflects the high moral standard in the code of conduct for German psychologists, mapped out in a broad canon of rules for the profession.

In paragraph 1.3 (Berufsverband Deutscher Psychologinnen und Psychologen 2016, p. 8), key statements about human rights and human dignity are quoted, referring to the *UN Human Rights Charta*. In paragraph 2, the ethical principles of the European Federation of Psychologists' Association (2005) are laid out as a *Meta Code on Ethics*. Foremost, the four principles of the dignity of man, competency standards, a special responsibility of psychologists for clients and the society, and questions of accountability in light of integrity and interdependency are addressed. In the further text about the application of the code, possible predicaments based on the broad bundle of demands placed on the profession are reflected critically, leading to the expectation: "Decisions must be made and action must be taken, even if contradicting aspects remain unsolved" (Berufsverband Deutscher Psychologinnen und Psychologen 2016, p. 10). This example makes it apparent that with the knowledge of the psychological profession, practitioners are awarded some sort of stewardship for the social processes they are part of. Such an aspirational professional code of conduct makes it difficult to look away from societal or interactional inadequacies.

The selected examples alone may illustrate for the non-psychologist how discerning and extensive the code of conduct for psychologists in Europe and Germany is. Accordingly, the choice of this profession leads to a certain way of life, contributing to forming the personality of a psychologist in a specific direction toward philanthropy, humanism, and perhaps some civil courage. Also, it becomes evident that the bulk of normative demands can lead in everyday life and in occupational life to difficult decisions, acknowledging that contradictions must perhaps be balanced within the psyche as well as in social interactions. Therefore, both in the structure of their psyche (inner world) and in their social abilities (outer world), a psychologist is obviously in need of constructive conflict management and self-management skills.

In other careers, the amount of normative theories bound to a chosen profession and vocation may not be as ethically demanding or complex as explained for the field of psychology. However, the example clearly shows that normative theory related to certain occupations must play an important role in adult life, which is – to a large extent – work life.[15]

---

[15] It might be of interest that normative theories underlying an occupation can also lead to issues between disparate professions, e.g., expressed in organisational subcultures and action styles (cf. Schottmayer 2002).

Further to the framework of convictions and occupational obligations discussed that far, the question arises as to which additional sets of rules, demands, and direction-giving paradigms are forming the inner compass for my research.

2.3 Sustainability Discourse as a Normative Theory

My research takes place at the *artec Sustainability Research Centre* at the University of Bremen (Germany). As a regulative idea, the political agenda of "sustainable development" has been unfolded by the United Nations over the last 40 some years.[16] With its sustainability programmatic, the UN aims to achieve an ultimately global social consensus on key subject areas and key objectives that cannot be sidestepped, in favour of the just distribution of opportunities as well as goods. This involves a commitment by UN member states to (mandatory) minimum standards needed in any discussion of social policy objectives. In a world where about 20 percent of all human beings use 80 percent of its goods, while 80 percent of humanity live under difficult conditions, where decisions made by companies shape societies more than of elected politicians, the UN acts in support of a better common future (cf. World Commission on Environment and Development 1987, Grunwald 2004, Grunwald and Kopfmüller 2006). Grunwald and Kopfmüller (2006, p. 7) stress in their summary on the subject that the idea of sustainability development is not a mere scientific concept but a societal-political and therefore *normative mission statement*. In actively taking on responsibility for global issues, the principle of sustainability is, as a guiding principle, *ethical* as well as *prudent*. Nevertheless, many developments oppose sustainability goals, be it for profit, power, conveniences, or customs.

Politically and scientifically, three key areas of sustainability are differentiated nowadays, the ecological, economic, and social dimensions (Deutsches Institut für Wirtschaftsforschung; Wuppertal-Institut, and Wissenschaftszentrum Berlin 2000). In these three areas, nations and organisations ought to take on their responsibility as actors of global efficacy. Often these three sustainability dimensions are visualised as three pillars holding up a shared roof, as intersect-

---

[16] Cf. milestones of the current understanding of sustainable development, the *Bruntland Report* (World Commission on Environment and Development 1987), the *Rio Declaration on Environment and Development* (United Nations 1992), in more recent years followed by nation-rooted action plans called *Agenda 21*, currently cf. United Nations Educational, Scientific and Cultural Organization (2018).

ing circles with overlapping fields, as a triangle, or an infinitive triangle in the kaleidoscopic style of a drawing by Maurits Cornelis Escher.[17]

In theory, all three areas demand investment, in order to pursue equality, fairness, and wellbeing. In practice, though, these three dimensions are anything but equally treated. Italian sustainability researcher Colantonio (2007, p. 4) states that the economic dimension has become more effective since the 1990s, while the ecological dimension is at least currently gaining more ground due to political pressure. Social issues still fall by the wayside too often, though. In organisations, people are working under increasingly economically optimised conditions, while work-related intensification and subjectification (cf. Pongratz and Voß 2002) resulting on a global scale in reaction formations of somatic and psychosomatic syndromes such as headache, backache, depression, anxiety disorder, and burnout (cf., e.g., Meyerhuber 2012). This is the point from which my own research sets out. Derived from the political target areas defined by the UN, key areas for "acting socially sustainably in organisations" are:

Table 1: Derivation of research issues in organisations from the political plane of social sustainability areas (cf. Meyerhuber 2017, p. 136 f.).

Deduction of areas for acting socially sustainably in organisations	
Political level of operation: societal and socially concerned with …	… and rendering to the level of work organisation …
(1) Structures of assets and income	(1) Decent workplace, fair and adequate salary setting and administration
(2) High level of culture and occupational training	(2) Socially responsible work culture, good apprenticeship, and in-service training for employees
(3) High level of health	(3) Salutogenetic work structure and interactions, socially apt leadership culture, occupational health management, work-life-balance
(4) Socially and ecologically compatible mobility	(4) Social- and health-adequate work mobility, time-related compensation

---

[17] The most prominent political development in this respect, the *Agenda 21 for Culture* and the *United Cities and Local Governments (UCLG) Executive Bureau*, were leading preparations of a policy statement, *Culture – Fourth Pillar of Sustainable Development*, passed on November 17th 2010 into the World Summit of Local and Regional Leaders in Mexico City (United Cities and Local Governments 2008). For more see, e.g., Hawkes (2001), Segghezzo (2009), European Commission (2011), General Assembly of the United Nations (2013), United Nations Educational, Scientific and Cultural Organization (2018), Meireis and Ripple (2019).

Table 1: Derivation of research issues in organisations from the political plane of social sustainability areas (cf. Meyerhuber 2017, p. 136 f.) *(Continued)*

Deduction of areas for acting socially sustainably in organisations	
Political level of operation: societal and socially concerned with ...	... and rendering to the level of work organisation ...
(5) Well-balanced population and settlement structure	(5) Well-balanced demographic structure of personnel (e. g., age, gender, interculturality), promotion opportunities, career development
(6) High level of safety	(6) Contractual security, reliable and fair manner of interaction, protection of legitimate expectations, participation, culture of acknowledgement
(Grunwald and Kopfmüller 2006, pp. 49 ff.)	(Meyerhuber 2017, pp. 136 f.)

This overview illustrates the subject matters that concern acting socially sustainably derived from the macro-level of politics for the meso- and micro-level of work and organisation, and that these subjects are, as a matter of fact, consistently relevant topics in every given organisation (cf. International Organization for Standardization 2009, Bundesministerium für Arbeit und Soziales 2009). Too often, these areas are not sufficiently reinforced in everyday proceedings though, (some due to a lack of understanding for group- and process dynamics). In Germany, frameworks such as labour law and collective bargaining law, as well as more recent legal regulations for labour-related threat analysis that include the requirement to evaluate psychological stress factors (cf. § 5 of the German *Act on the Implementation of Measures of Occupational Safety and Health to Encourage Improvements in the Safety and Health Protection of Workers at Work*; Bundesministerium der Justiz und für Verbraucherschutz 2015) ought to promote intensive engagement with such issues in organisations. However, the degree to which specific stakeholders in organisations address these topics in a socially sustainably manner remains up to them.

Over time, the following working definition has been developed for a social-psychological angle on organisational and work-related research:

> Acting socially sustainably in organisations includes all actions on the level of *structures*, *interactions* and *individuals* in support of workplace sociality. All actions or omissions with effects on the fabric of the social (positively or negatively) are socially efficacious, while *socially sustainably* activities aim for sustainable social effects – in the sense of a positive should-be perspective (Meyerhuber 2017, p. 139).

Accordingly, deliberate analysis of all research material concerning these three levels of the social fabric (structure, interaction, individual), their interconnectedness and ambiguity, emergent characteristics, fractures and contradictions are issues of interest in my psychological organisational research.

In summary, two things can be remarked on at the end of this merely brief glimpse into the normative theory frameworking behind my research approach of social sustainability in organisations. First, as delineated by example, a normative rule I follow for my research is that subject areas of research *have to be deduced plausibly and comprehensively*, as research must be conducted in a manner compatible to the already accessible. The work necessary to make sure that one's own research lives up to this standard becomes – in our world of "fake news" and multiplied publishing[18] – even more essential. Second, from my humanistic psychology angle, the topic areas derived above invite me to engage and partake wholeheartedly in different interesting aspects of organisational and work life. This is wonderful, making the sustainability debate of the UN not only normative, ethical, and prudent but also very interesting. Partaking in the explorations, conceptualisation, and evaluation of ways to "act socially sustainably in organisations" with respect to structures, social interactions, and the individual is in alignment with the previously presented cornerstones of social psychology, humanism, and the psychologists' code of conduct.

3 Normative Theory in Empirical Research

> Supreme truths have such beauty, that even the errors that turn our minds upon them have some charm, and the shadows that veiled them have a kind of radiance (Joubert 1899, p. 102).

Psychology ranks as a science,[19] substantiated by experiments, statistics, and elaborate research designs, and based on stringent regulations of conduct. Psychological empirical research and its publishing follow defined rules, principles, and justifications (Deutsche Gesellschaft für Psychologie 2016). The research approach I work with is rooted in qualitative methodology and reasoning. The nor-

---

18 Beside these classic three, recently different further dimensions have been suggested in this global political and scientific discourse. Some examples are Bohannon (2013), Shaw (2013), Prafer (2018), Funke and Mantzarlis (2018).
19 Not, as some non-psychologist think, an art, nor arbitrary: the psychology degree is a Master of Science.

mative theory that is contained in and enforced by this tradition in the social sciences will be outlined in the following.

3.1 Qualitative Research Paradigm

In sociology and social psychology, the *interpretation of social actions* is of foremost interest in order to understand processes as well as the effects of the social. The "understanding approach" has its own tradition. As a fundamental way of thinking, the paradigm for qualitative research was unfolded, e.g., by symbolic interactionist Thomas Wilson (1973).[20] *Symbolic interactionism* is especially designed to understand social situations and to lay them out in a way that the reader recognises parallels to their own experiences (cf. Helle 2001, p. 3).[21] In a famous essay, Wilson explains the main differences between the quantitative and the qualitative paradigm of sociological and social-psychological research. The main reasoning in the explanatory approach by Wilson:

> Following the interpretative paradigm, in contrast to the normative paradigm, definitions of situations and actions cannot be seen as once and for all, explicit or implicit, being set and established. [...] Rather definitions of situations and actions must be seen as interpretations, ratified or revised or restated by participating actors at singular "event points" (Wilson 1973, p. 61).

In this light, all interaction in social situations can and must be reconstructed in an understanding manner, from the acting individual's points of view and with respect to a specific interaction constellation. Occurrences are to be understood as neither objectively factual nor repeatable. Situations may seem similar but have their peculiars in meaning and importance from the viewpoint of the persons affected, which might lead to different further results. According to Wilson,

---

[20] The approach of symbolic interactionism developed as a branch of American sociology. It is a sociological theory of micro-sociology, analysing interaction between individuals in relation to specific situations. The symbolically conveyed process of communication respectively interaction yields meaning of social objects, situations, and relationships. Important representatives of the approach are Blumer (1969, 1981) and Mead (1978).

[21] "Comprehension" is a problem of epistemology, with roots in the world of ideas by Plato, the concept of reason by Kant, and later positivism and Neo-Kantianism. Understanding as pursuit here follows the idea of making traceable the process of attribution and assignment of significance (cf. Mead 1978), leading to Blumer and others for the research-oriented development of the theory of symbolic interactionism (cf. Helle 2001).

therefore all social interaction has to be understood as a process of interpretation instead of factual events. As such,

> explanations can not be construed in a deductive manner, but must be understood as acts in which agents are attributed with intentions and circumstances suitable to explain to the observer the meaning of monitored actions. This approach, to try to interpret the actions of agents in light of their intention and specific situation, is [...] a sensible and significant means of explanation. Our conclusion is therefore not that the sociological explanation of action patterns is impossible, but rather that they are profoundly different from explanations referring to phenomena which are not themselves construed by meaning and sense (Wilson 1973, p. 69).

With its analytical concept, the paradigm of symbolic interactionism clarifies that a person's gesture does not allow for a nomothetic-deductive[22] conclusion of its meaning, rather must it be *interpreted in its specific context*. E. g., a smile in a meeting does not imperatively indicate happiness, or sympathy, or approval, it can also indicate ruefulness, or cynicism, or rejection, or play-acting,[23] or that a person is thinking of something entirely different, like last night's lovemaking. Therefore, a careful reconstruction by means of indicators of what is actually going on is supported by this paradigm. Research depends on active participants with knowledge about the field the research takes place in, and the subjective perspective is understood as a level of analysis in its own right (cf. Leithäuser and Volmerg 1988, p. 94 ff., Meyerhuber 2009, p. 101). To this end, Wilson (1973, p. 55) argues that "taking action" or "acting" in the sense of the paradigm describes a complex and exploratory space, comprising much more than human "behaviour" as a predictable pattern. The term "acting" tethers the action to the sense the action comprises. In the tradition of the school of "understanding sociology" in Europe, German sociologist Max Weber differentiates this further:

> "Acting" should describe human behaviour if and when the person who acts connects this action to a distinct subjective meaning. "Social acting" though should describe the actions of one or more persons whenever the sense of the behaviour refers to actions of others and the action is oriented or related to an ongoing process (Weber 1980, p. 1).

---

[22] The term "nomothetic" developed from a Greek term for "lawgiving". It depicts an approach to science seeking lawfulness by testing hypotheses, applying research-supported general formulations to particular cases, and using a deductive approach to reasoning. In opposite to this paradigm, the idiographic, from the Greek term for "oneself" or "one's own" can be differentiated (cf. Salkind 2007).
[23] On the one hand one might think here also of Goffmann (2003), on the other hand of Hochschild (1983).

Since all actions of individuals occur socially contextualised, all acting is at least to some degree also social acting. In research about work and organisation, this viewpoint is particularly enlightening. For research, symbolic interactionism aims for social "understanding" instead of "explaining". Read as a normative theory, the approach guides a specific kind of research, demanding certain ways of collecting and analysing information about the fabric of sociality. The reader might recognise, even by such a brief introduction of cornerstones, how the paradigm is consistent with the humanistic demands, attitudes, and methods delineated above.

Research with this ambition is to be designed as a *participatory* process – understanding an unfamiliar living environment only becomes possible by entering into it, getting involved and going along with the logic offered by research partners and their field. This term expresses another aspect of the accompanying attitude in research designs that adhere to it; individuals in interviews or group discussions, et cetera are regarded as research partners and experts of subject matters in the study, not as test subjects or objects of study. In attitudes and methods, this leads to a respectful and interested manner of communication (in contrast to, e.g., monotonous and alienating questions and answers). For Wilson (1973, p. 55), all *interaction itself is an interpretive process*, and all actions are part of a larger process of interaction, action answering action; a macro-social phenomenon unfolding. Since all actions can be rationalised in retrospection, this kind of research needs an understanding of intention and everyday life theory,[24] in order to be able to reconstruct perspectives and meanings adequately.

While it would lead too far from the topic at hand if I were to describe this paradigmatic and theoretical background in more detail, at least one further normative framework of interest should be derived from Wilson. The author points out which *quality criteria of qualitative research* must be met. For all research must observe certain quality criteria and live up to a set of norms, standards and rules in its scientific community (as defined via paradigm). Research following the paradigm outlined above is not exactly the mainstream,[25] and therefore must justify the quality of its findings. A guideline on how to achieve preciseness, dependability, reflection of relevance, validity, reliability, and a certain representativity of results is of interest. And just expressing this point illustrates an-

---

[24] Cf. Leithäuser et al. (1981) about everyday life theory (German: "Theorie des Alltagsbewußtseins").
[25] For a meta-study on the worldwide increase of qualitative research in psychology cf. Carrera-Fernández, Guàrdia-Olmos, and Peró-Cebollero 2012.

other normative theory in the sciences, which researchers have to deal with in their work. Here are some exemplary key elements:
- For research from the angle of symbolic interactionism, Wilson (1973, p. 67) points out that the probing rendition is in itself a construction of context – a context nurtured by actions for which interpretation is construed. According to the author, based on later events or information, to a later point these interpretations can and should be *revised* as appropriate. In conclusion, the researcher must be aware of this fact and document the whole research process and all interpretation with great care.
- Furthermore, interpretation is to be construed in light of all information gained from the context, so that "indexical patterns" become apparent (as opposed to stand-alone assumptions or unjustifiable claims). Interpretation derived in this manner must than be *documented* and *passed back* to research partners and colleagues (Wilson 1973, p. 68), thereby allowing for the verification of *conclusiveness* and *appropriateness* (criteria) of the "interpretative documentary".
- Additionally, interpretations in sociological interactionism research are to be described with Blumer's (1954) "sensitizing concepts", so Wilson (1973, p. 69). The careful encoding of empirical text material itself is to be understood as an interpretative process (Wilson 1973, p. 70). Furthermore, the context and background of all interpretation must be documented, instead of only presenting or stating results. Since objectivity in the context of this approach is not possible, instead *complete traceability* is what is to be aspired.

Concluding, only some of the exemplary qualitative criteria in this research paradigm are laid out here. Nevertheless, this alone illustrates the careful and respectful dealings a researcher has to facilitate in order to achieve their goal. I assume that in all research, the inner compass of paradigm and methodology gives a researcher an important steering wheel allowing them to maintain an aspired course even in light of manifold "turbulences and wind shear" in the research field, the complexity of text material, and everyday life issues perplexing the mind.

Is finding and incorporating the "right" paradigm for one's research enough, though? As I understand it, this again is just another set of binding guidelines in which then particular methods of survey and analysis are brought to bear.

3.2 The Idiosyncrasies of Qualitative Research Methods – Text Analysis with the "Core-Sentence Method" by Leithäuser and Volmerg

Thus far I have elaborated on the fact that research in the field of work and organisation should be designed as research beneficial to partners in the field as well as to the sciences, although these are pursuable to different degrees.[26] At the same time, research must follow sets of norms and rules defined by the scientific community and the paradigm chosen by the researcher. To which strategic and operational framework does this lead in research? Over time, suitable research settings and methods operationalising the qualitative-interactionist paradigm have been developed and incrementally set out. Exemplarily, some of the main aspects of such methodological instruction and limitation will be introduced in the following to allow insights into the complexity of normative theory explicitly determining research, with definitions and instructions on how to use a method.

3.2.1 Introductory Thoughts About the Collection and Interpretation of "Text"

When *workplace-related research* has its foundations in the paradigm of symbolic interactionism, qualitative research requires an appropriate attitude and adequate proceedings while collecting information in the form of narrations, discussions, and sometimes also symbolisations, leading to text material and drawings for analysis and interpretation. These qualitative methods include unstructured or partially structured *interview methods* such as narrative, theme-centred, or expert interviews (cf. Bogner, Littek, and Menz 2002, Schorn 2000, Hitzler, Honer, and Maeder 1994), as well as methods as *group discussion* and role plays (cf. Volmerg, Senghaas-Knobloch, and Leithäuser 1986, Stahlke 2001). I expect that basics of these interview methods mentioned above are well known, and will, therefore, decline from explaining them in detail here or pointing out their nor-

---

26 The underlying distinction I follow here is: (1) *Basic research* is primarily interested in scientific issues and deals with them purely scientifically. (2) *Application-oriented basic research* is oriented towards scientific and practical issues simultaneously and works on them scientifically, offering results to be used in practice. (3) *Applied research* is primarily referencing to practical issues which are worked on purely scientifically. (4) *Transdisciplinary research* aims for scientific and practical problems and collaborates not only with different fields of expertise but also with actors beside the scientific community. (5) *Transformative research* primarily focuses on solving persistent societal problems.

mative theory aspects. Whereas basics of these qualitative interview- and group-settings are well described in books (cf., e.g., Meyring 1990, Kern 1982, Horn 1979), each time they are used they have to be modified to the specific field and situation of a study in order to fit the subject matter at hand. *Appropriate adaptation of these survey methods* is supported by normative guidelines elaborated on thus far.

While one can read about methods in books, their realisation with an appropriate attitude is a different matter. In the face of the paradigm outlined above, it became apparent that research concerned with subjective and interactional patterns, as well as their interpretation of ascribed sense and meaning in specific organisational situations must be based on *building an interested and respectful relationship* with organisational role owners as eye-level partners in the endeavour (cf. Meyerhuber 2013). In this respect, I find it most helpful to tune my communication in the style of *non-directed counselling* by Rogers (see subsection 2.1) during the survey process as well as for interpretation.[27] Most of all this means applying the non-directive communication attitude called "active listening", which is particularly congruent here due to its humanistic background. "Active listening" is an attitude and method stressing acknowledgement, empathy, and authenticity in communication, resulting in the experience of genuinely humane encounters with high healing potential for a client. This is achieved by carefully listening to and carefully mirroring back of what has been understood, and by respectfully asking questions closely related to what has been said without judgement. When practised in interviews, the research partner feels understood and accepted, and the narration can unfold consistently from the angle of the speaker. Accordingly opening up and giving detailed insights unfolds naturally. The interviewee often better understands and processes hitherto unresolved aspects of a situation spoken about. Hence both interlocutors profit from the familiar talk (cf. Meyerhuber 2019). Later, in the process of interpretation, the same attitude supports the researcher in focussing and staying open to what the material has to reveal, instead of falling into the trap of interpreting material foremost in light of their own viewpoints and expectations.

In the following, a *method for text analysis* called the "Core-Sentence Method" will be delineated, and exemplarily some aspects with normative character concerning how to conduct this method will be highlighted. I chose this method because, as far as I know, it has not yet been broadly translated from German

---

[27] Rogers was an influential American psychologist and counts among the most important representatives of humanistic psychology. His well-respected therapeutic approach is known as non-directive and client-centred, applied in therapy as well as in counselling.

into other languages. Therefore, I feel that it might be of interest for international readers to have a brief if only exemplarily look at some of the main ways this method operationalises the ideals of symbolic interactionism. It must be mentioned upfront that the methodological proceedings, as well as their theoretical background, are complex. They are designed to offer a workable and transparent answer to the demands of symbolic interactionism by weaving psychoanalytical, linguistic, and sociological aspects tightly into one logical framework, whereupon social interaction is understood as interpretation, and research as social interaction produces its own interpretation of those interpretations in a reflected manner. Accordingly, the aspired research product is a "documentary interpretation" (Wilson 1973, p. 62, based on Garfinkel 1962) based on the recognition and documentation of "indexical patterns" throughout the material, to be interpreted with attentive regard to the fabric of sociality. This philosophy in mind, German social psychologists Leithäuser and Volmerg introduced the "Core-Sentence Method" in 1988, working primarily with material gathered in interviews, group discussions, and additional collective drawings created during group discussions in order to symbolise and deepen certain aspects deemed as important in the discussion group (cf. Volmerg, Senghaas-Knobloch, and Leithäuser 1986).[28] In the following, some of the proceedings of this approach are outlined.

3.2.2 Hermeneutic Understanding in Text Interpretation

One principle of analysis in the Core-Sentence Method is "hermeneutic understanding", under the assumption that *understanding derives over time*, like an ongoing circle (cf., e.g., Gadamer 1960) or spiral (cf. Bolten 1985), while the researcher emerges in detail and thought, gaining a deeper understanding over time, which again stimulates further investigation of the material, and so forth.[29] In this process, the *learning process* of research partners and the researcher are not artefacts but prerequisite for success in hermeneutic research (Volmerg 1988, p. 132). A hermeneutic attitude while working with transcripts and drawings determines its own rules, such as:

---

[28] For research in or with groups as well as group discussions, the method and attitude supported by Theme-Centered Interaction is, in addition to active listening, very useful. This is solely mentioned as a further referral for the interested reader, for more detail, see Cohn (1975), Volmerg, Senghaas-Knobloch, and Leithäuser (1986), Schneider-Landolf, Spielmann, and Zitterbarth (2017), Meyerhuber, Reiser, and Scharer (2019).

[29] Ethno-psychoanalysis and other branches of ethno-psychology draw similar conclusions (cf. Nadig 1986, 2004).

- Reflecting on one's *own pre-assumptions* and modifying them in light of a developing and changing interpretation in the process. Accordingly, it is imperative to remain cognitively flexible and open as a researcher.
- In attitude, the hermeneutic researcher is *seeking out the sense of social interactions* in a given field – sense from the angle of the context and the research partners and their understanding. It is not one's own opinions but openness to the specifics of "sense in the field" that drives the interpretation. The underlying rule: All action makes somewhat sense and asks to be understood (Volmerg 1988, p. 131).
- In order to support this effort, a willingness to *partly becoming a member* of the research field and its rules is suggested. This allows for an empathic personal reflection on narrations: What does it mean for me professionally, cognitively, emotionally? Do I understand more by empathising with the field and its agents (Volmerg 1988, p. 131)?
- Furthermore, acceptance of and dealing with the *vagueness of meaning* (Volmerg 1988, p. 132) and the *flexibility of rules* in a social context are essential. The "vagueness of meaning" is a concept developed by language philosopher Wittgenstein.[30] Understanding rules as keys to the social fabric that are but flexible instead of fixed allows for better access to the expectable but difficult aspects within the material; such as change, friction, ambiguity, or contradiction.

Hermeneutic understanding supports a re-construction of the somewhat *disturbed or broken common understanding*, which is often not pure and incomplete (Volmerg 1988, p. 132). Awareness of implicit knowledge permeating the social code in normality, taboo, omission, and stereotype is sensible. The researcher is required to be continually aware that so-called neutrality is a myth and to reflect – ideally with post-scripts, field diaries, reflection with interlocutors – in order to support the reduction (not elimination) of blind spots in the interpretation process. This understanding of hermeneutic stems from the symbolic interactionist Gadamer and psychoanalysis.

Accordingly, any results are interpreted in a manner of "what has been understood so far" instead of "this is what is true".[31] This moderate demeanour invites experts from the field, colleagues, and research partners to retrace and comprehend how a certain interpretation came to pass instead of believing

---

[30] Wittgenstein was an Austrian and British philosopher. His works comprise reflections on logic and, i.a., the philosophy of language, mathematics, and the mind.
[31] Exactly this attitude "what has been understood so far" is also applied in active listening, another consistency.

the results presented to be factual; precisely in the spirit of qualitative research quality criteria described above.

3.2.3 Concrete Steps to Be Taken

Imagine that interviews or group discussions have taken place in a non-standardised way. Well attuned to a hermeneutic attitude, concrete steps are to be taken in order to *organise collected material*, so as to enter the process of interpretation.

- First, a *transcript* is to be written, including pauses and other rather nonverbal but crucial indicators for the following symbolic interactional understanding.
- Second, *narrations* in the flow of the text are distinguished: Where does the next topic or sub-topic start? For each of these text passages or narrations, a sort of headline is densified from the text, the so-called *core sentence* indicating exactly what this text passage is about at the core of its meaning (not so much mere topics but more the gist of it).
- Third, the interview is *virtually cut*, according to the narrations, so that the passages are distinguishable. Imagine this as a bunch of cards with text and a headline, the core sentence.
- Fourth, the researcher *clusters these cards*, the narrations, according to the proximity and logic of themes and their dynamic, into heaps.
- Fifth, *the most typical card/narration/core sentence*, representing its cluster best, is laid on top of a pile of sequences about a topic. The core sentence of this card best represents the sequences within the heap. Sometimes one narration fits into different clusters, due to a mixture of different aspects that text passage refers to. In this special case, the card can be *copied* as needed and added elsewhere, so that those connections into other clusters are not lost.
- Sixth, the overall topics tend to represent aspects of the more complex perspectives and dimension of experience related to the social field. These otherwise suppressed connections are now made explicit, and then an overall headline is found.

This sounds feasible, right? Well, imagine two hours of transcript leading to about 200 narrative units or cards before you, and after much contemplation and sensitivity spent, a sense-making pattern occurs. Generally speaking, single-case analysis leads to vertical hermeneutics (in-depth analysis), while reviews of several interviews and group discussions more often lead to horizontal hermeneutics (comparing and puzzling together overall issues). Offering a tangible example, the occurring pattern in a single-case analysis is shown based on a piece of my own research material (figure 1).

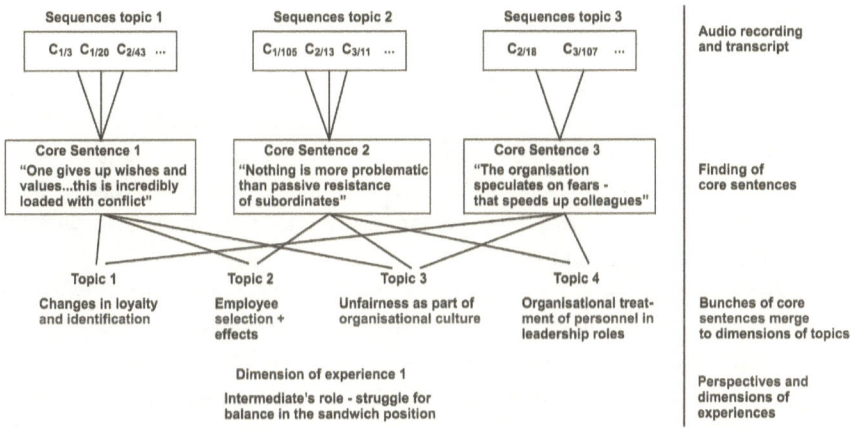

Figure 1: Steps of analysis and interpretation by example from an unpublished case study by Meyerhuber about experiences of an intermediate in times of change; diagram text material in clusters of meaning, illustrating the logic in an overall schema for text analysis by Leithäuser and Volmerg (1988, p. 248)

Singular narrations assemble "sequences of the same issue" and find themselves represented by the most comprehensive "core sentence" card of a cluster. In light of different clusters somewhat connected to each other, underlying themes become apparent, adding up to one "dimension of experience". There might be other dimensions with similar internal complexity. And these are again in specific relationships to each other. Thusly, from contemplation on the narrations in a chronological text, by disassembling and newly re-constructing the material, the complexity of the social field emerges in a clearer form and gives new insights via a more disclosing structure than the original succession.

3.2.4 Occurrence of Personal, Interactional, and Structural Barriers to Understanding

Staying open to occurring patterns instead of sorting cards according to how oneself thinks about the field is the first stumbling block. Here alone, conflicts in research groups can become insurmountable and instead of the truth of the field, dominant definitional power struggles impede the process of enlightenment. Accordingly, some researchers are more suitably open and ambiguity-tolerant, thus better able to uncover the potentials of the material. "Structurally, the entrance into a foreign research field is comparable to the entrance into a foreign culture", Volmerg (1988, p. 141) explains. People are different and differently able to cope with ambiguity and strangeness, mirrored in the interpretation process.

Another consequence is that field-appropriateness must be observed, moulding the method to field-prevalent rules, and asking questions such as: What do I know about the rules and culture of the interview partners and their field? How does my professional expertise and reputation fit into it? Last but not least, how does my own personality relate, my values and wishes; what can I do or grasp, and what not?

These thoughts lead to an overall reflection on the *barriers to understanding* in such qualitative research. From the viewpoint of psychology, barriers to understanding may derive from different sources in the context of research activities: (1) One's own *unconscious motives*, like personal interests, a lack of or wish for reflective distance, being involved as a person with individual thoughts and feelings. (2) *Anxieties* may occur, if anxiety from events in one's own history is touched on, or personal defence mechanisms become activated, the researcher loses her ability to empathise and act appropriately. (3) Moreover, anxieties can arise from the *social situation* within the research group itself. The researcher aims for a good standing with others while trying to stay true to her- or himself – not always simple in practice.

Not only personal and interactive-based barriers might become apparent. In their methodological book, Volmerg emphasises: "A reflection of the mechanisms – which through *determinations of the science production structure* are part of any research process – ought to be an integral part of psychoanalytical social psychology" (Volmerg 1988, p. 145). It is only in this way, the author argues, that one might gain an understanding of the activated psychic defences against anxieties in the research process, which derives from distortions of the subjectivity of the researcher in light of their research material and the intersecting social settings (figure 2).[32]

---

[32] I do not want to go into detailed explanations of psychoanalysis theory here, in short: In-depth psychology deals with strategies of the psyche active to protect the individual from anxieties and unacceptable impulses related to reality (the outside world), thrives (the It), and the conscience (the Over-I), functioning foremost unconsciously. Thus, the self (I) maintains stable. The topological model of the psyche by Sigmund Freud and further insights by, e. g., Anna Freud have proven useful for understanding the impulses within a person. Nowadays, psychoanalysis identifies many different defence mechanisms of the psyche, such as rationalisation, repression,

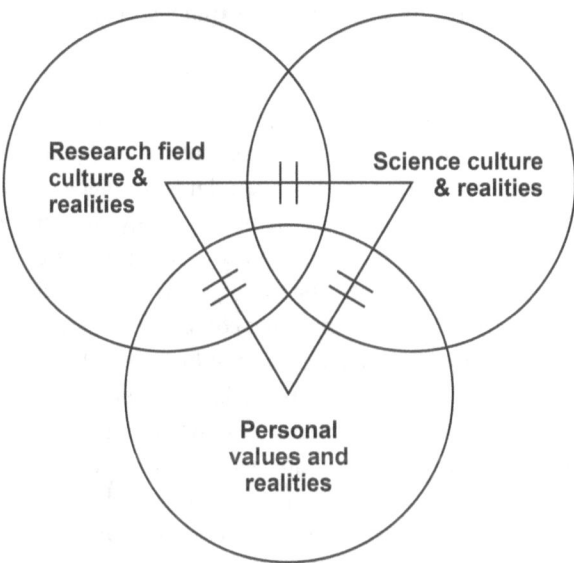

Figure 2: Reflecting "barriers to understanding" in and between researcher, research field, and scientific community as normal part of all empirical situations; visualisation with reference to Leithäuser and Volmerg (1988, p. 252)

As the visualisation indicates, the situation consequently connects different areas of the social, and thereby also bears several barriers to understanding, besides issues stemming from the research itself (Volmerg 1988, p. 142). *Field-specific* defences can be unconsciously raised against attempts at communication about taboos, specific interactions or talks, or the uncovering of certain aspects of the fields and their routines (in all directions). So, while a researcher must be able and willing to adapt to the field of research, the defence of the field against the research (there is always at least a bit of it) can in some ways form a threat to the identity of the researcher as well as artefacts in the material. Situations can threaten self-conceptions within the science culture, and of the personality. While this tangle is a *structurally* given problem in any research, artefacts from this constellation become more quickly apparent when the researcher is attuned to this fact. In conclusion, the ability and willingness of such reflection as

---

idealisation, identification with the aggressor, regression, shifting, sublimation, splitting, isolation, depersonalisation, devaluation, somatizising, and so on (cf. Laplance and Pontalis 1973, a classic book and testament of fruitful collaboration between a psychoanalyst and a philosopher).

a researcher appears to be substantial and is explicitly demanded in the qualitative research outlined here.

Moreover, the researcher needs experience in how to structure material in this way; being open to the logic emerging from the material, instead of following their own inner logic. Only then can the content fall into place, and the further analysis and interpretation of the text material takes place accordingly. But what if my questioning of the text misses the point entirely, or if the text answers in a way that I cannot grasp? This might indicate that aspects of the material make me anxious and cloud my understanding. Barriers to understanding do not only occur during the survey and in direct contact with an interview partner or research field. They have their meaning in the hermeneutic field of interpretation as well (Volmerg 1988, p. 256). Empathising and self-reflection in contact with the text material might lift the barrier to understanding, to a degree. Discourse in the interpretational group helps as well. Nevertheless, blind spots are human, and some aspects will continue to elude us. But in order to differentiate such issues from methodological blunder, a bit more understanding of how a text should be questioned is appropriate.

3.2.5 Interpreting – The Text is Not the Person – Four Levels of Questioning Text

Qualitative text interpretation is based on the *researcher's understanding of meaning and sense* by knowledge of the rules of everyday life and language (Volmerg 1988, p. 258). It is imperative to see that in contrast to everyday life, scientific understanding is produced systematically (Volmerg 1988, p. 256). "Systematically" means, with reference to the author, not being satisfied with a "nearly" or "vague" understanding or skipping over misunderstandings or annoyances. On the contrary, misunderstandings or vagueness in a text are to be recognised as indicators for examining those aspects further, comparing them to other text passages of similar contents; it is a journey of trying to make sense of them. This is why all the passages of the material are processed and sorted, instead of conveniently just picking a striking sequence for analysis.

"As a virtual counterpart, the text answers to our questions about meaning and sense", the author points out (Volmerg 1988, p. 256). For this purpose, the text and the text-producing person must be differentiated: "*The text is not the person.* Even if one person is spoken of as the key person in the text, or is the narrator in an interview, this person that we imagine based on the text is not the person him- or herself" (Volmerg 1988, p. 256). Even more, mostly in the context of organisational research, the question is: What does this mean, spoken by a representative of this work culture? What do we learn by this example about the field as a whole? Instead of personalising what is said in the text, content is regarded as an expression of the social fabric of workplace realities. In short, this "underworld of the text has to be distinguished from the personal unconsciousness of the individual" (Volmerg 1988, p. 254).

Layers of understanding in text material are to be lifted by systematically questioning the text. Figure 3 shows the levels of this systematic procedure.

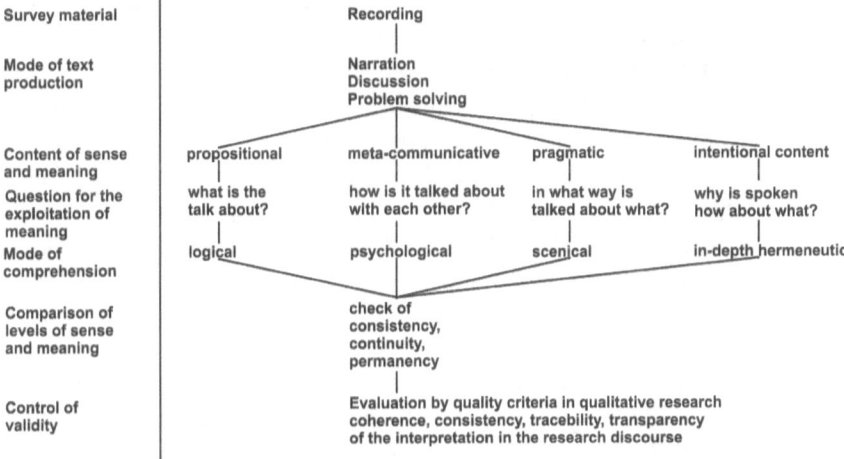

Figure 3: Schematic of steps of text analysis and interpretation by Leithäuser and Volmerg (1988, p. 257; own translation)

Accordingly, the content of sense and meaning is to be explored by four levels of questioning towards the text (with reference to linguistic text comprehension):
- *Propositional logical* understanding of factual messages of communication and interaction (understanding content of the spoken). This alone is a greatly rewarding endeavour throughout research material. The leading question: *What* is the talk about?
- *Psychological* understanding explores the meta-communicative substance with respect to the emotional content and in light of relationships (understanding the interlocutor), which is supported by the analysis of: *How* is it talked about with *whom*?
- *Scenic* understanding endeavours to analyse patterns of the scene which are part of the organisation. The linguistic pragmatic tries to understand the manifestations of life (understanding the situation), evaluating: *In what way* is talked about what exactly, throughout the text material?

– *In-depth hermeneutic* comprehension tries to unravel intentional content. Often unconsciously hidden in the speaker and cultural practices, understanding hidden wishes or defences within a scene is very interpretative. Nevertheless and in light of supporting indexical patterns throughout the text, here the leading question is: *Why* is spoken how about what (or not), and with whom?

Observation of the interpretative plane that one interprets on is one of the qualitative criteria in this kind of research. Only thus can contents of meaning be unearthed systematically in the excavation we call text interpretation. The proceedings are complex, time-consuming, they need intuition and detective work, more than simple handicraft. A very good sense of language and its nuances as well as (sub-)intercultural understanding is of the essence.

With reference to Lorenzer (1970), Volmerg (1988, p. 259) indicates that to her the most important aspect of a symbolic interactionist and psychoanalytical text understanding is the "scenic understanding". Being able to recognise overall occurring patterns within the narrations, and even more of the way in which things are spoken of (or not), this opens the door to a deeper understanding of the interactional *function and meaning of things in a certain context*, embedded in the form of how topics are handled throughout the text. Scenic patterns within text material are like offers to the interpreter, becoming more apparent with the time one spends on it. The four questions (planes/levels) for the systematic exploitation of sense and meaning support the researcher's balance of keeping a distance while allowing involvement. Thereby, one's *own and foreign sense-making* of the text can be differentiated; the author: "The scenic pattern always implies a relationship offer towards the interpreter too, only re-constructible to the same degree as the researcher's involvement" (Volmerg 1988, p. 260). The method needs a certain amount of training and probably "fitting" to practitioners. While most students of psychology somewhat master statistical factor analysis, I doubt that as many as them are aptly skilled for this method.

Overall, by these selected extracts alone it becomes apparent that the "core-sentence method" consists of a normative corpus of rules aimed at conducting and writing down a sensible, field-appropriate interpretation. Though exemplarily, this should be enough to provide an impression of how the approach leads to normative guidance and to successful empirical conduct in an "understanding" manner, by means of theory and methodology.

4 Conclusion

> Not only is there no goodness where there is no
> rule and law, but there is not even pleasure.
> Even the games of children have laws, and
> could not exist without them: these laws are a
> constraint, and yet, the more strictly they are
> observed, the greater is the enjoyment
> (Joubert 1988, p. 94).

The overall question in this volume concerns the relation in which we define normative theory and empirical research. How can their relatedness approximately be described, defined, or differentiated? As it became apparent in this chapter, I do not believe there is an opposition between the two. On the contrary, I argued throughout the text in favour of an integrative understanding of the two terms "normative theory" and "empirical research". Nevertheless, the normative framework must endure where real-life issues demand adaptation. While normative theory provides a compass, in research we are but using our compass (devised of emotional, cognitive, social, and professional guidelines), while sailing closely with the winds of our research field. Here we must adapt ourselves as well as our methods, within reasonable limits. By contrast, bending real-life issues to fit into normative theory would present the danger of producing ivory tower artefacts instead of appropriate understanding (e. g., of workplace-related issues), and this must be rejected.

As shown throughout my reasoning, from a psychologist's viewpoint a broader definition of what normative theory means was introduced (others might define this differently), delineating inner-worldly as well as professional, theoretical and methodological normative theories contributing to and build on "layers" of what the author, as a researcher, perceives as actually important compass components for her own empirical work. In accordance with the spirit of symbolic interactionism, I find it reasonable to address the issue on this broader scale in order to draw a picture of the normative landscape of a professional scientist travelling towards the goal of empirical research. Each reader's personal landscape will be a different one, but perhaps she or he now feels inspired to reflect on the levels of normative underpinnings in their own work, at least these which are consciously accessible?

Beside this strictly *subjective level of analysis* and in light of having normative theories influencing empirical research defined as value-and-belief systems that are comprised of personal, discipline- and subject-specific convictions, I need to point out that there is also a research tradition on values in social psychology as well as in philosophy. In this respect, this author's contribution can be understood as setting out parts of a subjective value structure, comprised from mostly consistent proportions of professional and personal conceptions. "Values are central points for orientation, they guide our actions and are at the base of culture", defines German social psychologist Witte (2008, p. 10). And his colleague and value researcher Klages (2008, p. 11) explains further: "While in the middle of the 20th century values were still mostly understood from a religious and philosophical tradition as undeniable reference points of morale, the development of a modern value- and value-change research scrutinizes values as variable concepts, different between cultures as well as individuals, and alterable over time".

According to Klages (2008, p. 12), in religion and philosophy values seem to have a more absolute character (right versus wrong), while psychological research stresses the relativity of values, their variability over time and context. This does not deny that they have also normative character for the time being. The cradle of modern social-psychological value research is seen by Klages (2008, p. 13) in the interdisciplinary large-scale project *Towards a General Theory of Action* (1951)[33] by sociologists Parsons and Shils, cultural anthropologist Kluckhohn, and psychologists Allport, Murray, Sears, and Tomann, to whom values were a connecting element: "Values have a central role in mediating between the macro- and micro-level, they are indispensable for analysing connections between person, culture and society", so Klages (2008, p. 13). While in about 100 years of value research different approaches emerged, a prominent one is the Rokeach Value Survey (RVS) from 1973, an instrument comprised of two lists of terminal and instrumental values which ought to be put into a subjective order.[34] Developing this further, an integrative meta-instrument was devised by Schwartz (1992) based on a structural model allowing researchers to sort and visualise many different values in one chart.[35] Bilsky (2008, p. 66 f.) writes:

---

[33] *Towards a General Theory of Action* from 1951 comprise contributions by members of the Department of Social Relations of the Harvard University, as well as by their visiting international collaborators. It is a famous and groundbreaking work, an interdisciplinary attempt to describe, clarify, and connect main principles and categories for a shared theory of the social sciences. Thus, the book outlines the common ground of the traditional disciplines of psychology, sociology, and cultural anthropology.

[34] Rokeach was an American social psychologist with Polish roots, located first at the Michigan State University and later the Washington State University.

[35] Schwartz is an American-Israeli social psychologist and researcher of interculturality who developed a theory of universal human values. German social psychologist Bilski published some works together with him.

Values are a relatively limited set of actions or goals, directing behaviour and events through according choices. Values are cognitive representations of central human goals and motives, and people must communicate about them because some are expressions of the individual and others of social expectations. [...] Schwartz assumes that values are organised in value systems and differ in their relative meaning for the person and society.

In his approach, Schwartz differentiates ten main motivational types of values, organised into a pie chart with similar values arranged next to each other and conflicting ones more or less opposite from each other (Bilsky 2008, p. 67).[36] The Schwartz Value Survey (SVS), as a further development of the RVS, has been tested and refined since the 1990s. "In analysis, 44 of 56 values have proven to be cross-culturally 'very consistent' [...] and therefore particularly suitable for cross-cultural comparisons", so Bilsky (2008, p. 68). This more *objective level of analysis* might be especially interesting to a reader who is curious about broader samples beside the single-case argument made in this chapter. Nevertheless, I assume that a creative researcher's normative inner landscape might be perhaps as unique as a fingerprint, while the items of the SVS reflect on a more generalised level for comparison in larger groups.

Throughout this text, musings from Joubert's *Thoughts* tuned the reader to the upcoming section. Judging by the selected quotations, the French moralist and essayist seems convinced that without the normative framework no freedom of thought is possible. In fact, laws and rules are to him "the thread in the labyrinth, the compass during the night" (Joubert 1899, p. 91). How does the reader at the end of this chapter define the relation between normative theory and empirical research? What are they to one another – restrictions or a framework, contradictions or the perfect team? In my professional life, I try to aim for the latter while being aware that frictions cannot always be avoided, and yet exceptions to the rule remain an option if need be.

---

[36] In the SVS "value circle", four main items are organised as a compass rose: universal values versus egocentric values and traditional versus self-actualising values. Between these four main elements, the following items are arranged for further differentiation: sociality, tradition, security, power, performance, hedonism, stimulation, autonomy, and universalism.

Bibliography

Aanstoos, Christopher; Serlin, Illene, and Greening, Thomas (2000): "A History of Division 32 (Humanistic Psychology) of the American Psychological Association". In: Dewsbury, Donald (ed.): *Unification Through Division. Histories of the Divisions of the American Psychological Association*. Vol. 5. Washington: American Psychological Association, pp. 1–48.

Antonovsky, Aaron (1979): *Health, Stress and Coping*. San Francisco: Jossey-Bass.

Badura, Albert (1977): "Self-Efficacy. Toward a Unifying Theory of Behavioral Change". In: *Psychological Review* 84 (2), pp. 191–215.

Berufsverband Deutscher Psychologinnen und Psychologen (2005): "Ethische Richtlinien der DGP und des BDP". In: *Berufsverband Deutscher Psychologinnen und Psychologen*. http://www.bdp-verband.org/bdp/verband/ethik.shtml, retrieved on November 22, 2018.

Bettelheim, Bruno (1984): *Freud and Man's Soul*. New York: Random House Vintage.

Bilsky, Wolfgang (2008): "Die Struktur der Werte und ihre Stabilität über Instrumente und Kulturen". In: Witte, Erich (ed.): *Sozialpsychologie und Werte*. Lengerich: Papst Science, pp. 63–89.

Blumer, Herbert (1969): *Symbolic Interactionism. Perspective and Method*. New Jersey: Englewood Cliffs.

Blumer, Herbert (1981): "Der methodologische Standort des symbolischen Interaktionismus". In: Arbeitsgruppe Bielefelder Soziologen (ed.): *Alltagswissen, Interaktion und gesellschaftliche Wirklichkeit*. Vol. 1. Reinbek bei Hamburg: Rowohlt, pp. 80–101.

Bogner, Alexander; Littek, Beate, and Menz, Wolfgang (eds.) (2002): *Das Experteninterview. Theorie, Methode, Anwendung*. Opladen: Leske & Budrich.

Bohannon, John (2013): "Who Is Afraid of Peer Review?". *Science* 343 (6154), pp. 60–65.

Bolten, Jürgen (1985): "Die hermeneutische Spirale. Überlegungen zu einer integrativen Literaturtheorie". In: *Poetica* 17 (3–4), pp. 355–371.

Bundesministerium der Justiz und für Verbraucherschutz (2015): "Act on the Implementation of Measures of Occupational Safety and Health to Encourage Improvements in the Safety and Health Protection of Workers at Work". In: *Bundesministerium für Arbeit und Soziales*. https://www.bmas.de/SharedDocs/Downloads/DE/PDF-Gesetze/arbschg-en.pdf, retrieved on November 18, 2018.

Bundesministerium für Arbeit und Soziales (2009): "Grundsätze des Nationalen CSR-Forums". In: *Was ist CSR?* http://www.csr-in-deutschland.de/DE/Was-ist-CSR/Grundlagen/grundlagen.html, retrieved on November 1, 2018.

Carrera-Fernández, María Jesús; Guàrdia-Olmos, Joan, and Peró-Cebollero, Maribel (2012): "Qualitative Methods of Data Analysis in Psychology. An Analysis of the Literature". In: *Qualitative Research* 14 (1), pp. 20–36.

Cohn, Ruth Charlotte (1975): *Von der Psychoanalyse zur Themenzentrierten Interaktion. Von der Behandlung einzelner zu einer Pädagogik für alle*. Stuttgart: Klett-Cotta.

Colantonio, Andrea (2007): "Measuring Social Sustainability. Best Practice for Urban Renewal in the EU". In: *EIBURS Working Paper Series* 1.

Deutsche Gesellschaft für Psychologie (2016): *Richtlinien zur Manuskriptgestaltung*. Göttingen: Hogrefe.

Deutsches Institut für Wirtschaftsforschung; Wuppertal-Institut, and Wissenschaftszentrum Berlin (eds.) (2000): *Arbeit und Ökologie*. Düsseldorf: DIW Papers.

European Commission (2011): *Communication from the Commission to the European Parliament, the Council, the European Economic and Social Committee and the Committee of the Regions. A Renewed EU Strategy 2011–2014 for Corporate Social Responsibility.* Brussels: European Commission.

European Federation of Psychologists' Associations (2005): "Meta-Code of Ethics". In: *European Federation of Psychologists' Associations*. http://ethics.efpa.eu/metaand-model-code/meta-code/, retrieved on November 19, 2018.

Freud, Anna (1966): *The Writings of Anna Freud. Vol. 2. 1936, The Ego and the Mechanisms of Defence.* New York: International Universities Press.

Freud, Sigmund (1959): *Abriß der Psychoanalyse. Das Unbehagen in der Kultur.* Frankfurt am Main: S. Fischer.

Freud, Sigmund (1969): *Vorlesungen zur Einführung in die Psychoanalyse und neue Folgen.* Frankfurt am Main: S. Fischer.

Freud, Sigmund (1989): "Das Unbehagen in der Kultur". In: id.: *Gesammelte Werke. Vol. 14. Werke aus den Jahren 1925–1931.* Frankfurt am Main: Lingam Press, pp. 433–474.

Funke, Daniel and Mantzarlis, Alexios (2018): "Fake Academic Journals Are Publishing Work from Real Researchers Alongside Junk Science". In: *Poynter*. https://www.poynter.org/news/fake-academic-journals-are-publishing-work-real-researchers-alongside-junk-science/, retrieved on November 14, 2018.

Gadamer, Hans-Georg (1960): *Wahrheit und Methode. Grundzüge einer philosophischen Hermeneutik.* Tübingen: Mohr Siebeck.

Garfinkel, Harold (1962): "Common Sense Knowledge of Social Structures. The Documentary Method of Interpretation". In: Manis, Jerome and Meltzer, Bernard (eds.) (1972): *Symbolic Interaction. A Reader in Social Psychology.* Boston: Allyn & Bacon, pp. 76–103.

General Assembly of the United Nations (2013): "Culture and Sustainable Development". In: *General Assembly of the United Nations*. http://www.un.org/en/ga/president/68/events/culture_sd.shtml, retrieved on November 23, 2018.

Goffmann, Erwing (2003): *Wir alle spielen Theater. Die Selbstdarstellung im Alltag.* Munich: Pieper.

Greening, Tom (2006): "Five Basic Postulates of Humanistic Psychology". In: *Journal of Humanistic Psychology* 46 (3), p. 239.

Grunwald, Armin (2004): "Strategic Knowledge for Sustainable Development". In: *International Journal of Foresight and Innovation Policy* 1 (1–2), pp. 150–167.

Grunwald, Armin and Kopfmüller, Jürgen (2006): *Nachhaltigkeit.* Frankfurt am Main: Campus.

Hawkes, Jon (2001): *The Fourth Pillar of Sustainability. Culture's Essential Role in Public Planning.* Illinois: Common Ground.

Helle, Horst Jürgen (2001): *Theorien der symbolischen Interaktion. Ein Beitrag zum verstehenden Ansatz in Soziologie und Sozialpsychologie.* Wiesbaden: Westdeutscher Verlag.

Hitzler, Ronald; Honer, Anne, and Maeder, Christoph (eds.) (1994): *Expertenwissen. Die institutionalisierte Kompetenz zur Konstruktion von Wirklichkeit.* Opladen: Westdeutscher Verlag.

Hochschild, Arlie Russel (1983): *The Managed Heart. Commercialization of Human Feeling.* Berkeley, Los Angeles, and London: University of California Press.
Hoff, Ernst (1992): *Arbeit, Freizeit und Persönlichkeit. Wissenschaftliche und alltägliche Vorstellungsmuster.* Heidelberg: Asanger.
Horn, Klaus (1979): *Aktionsforschung. Balanceakt ohne Netz?* Frankfurt am Main: Syndikat.
Hutterer, Robert (1998): *Das Paradigma der Humanistischen Psychologie.* Vienna and New York: Springer.
International Organization for Standardization (2009): "Grundsätze der internationalen Ethiknorm ISO 26000. Guidance on social responsibility ICS 03.100.01". In: *International Organization for Standardization.* https://isotc.iso.org/livelink/livelink/fetch/-8929321/8929339/8929348/3935837/ISO_DIS_26000_Guidance_on_Social_Responsibility.pdf, retrieved on November 19, 2018.
Joubert, Joseph (1899): *Joubert. A Selection from his Thoughts.* New York: Dodd, Mead and Company.
Kern, Horst (1982): *Empirische Sozialforschung.* Munich: C.H. Beck.
Klages, Helmut (2008): "Entstehung, Bedeutung und Zukunft der Werteforschung". In: Witte, Erich (ed.): *Sozialpsychologie und Werte.* Lengerich: Papst Science, pp. 11–29.
Krampen, Günter (1987): *Handlungstheoretische Persönlichkeitspsychologie.* Göttingen: Hogrefe.
Laplance, Jean and Pontalis, Jean-Bertrand (1973): *The Language of Psycho-Analysis.* London: Hogarth Press.
Leithäuser, Thomas (1988): "Die Bedeutung von Ich und Ich-Ideal in der Bewältigung gesellschaftlicher Rollenanforderungen". In: Leithäuser, Thomas and Volmerg, Birgit: *Psychoanalyse in der Sozialforschung.* Opladen: Westdeutscher Verlag, pp. 81–90.
Leithäuser, Thomas; Meyerhuber, Sylke, and Schottmayer, Michael (eds.) (2009): *Sozialpsychologisches Organisationsverstehen.* Opladen: Westdeutscher Verlag.
Leithäuser, Thomas and Volmerg, Birgit (1988): *Psychoanalyse in der Sozialforschung.* Opladen: Westdeutscher Verlag.
Leithäuser, Thomas; Volmerg, Birgit; Salje, Gunther; Volmerg, Ute, and Wutka, Bernhard (1981): *Entwurf zu einer Empirie des Alltagsbewußtseins.* Frankfurt am Main: Suhrkamp.
Levenson, Hanna (1974): "Activism and Powerful Others. Distinctions Within the Concept of Internal-External Control". In: *Journal of Personality Assessment* 38 (4), pp. 377–383.
Lorenzer, Alfred (1979): *Sprachzerstörung und Rekonstruktion. Vorarbeiten zu einer Metatheorie der Psychoanalyse.* Frankfurt am Main: Suhrkamp.
McGregor, Douglas (1960): *The Human Side of Enterprise.* New York: McGraw-Hill.
Mead, Georg Herbert (1978): *Geist, Identität und Gesellschaft.* Frankfurt am Main: Suhrkamp.
Meireis, Torsten and Rippl, Gabriele (2019): *Cultural Sustainability. Perspectives from the Humanities and Social Sciences.* New York: Routledge.
Meyerhuber, Sylke (2001): *Transparenz in Arbeitsorganisationen.* Wiesbaden: Westdeutscher Verlag.
Meyerhuber, Sylke (2009): "Das dynamische Paradigma der Arbeits- und Organisationspsychologie und analytische Konsequenzen". In: Leithäuser, Thomas; Meyerhuber, Sylke, and Schottmayer, Michael (eds.): *Sozialpsychologisches Organisationsverstehen.* Opladen: Westdeutscher Verlag, pp. 95–115.
Meyerhuber, Sylke (2012): "Soziale Nachhaltigkeit im Spannungsfeld postmoderner Arbeit. Systemische Zusammenhänge von Entgrenzung, Arbeitssucht, Burnout und Mobbing

sowie Vertrauen, Verantwortung und Achtsamkeit in Organisationen". In: Molter, Haja; Schindler, Rose, and von Schlippe, Arist (eds.): *Vom Gegenwind zum Aufwind. Der Aufbruch des systemischen Gedankens*. Göttingen: Vanderhoeck & Ruprecht, pp. 86–155.

Meyerhuber, Sylke (2013): "Wie ein Frosch in der Sahne. Identität im organisationalen Wandel am Beispiel eines unternehmensseitig angestoßenen Ausscheidens aus dem bisherigen Berufsleben". In: *Journal für Psychologie* 21 (3). https://www.journal-fuer-psychologie.de/index.php/jfp/article/view/306/338/, retrieved on November 3, 2018.

Meyerhuber, Sylke (2017): "CSR für sozial nachhaltiges Handeln. Psychologische Dynamik und die Vulnerabilität mittlerer Führungskräfte im permanenten Organisationswandel". In: Lopez, Irene (ed.): *CSR und Wirtschaftspsychologie*. New York and Berlin: Springer, pp. 135–163.

Meyerhuber, Sylke (2019): "'Active Listening' as a Key Competence in Intercultural Communication Education. An Example From an Academic Classroom With Conceptual and Theoretical Embedding". In: *Journal of Linguistic and Intercultural Education* 12 (2), pp. 91–114.

Meyerhuber, Sylke; Reiser, Helmut, and Scharer, Matthias (2019): *Theme-Centered Interaction in Higher Education*. Heidelberg, New York, Dorecht, and London: Springer.

Meyring, Phillipp (1990): *Einführung in die qualitative Sozialforschung*. Munich: Psychologie Verlags Union.

Nadig, Maya (1986): *Die verborgene Kultur der Frau*. Frankfurt am Main: S. Fischer.

Nadig, Maya (2004): "Transculturality in Process. Theoretical and Methodological Aspects Drawn from Cultural Studies and Psychoanalysis". In: Sandkühler, Hans Jörg and Lim, Hong-Bin (eds.): *Transculturality, Epistemology, Ethics, and Politics*. Frankfurt am Main: Peter Lang, pp. 9–21.

Parsons, Talcott and Shils, Edward (1951): *Toward a General Theory of Action*. Cambridge: Harvard University Press.

Perry, Ryan; Sibley, Chris, and Duckitt, John (2013): "Dangerous and Competitive Worldviews. A Meta-Analysis of Their Associations with Social Dominance Orientation and Right-Wing Authoritarianism". In: *Journal of Research in Personality* 47 (1), pp. 116–127.

Pongratz, Hans and Voß, Günther (2002): "From Employee to 'Entreployee'. Towards a 'Self-Entrepreneurial' Work Force?". In: *Concepts and Transformation* 8 (3), pp. 239–254.

Prater, Chrissy (2018): "8 Ways to Identify a Questionable Open Access Journal". In: *American Journal Experts*. https://www.aje.com/en/arc/8-ways-identify-questionable-open-access-journal/, retrieved on November 23, 2018.

Preiser, Siegfried (1992): "Beurteilungen in sozialen Interaktionen". In: Selbach, Ralf and Pullig, Karl-Klaus (eds.): *Handbuch Mitarbeiterbeurteilung*. Wiesbaden: Gabler, pp. 4–38.

Riebl, Schaun; Estabrooks, Paul; Dunsmore, Julie; Salva, Jyoti; Frisard, Madlyn; Dietrich, Andrea; Peng, Yiming; Zhang, Ciang, and Davy, Brenda (2015): "A Systematic Literature Review and Meta-Analysis. The Theory of Planned Behavior's Application to Understand and Predict Nutrition-Related Behaviors in Youth". In: *Eating Behaviors* 18 (1), pp. 160–178.

Rogers, Carl (1942): *Counselling and Psychotherapy*. Boston: Houghton Mifflin.

Rogers, Carl (1951): *Client-Centered Therapy*. Boston: Houghton Mifflin.
Rokeach, Milton (1973): *The Nature of Human Values*. New York: The Free Press.
Rotter, Julian (1966): "Generalized Expectations of Internal Versus External Control of Enforcement". In: *Psychological Monographs* 80 (1), 1–28.
Salkind, Neil (2007): *Encyclopedia of Measurement and Statistics*. Thousand Oaks: Sage.
Satir, Virginia (1976): *Making Contact*. Berkeley: Celestial Arts.
Schallberger, Urs (1989): "Identitäts- und Persönlichkeitsentwicklung". In: Greif, Siegfried; Holling, Heinz, and Nicholson, Neigel (eds.): *Arbeits- und Organisationspsychologie. Internationales Handbuch in Schlüsselbegriffen*. Munich: Psychologie Verlags Union, pp. 245–248.
Schein, Edgar (2010): *Organizational Culture and Leadership*. San Francisco: Jossey-Bass.
Schneider-Landolf, Mina; Spielmann, Jochen, and Zitterbarth, Walter (eds.) (2017): *Handbook of Theme-Centered Interaction (TCI)*. Göttingen: Vandenhoeck & Ruprecht.
Schorn, Ariane (2000): "The Theme-Centered-Interview. A Method to Decode Manifest and Latent Aspects of Subjective Realities". In: *Forum Qualitative Sozialforschung, Forum: Qualitative Social Research* 1 (2).
http://www.qualitative-research.net/index.php/fqs/article/viewArticle/1092/2395/, retrieved on November 14, 2018.
Schottmayer, Michael (2002): *Subkulturen im Betrieb*. Münster: Lit-Verlag.
Schwartz, Shalom (1992): "Universals in the Content and Structure of Values. Theoretical Advances and Empirical Tests in 20 Countries". In: Zanna, Marc (ed.): *Advances in Experimental Social Psychology*. Vol. 25. New York: Academic Press, pp. 1–65.
Seghezzo, Lucas (2009): "The Five Dimensions of Sustainability". In: *Environmental Politics* 18 (4), pp. 539–556.
Sennett, Richard (1990): *Autorität*. Frankfurt am Main: S. Fischer.
Sennett, Richard (1998): *Der flexible Mensch. Die Kultur des neuen Kapitalismus*. Berlin: Berlin Verlag.
Sennett, Richard (2002): *Respekt im Zeitalter der Ungleichheit*. Berlin: Berlin Verlag.
Shaw, Claire (2013): "Hundreds of Open Access Journals Accept Fake Science Paper". In: *The Guardian*.
https://www.theguardian.com/higher-education-network/2013/oct/04/open-access-journals-fake-paper/, retrieved on November 15, 2018.
Stahlke, Iris (2001): *Das Rollenspiel als Methode der qualitativen Sozialforschung*. Berlin: Waxmann.
United Cities and Local Governments (2008): "Agenda 21 for Culture". In: *Agenda 21 for Culture*.
http://www.agenda21culture.net/documents/culture-the-fourth-pillar-of-sustainability/, retrieved on November 15, 2018.
United Nations (1992): "Rio Declaration on Environment and Development". In: *United Nations Department of Economic and Social Affairs*.
https://www.un.org/documents/ga/conf151/aconf15126-1annex1.htm, retrieved on November 19, 2018.
United Nations (2018): "Transforming our World. The 2030 Agenda for Sustainable Development". In: *Sustainable Development Goals*.
https://sustainabledevelopment.un.org/post2015/transformingourworld/, retrieved on November 26, 2018.

United Nations Educational, Scientific and Cultural Organization (2018): Culture for the 2030 Agenda. In: *United Nations Educational, Scientific and Cultural Organization*. http://www.unesco.org/culture/flipbook/culture-2030/en/mobile/index.html, retrieved on November 3, 2018.

Volmerg, Birgit (1988): "Erkenntnistheoretische Grundsätze interpretativer Sozialforschung in der Perspektive eines psychoanalytisch reflektierten Selbst- und Fremdverstehens". In: Leithäuser, Thomas and Volmerg, Birgit (eds.): *Psychoanalyse in der Sozialforschung*. Opladen: Westdeutscher Verlag, pp. 131–179.

Volmerg, Birgit (1988): "Methoden der Auswertung". In: Leithäuser, Thomas and Volmerg, Birgit (eds.): *Psychoanalyse in der Sozialforschung*. Opladen: Westdeutscher Verlag, pp. 234–261.

Volmerg, Birgit; Senghaas-Knobloch, Eva, and Leithäuser, Thomas (1986): *Betriebliche Lebenswelt. Eine Sozialpsychologie industrieller Verhältnisse*. Opladen: Westdeutscher Verlag.

von Lewinski, Manfred (2006): *Wie einsam bleibt der Mensch*. Berlin: Pro Business.

Weber, Max (1980): *Wirtschaft und Gesellschaft*. Tübingen: Mohr Siebeck.

Wilson, Thomas (1973): "Theorien der Interaktion und Modelle soziologischer Erklärung". In: Arbeitsgruppe Bielefelder Soziologen (ed.): *Alltagswissen, Interaktion und gesellschaftliche Wirklichkeit. Vol. 1. Symbolischer Interaktionismus und Ethnomethodologie*. Reinbek bei Hamburg: Rowohlt, pp. 54–79.

Witte, Erich (ed.): *Sozialpsychologie und Werte*. Lengerich: Papst Science.

Witttgenstein, Ludwig (2001): *Philosophische Untersuchungen. Kritisch-genetische Edition*. Frankfurt am Main: Wissenschaftliche Buchgesellschaft.

World Commission on Environment and Development (1987): *Report of the World Commission on Environment and Development. Our Common Future*. Oxford: UN Documents.

Jannis Kreienkamp, Maximilian Agostini, Marvin Kunz, Malte Ingo Meyerhuber, and Carlos A. de Matos Fernandes

Normative Influences in Science and Their Impact on (Objective) Empirical Research[1]

Abstract: Empirical research has the ultimate goal to inform us about the "objectively true" state of the world. This ambition especially holds for the natural sciences, but also extends to the social sciences. In the context of recent developments and theoretical discussions, the authors aim to contribute to the discussion of objectivity in empirical research from a junior researcher's perspective, debating the influence of normative assumptions on empirical research. They analyse normative influences within the six conceptual steps of the empirical research process: (1) idea generation, (2) research funding, (3) research planning, (4) data collection, (5) data analysis, and (6) scientific output. The authors end with a summary of current directions that may help move to a more reflective, nuanced, and transparent scientific process.

1 Introduction – A Reflexivity Perspective

This chapter on normative influences in empirical research was a result of normative influences on us. All five authors enjoyed an education in the social sciences, varying in degree between psychology and sociology. This means that the examples we will draw upon are examples closely related to these disciplines.

As junior researchers, we are both in the most and least favourable position to write about normative influences; the least favourable because our limited research experience provides us only bounded insight into the normative research culture; and the most favourable because our limited experience leaves us mostly untouched by many of the normative influences of the research culture. We do not offer a complete picture, nor do we pretend to comprehensively understand the snapshot we are presenting. Yet, we attempt to present a new angle, showing how the bigger picture of gaining scientific insights is perceived by a new generation that will continue the venerable tradition of empirical research.

During our university education we were the recipients of lines of thoughts that were influenced by a field in uproar: social science research did not repli-

---

[1] We stipulate that writing this chapter was a collective enterprise and all authors contributed equally to it.

https://doi.org/10.1515/9783110613797-007

cate (Open Science Collaboration 2015), prominent researchers were convicted of fraud (Carey 2011), and the underlying statistical framework of "standard inference" was being challenged (Simmons, Nelson, and Simonsohn 2011). As a result, our education was heavily influenced by a changing field, focussed on teaching us how to avoid the mistakes of the past.

In 2011, Diederik Stapel was accused and later convicted of scientific misconduct for fabricating data (see, e.g., Bhattacharjee 2013). This case stirred up the scientific community, especially at the universities where Stapel was previously employed as a researcher. One of these universities was the University of Groningen, where we were educated to become (empirical) researchers. The realisation of the susceptibility of the scientific community to misconduct influenced academic staff and the teaching methods at our university. In this climate of raised awareness, it was communicated that we, as a new generation of social scientists, are required to understand and safeguard against the exploitation and misuse of empirical research. This facet of our scientific education has influenced our thinking and is central to our discussion of normative influences in, and on, empirical research.

2 Background

According to Richard Dawkins (as quoted by Singh 2004, p. 497), science is the "disinterested search for the objective truth about the material world", offering us insights into the truth of the world we live in and the entities we are. The method of choice for this "disinterested search" – in many fields – is empirical research,[2] generally due to its methodological rigour and adherence to certain standards of scientific conduct. The way for the march of empirical research has only been paved in the 18th-century Enlightenment, when philosophers, like John Locke and David Hume, formed theories that aimed to pave a road towards a world knowable through empiricism. While this view has become somewhat diluted in recent years, many still assume scientific findings to approach objectivity. Such research has not always been in the hands of empirical approaches and may be less justified than is often assumed. Consider, e.g., the work of Kant (1964), who tried to find *a priori* insights to the way our reasoning and our perception of the world function; relying on his pure thinking rather than on methodical empirical observations. Thus, while gaining more influence

---

[2] With "empirical research" we, here, mean the positivistic research tradition that relies on the analysis of (directly and indirectly) observable data.

in scientific inquiries, in this chapter we argue that empirical research cannot stand autonomously for itself; rather it is interwoven with and must acknowledge the political, cultural, and subjective context (i.e., normative influences), especially when interpreting the social world.

Normative influences in, and on, empirical research are a topical debate (see, e. g., the checklist discussed by Munafò and Smith 2018), due to their essentiality for researchers, for those who rely on the empirical findings, and for those who are studied. Two key aspects can be identified in the debate:
- Ought: Should there be normative influences in, and on, empirical research?
- Is: What normative influences exist within empirical research?

In general, the social sciences have been especially ambivalent regarding the first question, exemplifying both sides of the debate. E. g., parts of psychology have striven to move towards an objective, norm-free science. Ambitions in philosophy (*Vienna Circle*), theory (*behaviourism*), and methodology (*randomised controlled experiments*) worked towards general laws and a nomothetic natural science, aiming to make science free from the influence of politics, culture, and the subjective individual that uncovers positivistic truths (Popper 1973, Porter 1995). However, several voices have claimed that value-free science may be impossible (Gergen 1973); e. g., anthropological theories, as well as qualitative research methods have explicitly built upon the subjectivity of study objects and researchers. Whilst the first question (ought) is important, it may be less relevant to the practitioners and users in the field, as most of them are likely to adopt a more pragmatic and instrumentalist position.

In contrast to the first question, the second question of *what kind of normative influences exist* is thus of greater importance to both researchers and practitioners. Accurate scientific knowledge is relevant to the generating field, as well as individuals who experience direct or indirect consequences from it. As an example, the field of empirically informed ethics attempts to improve ethical theories by incorporating empirical results into the theory building process. These theories may then find implementation in medical or elderly care facilities, such as when a new finding is implemented to – potentially – improve elderly care. However, which empirical results are trustworthy? And which should be implemented? While empirical results can assist in advancing knowledge, it is precarious to rely on each piece of empirical data as if it represented the truth (cf. meta-analysis which accounts for multiple pieces of empirical data; see, e. g., Postmes and Spears 1998, Zimbardo 1969). This holds especially for scientific debates in which both sides provide empirical evidence for opposing claims.

The aim of this chapter is to inform philosophers, but also empiricists, about the implications of normative influences on empirical scientific processes. Our goal is not to discourage using empirical results altogether, but to place them into perspective and inspect them within their specific context.

3 The Six Conceptual Stages of Research

In general, we will investigate six *interwoven* stages, which we deem prominent in conducting empirical research and that appear relevant for scholars in general. Specifically, we will discuss: (1) idea generation, (2) research funding, (3) research planning, (4) data collection, (5) data analysis, and (6) scientific output. In the following sections, we will explore how normative assumptions can influence seemingly objective empirical research (for a graphical illustration see: https://www.doi.org/10.17605/OSF.IO/GYDB8).

3.1 Idea Generation

The first step in the research process is to decide on a phenomenon of systematic analysis. In this step, normative influences are often very direct and overt. One direct normative influence on research idea generation is, e.g., the political diversity (or lack thereof) within a scientific field. Most fields have a certain implicit outlook on society and recreate their political perspective through the people they attract (and keep within the field). E.g., when social psychologists recently investigated their field's political diversity, they realised that their field predominantly consisted of liberal voices, which may hinder the advancement of certain social psychology research domains (Crawford et al. 2015, Duarte et al. 2015). Liberal values may be ingrained into research questions and methods and may result in an one-sided approach to (politically) controversial topics. Moreover, the authors claim that conservative voices trying to get into the field experience a hostile climate and – sometimes – outright discrimination. Similarly, philosophy seems to be having issues with getting (and keeping) minorities and women in the field (Lombrozo 2013). The often-implicit political attitude and self-selection can, therefore, be problematic for the general validity of research, as it may strongly influence the kinds of questions scientists (dare to) ask and the results they find.

Apart from direct influences, such as liberal biases, more indirect influences are observable as well. E.g., a tendency in the social sciences is to avoid broad theorising to explain the observed phenomena (Kruglanski 2001); with the development of comprehensive theoretical frameworks being undervalued. The current trend away from broader theories has been referred to as the *Post-Normal*

Science of Precaution (Ravetz 2004).[3] Some argue that this shift leads towards circular research, a scattered field, and has increased the distance to the societal dialogue (Kruglanski 2001, Sarewitz 2016). The fear of theorising is especially apparent on a smaller scale: the model scale. As an example from the psychological discipline, developmental psychologists may focus on the development of the self, neuropsychologists focus on the neurological processes of the self, and social psychologists on the interplay of situational cues and changes of the self. An integrative underpinning of what the self actually consists of, however, is missing. Instead, every domain tends to undertake (mainly) its own theorising; van Zomeren (2016, p. 13) summarises this by arguing that

> without theoretically integrative efforts, science is blind; and a blind science is nothing more than a very large storage container of empirical trivia. It is and does what a very large storage container is and does: it is very large, and it contains and stores things. And within, it is divided into so many sections and subsections that one may spend a lifetime counting or easily lose count.

Notably, this was already highlighted by McGuire (1973), when he argued that only using societally relevant problems, such as a sequential cause-effect model without underlying theory, disregards the complex nature of human behaviour. The apparent lower model scale would, therefore, benefit from broad interdisciplinary theorising that is able to span the different subdomains, achieving successful integration. In turn, an additional effort integrating the Post-Normal Science of Precaution might also help showcase and address the normative inconsistencies of small scale models, methods, and sub-disciplines.

3.2 Funding

While pursuing a promising research idea, researchers discover they are dependent on grants from public, commercial, or private funding sources to realise their research. The funding of a promising research idea has become an increasing concern for both experienced and aspiring researchers. In 2006, biochemist Roger Kornberg received the Nobel Prize for his research on the copy process of information in DNA. Following this award, he declared before the United States Senate that the current funding practices hinder important research projects and discourage scientists (Edwards and Roy 2017). Kornberg stated that his

---

[3] Note that Ravetz sees this shift as positive, opening doors for new interdisciplinary collaborations.

fundamental research would have been impossible if he was raised a decade later, within the current funding environment. The following paragraphs will illustrate several normative influences on the funding process.

The allocation of funds is usually based on the quality of scientific proposals through peer review. This system may, however, be an ineffective method of financial redistribution. Some scientists claim that due to restrictions in review panels' size and available time, most panels are unable to accurately rank the quality of research proposals (Fang, Bowen, and Casadevall 2016). Additionally, 85 percent of reviewers in the field of medicine report an absence of training in reviewing grant proposals. For allocating funds in empirical research, a typical study selection is commonly limited to two or three reviewers reading a study proposal in-depth, a number too low to provide an acceptable level of accuracy (Kaplan, Lacetera, and Kaplan 2008). Funding and review panels thus often appear to lack the effective structure to adequately judge the quality of research proposals – introducing their personal normative agendas as a heuristic to decide between the large numbers of studies.

The problems with funding extend beyond individual and collective normative influences of review panels. Edwards and Roy (2017) criticise academia's contemporary incentive and reward structure for fostering unhealthy competition and unethical behaviour. They argue that a focus on quantitative performance metrics (such as the h-index) results in these indices being a target rather than a measure. According to *Goodhart's Law* (see, e.g., Elton 2004), a measure that becomes a target is no longer an adequate measure. For researchers, many factors such as hiring, promotion, funding, and awards depend on quantitative measures, which is why researchers are pressured to emphasise quantity of publications over quality. One consequence of this increasing pressure may be the temptation of questionable research practices (QRPs). The usage of QRPs gives researchers a competitive advantage over their colleagues, wherewith they more often publish successfully, and attract new funding. This results in a feedback loop, further promoting the application of QRPs and promising researchers utilising these practices an advantage. Moreover, according to Edwards and Roy, incentive structures in academia often lead researchers and other stakeholders to neglect the existence of QRPs. As long as the funding and incentive structure promotes and rewards the usage of QRPs, engaging in these practices will improve a researcher's chance to receive funding.

Cushman and colleagues (2015) illustrate further problematic funding structures. In their analysis, they reveal that although proposal quality, proposer demographics, requested amount of funding, and number of submitted proposals per researcher remained unaltered, the likelihood of receiving funding has substantially decreased for the last decades (see also Alberts et al. 2014). This is consistent with the observation that funding budgets remained stagnant or decreased, while the number of researchers has rapidly grown (Kimble et al. 2015). According to Cushman and colleagues, the likelihood of acquiring funding per application might decrease to or below six percent if the current trend continues. The six percent threshold illustrates a tipping point at which the time required to write proposals will take more working hours than the grant's financial payoff will allow a researcher to continue working. This scenario turns the process of applying for scientific funding into an endeavour that leaves scientists wondering whether they can afford to pursue their own interests and forces them to satisfy the expectations of external funding agencies. This could result in researchers serving the interest of private corporations for the sake of future funding (and thus financial stability; see, e.g., Sismondo 2008), or a focus on irrelevant in vogue topics. It should be noted that proponents of the currently existing funding structure state that the competition between researchers will subsequently provide better results and better research, similar to competition on the free market. A comparison between countries, funding structures, and scientific output has, however, not found any compelling evidence for this claim (Auranen and Nieminen 2010).

3.3 Research Planning

After receiving funding for one's research, implementing the research idea requires a detailed plan (while receiving funding also often requires a specific research plan, this section is related to all aspects of research that need planning, above and beyond just arriving at a plan that allows applying for funding). Normative assumptions also influence this process of planning and conceptualising empirical studies, sometimes leading to systematic influences in scientific results. Planning is, e.g., influenced by paradigmatic norms, habits, types of research, and the choice of research participants.

In particular, research planning is often a series of (conscious) decisions by researchers; these decisions, however, never occur in a normative vacuum. E.g., previous research is highly influential in research planning. If previous work, however, was limited to certain aspects, it may lead a researcher to neglect some relevant lines of enquiry for several reasons: First, analysing data with new (un-paradigmatic) questions is inherently precarious, which is why scientists may over-focus on a limited aspect of their research paradigm (Kuhn 1962). Second, due to the difficulty of publishing non-significant quantitative research findings (*file drawer problem*; Rosenthal 1979), scientists may be unaware of certain relations and may thus not investigate them. Third, a strong focus on linear cause-and-effect relations in social science research may lead to the neglect of many of the complexities within a studied system (McGuire 1973), further restricting the type of research project that is deemed to be of value. Lastly, many concepts can be defined very differently. These definitions are, however, at the core of the research process and not only influence a study's outcomes but also create a normative frame of key concepts. E.g., "the difference between a terrorist and a freedom fighter is a matter of perspective: It all depends on the observer and the verdict of history" (Linkola 2009, p. 160). If one were to study terrorists' attitudes, it is hard to imagine that stating, "You as a terrorist …" and "You as a freedom fighter …" led to the same responses.

Moreover, the subjects included in a study may also have an impact on outcomes. Research in the social sciences is often not as representative and generalisable as might be expected. E.g., between 2003 and 2007, 96 percent of participants in six psychology journals came from industrialised Western countries, which, however, only comprises 12 percent of the global population (Henrich, Heine, and Norenzayan 2010). Hence, study samples in the social sciences are often WEIRD (Western, Educated, Industrialized, Rich, and Democratic). Furthermore, the majority of these participants are undergraduate psychology students (Arnett 2008, Gallander Wintre, North, and Sugar 2001, Peterson 2001). While it is convenient to sample students from one's own university, it is also questionable whether claims regarding individuals can be abstracted from such a specific group. In some cases, e.g., when the underlying theory assumes a mechanism to be fundamental to all human beings, generalisation may be possible (Stroebe, Gadenne, and Nijstad 2018); however, in others not (Anderson and Stamoulis 2007, Gendron et al. 2014). As most psychological theories were constructed utilising such samples, the question of cross-cultural validity (or even within culture generalisability) often remains unanswered. Moreover, the theories and theorists themselves are often also WEIRD when theories and theorising rely on a very limited set of assumptions (for an exception, see Guo et al. 2013, van Zomeren 2016). In summary, research planning – and thus also the results – of empirical research are seldom as objective and "straightforward" as they seem to be. Once a researcher has planned a study, one has to collect data, a process which once more can be subject to normative influences.

3.4 Data Collection

Many claim that empirical data collection in the social sciences has moved the field away from subjective influences towards a more objective representation of reality or at least of the data. Randomised controlled trials (RCTs) have long been the prime example of this apparent cut with individual, political, or cultural influences in empirical sciences. They have often been called the gold standard of research in social sciences that allow for experimental manipulation (for a review, see Cartwright 2007, Meldrum 2000). The reason why RCTs are considered as such, was the introduction of several key components to safeguard against a range of biases: Randomisation, (placebo-)control, and masking are three key elements to the RCT method, each of which is a solution to a form of systematic bias researchers faced in the past (Kaptchuk 2001).

The element of a control group was introduced as evidence for the effectiveness of an intervention (Dehue 2005). A control group is the benchmark to which the treatment group is compared. If one can show that the intervention was the only thing that differed between two groups, this might be considered strong evidence for the intervention. To ensure that the two groups are as similar as possible and only differ by the factor of intervention the second element, randomisation, was introduced. By randomly assigning participants to either the treatment or the control group, one can assume that, given a reasonable sample size and random sampling, chance will allocate individual differences roughly equally, minimising the mean differences between the groups (for a historical review, see Dehue 1997, Hacking 1988). In short, this method would unfetter the design from conscious or unconscious allocation-decisions of the experimenter (Kaptchuk 2001). Lastly, masking describes the idea that neither the participants nor the researchers are aware of the participant's experimental group affiliation. This element controls for deliberate influences by the experimenter as well as for several well-known unconscious psychological effects. An example would be the *experimenter's bias*, the idea that the researcher's expectations unconsciously change his or her behaviour towards the study object. While RCTs produce useful results and develop the sciences in which they are applied, the question remains whether they can stick up to the reputation of eliminating normative influences.

RCTs, although (seemingly) promising as an extensive effort to move towards a more objective methodology, also introduce their own problems. Many have pointed out that even the simplest RCT experiment is never free of (normatively influenced) choices made by the scientists in the research process. Many of these decisions relate to the previous stages of research where someone had to define, operationalise, and measure a concept. Zwaan (2013), in his blog post "50 Questions About Messy Rooms", argues that in many cases already setting up control and experimental conditions is not as clear and objective as it is often claimed, and highlights that many aspects of study setups are subjective and influenced by personal (normative) biases and expectations.

Another type of scientific standard, at least in many social sciences, seems to be a preference to favour quantitative over qualitative data – something which also holds for the way that RCT experiments are typically set up. Quantitative research methods that rely on numerical results and statistics seem to be valued more than qualitative research methods that rely on more personal investigations of words, pictures, and objects. Such a development is especially apparent when considering the methodological courses offered at research-oriented universities and when considering what kind of research is published in the highest ranking and most cited journals. Both university education and top-tier journals focus largely on quantitative research methods and lack the inclusion of qualitative research (see, e.g., Shuval et al. 2011). Again, the argument many educators and philosophers of science offer is that quantitative results are clear, solid, and most importantly less affected by normative influences (yet, see also Tetlock 1994). Alan Bryman (1984) famously observed that the debate between quantitative and qualitative researchers is less methodological and more metaphysical, asking the important question of epistemological positions. Bryman writes that qualitative methods are often seen as phenomenological and constructivist by proponents of quantitative research, while quantitative research methods are described as positivistic from the perspective of researchers utilising qualitative research methods. Consequently, a social science that tries to lose its relativistic connotation, looking for hard facts, came to systematically favour a quantitative approach in order to show its positivistic effort to uncover the reality as it is without any normative connotation. In sum, the philosophers of science and research practitioners in the social sciences have gone to great lengths to build an argument for a purely empirical and somewhat "objective" and "quantitative" research process. Therefore, this process is in itself an important systemic influence on data collection that implicitly and explicitly restricts researchers to a limited valued frame of operation.

The problems with qualitative research that these researchers point out hold, however, also for quantitative research: In the case of developmental research, according to Peterson (2016), researchers cannot rely on strictly following standard procedures, as babies and children can easily violate standard protocols (e.g., throwing temper tantrums, being too tired, or being too excited). Excluding every infant that breaks protocol may result in the need for very large initial samples, only to reach a very small (and highly specific, thus even more biased) final sample – something that often is logistically impractical or impossible. Peterson claims that in order to gain meaningful insights (and statistical significance), certain factors are required: Flexibility with protocols, early analyses of the data, consideration of failure as a way to detect boundary conditions, and the analysis of unexpected statistically significant results. For many researchers, these factors may raise (or even constitute) red flags for "bad" research. However, most people would also agree that such developmental research has yielded some beneficial insights into the development of humans. Therefore, the process of collecting data may be (severely) influenced by a field's ideals and standards, and while questioning each one of these should be done in moderation, reflecting on them may nonetheless be beneficial.

3.5 Data Analysis

The next research stage of interest, logically following after data collection, is the analysis of the gathered data. One may assume that at least this process should be free from normative influences, as statistical methods are mathematical equations and therefore "objective" in their nature. However, also in the process of data analysis, normative influences and personal judgements play a large role. For instance, Kahneman (2011), in his popular-scientific book *Thinking, Fast and Slow*, exemplifies that scholars are taken in by human biases as well – also influencing how they use statistics to answer specific questions. In his research on heuristics and biases, he argues that lay people, as well as experts in statistics (e.g., statistics professors), maintained biases or heuristics that lead to incorrect statistical inferences. Kahneman implicitly makes an argument that scholars, in general, can (and should) improve their "how-to" knowledge on data analysis. It appears that certain normative influences on data analysis are influenced by either a lack of statistical knowledge or a rather unintentional reliance on internalised heuristics and biases (and thus also one's "go-to" methods of analysis). We will address two aspects in more detail: Normative influences in (1) finding statistical results, and in (2) describing statistical results.

Firstly, the process of data analysis can be influenced by statistical interpretation of the findings. A normative challenge arises when scholars interpret the statistical output of the data, for instance, to distinguish between the magnitude of the statistical certainty (probability value or p-value) and the practical impact of the finding (Cohen 1992, Kirk 1996). Plainly, it appears that during data analysis a certain grey-zone of statistical interpretation arises wherein scholars have to navigate. E.g., a non-significant statistic can be observed (i.e., a high p-value), even when the effect size (i.e., the comparative practical size of the effect; see Cohen 1992) can be substantial. Furthermore, small non-significant effect sizes (e.g., due to small samples) can be meaningful – and in practice even save lives. Or, the other way around, an effect can be statistically significant but irrelevant in reality. The leeway of scholars occurs within the bounds of practical or statistical relevance and tends to favour statistical over practical significance (e.g., Roberts 2015). Furthermore, one can remove unfortunate outliers, transform the data, or interpret statistical assumptions loosely to "improve" the likelihood of finding statistically significant results – all without having violated formal guidelines. The aforementioned points relate to the issue raised by Roberts (2015), who discusses the importance of a statistically significant result, and why scholars tend to pursue a statistically significant result. The success of researchers seems to depend on a p-value below 0.05.[4] With non-significant research findings ($p > 0.05$) scientific journals are less likely to give coverage to one's results, even if they are highly relevant in practice. All in all, there is a seemingly normative pressure on researchers to pursue findings in their studies with "good" (i.e., significant) statistical results (see Cohen 1992, Kirk 1996).

Secondly, another strand of normative influences on data analysis considers the notion of "hypothesising after the results are known" (i.e., HARKing; see Kerr 1998, p. 196). One speaks of HARKing when a researcher hypothesises based on data (i.e., post hoc), but presents the findings as if they were predicted before the data was collected (Edwards and Roy 2017). This is problematic, because Type I errors (finding an effect that does not exist) may be translated into theory and the process of scientific research may be misrepresented (Rubin 2017). The scope of HARKing has been investigated in several qualitative and quantitative studies. For instance, qualitative investigations of social scientists report severe transgressions of scientific dishonesty, such as questionable lab protocols and scheduled HARKing meetings (Peterson 2016). Quantitative studies, looking at a broader group of scientists, indicate similar results (John, Loewenstein, and Prelec 2012). Explicitly, 74 percent of researchers stated to not always report all the measures they used, and 71 percent continued data collection until statistical significance was reached (John, Loewenstein, and Prelec 2012). Thus, what is considered as a good statistical result can influence the a priori described aim of the empirical study. This shifts the supposed right way of deductive research towards a more inductive way of hypothesising because the interpretation of statistics by researchers can be value-laden.

HARKing has often been described as a practice of malicious intent – researchers using their data to cheat. Issues of at least equal importance are the data analysis decisions that are made unintentionally or theory-guided but are still data contingent and neglect the implications of potential analyses testing the same question. A recent article by Gelman and Loken (2013) argues that the same issue that underlies HARKing – namely doing analyses until one finds a statistically significant result – can still be problematic even if one

---

[4] A p-value below 0.05 suggests that if we drew infinitely random samples from the population, 95 percent of the samples would reject the null hypothesis (frequentist understanding), or as a theoretical statement, the finding has a probability of 0.95 of correctly rejecting the null hypothesis (Kass 2011).

only does a single analysis. Especially when the analysis depends heavily on the data structure, even a single analysis is problematic because there are many possible analyses that could have been done with the same data and still answer the same research question.[5] This includes two main aspects. (1) One influence is the arbitrary decision of how a hypothesis is tested. Gelman and Loken offer a series of examples to illustrate this point. One compelling example especially highlights this "garden of forking paths" (Gelman and Loken 2013, p. 1) – the assertion that a specific analysis testing a research hypothesis could be contrary to a series of other analyses testing the same hypothesis. Especially broad or vague hypotheses, such as "political orientation has an influence on voting turnout". There are multiple ways in which we could test such a hypothesis – all of which would be based on theoretical grounds. If we were to find a political orientation effect among men (because, e.g., men are more ideological) we would see the hypothesis confirmed. If we were to find an effect only in state elections but not in county elections (because ideological issues often arise on a state level), we would also see our hypothesis confirmed. Choosing any specific analysis is in parts an often-unacknowledged arbitrary choice. (2) A second form of unintentional influence on the analysis performed is the arbitrary decision made during the analysis process (Steegen et al. 2016). E.g., a researcher might decide to define a person as poor if they earn less than 60 percent of the median income. This can be a reasonable definition and analysis choice, yet, defining someone as poor if they cannot afford basic necessities might be just as valid of a definition of poverty. Deciding between the two options often does not solely depend on theory (both decision rules have theoretical and empirical backing) but it is an arbitrary decision by the researcher that might have led to different results if they had chosen a different method.

Consequently, normative influences (e.g., subjective expectations and biases) remain prevalent in finding and describing statistical results in the process of data analysis (see, e.g., Gelman and Loken 2013). The topic of statistical analysis relates closely to the subsequent section of scientific output in general.

---

[5] A recent study exemplifies this point. Scholars received the same dataset and the same question: "[are] soccer players with dark skin tone [...] more likely than those with light skin tone to receive red cards from referees" (Silberzahn et al. 2018, p. 338). They found that analytic choices within each scientific field resulted in different outcomes.

3.6 Output

Every process of scientific inquiry aims to be shared in one way or another with the scientific community or the society at large. Scientific communication ranges from journal publications to conference proceedings, or output aimed at the general public. Scientific communication, or scientific output as we shall label it, is a necessary part of every scientific process. The creation of scientific output overarches many of the processes we have discussed thus far.

Such output may be influenced by the norms or expectations within the researchers' academic communities and institutions (university or otherwise). The communal judgement of academic output (e. g., through peer-review), often, has a general tendency to support a certain status quo. Take, e. g., the research by Nobel-prize winner George Akerlof, who studied a special problem of asymmetric information for markets. This later led to a paradigm shift in economics. Before this occurred, though, the publication of his research was turned down by several referees of well-known journals: *The Academic Economic Review* and *The Review of English Studies* both rejected it for "triviality", a reviewer of the *Journal of Political Economy* stated: "If this paper would be correct, no goods could be traded at all" (Akerlof 2003, par. 14). There are, thus, systemic restrictions in the publishing process that (normatively) value certain paradigm-corroborating papers over others (at times at the expense of important research findings).

Apart from finding acceptance for one's findings by journals, researchers may also experience normative pressures from their universities and funding agencies. Academic institutions may only grant rewards for researchers' efforts when they succeed in publishing a certain number of scientific articles in certain high-tier journals (Edwards and Roy 2017, Roberts 2015). These kinds of productivity norms can often be manipulated. E. g., researchers' output can be quantified using a measure that calculates the personal productiveness and impact of publications: the h-index (Hirsch 2005).[6] While the h-index takes into account the quantity of published studies, it can be easily manipulated by self-citation (Gálvez 2017). Edwards and Roy (2017) argue that a focus on quantity over quality, when linked to quantitative performance measures, such as the h-index, causes these measures to be a target rather than a measure. For researchers, many factors – such as hiring, promotion, funding, and awards – depend on these quantitative measures, which is why they are seemingly pressured to em-

---

[6] The h-index quantifies the number of an author's publications and their citations (Hirsch 2005). With one published paper being cited once, the h-index will be 1, with two published papers, both of them being cited twice, the h-index is 2, and so on.

phasise quantity of publications over their quality. Hence, there is pressure on researchers who do empirical studies, through certain expectations of the institutions they rely on (see also subsection 3.2 on *Goodhart's Law*).

Moreover, the aforementioned form of pressure strongly relates to the possible personal (i.e., subjective) goals of a researcher in comparison to the collective goal of building a foundation for future research. For instance, a researcher can become widely known after publishing counterintuitive or "flashy" findings. Although pursuing counterintuitive findings may not be obscured by normative influences, it could diminish the objectivity of a researcher when the two collide. Roberts describes this as "clickbait worthy research" (Roberts 2015, p. 2). His argument centres on the tendency to neglect certain long-lasting problems, but rather pursuing something "flashy" that might result in popularity for the scholar publishing the findings. However, "researchers [should] seek to answer some of the most fundamental questions that humans can ask about nature" (National Academies 2009, p. 1). Pursuing clickbait-worthy findings conflicts with a core view that the National Academies and others postulate and can make way for value-laden judgements which relate back to the stage of idea generation. In the end, pursuing personal (subjective) goals, influenced by the institutional context, may influence what kind of output is generated, instead of asking oneself what a study may contribute to the literature.

Output does not only relate to the scientific system as a whole, it also has very real-life implications on the presented output itself (e.g., papers, presentations, and so forth); the underlying pressure for it often being the drive to publish one's findings. When publishing, however, many hurdles have to be taken. One of these hurdles may be the need to present a clear and understandable narrative – something that, in theory, should not pose a problem, as one should just write down how the research was conducted. Research should be presented in a clear fashion with a clear introduction, followed by a fitting method, and ended with significant findings that correspond to the hypotheses in the introduction. This is because a clear and understandable narrative often helps a different person (e.g., reviewers, editors, or readers) to understand one's findings. However, this can become dangerous if the suggestion of a clear narrative becomes a need or even a "tyranny" (Roberts 2015, p. 2). The argument that underlies the clean narrative is that it might be beneficial to rotate the order and writing or changing a previous narrative to be more consistent with one's findings (i.e., HARKing; see Kerr 1998). People may thus be prone to not honestly report on all the hurdles and inspirations on the way, but rather try to present the most coherent story – something that often does not reflect the actual research process. Thus, there are subjective expectations in sciences concerning the narrative of empirical studies which can, partially, deter the objectivity of findings, for instance as we discussed with the example of HARKing (see subsection 3.5).

4 Moving Forward – The Next Steps

When reflecting on how these research stages deal with normative influences, one is quickly faced with several questions: Is there no objectivity in empirical research? And should we, if that were the case, stop doing empirical research altogether? The latter question would be answered with a determined "no" by most scientists (ourselves included). We hope that theorists and practitioners can use the six steps of the research process to reflect upon empirical results and thereby understand and use the inferences from research, while being aware of the normative influences. We would also like the reader to further consider the following points.

Firstly, we would like to propose an active and public discussion about the normative influences of the academic system and its incentive structures. Secondly, we suggest utilising multiple research (method) perspectives in the research process. Thirdly, we want to propose some concrete ways in which individual researchers can develop a nuanced understanding of their scientific output's normative influences. To communicate these points, we will use the remainder of this chapter to suggest concrete measures both on a structural and individual level.

4.1 Change the System – Addressing the Incentive Structure

We recognise the enormous effort necessary to change an established system. However, recently several strings of thought have emerged to propose systemic alternatives. For instance, some have called for a renaissance of a "democratic educator" tradition (Rustin 2016, p. 147), others focussed on the values (e. g., cultural and intellectual purpose) universities should strive for (Collini 2012, Miedema 2012, Thomas 2010), and again others argue for more transparent journal procedures (e. g., pre-registration, openness of peer-reviews; see Gonzales and Cunningham 2015, Polka et al. 2018). In the following paragraphs, we would like to highlight some of these developments and discuss how the larger scientific incentive system and the research process could profit from them.

Many thinkers mention a reconstructing of governmental funding for the academic incentive system. For instance, one funding system that is not entirely novel but might help offer a more independent, low-pressure research environment, could be long-term institutional grants (like the *Harnack Principle* of the Max Planck Society in Germany). Some have argued that larger, independent, and unconditional grants for relevant topics might give researchers the leeway to spend some of their resources on free and bold theorising (which links back to the idea generation stage). It might introduce a different notion of scientific freedom than the current situation and also offer a space for the large-scale theorising the social sciences dearly need to develop, even though a fair and unbiased distribution of funds may be a challenge in itself. Recognising this need, some research councils have already implemented changes that lead to longer grant durations (e.g., Burgio 2017) or larger researcher freedom due to a broadened scope of evaluation panels (e.g., Hornyak 2017), emphasising original research and merit thereof over pure quantity of publication. Inspired by such approaches, we propose that rethinking governmental funding might have the potential to positively change normative assumptions in the process of empirical research and the six stages therein.

With a change in (governmental) funding, we also have to ask the question who should profit from these investments. We believe that research funded by society, through governmental channels, should be reported back to and impact society. An interesting development in this area is the publication process in open science formats (e.g., Butler 2016, Waldrop 2008),[7] allowing interested individuals to read scientific output and to investigate data themselves (for more information, see the initiative "Science Without Publication Paywalls" by cOAlition S; see Schiltz 2018). This allows for transparency of the data, enables new collaborations, and makes efficient use of the data (see also Else 2018). A complementary approach is to use the open access channels to include other disciplines and their expertise. E.g., in a recent paper, a collaboration of 84 people from multiple disciplines worked on an openly accessible paper, providing expertise from multiple angles (Lakens et al. 2018). With today's technology, these endeavours do not prove to be impossible anymore, as many software and internet services allow for a contemporaneous collaboration, no matter where on the world researchers are based. From this, we argue that changing the standards of how scientific results are accessed and communicated can benefit society as a whole and might in the process create an awareness of the limitations of any individual scientific discipline.

An additional issue closely linked to this is the journal-based review process. We will not take an absolute stance in the discussion on what kind of review

---

[7] There are different formats of open science, some scholars advocate for open data formats; for a review, see Arzberger et al. (2004), Janssen, Charalabidis, and Zuiderwijk (2012).

process may be the best (see, e. g., the discussion between Fiske 2016 and Gelman 2016), but the process of reviewing certain scientific output can possibly be made less value-laden.[8] For instance, citation pushing (e. g., reviewers suggesting their own work when commenting on a paper, even though it is not relevant in that context) may be deterred if one knows who is reviewing. One could also imagine that if the reviewing and editing process would be "rewarded", a reviewer could gain credit through the possibility of adding her name to a section of the paper. This would hopefully encourage the reviewer to provide useful feedback as she gets partly responsible for the research project. Another possibility would be to "pay" reviewers from the journal income. Any payment that reviewers receive should, however, be strictly limited to funding for their own future research projects. One could argue that paying a reviewer would bias the reviewer to support a possible manuscript. One possible solution to this would be to make the outcome of the review independent of the payment process. Reviewers who do not live up to the expectations may, however, not be invited for reviews in the future. Nonetheless, crediting the reviewers may be an interesting development that could help change the academic reward system, but then again, ironically, it may also fuel other biases. Although we realise that solely generating research without any value-laden judgement is untenable, a step forward could be openness in the process.

Others have argued, more philosophically, that scholarship and learning are intrinsic values in themselves and what universities should again strive for (Collini 2012), or that universities have a cultural and intellectual purpose of free speculations and inter-generational transmission (Thomas 2010). Still others have started building a (mostly) new vision of academia – in symbiosis with the current system and the broader society (Miedema 2012). These new initiatives do their best to propose more democratic and inclusive environments, which, in our minds, should also aid a more open and reflective research climate.

All the previous points result in the question of what academic output is and what it ought to be. With a change of the incentive system, (more) people may realise that doing academic work and getting academic achievements do not have to be zero-sum, and that, e. g., very often publication- and citation-numbers are not ideal in determining the value of a project to society. One should be aware that the excellence of different people might become evident in different measurements. Limiting academic output solely to the production and publishing of papers fails to address science in its complexity. Educator, theoriser, practitioner, reviewer, communicator, and connector are academic roles that are not

---

[8] For an interesting podcast episode on incivility in reviewing, see Inbar and Inzlicht (2018).

sufficiently rewarded by the current academic system. It could, thus, be beneficial (and fair) to change the incentive system so that not a single measurement or a single dimension of measurement is applied, but that a multitude of measures provides a better picture.

4.2 Robust Research

There are also very practical possibilities for researchers to disentangle normative influences from empirical research: e.g., by changing how scholars conduct research (e.g., Munafò and Smith 2018), as well as how they handle and present data (e.g., Weissgerber et al. 2015). We will thus elaborate on how individuals can reflect on influences on the research process.

Collaborating with multiple disciplines is inherent to the recently encouraged triangulation approach (Munafò and Smith 2018). In this approach, any research question is investigated by a team consisting of multiple disciplines, applying multiple methods, and using theories from different angles. The use of mixed methods may help to reveal much more than a single method could (e.g., Pool et al. 2010), and may yield insights that would be ignored when employing only one method.[9] This basically means that the process of replication is conducted from different fields (for an overview on replication, see Open Science Collaboration 2015). Particularly, triangulation calls for a stronger, possibly bolder, and more integrative theoretical and statistical approach to empirical research. An interesting addition to this would be a combination with a change to the incentive system. Munafò and Smith (2018) suggest crediting every person involved in the triangulation process, specifically defining which person contributed in which way. This would acknowledge every person involved in the project, giving credit to people that may sometimes be left behind in the current system.

In terms of data handling, researchers should try to avoid normative default options and use the statistical methods and standards most suitable. E.g., the notion of setting the Type I error rate (i.e., the chance of inferring an effect that is not there; also known as the *alpha level*) to 5 percent has become almost a doctrine in the scientific domains. In light of the recent replication crisis, some have suggested to set the "new" alpha to 0.5 percent, requiring "stronger" findings in order to achieve statistical significance (Benjamin et al. 2018). On the opposite side, other voices have called for abandoning alpha levels all together and

---

[9] An interesting approach can be to combine the theoretical design with the statistical design, e.g., in *dynamic systems modelling*; see Kunnen (2012).

looking at the size of the actual effects instead (following the seminal paper by Cohen 1992, Sullivan and Feinn 2012). Another interesting approach argues to "give p's a chance" and to let researchers reflect on their results (Albers 2017, par. 1, see also Lakens et al. 2018). This would give a researcher the freedom to set the alpha level in accordance with one's study. If a Type I error has to be avoided at all costs (e.g., if a medical treatment has strong negative side effects) the researcher can set their Type I error more rigidly (e.g., alpha to 0.1 percent). However, if this is not the case, a more lenient Type I error rate can be utilised. Sincerely reporting on these choices, in combination with an indication of statistical power, would provide a broader picture of the investigated reality. The move away from strong normative default options to more individual decision making can also be found when applying general research methods. E.g., Dehue (2002) argues that we should refrain from using a randomised control trial in every situation, because qualitative and mixed methods research can be superior in some situations. All these options have in common that they encourage the researcher to use the methods most suitable for the research question at hand (while justifying their use) and refrain from normative defaults assumed to be "good".

Moreover, a scholar can try to present the data more thoroughly and comprehensively with less normative decisions (e.g., Weissgerber et al. 2015). E.g., a recent study shows that bar charts and simple slope graphs (a graph of predicted effects at very high or low values of the predictor) remain prevalent (47 percent of total observed) as visualisation methods in psychology (Stulp 2017). They provide descriptive visual information but might overstate the results (e.g., because it does not show the large variation in the data) or misrepresent the data and relationships to the human eye. The choice for visualising the data with these kinds of plots can be problematic (e.g., Anscombe 1973). The graphs used are often too simplistic to portray the vast complexity of the underlying data (see, e.g., the *Datasaurus Dozen* visualised by Locke and D'Agostino McGowan 2017). Weissgerber and colleagues (2015) argue that presenting the data in a more complete manner can show, for instance, the distribution of data rather than just presenting a simple slope (as Anscombe visualised by presenting four same slopes with different data points in each graph). Scholars can still convey their message but presenting the data more comprehensibly can leave some of the subjective interpretation of the data to the reader, and thus divert some of the interpretation to the reader without prematurely excluding alternative explanations. It is, however, not a new suggestion, as illustrated by a quote by Edward Tufte (2001, p. 105), who demanded early on: *"above all else show the data"*.

4.3 Reflexivity

We finally want to advocate for a method that could sit at the core of our previous points. At the beginning of our chapter, we introduced ourselves and explained our own view on normative influences and the normative influences in, and on, our education. By doing so, we tried to give our readers an understanding of our own background, making our arguments not an objective representation of truth but a subjective interpretation of the current field. We believe that such a reflexivity approach can also benefit research in such a way that it would give researchers and their audience agency to understand why specific decisions in the research process were made and their potential consequences.

Reflexivity has been a key term in qualitative social science research in the last decades, especially in the field of sociology, but the concept has been applied in many different ways (Holland 1999). The concept is, however, old. Mead (1934, p. 134) defined reflexivity as "the turning back of the experience of the individual upon [her- or himself]". In recent years, reflexivity was argued to be one of the most appealing buzzwords of sociology and epistemology (Tsekeris 2010). Reflexivity has generally been understood in the social sciences and in recent years as "awareness of the influence the researcher has on the people or topic being studied, while simultaneously recognising how the research experience is affecting the researcher" (Probst 2015, p. 37). It has been argued to be essential in qualitative research (Ahmed, Hundt, and Blackburn 2011, Blaxter, Hughes, and Tight 2001, D'Cruz, Gillingham, and Melendez 2007, Gilgun 2008, Koch and Harrington 1998, Lazard and McAvoy 2017), as a means to, and end to, overcome the criticism that qualitative research was anecdotal and subject to researcher's bias (Patniak 2013). Reflexivity in qualitative research aims to monitor the effects of a researcher's involvement in the research, thus improving both the research's accuracy as well as the findings' credibility and context by clarifying the researcher's biases, values, and beliefs (Cutcliffe 2003). There are many ways in which this may be done and there is no standardised procedure for doing so. Attia and Edge (2017) recently argued that reflexivity should be considered as consisting of both a prospective and a retrospective component. The former is concerned with the impact of the researcher on the study, while the latter is concerned with the impact of the study on the researcher.

As we have illustrated throughout this chapter, quantitative research can also, against its best efforts and intentions, be subjected to all kinds of biases, and the introduction of reflexivity throughout empirical research may, therefore, be highly beneficial. E.g., Dehue (2002, p. 86) argues that "the designing of surveys and tests demands the taking of decisions as to which categories to use, and how to further specify them in survey questions and test items. After a research project, the original decisions are removed from the construction like redundant moulds".

Moreover, this would allow others to somewhat control for researchers' values and beliefs when pooling together results from many different studies, such as utilising meta-analyses. However, this has barely been done, with a few exceptions (Ryan and Golden 2006, Walker, Read, and Priest 2013). Nonetheless, journals seem to require such processes more and more (see, e. g., Nature 2018). Therefore, embracing, or at least actively acknowledging, decisions potentially influenced by the normative framework instead of removing them, could provide a broader and more holistic view on the research process. Such an embracement could provide important information and help not only the practitioners of science but also the users of science (e. g., philosophers). With our reflexivity example at the beginning of this chapter, we elucidate one way to implement reflexivity, nevertheless, this is by all means not the only way to do so.

5 Conclusion

In this chapter we aimed to raise an argument that in each step of the research process, in (1) idea generation, (2) research funding, (3) research planning, (4) data collection, (5) data analysis, and (6) scientific output, normative influences play a role. Furthermore, we aimed to answer the "is" question postulated at the beginning of this piece: What normative influences exist within empirical research? These stages are, moreover, not independent of each other. Systemic influences often intertwine these domains. Finally, we propose that addressing the incentive system, robust research, and reflecting on normative influences could provide a more holistic picture of the overall interwoven research process.

Acknowledgements

We express our sincerest appreciation to Martijn van Zomeren, Trudy Dehue, and Alexander Max Bauer, for intellectual support and advice from the start of this process.

Bibliography

Ahmed, Dunya Ahmed Abdulla; Hundt, Gillian Lewando, and Blackburn, Clare (2011): "Issues of Gender, Reflexivity and Positionality in the Field of Disability. Researching Visual Impairment in an Arab Society". In: *Qualitative Social Work* 10 (4), pp. 467–484.

Akerlof, George (2003): "Writing the 'The Market for "Lemons"'. A Personal and Interpretive Essay". In: *The Nobel Prize*. https://www.nobelprize.org/prizes/economics/2001/akerlof/article/, retrieved on November 23, 2018.

Albers, Casper (2017): "All We Are Saying is Give p's a Chance". In: *Mindwise Psychometrics*. http://mindwise-groningen.nl/all-we-are-saying-is-give-ps-a-chance/, retrieved on November 24, 2018.

Alberts, Bruce; Kirschner, Marc; Tilghman, Shirley, and Varmus, Harold (2014): "Rescuing US Biomedical Research from Its Systemic Flaws". In: *Proceedings of the National Academy of Sciences* 111 (16), pp. 5773–5777.

Anderson, Leigh and Stamoulis, Kostas (2007): "Applying Behavioural Economics to International Development Policy". In: Mavrotas, George and Shorrocks, Anthony (eds.): *Advancing Development*. London: Palgrave Macmillan, pp. 664–685.

Anscombe, Francis (1973): "Graphs in Statistical Analysis". In: *The American Statistician* 27 (1), p. 17.

Arnett, Jeffrey (2008): "The Neglected 95%. Why American Psychology Needs to Become Less American". In: *American Psychologist* 63 (7), pp. 602–614.

Arzberger, Peter; Schroeder, Peter; Beaulieu, Anne; Bowker, Geof; Casey, Kathleen; Laaksonen, Leif; Moorman, David; Uhlir, Paul, and Wouters, Paul (2004): "An International Framework to Promote Access to Data". In: *Science* 303 (5665), pp. 1777–1778.

Attia, Mariam and Edge, Julian (2017): "Be(com)ing a Reflexive Researcher. A Developmental Approach to Research Methodology". In: *Open Review of Educational Research* 4 (1), pp. 33–45.

Auranen, Otto and Nieminen, Mika (2010): "University Research Funding and Publication Performance. An International Comparison". In: *Research Policy* 39 (6), pp. 822–834.

Benjamin, Daniel; Berger, James; Johannesson, Magnus; Nosek, Brian; Wagenmakers, Eric-Jan; Berk, Richard; Bollen, Kenneth; Brembs, Björn; Brown, Lawrence; Camerer, Colin; Cesarini, David; Chambers, Christopher; Clyde, Merlise; Cook, Thomas; de Boeck, Paul; Dienes, Zoltan; Dreber, Anna; Easwaran, Kenny; Efferson, Charles; Fehr, Ernst; Fidler, Fiona; Field, Andy; Forster, Malcolm; George, Edward; Gonzalez, Richard; Goodman, Steven; Green, Edwin; Green, Donald; Greenwald, Anthony; Hadfield, Jarrod; Hedges, Larry; Held, Leonhard; Ho, Teck-Hua; Hoijtink, Herbert; Hruschka, Daniel; Imai, Kosuke; Imbens, Guido; Ioannidis, John; Jeon, Minjeong; Jones, James Holland; Kirchler, Michael; Laibson, David; List, John; Little, Roderick; Lupia, Arthur; Machery, Edouard; Maxwell, Scott; McCarthy, Michael; Moore, Don; Morgan, Stephen; Munafò, Marcus; Nakagawa, Shinichi; Nyhan, Brendan; Parker, Timothy; Pericchi, Luis; Perugini, Marco; Rouder, Jeff; Rousseau, Judith; Savalei, Victoria; Schönbrodt, Felix; Sellke, Thomas; Sinclair, Betsy; Tingley, Dustin; van Zandt, Trisha; Vazire, Simine; Watts, Duncan; Winship, Christopher; Wolpert, Robert; Xie, Yu; Young, Cristobal; Zinman, Jonathan, and

Johnson, Valen (2018): "Redefine Statistical Significance". In: *Nature Human Behaviour* 2 (1), pp. 6–10.
Bhattacharjee, Yudhijit (2013): "The Mind of a Con Man". In: *The New York Times*. http://www.nytimes.com/2013/04/28/magazine/diederik-stapels-audacious-academic-fraud.html, retrieved on November 25, 2018.
Blaxter, Loraine; Hughes, Christina, and Tight, Malcolm (2001): *How to Research*. Buckingham: Open University Press.
Bryman, Alan (1984): "The Debate About Quantitative and Qualitative Research. A Question of Method or Epistemology?". In: *The British Journal of Sociology* 35 (1), pp. 75–92.
Burgio, Gaetan (2017): "The NHMRC Program Grant Overhaul. Will It Change the Medical Research Landscape in Australia?". In: *The Conversation*. https://theconversation.com/the-nhmrc-program-grant-overhaul-will-it-change-the-medical-research-landscape-in-australia-78343/, retrieved on November 14, 2018.
Butler, Declan (2016): "Dutch Lead European Push to Flip Journals to Open Access". In: *Nature* 529 (7584), p. 13.
Carey, Benedict (2011): "Fraud Case Seen as a Red Flag for Psychology Research". In: *The New York Times*. http://www.nytimes.com/2011/11/03/health/research/noted-dutch-psychologist-stapel-accused-of-research-fraud.html, retrieved on November 14, 2018.
Cartwright, Nancy (2007): "Are RCTs the Gold Standard?". In: *BioSocieties* 2 (1), pp. 11–20.
Cohen, Jacob (1992): "A Power Primer". In: *Psychological Bulletin* 112 (1), pp. 155–159.
Collini, Stefan (2012): *What Are Universities For?* London: Penguin.
Crawford, Jarret; Duarte, José; Haidt, Jonathan; Jussim, Lee; Stern, Charlotta, and Tetlock, Philip (2015): "It May Be Harder than We Thought, But Political Diversity Will (Still) Improve Social Psychological Science". In: *Behavioral and Brain Sciences* 38, e164.
Cushman, Priscilla; Hoeksema, Todd; Kouveliotou, Chryssa; Lowenthal, James, and Peterson, Bradley (2015): "Impact of Declining Proposal Success Rates on Scientific Productivity". In: *ArXiv E-Prints*, arXiv:1510.01647.
Cutcliffe, John (2003): "Reconsidering Reflexivity. Introducing the Case for Intellectual Entrepreneurship". In: *Qualitative Health Research* 13 (1), pp. 136–148.
D'Cruz, Heather; Gillingham, Philip, and Melendez, Sebastian (2007): "Reflexivity, Its Meanings and Relevance for Social Work. A Critical Review of the Literature". In: *British Journal of Social Work* 37 (1), pp. 73–90.
Dehue, Trudy (2002): "A Dutch Treat. Randomized Controlled Experimentation and the Case of Heroin-Maintenance in the Netherlands". In: *History of the Human Sciences* 15 (2), pp. 75–98.
Dehue, Trudy (1997): "Deception, Efficiency, and Random Groups. Psychology and the Gradual Origination of the Random Group Design". In: *Isis* 88 (4), pp. 653–673.
Dehue, Trudy (2005): "History of the Control Group". In: Everitt, Brian and Howell, David (eds.): *Encyclopedia of Statistics in Behavioral Science*. Vol. 2. Chichester: Wiley & Sons, pp. 829–836.
Duarte, José; Crawford, Jarret; Stern, Charlotta; Haidt, Jonathan; Jussim, Lee, and Tetlock, Philip (2015): "Political Diversity Will Improve Social Psychological Science". In: *Behavioral and Brain Sciences* 38, e130.

Edwards, Marc and Roy, Siddhartha (2017): "Academic Research in the 21st Century. Maintaining Scientific Integrity in a Climate of Perverse Incentives and Hypercompetition". In: *Environmental Engineering Science* 34 (1), pp. 51–61.

Else, Holly (2018): "Radical Open-Access Plan Could Spell End to Journal Subscriptions". In: *Nature* 561, pp. 17–18.

Elton, Lewis (2004): "Goodhart's Law and Performance Indicators in Higher Education". In: *Evaluation & Research in Education* 18 (1–2), pp. 120–128.

Fang, Ferric; Bowen, Anthony, and Casadevall, Arturo (2016): "NIH Peer Review Percentile Scores Are Poorly Predictive of Grant Productivity". In: *eLife* 5, e13323.

Fiske, Susan (2016): "A Call to Change Science's Culture of Shaming". In: *Association for Psychological Science*. https://www.psychologicalscience.org/observer/a-call-to-change-sciences-culture-of-shaming/, retrieved on November 14, 2018.

Gallander Wintre, Maxine; North, Christopher, and Sugar, Lorne (2001): "Psychologists' Response to Criticisms About Research Based on Undergraduate Participants. A Developmental Perspective". In: *Canadian Psychology, Psychologie Canadienne* 42 (3), pp. 216–225.

Gálvez, Ramiro (2017): "Assessing Author Self-Citation as a Mechanism of Relevant Knowledge Diffusion". In: *Scientometrics* 111 (3), pp. 1801–1812.

Gelman, Andrew (2016): "What Has Happened Down Here Is the Winds Have Changed". In: *Statistical Modeling, Causal Inference, and Social Science*. http://andrewgelman.com/2016/09/21/what-has-happened-down-here-is-the-winds-have-changed/, retrieved on November 14, 2018.

Gelman, Andrew and Loken, Eric (2013): "The Garden of Forking Paths. Why Multiple Comparisons Can Be a Problem, Even When There Is No 'Fishing Expedition' or 'p-Hacking' and the Research Hypothesis Was Posited Ahead of Time". In: *Department of Statistics, Columbia University in the City of New York*. http://www.stat.columbia.edu/~gelman/research/unpublished/p_hacking.pdf, retrieved on November 14, 2018.

Gendron, Maria; Roberson, Debi; van der Vyver, Jacoba Marietta, and Barrett, Lisa Feldman (2014): "Perceptions of Emotion from Facial Expressions Are Not Culturally Universal. Evidence from a Remote Culture". In: *Emotion* 14 (2), pp. 251–262.

Gergen, Kenneth (1973): "Social Psychology as History". In: *Journal of Personality and Social Psychology* 26 (2), pp. 309–320.

Gilgun, Jane (2008): "Lived Experience, Reflexivity, and Research on Perpetrators of Interpersonal Violence". In: *Qualitative Social Work* 7 (2), pp. 181–197.

Gonzales, Joseph and Cunningham, Corbin (2015): "The Promise of Pre-Registration in Psychological Research". In: *American Psychological Association*. http://www.apa.org/science/about/psa/2015/08/pre-registration.aspx, retrieved on November 14, 2018.

Guo, Lan; Stone, Dan; Bryant, Stephanie; Wier, Benson; Nikitkov, Alex; Ren, Chunyan; Riccio, Edson Luiz; Shen, Milton; Trabelsi, Samir, and Zhang, Li Fang (2013): "Are Consumers' Financial Needs and Values Common Across Cultures? Evidence from Six Countries". In: *International Journal of Consumer Studies* 37 (6), pp. 675–688.

Hacking, Ian (1988): "Philosophers of Experiment". In: *Proceedings of the Biennial Meeting of the Philosophy of Science Association* 2 (1), pp. 147–156.

Henrich, Joseph; Heine, Steven, and Norenzayan, Ara (2010): "The Weirdest People in the World?". In: *Behavioral and Brain Sciences* 33 (2–3), pp. 61–83.
Hirsch, Jorge (2005): "An Index to Quantify an Individual's Scientific Research Output". In: *Proceedings of the National Academy of Sciences* 102 (46), pp. 16569–16572.
Holland, Ray (1999): "Reflexivity". In: *Human Relations* 52 (4), pp. 463–484.
Hornyak, Tim (2017): "Japan Shakes up Research Funding System". In: *Nature Index*. https://www.natureindex.com/news-blog/japan-shakes-up-research-funding-system/, retrieved on November 14, 2018.
Inbar, Yoel and Inzlicht, Michael (2018): "You're Not Wrong Walter, You're Just an A$$hole". In: *Two Psychologists Four Beers*. http://michaelinzlicht.com/getting-better/2018/5/24/two-psychologists-four-beers-in-search-of-the-campus-free-speech-crisis-pe9hd/, retrieved on November 14, 2018.
Janssen, Marijn; Charalabidis, Yannis, and Zuiderwijk, Anneke (2012): "Benefits, Adoption Barriers and Myths of Open Data and Open Government". In: *Information Systems Management* 29 (4), pp. 258–268.
John, Leslie; Loewenstein, George, and Prelec, Drazen (2012): "Measuring the Prevalence of Questionable Research Practices with Incentives for Truth Telling". In: *Psychological Science* 23 (5), pp. 524–532.
Kahneman, Daniel (2011): *Thinking, Fast and Slow*. New York: Farrar, Straus and Giroux.
Kant, Immanuel (1964): *Groundwork of the Metaphysic of Morals*. London: Harper Torchbooks.
Kaplan, David; Lacetera, Nicola, and Kaplan, Celia (2008): "Sample Size and Precision in NIH Peer Review". In: *PLoS ONE* 3 (7), e2761.
Kaptchuk, Ted (2001): "The Double-Blind, Randomized, Placebo-Controlled Trial. Gold Standard or Golden Calf?". In: *Journal of Clinical Epidemiology* 54 (6), pp. 541–549.
Kass, Robert (2011): "Statistical Inference. The Big Picture". In: *Statistical Science* 26 (1), pp. 1–9.
Kerr, Norbert (1998): "HARKing. Hypothesizing After the Results Are Known". In: *Personality and Social Psychology Review* 2 (3), pp. 196–217.
Kimble, Judith; Bement, William; Chang, Qiang; Cox, Benjamin; Drinkwater, Norman; Gourse, Richard; Hoskins, Aaron; Huttenlocher, Anna; Kreeger, Pamela; Lambert, Paul; Mailick, Marsha; Miyamoto, Shigeki; Moss, Richard; O'Connor-Giles, Kate; Roopra, Avtar; Saha, Krishanu, and Seidel, Hannah (2015): "Strategies from UW-Madison for Rescuing Biomedical Research in the US". In: *eLife* 4, e09305.
Kirk, Roger (1996): "Practical Significance. A Concept Whose Time Has Come". In: *Educational and Psychological Measurement* 56 (5), pp. 746–759.
Koch, Tina and Harrington, Ann (1998): "Reconceptualizing Rigour. The Case for Reflexivity". In: *Journal of Advanced Nursing* 28 (4), pp. 882–890.
Kruglanski, Arie (2001): "That 'Vision Thing'. The State of Theory in Social and Personality Psychology at the Edge of the New Millennium". In: *Journal of Personality and Social Psychology* 80 (6), pp. 871–875.
Kuhn, Thomas (1962): *The Structure of Scientific Revolutions*. Chicago: The University of Chicago Press.
Kunnen, Saskia (2012): *A Dynamic Systems Approach to Adolescent Development*. London: Psychology Press.
Lakens, Daniel; Adolfi, Federico; Albers, Casper; Anvari, Farid; Apps, Matthew; Argamon, Shlomo; Baguley, Thom; Becker, Raymond; Benning, Stephen; Bradford, Daniel;

Buchanan, Erin; Caldwell, Aaron; van Calster, Ben; Carlsson, Rickard; Chen, Sau-Chin; Chung, Bryan; Colling, Lincoln; Collins, Gary; Crook, Zander; Cross, Emily; Daniels, Sameera; Danielsson, Henrik; DeBruine, Lisa; Dunleavy, Daniel; Earp, Brian; Feist, Michele; Ferrell, Jason; Field, James; Fox, Nicholas; Friesen, Amanda; Gomes, Caio; Gonzalez-Marquez, Monica; Grange, James; Grieve, Andrew; Guggenberger, Robert; Grist, James; van Harmelen, Anne-Laura; Hasselman, Fred; Hochard, Kevin; Hoffarth, Mark; Holmes, Nicholas; Ingre, Michael; Isager, Peder; Isotalus, Hanna; Johansson, Christer; Juszczyk, Konrad; Kenny, David; Khalil, Ahmed; Konat, Barbara; Lao, Junpeng; Larsen, Erik Gahner; Lodder, Gerine; Lukavský, Jiří; Madan, Christopher; Manheim, David; Martin, Stephen; Martin, Andrea; Mayo, Deborah; McCarthy, Randy; McConway, Kevin; McFarland, Colin; Nio, Amanda; Nilsonne, Gustav; de Oliveira, Cilene Lino; de Xivry, Jean-Jacques Orban; Parsons, Sam; Pfuhl, Gerit; Quinn, Kimberly; Sakon, John; Saribay, Adil; Schneider, Iris; Selvaraju, Manojkumar; Sjoerds, Zsuzsika; Smith, Samuel; Smits, Tim; Spies, Jeffrey; Sreekumar, Vishnu; Steltenpohl, Crystal; Stenhouse, Neil; Świątkowski, Wojciech; Vadillo, Miguel; van Assen, Marcel; Williams, Matt; Williams, Samantha; Williams, Donald; Yarkoni, Tal; Ziano, Ignazio, and Zwaan, Rolf (2018): "Justify Your Alpha". In: *Nature Human Behavior* 2 (3), pp. 168–171.

Lazard, Lisa and McAvoy, Jean (2017): "Doing Reflexivity in Psychological Research. What's the Point? What's the Practice?". In: *Qualitative Research in Psychology* (Early Access), pp. 1–19.

Linkola, Pentti (2009): *Can Life Prevail? A Radical Approach to the Environmental Crisis*. London: Integral Tradition Publishing.

Locke, Steph and D'Agostino McGowan, Lucy (2017): "DatasauRus. Datasets from the Datasaurus Dozen". In: *Datasaurus*. https://itsalocke.com/datasaurus/, retrieved on November 14, 2018.

Lombrozo, Tania (2013): "Name Five Women in Philosophy. Bet You Can't". In: *NPR*. https://www.npr.org/sections/13.7/2013/06/17/192523112/name-ten-women-in-philosophy-bet-you-can-t/, retrieved on November 14, 2018.

McGuire, William (1973): "The Yin and Yang of Progress in Social Psychology. Seven Koan". In: *Journal of Personality and Social Psychology* 26 (3), pp. 446–456.

Mead, George (1934): *Mind, Self, and Society*. Chicago: The University of Chicago Press.

Meldrum, Marcia (2000): "A Brief History of the Randomized Controlled Trial. From Oranges and Lemons to Gold Standard". In: *Hematology, Oncology Clinics of North America* 14 (4), pp. 745–760.

Miedema, Frank (2012): *Science 3.0. Real Science, Real Knowledge*. Amsterdam: Amsterdam University Press.

Munafò, Marcus and Smith, George Davey (2018): "Repeating Experiments Is Not Enough". In: *Nature* 553 (7689), pp. 399–401.

National Academies (2009): *On Being a Scientist. A Guide to Responsible Conduct in Research*. Washington: National Academies Press.

Nature (2018): "Nature Journals Tighten Rules on Non-Financial Conflicts". In: *Nature* 554 (7690), p. 6.

Open Science Collaboration (2015): "Estimating the Reproducibility of Psychological Science". In: *Science* 349 (6251), aac4716.

Patniak, Esha (2013): "Reflexivity. Situating the Researcher in Qualitative Research". In: *Humanities and Social Science Studies* 2 (2), pp. 98–106.

Peterson, David (2016): "The Baby Factory. Difficult Research Objects, Disciplinary Standards, and the Production of Statistical Significance". In: *Socius, Sociological Research for a Dynamic World* 1 (2), pp. 1–10.

Peterson, Robert (2001): "On the Use of College Students in Social Science Research. Insights from a Second-Order Meta-Analysis". In: *Journal of Consumer Research* 28 (3), pp. 450–461.

Polka, Jessica; Kiley, Robert; Konforti, Boyana; Stern, Bodo, and Vale, Ronald (2018): "Publish Peer Reviews". In: *Nature* 560 (7720), pp. 545–547.

Pool, Robert; Montgomery, Catherine; Morar, Neetha; Mweemba, Oliver; Ssali, Agnes; Gafos, Mitzy; Lees, Shelley; Stadler, Jonathan; Crook, Angela; Nunn, Andrew; Hayes, Richard, and McCormack, Sheena (2010): "A Mixed Methods and Triangulation Model for Increasing the Accuracy of Adherence and Sexual Behaviour Data. The Microbicides Development Programme". In: *PLoS ONE* 5 (7), e11600.

Popper, Karl (1973): *Objective Knowledge. An Evolutionary Approach.* Oxford: Clarendon Press.

Porter, Theodore (1995): *Trust in Numbers. The Pursuit of Objectivity in Science and Public Life.* Princeton: Princeton University Press.

Postmes, Tom and Spears, Russell (1998): "Deindividuation and Antinormative Behavior. A Meta-Analysis". In: *Psychological Bulletin* 123 (3), pp. 238–259.

Probst, Barbara (2015): "The Eye Regards Itself. Benefits and Challenges of Reflexivity in Qualitative Social Work Research". In: *Social Work Research* 39 (1), pp. 37–48.

Ravetz, Jerry (2004): "The Post-Normal Science of Precaution". In: *Futures* 36 (3), pp. 347–357.

Roberts, Brent (2015): "The Perverse Incentives That Stand as a Roadblock to Scientific Reform". In: *The Inquisitive Mind* 25 (3). http://www.in-mind.org/article/the-perverse-incentives-that-stand-as-a-roadblock-to-scientific-reform/, retrieved on November 14, 2018.

Rosenthal, Robert (1979): "The File Drawer Problem and Tolerance for Null Results". In: *Psychological Bulletin* 86 (3), pp. 638–641.

Rubin, Mark (2017): "When Does HARKing Hurt? Identifying When Different Types of Undisclosed Post Hoc Hypothesizing Harm Scientific Progress". In: *Review of General Psychology* 21 (4), p. 308.

Rustin, Michael (2016): "The Neoliberal University and Its Alternatives". In: *Soundings* 63 (3), pp. 147–176.

Ryan, Louise and Golden, Anne (2006): "'Tick the Box Please'. A Reflexive Approach to Doing Quantitative Social Research". In: *Sociology* 40 (6), pp. 1191–1200.

Sarewitz, Daniel (2016): "Saving Science". In: *The New Atlantis* 49 (1), pp. 4–40.

Schiltz, Marc (2018): "Science Without Publication Paywalls. cOAlition S for the Realisation of Full and Immediate Open Access". In: *PLoS Med* 15 (9), e1002663.

Shuval, Kerem; Harker, Karen; Roudsari, Bahman; Groce, Nora; Mills, Britain; Siddiqi, Zoveen, and Shachak, Aviv (2011): "Is Qualitative Research Second Class Science? A Quantitative Longitudinal Examination of Qualitative Research in Medical Journals". In: *PLoS ONE* 6 (2), e16937.

Silberzahn, Raphael; Uhlmann, Eric; Martin, Daniel; Anselmi, Pasquale; Aust, Frederik; Awtrey, Eli; Bahník, Štěpán; Bai, Feng; Bannard, Colin; Bonnier, Evelina; Carlsson, Rickard; Cheung, Felix; Christensen, Garret; Clay, Russ; Craig, Maureen; Rosa, Anna

Dalla; Dam, Lammertjan; Evans, Mathew; Cervantes, Ismael Flores; Fong, Nathan; Gamez-Djokic, Monica; Glenz, Andreas; Gordon-McKeon, Shauna; Heaton, Tim; Eriksson, Karin Hederos; Heene, Moritz; Mohr, Alicia Hofelich; Högden, Fabia; Hui, Kent; Johannesson, Magnus; Kalodimos, Jonathan; Kaszubowski, Erikson; Kennedy, Deanna; Lei, Ryan; Lindsay, Thomas; Liverani, Silvia; Madan, Christopher; Molden, Daniel; Molleman, Eric; Morey, Richard; Mulder, Laetitia; Nijstad, Bernard; Pope, Bryson; Pope, Nolan; Prenoveau, Jason; Rink, Floor; Robusto, Egidio; Roderique, Hadiya; Sandberg, Anna; Schlüter, Elmar; Schönbrodt, Felix; Sherman, Martin Felix; Sommer, Amy; Sotak, Kristin; Spain, Seth; Spörlein, Christoph; Stafford, Tom; Stefanutti, Luca; Täuber, Susanne; Ullrich, Johannes; Vianello, Michelangelo; Wagenmakers, Eric-Jan; Witkowiak, Maciej; Yoon, Sangsuk, and Nosek, Brian (2018): "Many Analysts, One Data Set. Making Transparent How Variations in Analytic Choices Affect Results". In: *Advances in Methods and Practices in Psychological Science* 1 (3), pp. 337–356.

Simmons, Joseph; Nelson, Leif, and Simonsohn, Uri (2011): "False-Positive Psychology. Undisclosed Flexibility in Data Collection and Analysis Allows Presenting Anything as Significant". In: *Psychological Science* 22 (11), pp. 1359–1366.

Singh, Simon (2004): *Big Bang. The Most Important Scientific Discovery of All Time and Why You Need to Know About It.* London and New York: Fourth Estate.

Sismondo, Sergio (2008): "How Pharmaceutical Industry Funding Affects Trial Outcomes. Causal Structures and Responses". In: *Social Science & Medicine* 66 (9), pp. 1909–1914.

Steegen, Sara; Tuerlinckx, Francis; Gelman, Andrew, and Vanpaemel, Wolf (2016): "Increasing Transparency Through a Multiverse Analysis". In: *Perspectives on Psychological Science* 11 (5), pp. 702–712.

Stroebe, Wolfgang; Gadenne, Volker, and Nijstad, Bernard (2018): "Do Our Laws Only Apply to Students? The Problem with External Validity". In: *Basic and Applied Psychology* 40, pp. 384–395.

Stulp, Gert (2017): "Visualising Differences in Visualisations in Social Psychology". Talk given at the University of Groningen.

Sullivan, Gail and Feinn, Richard (2012): "Using Effect Size or Why the p Value Is Not Enough". In: *Journal of Graduate Medical Education* 4 (3), pp. 279–282.

Tetlock, Philip (1994): "Political Psychology or Politicized Psychology. Is the Road to Scientific Hell Paved With Good Moral Intentions?". In: *Political Psychology* 15 (3), p. 509.

Thomas, Nancy (2010): "The Politics of Academic Freedom". In: *New Directions for Higher Education* 152, pp. 83–90.

Tsekeris, Charalambos (2010): "Reflections on Reflexivity. Sociological Issues and Perspectives". In: *Contemporary Issues* 3 (1), pp. 28–37.

Tufte, Edward (2001): *The Visual Display of Quantitative Information.* Cheshire: Graphics Press.

Waldrop, Mitchell (2008): "Science 2.0". In: *Scientific American* 298 (5), pp. 68–73.

Walker, Susan; Read, Susan, and Priest, Helena (2013): "Use of Reflexivity in a Mixed-Methods Study". In: *Nurse Researcher* 20 (3), pp. 38–43.

Weissgerber, Tracey; Milic, Natasa; Winham, Stacey, and Garovic, Vesna (2015): "Beyond Bar and Line Graphs. Time for a New Data Presentation Paradigm". In: *PLoS Biology* 13 (4), e1002128.

Zimbardo, Philip (1969): "The Human Choice. Individuation, Reason, and Order Versus Deindividuation, Impulse, and Chaos". In: *Nebraska Symposium on Motivation* 17, pp. 237–307.

van Zomeren, Martijn (2016): *From Self to Social Relationships. An Essentially Relational Perspective on Social Motivation.* Cambridge: Cambridge University Press.

Zwaan, Rolf (2013): "50 Questions About Messy Rooms and Clean Data". In: *Rolf Zwaan.* https://rolfzwaan.blogspot.com/2013/08/50-questions-about-messy-rooms-and.html, retrieved on November 14, 2018.

Guillermina Jasso
Is and Ought

From Ideas to Theory to Empirics

Abstract: Understanding the relation between Is and Ought questions and their relation to theory and empirics is a central task for social science. This chapter makes several contributions. First, it presents two substantive approaches, a deeper forces approach (including two engines of behaviour – to know the causes of things and to judge the goodness of things – leading directly to Is and Ought questions, respectively) and a middle-range theory which recently unified theories of justice, status, and power. Second, it reviews three theory types (two deductive, one nondeductive). Third, it examines postulates and predictions from the new unified theory and its component theories. Fourth, it provides five illustrations tracing the path from ideas to theory to empirics – (1) five types of persons and five types of societies in the new unified theory, (2) three questions on inequality, (3) justice and impartiality, (4) salary secrecy, and (5) theft and punishment. Along the way the chapter notes the classical sources for the ideas, the special tools such as probability distributions for theory and factorial surveys for empirics, and the major embedded Is and Ought questions and behaviour. The chapter also introduces a new kind of question – Is-about-Ought – which represents the scientific search for knowledge about the normative views to which persons subscribe.

1 Introduction

There was a time when philosophers were scientists and scientists were philosophers. Aristotle wrote both *Meteorology* (1952a) and the *Nicomachean Ethics* (1952b). However one sees the historical balance between the impulse to know and the impulse to judge – or between questions susceptible of definite knowledge and questions susceptible only of speculation, remaining insoluble, as Russell (1945) put it – it is a fact that some of the greatest minds yet produced addressed both kinds of questions. And thus, for a scientist, the road to reliable knowledge starts in philosophy. This is especially true for a social scientist, for much of the definite knowledge is yet to come and the earliest ideas are rich and vivid. Yet, even in the study of the physical world and of mathematics, there is glory in the philosophical origins of such basic ideas as continuity and infinity.[1]

A recent effort to codify the basic engines of human behaviour, grounded in Plato's and Aristotle's idea that the ways and means of seeking happiness generate distinctive types of persons and distinctive types of societies, lists four basic drivers and three midlevel drivers (Jasso 2015). In the language of happiness, and using Merton's (1968) as well as Rayo and Becker's (2007) evocative words, the midlevel approach is based on three middle-range carriers of happiness and the other on four deeper carriers of happiness. The four deeper drivers are:
- to know the causes of things
- to judge the goodness of things
- to be perfect
- to be free

Of these, the first two provide a foundation for the Is and the Ought, respectively (Jasso 2006, p. 337). With respect to the Is, social scientists are interested in two distinct manifestations – what actually is and what individuals *believe* actually is – viz., social scientists' collective and systematic approximations to "truth" (called Type I equations) and lay scientists' solitary and less systematic approximations (called Type II or positive-beliefs equations). With respect to the Ought, there are again two manifestations of interest – what philosophers and normative social scientists (such as welfare economists) judge ought to be and what ordinary individuals judge ought to be – both called Type III or normative-judgements equations. This latter manifestation can be viewed from the individual's perspective – as an Ought claim – or from the scientist's perspective – as what may be termed an Is-about-Ought proposition.

The Is propositions and Ought claims are interrelated, most commonly when an Is proposition is used as the basis for an Ought claim. Indeed, when philosophers and normative social scientists present Ought claims they invoke special knowledge, obtained either by trying to get inside the mind of a special observer – from Plato's (1952) "guardians" to Smith's (1976) "spectator" to Firth's (1952) "ideal observer" and Hare's (1981) "archangel" – or by comprehensive scientific work.

---

[1] E.g., philosophical and theological discussions of such matters as "How does an angel move through space?" and "How does love grow?" were integral to developments in mathematics and physics (Grant 1974, Shapere 1974). And Georg Cantor, founder of set theory, credited Augustine with formulating an accurate description of infinity (Struik 1987).

Meanwhile, the three middle-range carriers of happiness – justice,[2] status,[3] and power – which are believed, but not yet demonstrated, to be generated by the four deeper carriers, have received sustained theoretical development and mathematical expression. At least two of the three midlevel sociobehavioural processes (justice and status) have been formalised, producing for each a deductive theory, with a basic postulate – the justice evaluation function and the status function – and yielding an abundance of deduced testable predictions.

Recently the three theories have been integrated into a new unified theory (NUT) generating identity and happiness and generating as well new testable predictions (Jasso 2008). The predictions obtained from each of the component theories and from the unified theory comprise a large set of Is propositions. Moreover, at least some of the predictions obtained from the component justice theory lead to Ought claims; these are, notably, predictions about things that increase well-being, for such things will be preferred and sought, sometimes assuming the character of moral imperatives. Further theoretical analysis of both the component theories and the NUT is likely to obtain both new Is propositions, new Ought claims, and new Is-about-Ought propositions.

Thus, the basic engines of behaviour provide foundational links to the Is and the Ought, and the midlevel engines of behaviour, singly and via the NUT, provide testable predictions about Is and Ought behaviour. The pages that follow will trace the path from ideas to theory to empirics, providing illustrative examples and noting their Is or Ought character. To make the exposition as clear as possible, section 2 provides a brief overview of three main forms of scientific theory, two deductive and one nondeductive. Section 3 provides an overview of the new unified theory, from which most of the examples will be drawn, including selected predictions. Section 4 shows how philosophical ideas motivate postulates or anticipate predictions and as well discusses pertinent empirical work; five topical domains are examined – the new unified theory's five types of persons and five types of societies, echoing Plato and Aristotle; three ques-

---

[2] The term "justice" is used as shorthand for "justice and the other comparison processes, such as self-esteem and relative deprivation". As will be seen, the hallmark of justice theory, and comparison theory more generally, is that the outcome depends on two variables, often called the actual reward and the just reward (or, more generally, the comparison reward). The direction of the effects of the actual reward and the just reward depends on whether the reward is considered a good (more is preferred to less) or a bad (less is preferred to more). When the reward is a good, the outcome increases with the actual reward and decreases with the comparison reward. E.g., this was the form described by William James (1952) for self-esteem. When the reward is a bad, the directions of the two effects are reversed.

[3] "Status" refers to evaluations of the worth of individuals and their characteristics; synonyms include "honor, esteem, respect, and prestige" (Zelditch 1968, pp. 250, 253).

tions on inequality; justice and impartiality; salary secrecy; and theft and punishment. A short note concludes.

2 Types of Theories

The word "theory" is used in many senses, some scientific, some not. Some favourite theories are indeed not scientific theories; probability theory and music theory come readily to mind. This chapter uses "theory" exclusively in the scientific sense. Three types of scientific theories are distinguished. Two are deductive (termed Type 1.A and 1.B), the third nondeductive (termed Type 2). The two deductive forms have similar structure. They each begin with a small set of premises which yield a number of deduced consequences. But there the similarity ends. Their very souls differ, visible in the character of the premises and the parts that are tested.

Theory Type 1.A: In the first deductive form – the gold-standard hypothetico-deductive form invented by Newton (and discussed by Toulmin 1978, pp. 378–379) – the premises (often called postulates) are "genuine guesses about the structure of the world" (Popper 1963, p. 245) and the deduced consequences (often called predictions) display the "marvellous deductive unfolding" which not only yields a wealth of implications but also reaches novel predictions (Popper 1963, p. 221, see also pp. 117, 241–248). The postulates' fruitfulness is evident in the "derivations far afield from the original domain", which "permit an increasingly broad and diversified basis for testing the theory" (Danto 1967, p. 299f.). Tests of the predictions reveal the postulates' fidelity to the real world. When the predictions are consistent with the theory – and it is no easy matter to decide how many tests, of how many predictions, with what combination of results is necessary – the starting postulates may come to be known as laws of nature.[4]

Theory Type 1.B: In the second deductive form, the premises are true or subject to human/social control, and the deduced consequences follow necessarily whenever the premises hold. There are no guesses about the nature of the world. The empirical task is to discern the conditions under which the premises hold.

---

[4] For description of the hypothetico-deductive theory form (Type 1.A), see also Jasso (1988) and the references cited therein.

Theory Type 2: In the nondeductive form (owed to Toulmin 1953, see also Fararo 1989), propositions are constructed by linking terms in a theory with observable outcomes; the empirical task is to test the propositions.[5]

A given assumption may appear in more than one theory form. E. g., justice and status theories each have both a hypothetico-deductive part and a nondeductive part, as will be seen below. They are thus hybrid theories. Of course, the propositions in the nondeductive part may in time be seen to be deducible from the assumptions and move to the hypothetico-deductive part.

3 Brief Overview of the New Unified Theory

The first task is to assemble the building blocks for the new unified theory, offering a "before" and "after" picture. Before the NUT – roughly, before 2006 – there were four main building blocks: (1) justice theory; (2) status theory; (3) identity theory; and (4) Homans' (1976, p. 231, 240 f.) idea that "there is only one theory we want to develop – a theory of human behavior" and it must address "the relations between equity, status, and power".

Comprehensive review of the theories of justice, status, and identity revealed that they share a common core of three elements (Jasso 2007, pp. 360–362): First, each theory involves a primordial sociobehavioural outcome (PSO), such as status, self-esteem, or the sense of justice. Second, in each theory the PSO is generated from personal quantitative characteristics, including both cardinal things like wealth and ordinal things like beauty. Third, in each theory the PSO is generated within groups formed by personal qualitative characteristics, such as race, religion, or place. E. g., status may be generated from wealth within a city, and self-esteem may be generated from academic skill within a classroom. Each bundle of elements – say, status-bravery-regiment – simultaneously generates an identity and a magnitude of happiness.

But how many PSOs are there? And what are they? It was obvious that any quantitative characteristic can be paired with any PSO. What makes each pair distinctive? E. g., what is the precise difference between "wealth generates status" (owed to Veblen 1953) and "wealth generates self-esteem"? Homans' (1976, p. 231) implicit idea of a trio of PSOs – justice, status, power – strikes a chord, for in nature there are three rates of change. Restricting attention to in-

---

[5] For description of the nondeductive theory form (Type 2), see also Jasso (2004).

creasing relations, a PSO can increase at an increasing rate or at a decreasing rate or at a constant rate.⁶

The sociological literature, in work dating to the early 1950s, suggests that as the quantitative characteristic increases, status increases at an *increasing* rate (Bales et al. 1951, Goode 1978, Sørensen 1979, Stephan 1952, Stephan and Mishler 1952) and the comparison outcomes (self-esteem, relative deprivation, the justice evaluation, et cetera) at a *decreasing* rate (Blau 1964, Jasso 1978, Wagner and Berger 1985). Interestingly, the literature does not provide a functional form for the relation between the personal quantitative characteristics and power (Webster 2006). Thus, if, mirroring the rates of change, the number of PSOs is three, and if Homans identified them correctly – i.e., if power is not merely a synonym for justice or status – then power must have a constant rate of change.

The sociological literature goes beyond the rate of change and suggests specific functional forms for the status and comparison PSOs. For status, Sørensen (1979) proposed the following function, a function which embeds Goode's (1978) convexity condition:

$$S = \ln\left(\frac{1}{1-r_X}\right), \tag{1}$$

where S denotes status, X denotes the valued good, and r denotes the relative rank on the valued good. Although the valued good can be cardinal or ordinal, the status function notices only its relative rank.

In the case of justice and the other comparison processes, Jasso (1978, 1990) proposed the following function:

$$Z = \theta \ln\left(\frac{X}{X^*}\right), \tag{2}$$

where Z denotes any of the comparison outcomes, such as self-esteem or the justice evaluation, X is as above the valued attribute or possession (called in this literature the actual reward), X^* denotes the comparison referent (called the just reward in the special case of justice), and θ is the signature constant whose sign indicates whether the reward is viewed as a good or a bad and whose absolute value denotes expressiveness.⁷ When the actual reward equals the comparison referent, the outcome is zero (a neutral point which in the

---

6 For visual illustration, see Jasso (2015, p. 880).
7 As noted above, goods are things of which more is preferred to less; bads are things of which less is preferred to more. These preferences are observer-specific. E.g., most people prefer more money to less, but there are famous exceptions (such as St. Francis of Assisi) and factorial surveys typically find a few "contrarians".

case of justice is called the point of perfect justice); when the actual reward exceeds the comparison referent, the outcome is positive (representing overreward), and when the actual reward is less than the comparison referent, the outcome is negative (representing underreward).

The expressiveness part of the signature constant θ plays an important part in empirical work but can be safely ignored in much theoretical work (though definitely not in empirical work). The framing part of the signature constant is always important, but in theoretical exercises can safely be set as positive, given that results for bads are readily established from results on goods.[8]

The actual reward in the comparison function is often denoted A instead of X, and the comparison referent C instead of X^*. In the special case of justice, the comparison function is called the justice evaluation function (JEF) and written:

$$J = \theta \ln\left(\frac{A}{C}\right), \tag{3}$$

where J denotes the justice evaluation.[9] When the reward is cardinal the situation is called "materialistic" and when the reward is ordinal the situation is called "nonmaterialistic".

The comparison function has accumulated several appealing properties (Jasso, Törnblom, and Sabbagh 2016, p. 208). The first four noticed were (Jasso 1978): (1) exact mapping from combinations of A and C to Z; (2) the outcome it yields is in units of the outcome (not reward units); (3) integration of rival conceptions of Z as a ratio and as a difference (Berger et al. 1972); and (4) deficiency aversion, viz., deficiency is felt more keenly than comparable excess (and loss aversion, viz., losses are felt more keenly than gains). These properties were quickly discussed (e.g., Wagner and Berger 1985) and remain the most often cited (Liebig and Sauer 2016, Turner 2005, 2007, Whitmeyer 1994). But, as will be seen below, a new theory for which the justice evaluation function served as a first postulate was yielding a large number of implications for a wide variety of behavioural domains, and a stronger foundation was needed. In the course of renewed scrutiny of the JEF, two new properties emerged: (5) scale in-

---

[8] Note, however, that goods and bads may operate differently, and less is known about bads than about goods, as discussed in Jasso (2017).

[9] The comparison function originated as a specification of the justice evaluation function (Jasso 1978). Subsequent theoretical development made clear that justice is a special case of comparison processes, and the function was generalised to the comparison function (Jasso 1990). Nowadays the term "justice evaluation function" is used interchangeably with the term "comparison function" except when reference is specifically to the large set of comparison processes or to the special case of justice.

variance; and (6) additivity, such that the effect of A on Z is independent of the level of C, and conversely (Jasso 1990). The logarithmic-ratio form is the only functional form which satisfies both scale invariance and additivity. Six years later two other desirable properties were noticed: (7) symmetry, such that interchanging A and C changes only the sign of Z; and (8) the fact that the log-ratio form of the comparison function is the limiting form of the difference between two power functions,

$$\lim_{k \to 0} \left(\frac{A^k - C^k}{k} \right) = \ln\left(\frac{A}{C}\right), \tag{4}$$

which both strengthens integration of the ratio and difference views and also integrates power-function and logarithmic approaches (Jasso 1996). More recently, a ninth property has emerged, linking the JEF and the Golden Number, $(\sqrt{5} - 1)/2$, or approximately 0.618 (van den Bos et al. 2015, pp. 239, 241 ff.).

Turning to power, if the reasoning above is provisionally accepted and if power is a sociobehavioural force in its own right, different from either justice or status, then it may be represented by a linear function:

$$P = a + bX, \tag{5}$$

where P denotes power and a and b are the intercept and slope, respectively. In the special case in which the intercept is zero and the slope is one, the function reduces to an identity function. Like the comparison PSO, power notices both ranks and amounts and thus appears in both materialistic and nonmaterialistic situations.

Both justice and status have given rise to a hypothetico-deductive theory (Type 1.A) and a nondeductive theory (Type 2), and the rich work on power in the literature can be re-stated to parallel justice and status. Four special techniques of theoretical derivation have been developed, called the micromodel, macromodel, mesomodel, and matrixmodel (Jasso 2008, p. 419). Because justice theory has been under development for a longer period of time, there is a large literature with derivation of theoretical predictions, including both standalone articles on prediction subsets as well as lists of predictions arranged by topic or by derivation procedure or by whether they refer to materialistic or nonmaterialistic societies. Examples of such predictions – which exemplify the hallmark traits discussed by Popper and Danto of derivation "far afield from the original domain" and "novel predictions" – include:[10]

---

[10] For further predictions of justice theory, see, i.a., Jasso (1988, 1996, 2004).

J.1: A thief's gain from theft is greater when stealing from a fellow group member than from an outsider, and this premium is greater in poor groups than in rich groups.
J.2: Parents of two or more non-twin children will spend more of their toy budget at an annual gift-giving occasion than at the children's birthdays.
J.3: Blind persons are less at risk of eating disorders than are sighted persons.
J.4: Veterans of wars fought away from home are more vulnerable to post-traumatic stress than veterans of wars fought on home soil.
J.5: In populations (or subpopulations) where husbands earn more than their wives, marital cohesiveness increases with husbands' earnings inequality and wives' mean earnings and decreases with wives' earnings inequality and husbands' mean earnings.

The hypothetico-deductive form of status theory is younger than that of justice theory by twenty years and thus the number of predictions deduced to date is smaller. Nonetheless, they include:[11]

S.1: Suppose that an interdisciplinary course enrols first-year graduate students from discipline A and third-year graduate students from discipline B. If competence is valued and if it increases with years of study, then a status hierarchy develops among the disciplines, with discipline B having higher status.
S.2: If two personal quantitative characteristics (such as wealth and beauty) are perfectly negatively associated and each is perfectly associated with gender and if the gender split is fifty-fifty, then average status will be the same among males and females and gender will not become a status characteristic.
S.3: In self-report surveys, the higher-ranking on a quantitative characteristic in each subgroup formed by a qualitative characteristic (such as race or ethnicity) will be less likely to answer subgroup-identification questions; thus, average schooling, skills, and income will be underestimated in all subgroups.
S.4: Personal quantitative characteristics have hierarchies and they confer status. But if not everyone values a characteristic, the associated status hierarchy will be unstable and may crumble. If a given quantitative characteristic is perfectly associated with a qualitative characteristic, such as race or sex, maintenance of a status hierarchy – and gender status differentiation – requires that the subgroups all value the quantitative characteristic.

---

[11] For further predictions of status theory, see, i.a., Jasso (2001b, 2004).

S.5: Economic inequality has no effect on status phenomena.

Recent work since the unification of justice, status, and power has produced new predictions, also displaying the hallmark traits of predictions in far-flung domains and novel predictions. These include:

NUT.1: When justice is the active PSO in a society, each person is closer to the neighbour above than to the neighbour below, while in a status society, each person is closer to the neighbour below than to the neighbour above, and in a power society, each person is equally close to the neighbours above and below.

NUT.2: In a materialistic society (viz., either justice-materialistic or power-materialistic) with two nonoverlapping subgroups, social distance between the subgroups always increases with economic inequality, but in a non-materialistic society (viz., justice-nonmaterialistic or status or power-nonmaterialistic) economic inequality has no effect on social distance between the subgroups.

NUT.3: In a group with two nonoverlapping subgroups, the lower-ranking in each subgroup will attach to the subgroup and the higher-ranking in each subgroup will think of themselves as individuals and band together in a third (emergent) subgroup. Thus, in a polarisation application, the lower-ranking from each subgroup become segregationists, while the higher-ranking from each subgroup become integrationists. This suggests that "the best and the brightest" in each subgroup cannot be trusted with important work for the subgroup.

NUT.4: Loss aversion is an exclusive property of the justice sociobehavioural force (because it requires a negative second derivative). Accordingly, the occurrence of loss aversion in a particular context provides evidence that justice is at work.

NUT.5: An ongoing project deriving predictions for the change in well-being when a top appointment is made in a workplace provides some initial contrasts between justice and status. When justice is the active force, all members experience a loss in well-being except the appointee. When status is the active force, members' well-being may increase, decrease, or remain the same depending on whether the appointee is an insider or outsider and on members' rank before and after the appointment.

Meanwhile, propositions constructed in the nondeductive version of the theories (Type 2) include: (1) healthiness increases with status; (2) the propensity to revolution depends jointly on justice evaluations about self and justice evaluations about others, decreasing with the former and increasing with the latter. Notice that the propositions in nondeductive theories remain in the postulate's domain, while the predictions derived in hypothetico-deductive theories may range to distant domains.

Note that all the predictions and propositions in this section are of the Is variety. However, some of them can lead to Ought claims. E.g., consider prediction S.1. Persons wishing to prevent the rise of differential status across disciplines may develop Ought claims restricting enrolment in the interdisciplinary course to students in the same year of their program. Similarly, prediction J.2 may lead societal "guardians" – wishing to maintain sibship cohesion and happiness – to exhort parents to give their children gifts at the same time.

Besides yielding predictions and propositions, the NUT and its component theories also yield interpretations of rare or nonrecurring events. E.g., justice theory suggests that both the rise of the mendicant orders in the early 13th century and the invention of detective fiction in 19th-century England are linked to a switch from valuing ordinal goods (like birth and nobility) to valuing cardinal goods (like wealth).

Moreover, the NUT and its component theories can be useful in other ways. E.g., the justice evaluation function provides the framing representations that enable proof of a theorem on inequality in goods and bads: "If an observer regards a cardinal thing as a good, then that observer implicitly regards inequality in the distribution of that thing as a bad; and if an observer regards a cardinal thing as a bad, then that observer implicitly regards inequality in the distribution of that thing as a bad" (Jasso 2017, p. 3).

As for testing theoretical predictions, some of the predictions have been explicitly tested, others are consistent with empirical research, and many others await test. E.g., the prediction about parental gift-giving is consistent with known patterns of toy sales in the United States (Jasso, Törnblom, and Sabbagh 2016, p. 211), and the prediction of earnings distribution effects on divorce rates is consistent with Bellou's (2017) finding that as male wage inequality increases, the divorce rate decreases. The prediction that the rate of vocations to the religious life is higher in societies with greater poverty and inequality is consistent with Ebaugh's (1993) findings concerning the dearth of religious vocations in the United States and the abundance in third-world countries.

Some predictions are consistent with notions that although not rigorously tested appear to be widely believed. These include the prediction that the incidence of gift-giving is greater during courtship than after marriage and greater in wartime than in peacetime.

Finally, some predictions are novel, and there seems to be no hint of them in any literature, technical or lay. These include the prediction that post-traumatic stress is less severe among veterans of wars fought on home soil than among veterans of wars fought away from home. A journalistic account notes that Vietnamese veterans of the Vietnam War appear to be better adjusted than American veterans of the Vietnam War but does not make the connection to the battleground's location (Sheehan 1991). Another novel prediction is that blind persons are less vulnerable to eating disorders than are nonblind persons. Still another novel prediction is the prediction that games of chance are salutary, contrary to the view that gambling is a vice. A final novel prediction is that the parent who dies first is mourned more, suggesting that in wartime fathers are mourned more than mothers but in times and places with high numbers of deaths in childbirth mothers are mourned more than fathers.

It is evident that the testing task will take time. The predictions must be disseminated to experts in the relevant topical domains, who, if interested, must then search for appropriate data.

4 Is and Ought – From Ideas to Theory to Empirics

The classic ideas of philosophy include both Is propositions and Ought claims. Sometimes they inspire social science inquiry, sometimes they echo in social science developments. This section discusses some selected examples.

4.1 Five Types of Persons and Five Types of Societies

Consider these classic words of Plato and Aristotle:
- From Plato (1952b, p. 402), *The Republic*, book 8, as words of Socrates: "[G]overnments vary as the dispositions of men vary, [...] there must be as many of the one as there are of the other. [...] [T]he States are as the men are; they grow out of human characters. [...] [I]f the constitutions of States are five, the dispositions of individual minds will also be five".
- From Aristotle (1952c, p. 532, 1328a40 – 1328b1), *Politics*, book 7, chapter 8: "Different men seek after happiness in different ways and by different means, and so make for themselves different modes of life and forms of government".

In the new unified theory persons seek after happiness via the three middle-range forces – justice, status, and power – in which the primordial sociobehavioural outcomes which give each force its name are generated by distinctive mechanisms from personal quantitative characteristics within groups formed by categories of qualitative characteristics. The distinctive mechanisms comprise the functions that convert the quantitative characteristic into the PSO. Quantitative characteristics can be cardinal (like wealth and land) or ordinal (like beauty and skill). But status, alone of the three forces, notices only the ordinal dimension of cardinal things. Accordingly, the bundles of PSO cum quantitative characteristic cum qualitative characteristic – viz., the identities – may be of five kinds, which, as above, using "materialistic" and "nonmaterialistic" to refer to cardinal and ordinal things, may be called: justice-materialistic, justice-nonmaterialistic, status, power-materialistic, and power-nonmaterialistic.

Persons may be thought of as collections of identities; they come to be characterised by the configuration of elements in their personal time series of bundles, termed *personality*. Similarly, societies are collections of persons; they come to be characterised by their configuration of elements in their members' identities, termed *culture*. Some individuals cycle over many different bundles, others fixate on one or another element, becoming, say, status-fixated or wealth-obsessed or race-conscious. In the same way, societies can become permeated by jock culture or a racialist culture.

Thus, the new unified theory provides concrete expression for the foundational insights in Plato and Aristotle that there are five types of persons and, correspondingly, five types of societies – justice-materialistic, justice-nonmaterialistic, status, power-materialistic, and power-nonmaterialistic.

Of course, these five are the major types. There are also subtypes (Jasso 2015, p. 881f.). For the two materialistic types, there are subtypes reflecting the distributional form of the cardinal reward. E.g., if a cardinal good is represented by a lognormal distribution, the justice distribution is normal, and if the cardinal good is represented by a Pareto or power-function distribution, the justice distribution is a negative or positive exponential, respectively. And when two or more goods, whether cardinal or ordinal, are valued simultaneously, the outcome distribution can assume a dazzling variety of forms, such as the equal, Laplace, logistic, and Erlang distributions, depending on whether the goods are independent, negatively associated, or positively associated. Importantly, the distributional form of the cardinal reward shapes and influences a wide variety of behavioral and social consequences.

Indeed, the door is opened to further discovery, even of tools. E. g., the case in which status arises from multiple negatively associated goods leads to a new family of distributions, the mirror-exponential (Jasso and Kotz 2007).[12]

4.2 Three Questions on Inequality

Three questions on inequality have fired the imagination. Two are Is questions: How does inequality grow? How fast does inequality grow? The third is an Ought question, or more precisely, Is-about-Ought: How much inequality is too much? In this case, there are fascinating classical ideas and accumulating definite knowledge.

4.2.1 How Does Inequality Grow?

Plato, in his *Laws* (1952a, p. 695), has the Athenian Stranger speculate about how a person acquires riches beyond the initial equal holding: "whether he has found them, or they have been given to him, or he has made them in business, or has acquired by any stroke of fortune". Other early accounts discuss losing money, e. g., the *Parable of the Prodigal Son* (Luke 15: 11–32).

Today it is understood that inequality increases when the poor become poorer and the rich become richer, as visible in inequality measurement. Setting aside mechanisms for redistribution (taxation), the challenge is to understand with precision the primary mechanisms by which poor become poorer and rich become richer. Of course, the situations described by the Athenian Stranger can be reversed and applied to the poor – bad luck, illness, and so on.

In a major theoretical work, Piketty (2014) links inequality to the discrepancy between capital return and the rate of economic growth. In another theoretical effort, Jasso (2009, 2018) formulates two models (of Theory Type 1.B). The first is a voting model of wagesetters in which wage inequality decreases (1) as the number of wagesetters (not perfectly likeminded) increases, and (2) as the covariances among the recommended wage distributions move from positive to zero to negative. The second model focuses on compensation in the workplace, showing that wage inequality decreases (1) as the number of wage-relevant worker characteristics (not perfectly positively associated) increases, and (2) as the co-

---

[12] This exemplifies the case discussed by Clogg (1992) in which work addressing a social science question makes contributions to the tools disciplines like statistics.

variances among wage-relevant worker characteristics move from positive to zero to negative.

Empirically, the study of inequality has been transformed by the landmark work of Piketty (2001, 2003) and Piketty and Saez (2003), who pioneered development of a new data infrastructure which combines all available data (national accounts, household surveys, tax systems, et cetera) to provide newly precise evidence of inequality and its trajectory. Through the collective efforts of researchers around the world, the new inequality landscape has grown from the studies of 22 countries summarised in Atkinson, Piketty, and Saez (2011) to a formidable worldwide database (see https://wid.world/) with a team of over a hundred researchers covering more than 70 countries (Alvaredo et al. 2018). These new data hold the promise for producing new definite knowledge on the question of how inequality grows.

4.2.2 How Fast Does Inequality Grow?

The Biblical prescription for a Jubilee Year (Leviticus 25: 8–13) every fiftieth year when slaves are freed and land reverts to its original owners suggests the belief that inequality grows rapidly – that 50 years is all it takes for inequality to be intolerable. The challenge is to obtain reliable scientific information.

Of course, the pace of inequality growth no doubt depends on a range of social and economic factors. The new data discussed above – the World Inequality Database – will no doubt be instrumental in helping scientists establish definite knowledge on the pace of inequality growth.

4.2.3 How Much Inequality Is Too Much?

The Athenian Stranger (Plato 1952a, p. 695) had a simple answer to this question: when the maximum is more than four times greater than the minimum. And the rationale was similarly simple: "[T]here should exist among the citizens neither extreme poverty, nor, again, excess of wealth, for both are productive of both these evils [faction and distraction]".

Contemporary social science provides much information concerning Ought views on inequality. The literature distinguishes two types of inequality (Jasso and Kotz 2008) – inequality between persons (such as that measured by the Gini coefficient, Atkinson inequality, Theil index, Theil MLD, et cetera) and inequality between subgroups (such as gender and race gaps and top and bottom shares). Research using factorial survey approaches routinely estimates Ought views for both types of inequality among samples of respondents judging samples of fictitious workers (Jasso 2006).

E.g., aggregate just gender wage gaps for entire respondent samples have been estimated at least since Jasso and Rossi (1977), most recently by Shamon and Dülmer (2014) as well as Auspurg, Hinz, and Sauer (2017), and respondent-specific just gender wage gaps at least since Jasso (1994), most recently by Jasso, Shelly, and Webster (2018). Results indicate that aggregate just gender wage gaps favour men in probability samples of adult populations but are closing or favour women in samples of college students or samples with educated young adults, but respondent-specific just gender wage gaps range widely, with subsets of respondents favouring one or the other gender.

4.3 Justice and Impartiality

Impartiality is a central ethical standard, dating at least as far back as the *New Testament* (e.g., Acts 10: 34) and analysed by philosophers at least since John Locke (1952) and by classical social scientists at least since Adam Smith (1976). The heart of impartiality is the requirement that there be no "distinction of persons" or "respect to persons".

Recent developments in justice theory show that there are six opportunities for impartiality, four for observers and two for allocators, generating the person-specific impartiality profile, including separate subprofiles for observer and allocator activities and characterising groups and societies by the impartiality profiles of their members (Jasso, Shelly, and Webster 2018). The Smithian (1976) impartial spectator is both an observer and an allocator, so that, invoking ideas from identity theory, it may be said that the Smithian impartial spectator has two selves, an observer self and an allocator self and proceed to study the six possibilities for impartiality. Rawls' (1972) veil of ignorance may be seen as a natural way to enable impartiality in the Smithian spectator.

Empirically, a new technique in the factorial survey family makes it possible to analyse three of the observer impartiality processes (Jasso, Shelly, and Webster 2018), including two recently-identified types of impartiality – framing impartiality and expressiveness impartiality.

Framing impartiality means that the observer frames rewards (as goods or bads) in the same way for all rewardees. E.g., if an observer frames income as a good for self but as a bad for another, or as a good for some rewardees and a bad for others, that observer lacks framing impartiality. Expressiveness impartiality means that the observer expresses a given magnitude of the justice evaluation in the same way for all rewardees. E.g., if an observer, for given justice evaluation, displays different expressiveness for self or other, or across rewardees, shouts the justice evaluation for one but whispers it for the other, that observer lacks expressiveness impartiality.

Understanding these two new forms of observer impartiality is important because their absence could destroy the good effects of impartiality in other elements of the justice situation, such as the just reward process. The only results obtained to date are for three samples of college students in the United States, and these indicate that framing impartiality is nearly universal, but expressiveness impartiality ranges from 28 to 30 percent in two of the samples to 57 percent in the third, with an intriguing mix of results by sample and respondent gender (Jasso, Shelly, and Webster 2018). These findings suggest, tentatively, that there may be "little cultures" of perceived fairness on college campuses, with distinct and nuanced profiles relevant to justice and impartiality.

4.4 Salary Secrecy

In some employment sectors, in some countries, salaries are public, and in others they are private, at least within the range of applicable law. A recent newspaper article in the United States urges workers to share their salary information, observing that pay transparency is "a powerful tool to fight pay inequity" (Herrera 2018, par. 11). Do the theories examined in this chapter provide any evidence of a behavioural basis for supporting or opposing pay transparency?

Analysis based on comparison theory, in the case where salary rank is known, indicates that the exact structure of well-being – and hence preference – depends on the salary distributional pattern (Jasso 1987, pp. 100 ff.). E. g., if salary is distributed as a lognormal or a Pareto, then the lowest-paid and the highest-paid persons prefer to have the information revealed, forming a coalition against the middle-paid persons; the middle faction commands a majority. In contrast, if salary is distributed as a power-function, there are only two factions; the lower faction is dominant and prefers to have the salary information revealed. In the fourth case examined, where salary is distributed as a quadratic, there are again two factions, but in this case there is a fifty-fifty split between proponents and opponents of pay transparency.

4.5 Theft and Punishment

"Thou shalt not steal", admonishes the seventh commandment in the Judaeo-Christian tradition. Might this Ought rule be related to the theories discussed in this chapter? One of the first set of predictions derived from comparison theory pertained to theft (Jasso 1988), as seen in prediction J.1 above. It is thus natural to examine the theft predictions and assess support for the seventh commandment and other candidates for theft rules. Jasso (2001a) reports this analysis, focussing on four kinds of actors – Thieves, Victims, Others, and Guardians – separately in homogeneous and heterogeneous societies.

Homogeneous societies have only one group; heterogeneous societies have two or more groups. In heterogeneous societies, Thief and Victim may come from different groups, in which case the theft is called cross-group. In heterogeneous societies, the Others are divided into Others in Thief's Group and Others in Victim's Group.

For each kind of actor in each society, the comparison function is defined for two time points, before and after the theft. Thus, the theory predicts whether the actor is made better off, worse off, or untouched by the theft. Support for anti-theft rules and punishments is then predicted for actors who become worse off because of the theft, and opposition is predicted for actors who become better off.

To illustrate, in cross-group theft, Thief and Others in Victim's Group become better off, while Victim and Others in Thief's Group become worse off. Hence, Thief and Others in Victim's Group are predicted to oppose an anti-theft rule, while Victim and Others in Thief's Group are predicted to support an anti-theft rule. Meanwhile, in homogeneous societies and in within-group theft, the Others are indifferent. (Additional predictions are based on other factors, such as own wealth, group wealth, and amount stolen.)

Predictions for Guardians are based on two criteria – maximising average well-being in the society and minimising Victim losses. E. g., Guardians are predicted to favour the anti-theft rule, as it minimises Victim losses, echoing the Athenian Stranger's words in the continuation of the passage cited in subsection 4.2.3 above: "[The minimum lot] ought to be preserved, and no ruler, nor any one else who aspires after a reputation for virtue, will allow the lot to be impaired in any case" (Plato 1952a, p. 695).

The strength of the constituency for or against a rule is represented by the number of members of the society who support or oppose it (excluding Guardians). In a heterogeneous society, no one is indifferent, because their well-being is always affected by the theft (as described above). So it may happen that constituencies in homogeneous groups are small.

However, if thieving is widespread, involving many members, then constituencies can grow. Results of the analysis, based on comparison theory, indicate that only one candidate-rule appears likely to arise in all societies, homogeneous or heterogeneous, and to be without opposition (Jasso 2001a, pp. 383f.):

§ Punish Thief more severely, the poorer the Victim.

It is possible to reason further that, to the extent that insider theft in heterogeneous societies operates the same way as theft in homogeneous societies, all societies may adopt the subset of homogeneous-society rules that do not have opposition in cross-group theft. These are:
§ Never steal from someone poorer than yourself.
§ When stealing from someone richer than yourself, never leave him poorer than you were before the theft.
§ If Victim is poorer than Thief, punish Thief more severely, the larger the amount stolen.
§ If Victim is richer than Thief, punishment severity is nonmonotonically related to amount stolen.

Finally, in all societies Guardians will propose the rule:
§ Thou shalt not steal.

But this rule is not without opposition, and may have to be imposed from above. Indeed, it is not without interest that in the Biblical story, the commandment does not come from Moses but rather from the Super-Guardian on Mount Sinai (Jasso 2001a, p. 388).

5 Conclusion

Understanding the relation between Is and Ought questions and their relation to theory and empirics is a central task for social science. This chapter made several contributions. First, it presented two substantive approaches, a deeper forces approach (including two engines of behaviour – to know the causes of things and to judge the goodness of things – leading directly to Is and Ought questions, respectively) and a middle-range theory which recently unified theories of justice, status, and power. Second, it reviewed three theory types (two deductive, one nondeductive). Third, it examined postulates and predictions from the new unified theory and its component theories. Fourth, it provided five illustrations tracing the path from ideas to theory to empirics – (1) five types of persons and five types of societies in the new unified theory, (2) three questions on inequality, (3) justice and impartiality, (4) salary secrecy, and (5) theft and punishment. Along the way the chapter noted the classical sources for the ideas, the special tools such as probability distributions for theory and factorial surveys for empirics, and the major embedded Is and Ought questions and behaviour. The chapter also introduced a new kind of question – Is-about-Ought – which represents the scientific search for knowledge about the normative views to which persons subscribe.

Acknowledgments

Earlier versions of portions of this chapter were presented at the NSF-inspired Empirical Implications of Theoretical Models (EITM) Summer Institutes at the Hobby School of Public Affairs, University of Houston. For many valuable discussions of Is and Ought matters, I thank the faculty and students at the EITM Institutes and especially James S. Granato, Director, and the pioneering spirits, William P. Hobby Jr. and Frank P. Scioli, as well as the editors of this far-seeing volume, Alexander Max Bauer and Malte Ingo Meyerhuber. I also gratefully acknowledge the intellectual and financial support of New York University.

Bibliography

Alvaredo, Facundo; Chancel, Lucas; Piketty, Thomas; Saez, Emmanuel, and Zucman, Gabriel (2018): *World Inequality Report 2018*. Paris: World Inequality Lab.

Aristotle (1952a): "Meteorology". In: id.: *The Works of Aristotle*. Vol. 1. Chicago: Britannica, pp. 443–494.

Aristotle (1952b): "Nicomachean Ethics". In: id.: *The Works of Aristotle*. Vol. 2. Chicago: Britannica, pp. 333–436.

Aristotle (1952c): "Politics". In: id.: *The Works of Aristotle*. Vol. 2. Chicago: Britannica, pp. 437–548.

Atkinson, Anthony; Piketty, Thomas, and Saez, Emmanuel (2011): "Top Incomes in the Long Run of History". In: *Journal of Economic Literature* 49 (1), pp. 3–71.

Bales, Robert; Strodtbeck, Fred; Mills, Theodore, and Roseborough, Mary (1951): "Channels of Communication in Small Groups". *American Sociological Review* 16 (1), pp. 461–468.

Bellou, Andriana (2017): "Male Wage Inequality and Marital Dissolution. Is There a Link?". *Canadian Journal of Economics* 50 (1), pp. 40–71.

Berger, Joseph; Zelditch, Morris; Anderson, Bo, and Cohen, Bernard (1972): "Structural Aspects of Distributive Justice. A Status-Value Formulation". In: Berger, Joseph; Zelditch, Morris, and Anderson, Bo (eds.): *Sociological Theories in Progress*. Vol. 2. Boston: Houghton Mifflin, pp. 119–246.

Blau, Peter (1964): *Exchange and Power in Social Life*. New York: Wiley.

Clogg, Clifford (1992): "The Impact of Sociological Methodology on Statistical Methodology". In: *Statistical Science* 7 (2), pp. 183–196.

Danto, Arthur (1967): "Philosophy of Science, Problems of". In: Edwards, Paul (ed.): *Encyclopedia of Philosophy*. Vol. 6. New York: Macmillan, pp. 296–300.

Ebaugh, Helen Rose (1993): "The Growth and Decline of Orders of Women Worldwide. The Impact of Women's Opportunity Structures". In: *Journal for the Scientific Study of Religion* 32 (1), pp. 68–75.

Fararo, Thomas (1989): *The Meaning of General Theoretical Sociology. Tradition and Formalization*. Cambridge: Cambridge University Press.

Firth, Roderick (1952): "Ethical Absolutism and the Ideal Observer". In: *Philosophy and Phenomenological Research* 12 (3), pp. 317–345.

Goode, William (1978): *The Celebration of Heroes. Prestige as a Control System*. Berkeley: University of California Press.

Grant, Edward (1974): *A Source Book in Medieval Science*. Cambridge: Harvard University Press.

Hare, Richard (1981): *Moral Thinking. Its Levels, Method, and Point*. Oxford: Clarendon Press.

Herrera, Tim (2018): "Why You Should Tell Your Co-Workers How Much Money You Make". In: *The New York Times*. https://www.nytimes.com/2018/08/31/smarter-living/pay-secrecy-national-labor-rights-act.html, retrieved on November 14, 2018.

Homans, George (1976): "Commentary". In: Berkowitz, Leonard and Walster, Elaine (eds.): *Advances in Experimental Social Psychology*. Vol. 9. New York: Academic Press, pp. 231–244.

Jasso, Guillermina (1978): "On the Justice of Earnings. A New Specification of the Justice Evaluation Function". In: *American Journal of Sociology* 83 (6), pp. 1398–1419.

Jasso, Guillermina (1987): "Choosing a Good. Models Based on the Theory of the Distributive-Justice Force". In: *Advances in Group Processes, Theory and Research* 4 (1), pp. 67–108.

Jasso, Guillermina (1988): "Principles of Theoretical Analysis". In: *Sociological Theory* 6 (1), pp. 1–20.

Jasso, Guillermina (1990): "Methods for the Theoretical and Empirical Analysis of Comparison Processes". In: *Sociological Methodology* 20 (1), pp. 369–419.

Jasso, Guillermina (1994): "Assessing Individual and Group Differences in the Sense of Justice. Framework and Application to Gender Differences in Judgments of the Justice of Earnings". In: *Social Science Research* 23 (4), pp. 368–406.

Jasso, Guillermina (1996): "Exploring the Reciprocal Relations Between Theoretical and Empirical Work. The Case of the Justice Evaluation Function (Paper in Honor of Robert K. Merton)". In: *Sociological Methods and Research* 24 (3), pp. 253–303.

Jasso, Guillermina (2001a) "Rule-Finding about Rule-Making. Comparison Processes and the Making of Norms". In: Hechter, Michael and Opp, Karl-Dieter (eds.): *Social Norms*. New York: Russell Sage, pp. 348–393.

Jasso, Guillermina (2001b): "Studying Status. An Integrated Framework". In: *American Sociological Review* 66 (1), pp. 96–124.

Jasso, Guillermina (2004): "The Tripartite Structure of Social Science Analysis". In: *Sociological Theory* 22 (3), pp. 401–431.

Jasso, Guillermina (2006): "Factorial Survey Methods for Studying Beliefs and Judgments". In: *Sociological Methods and Research* 34 (3), pp. 334–423.

Jasso, Guillermina (2007): "Theoretical Unification in Justice and Beyond". In: *Social Justice Research* 20 (3), pp. 336–371.

Jasso, Guillermina (2008): "A New Unified Theory of Sociobehavioral Forces". In: *European Sociological Review* 24 (4), pp. 411–434.

Jasso, Guillermina (2009): "A New Model of Wage Determination and Wage Inequality". In: *Rationality and Society* 21 (1), pp. 113–168.

Jasso, Guillermina (2015): "Societies, Types of". In: Wright, James (ed.): *The International Encyclopedia of the Social and Behavioral Sciences*. Vol. 22. London: Elsevier, pp. 878–886.

Jasso, Guillermina (2017): "Inequality in the Distribution of a Good Is a Bad, and Inequality in the Distribution of a Bad Is a Good". In: *European Sociological Review* 33 (4), pp. 604–614.

Jasso, Guillermina (2018): "What Can You and I Do to Reduce Inequality?". In: *Journal of Mathematical Sociology* 42 (4), pp. 186–204.

Jasso, Guillermina and Kotz, Samuel (2007): "A New Continuous Distribution and Two New Families of Distributions Based on the Exponential". In: *Statistica Neerlandica* 61 (3), pp. 305–328.

Jasso, Guillermina and Kotz, Samuel (2008): "Two Types of Inequality. Inequality Between Persons and Inequality Between Subgroups". In: *Sociological Methods and Research* 37 (1), pp. 31–74.

Jasso, Guillermina and Rossi, Peter (1977): "Distributive Justice and Earned Income". In: *American Sociological Review* 42 (4), pp. 639–651.

Jasso, Guillermina; Törnblom, Kjell, and Sabbagh, Clara (2016): "Distributive Justice". In: Sabbagh, Clara and Schmitt, Manfred (eds.): *Handbook of Social Justice Theory and Research*. New York: Springer, pp. 201–218.

Liebig, Stefan and Sauer, Carsten (2016): "Sociology of Justice". In: Sabbagh, Clara and Schmitt, Manfred (eds.): *Handbook of Social Justice Theory and Research*. New York: Springer, pp. 37–59.

Locke, John (1952): *Concerning Civil Government. Second Essay*. Chicago: Britannica.

Merton, Robert (1968): *Social Theory and Social Structure*. New York: Free Press.

Piketty, Thomas (2001): *Les Hauts Revenus en France au XXe Siècle. Inégalités et Redistributions, 1901–1998*. Paris: Grasset.

Piketty, Thomas (2003): "Income Inequality in France, 1901–1988". In: *Journal of Political Economy* 111 (5), pp. 1004–1042.

Piketty, Thomas (2014): *Capital in the Twenty-First Century*. Cambridge: Belknap Press.

Piketty, Thomas and Saez, Emmanuel (2003): "Income Inequality in the United States, 1913–2002". In: *Quarterly Journal of Economics* 118 (1), pp. 1–39.

Plato (1952a): "Laws". In: id: *The Dialogues of Plato*. Chicago: Britannica, pp. 640–799.

Plato (1952b): "The Republic". In: id: *The Dialogues of Plato*. Chicago: Britannica, pp. 295–441.

Popper, Karl (1963): *Conjectures and Refutations. The Growth of Scientific Knowledge*. New York: Basic Books.

Rawls, John (1971): *A Theory of Justice*. Cambridge: Harvard University Press.

Rayo, Luis and Becker, Gary (2007): "Evolutionary Efficiency and Happiness". In: *Journal of Political Economy* 115 (2), pp. 302–337.

Russell, Bertrand (1945): *History of Western Philosophy*. New York: Simon and Schuster.

Shamon, Hawal and Dülmer, Hermann (2014): "Raising the Question on 'Who Should get What?' Again. On the Importance of Ideal and Existential Standards". In: *Social Justice Research* 27 (3), pp. 340–368.
Shapere, Dudley (1974): *Galileo. A Philosophical Study.* Chicago: The University of Chicago Press.
Sheehan, Neil (1991): *After the War was Over. Hanoi and Saigon.* New York: Random House.
Smith, Adam (1976): *The Theory of Moral Sentiments.* Oxford: Clarendon Press.
Sørensen, Aage (1979): "A Model and a Metric for the Analysis of the Intragenerational Status Attainment Process". In: *American Journal of Sociology* 85 (2), pp. 361–384.
Stephan, Frederick (1952): "The Relative Rate of Communication Between Members of Small Groups". In: *American Sociological Review* 17 (1), pp. 482–486.
Stephan, Frederick and Mishler, Elliot (1952): "The Distribution of Participation in Small Groups. An Exponential Approximation". In: *American Sociological Review* 17 (5), pp. 598–608.
Struik, Dirk Jan (1987): *A Concise History of Mathematics.* New York: Dover.
Toulmin, Stephen (1953): *The Philosophy of Science. An Introduction.* London: Hutchinson.
Toulmin, Stephen (1978): "Science, Philosophy of". In: *The New Encyclopaedia Britannica, Macropaedia 16.* Chicago: Britannica, pp. 375–393.
Turner, Jonathan (2005): "The Desperate Need for Grand Theorizing in Sociology". Talk given at the Social Justice Conference, University of Bremen, Germany, March 2005.
Turner, Jonathan (2007): "Justice and Emotions". In: *Social Justice Research* 20 (3), pp. 288–311.
van den Bos, Kees; Cropanzano, Russell; Kirk, Jessica; Jasso, Guillermina, and Okimoto, Tyler (2015): "Expanding the Horizons of Social Justice Research. Three Essays on Justice Theory". In: *Social Justice Research* 28 (2), pp. 229–246.
Veblen, Thorstein (1953): *The Theory of the Leisure Class. An Economic Study of Institutions.* New York: New American Library.
Wagner, David and Berger, Joseph (1985): "Do Sociological Theories Grow?". In: *American Journal of Sociology* 90 (4), pp. 697–728.
Webster, Murray (2006): "Status Research Since 2000". Paper presented at the annual Group Processes Conference, Montreal, Canada, August 2006.
Whitmeyer, Joseph (2004): "Past and Future Applications of Jasso's Justice Theory". In: *Sociological Theory* 13 (1), pp. 432–444.
Zelditch, Morris (1968): "Status, Social". In: Sills, David (ed.): *International Encyclopedia of the Social Sciences.* Vol. 15. New York: Macmillan, pp. 250–257.

Albert W. Musschenga
Empirically Informed Moral Intuitionism

Abstract: This chapter investigates whether the model of an empirically informed theory is also useful for connecting philosophical and psychological moral intuitionism. The authors exploration takes place in successive steps. Section 2 presents the author's view on (moral) intuitions. Sections 3 and 4 offer an account of (moral) psychological intuitions as the product of unconscious and automatic processes. Section 5 discusses how psychological moral intuitions relate to philosophical moral intuitions. Section 6 deals with the relation between the justification of intuitions and their reliability, and discusses whether we need reasons to trust our intuitions. Section 7 deals with the reliability of unconscious and automatic processes in general. Section 8 discusses the reliability of psychological moral intuitions. Finally, section 9 offers some conclusions about sense and feasibility of an empirically informed moral intuitionism.

1 Introduction

Intuitions are an object of study for philosophers as well as psychologists. Although intuitionists in philosophy (φ-intuitionists) may disagree about the nature of intuitions, they share the belief that intuitions have a specific epistemological function: The intuition that p provides reasons or evidence for believing that p – the intuition's propositional content. Psychological intuitionism (ψ-intuitionism) holds that the majority of our judgements result from unconscious and automatic, intuitive processes. Some psychologists have argued that this also applies to moral judgements (Haidt 2001, 2007, 2012, Haidt and Bjorklund 2008).

When two disciplines use the same term for referring to an object that is central to their research, it is reasonable to assume that these objects are also the same, or at least similar, until it is shown that the contrary is supported by better reasons. But even if two disciplines study the same object, their findings need not be mutually relevant. Art historians and evolutionary biologists may both study cows. However, findings of art historians on how the way cows are represented changed throughout the ages lack relevance for the biologists' study into the evolution of cows. They are independent disciplines. According to Sinnott-Armstrong, moral ψ-intuitionism and moral φ-intuitionism are independent positions. Moral φ-intuitionism is openly normative and epistemic – it specifies when moral beliefs are justified – while moral ψ-intuitionism is a descriptive psychological theory about how moral beliefs are formed (Sinnott-Armstrong 2008, p. 50). Thus, accepting the psychological theory of moral ψ-intuitionism does not commit one to accept the epistemological theory of moral φ-intuitionism. I agree with him. However, when examining the origin of φ- intuitions, adherents of moral φ-intuitionism cannot ignore the findings of psychological studies on the origin of moral ψ-intuitions. Neither can moral φ-intuitionism go by the findings of psychological studies on the reliability of moral ψ-intuitions. Moral ψ-intuitionism and moral φ-intuitionism are interconnected.

In recent years, a growing number of authors plead for integrating empirical findings in ethical theorising. John Doris and Stephen Stich (2005, p. 114) speak of "informing ethical theorising richly with empirical considerations". The aim of empirically informed ethical theorising is to see to it that empirical claims within ethical theories find support in, or at least do not conflict with, findings of empirical sciences. Examples of ethical theories that seek support from empirical finding are the theories of virtue ethics developed by Nancy Snow (2010) and Daniel Russell (2009). In this chapter, I investigate if it makes sense, and what it requires, to develop an empirically informed theory of moral φ-intuitionism.

My exploration of the sense and the feasibility of an empirically informed moral φ-intuitionism takes place in successive steps. In section 2, I present the philosophical view on (moral) intuitions. Sections 3 and 4 present an account of (moral) ψ-intuitions as the product of unconscious and automatic processes. Section 5 discusses how moral ψ-intuitions relate to moral φ-intuitions. In section 6, I examine the relation between the justification of ψ-intuitions and their reliability, and discuss whether we need reasons to trust our φ-intuitions. Section 7 deals with the reliability of unconscious and automatic processes in general. In section 8, I discuss the reliability of moral ψ-intuitions. Section 9 offers some conclusions about sense and feasibility of an empirically informed moral intuitionism.

2 The Philosophical View on (Moral) Intuitions

How do philosophers characterise moral intuitions? Some of them equate intuitions with beliefs, others with seemings. For Robert Audi (2004), intuitions are doxastic; they are a kind of belief. Audi draws a distinction between doxastic intuitions and non-doxastic intuitions or "intuitive seemings".[1] What then is a "seeming"? Normally, we do not speak of an intuition that *p*, without presuppos-

---

[1] In a recent publication, Audi (2015, p. 61) calls seemings "episodic intuitions".

ing that the cognition that *p* entails belief. If we are aware that we do not believe *p*, but that *p* non-inferentially seems to be true by virtue of a kind of credibility of its own, we are likely to say that it seems to be true, or that it seems intuitive.

For some philosophers, this non-doxastic sense of the intuitive truth of a proposition is the primary concept of intuition (Bealer 2002, Huemer 2005, 2008). Michael Huemer sees intuitions as a type of mental states which he calls "appearances". "Appearance" is a broad category that includes mental states involved in perception, memory, introspection, and intellection. Statements such as "It seems to me that *p*", "It appears to me that *p*", or "It is obvious that *p*", all refer to appearances. Although appearances have propositional content and usually lead us to form beliefs, they should be distinguished from beliefs. Otherwise, a statement such as "The arch seems wide, but I do not think it is" would not be intelligible (Huemer 2005, p. 99).[2] An intuitive seeming that *p* can, but need not, be an evidential ground for believing *p*. According to Huemer, moral intuitions – he speaks of ethical intuitions – belong to the category of intellectual seemings. Intellectual seemings articulate "how things appear to us prior to reasoning". Without such initial appearances, reasoning would not get started. An intellectual appearance is "an intuition that *p* is a state of its seeming to one that *p* is not dependent on inference from other beliefs and that results from thinking about *p*, as opposed to perceiving, remembering, or introspecting. An ethical intuition is an intuition whose content is an evaluative proposition" (Huemer 2005, p. 102).

Not all (moral) intuitions are equal; some are stronger than others, seem to be truer or at least more credible than others. The intuitive propositions are, according to Huemer, *prima facie* justified. This is what Huemer calls "phenomenal conservatism"; things are as they seem to be, in the absence of evidence doubting it (Huemer 2005, p. 99).

In this chapter, I will focus on intuition as intuitive seeming. I think that Huemer's concept is more appropriate for connecting philosophical and psychological discussions on intuition than the doxastic concept. Matthew Bedke added an important improvement to Huemer's theory. In Huemer's view, the content of a moral intuition is an evaluative proposition. The seemingness of seemings consists in special attitudes towards (propositional) contents. According to Bedke, this view does not sufficiently address where to locate the seeming. For any given seeming, he says, one should ask whether it is located in a special seemingish attitude taken towards content, whether it is located in the very content

---

[2] According to Audi (2015, p. 61) seemings entail inclinations to belief, but they are not beliefs, nor do they entail forming beliefs.

under consideration, whether it is located somewhere else entirely, perhaps as a phenomenologically salient character that attends the attitude-content pair (which by itself does not make anything seem to be the case), or whether seemings consist in a combination of these options (Bedke 2008, p. 253f.).

Bedke argues that the diverse categories of seemings differ in the location of the seeming. In the case of sensory seemings, the contents of the sensory experiences are laden with seemingness. When someone sees a stick placed in water, this person may form the belief that the stick is bent. It is the content of the sensory experience that justifies this belief. In Bedke's view, intellectual seemings present a striking contrast to seemings of sensory experience. Intellectual seemings differ from those in sensory experiences in that the intellectual seeming is not part of the content. Some intellectual seemings have to do with competent understanding and application of either a procedural rule or a concept. In the view of Bedke, competence should be thought of as a kind of successful non-inferential performance that *enables* the extra justificatory power of an intellectual seeming. Bedke's theory retains the view that the seeming itself is justification conferring, while acknowledging the epistemic relevance of other factors that must be met for the seeming to confer justification (Bedke 2008, p. 260).

According to Bedke (2008, p. 260ff.), moral intuitions, although belonging to the intellectual seemings, are *not* competence driven. Their seemingness – the attitude of consideration towards the evaluative proposition – is completely constituted by special phenomenological features such as a felt veridicality, appropriateness, familiarity, or confidence. If Bedke is right in saying that moral intuitions are not competence-driven, all the epistemic work of justification is done by their special phenomenological features such as a felt veridicality, appropriateness, familiarity, or confidence. Bedke (2008, p. 262) concedes that competence might be relevant for the application of thicker moral concepts, such as torture and cruelty, but he thinks that this competence only regards applying the descriptive criteria of thick concepts. Bedke's view that competence may only be needed to apply thick moral concepts because of their descriptive features, assumes that the descriptive and the evaluative aspect can be separated. I do not think that this assumption is valid but will not pursue the issue here.[3] Moral psychologists regard moral development as a process of maturation in which a person's moral competence is increasing (Kohlberg 1976, Rest 1986, Hoffman 2000). In Bedke's view, growth of competence does not lead to an increase of the justificatory force of moral intuitions – which is counter-intuitive. I

---

3 In Musschenga (2010) I discuss whether the descriptive and the evaluative aspect can be separated.

do not know whether Bedke finds that people's general moral competence increases in the course of their moral development, but if he does, he should also endorse the view that their moral intuitions gain in justificatory power.

3 Psychological Intuitions as the Product of Intuitive Processes

Most psychologists agree that there are two types of cognitive processes or "reasoning systems". Roughly, one system is associative, and its computations reflect similarity and temporal structure; the other system is symbolic, and its computations reflect a rule structure (Sloman 1996). Keith Stanovich and Richard West (2000) labelled these systems or types of processes "System I" and "System II". There is now considerable agreement on the characteristics that distinguish the two systems. The operations of System I are fast, automatic, effortless, associative, and difficult to control or to modify. The operations of System II are slower, serial, effortful, and deliberately controlled; they are also relatively flexible and potentially rule-governed. The perceptual system and the intuitive operations of System I generate *impressions* of the attribute of objects of perception and thought. These impressions are not voluntary and need not be verbally explicit. In contrast, *judgements* are always explicit and intentional, whether or not they are overtly expressed. The label "intuitive" is applied to those judgements that directly reflect impressions. As in several other dual-process models, one of the functions of System II is to monitor the quality of both mental operations and overt behaviour (Kahneman 2003, pp. 1450 ff.).

Recent studies show that most of our judgements are not simply the outcome of conscious (i.e., System II) reasoning. To a large extent, they are intuitive and automatic (i.e., System I) responses to challenges, elicited without awareness of underlying mental processes (Bargh 1996, Bargh and Chartrand 1999). Moreover, people are often not very adept at describing how they actually reached a particular judgement (Nisbett and Wilson 1977). In his by now famous article "The Emotional Dog and its Rational Tail – A Social Intuitionist Approach to Moral Judgment", Jonathan Haidt (2001) extends these findings to the area of morality. He defines moral intuition as

> the sudden appearance in consciousness of a moral judgment, including an affective valence (good–bad, like–dislike), without any awareness of having gone through steps of searching, weighing evidence, or inferring a moral conclusion. Moral intuition is therefore the psychological process that the Scottish philosophers talked about, a process akin to

aesthetic judgment. One sees or hears about an event and one instantly feels approval or disapproval (Haidt 2001, p. 818).

John Bargh (1989, p. 6) distinguishes between several kinds of unconscious and automatic processes.[4] According to him automaticity has been invoked to explain the following process effects: (1) effects of which a person is *not aware*, (2) effects that are relatively *effortless*, such that they will operate when attentional resources are scarce, (3) effects that are *non-intentional*, i.e., they occur even in the absence of explicit intentions or goals, (4) effects that are *autonomous* in that they will run themselves to completion without the need for conscious attentional monitoring, and (5) effects that are *involuntary* or *uncontrollable*, even when one is aware of them. Attention, awareness, intention, and control do not necessarily occur together in an all or none fashion. They are to some extent independent qualities that may appear in various combinations. Bargh argues that these automatic effects fall into regular classes: those that occur prior to conscious awareness ("preconscious automaticity"); those that require some form of conscious processing but produce an unintended outcome ("postconscious automaticity"); and those that require a specific type of intentional, goal-directed processing ("goal-dependent automaticity") (Bargh 1989, p. 7).

In order to identify what kinds of automatic processes are responsible for generating intuitions, we need to have a closer look at these three classes of automaticity. The first class, *preconscious automaticity*, operates uncontrollably, autonomously, involuntarily, and nearly effortlessly. These processes require only the triggering of a proximal stimulus event and occur prior to or in the absence of any conscious awareness of that event. Preconscious automaticity is considered to be responsible for the strong feelings of certainty regarding (some of) our judgements. They are trusted by a subject as accurate and valid just because the constructs are generated preconsciously, without awareness of inferential activity or cognitive effort (Bargh 1989, p. 11).[5]

A second class of automaticity is *postconscious automaticity* (Bargh 1989, p. 14). People are aware of an environmental stimulus, but not of the processes it activates. A triggering event induces conscious awareness or attention but has "postconscious" cognitive consequences that are generated automatically and

---

[4] For a discussion on automaticity and virtues, see Snow (2010, chapter 2).

[5] One wonders why Bargh suggests that lack of awareness *explains* why a person trusts the validity and accuracy of an intuitive judgement. He may mean that persons who consciously draw inferences, might not claim accuracy and validity for their judgements because they realise that inferences are fallible human activities.

outside of conscious awareness. E.g., when people are primed by an environmental stimulus, they are aware of the stimulus, but not of its influences on later judgements.

A third class of automaticity is *goal-dependent automaticity*. Goal-dependent automaticity appears in an unintended and an intended form. In goal-dependent automaticity with *unintended* effects, the perceiver is aware of the stimulus but not necessarily of its effects on cognitive processes; such effects nevertheless require some cognitive capacity and depend on the perceiver's goal. Thus, e.g., inferring a trait from a written description of behaviour seems to occur spontaneously at encoding; it occurs without intent or awareness, is subjectively effortless, and is difficult to disrupt with a concurrent task (Bargh 1989, p. 20). *Intended* goal-dependent automaticity occurs autonomously and outside awareness, but the output was intended by the goal of the current processes. An important example of intended goal-dependent automaticity is the skilful behaviour of experts. Well-learned situational scripts or thoroughly routine action sequences typically operate autonomously, with little need for conscious control or significant attentional resources (Bargh 1989, p. 24).

4 Automaticity and Moral Intuitions

It is plausible to assume that all three classes of automatic processes are also operating in the moral domain.[6] People often "just know", without discussion and deliberation, what is morally seen the right thing to do. The feelings of certainty we have regarding (some of) our moral judgements also explain why counterarguments often fail to undermine them. This seems to be the class of moral intuitions studied by Haidt. Among the many types of enduring goals and commitments that are likely to be chronically held and the representations of which could become automatically activated are those related to moral values such as equity and truth (preconscious automaticity) (Bargh 1990, pp. 113f., 118). Priming effects (postconscious automaticity) also influence intuitive moral judgements, both in a positive and in a negative way. Darcia Narvaez and Daniel Lapsey (2005) point out that priming effects offer surprising insight in a practice of character education programs, common in the US, that attempt to teach a virtue of the week or the month by prominently posting the trait word or its example around the classroom or school (i.e., morally positive effect of priming). A neg-

---

[6] For the relevance of the three classes of automaticity for moral psychology, see Narvaez and Lapsey (2005).

ative effect of priming occurs when, e. g., subjects who were subliminally primed with faces of criminals, coincidentally all black Americans, show a greater hostility to black Americans than to whites. Expert judgements are an example of Bargh's goal-dependent automaticity.

5 How Do Philosophical Moral Intuitions Relate to Psychological Moral Intuitions?

Psychologists study the nature and the origin of intuitions. In their view, intuitions result from unconscious and automatic, intuitive processes. Although φ-intuitionists are primarily interested in the epistemological role of intuitions, they also discuss their nature and origin. The controversy between rationalism and sentimentalism within philosophy also has an effect on the view on the nature of intuitions. According to René Descartes, intuition results from reason.[7] In the tradition of the sentimentalism of David Hume and Adam Smith, intuitions are conceived as experiences constituted by the emotional manifestation of moral sentiments (Kauppinen 2013). Philosophers Alison Gopnik and Eric Schwitzgebel (1998) agree with psychologists that intuitions originate from unconscious processes. Antti Kauppinen, also a philosopher, takes a contrary position. He claims that the output of System I processes are not φ-intuitions. He calls these ψ-intuitions "pseudo-intuitions" (Kauppinen 2015, p. 239). I agree with him that not all intuitive judgements resulting from automatic, intuitive processes are intuitions as conceived by philosophers. However, how do (moral) φ-intuitions originate if they are neither the product of conscious reasoning nor of intuitive processes? I hypothesise that φ-intuitions *indirectly* result from intuitive processes. For clarifying this, I return to Huemer and his definition of a moral intuition:

> An intellectual appearance is an intuition that *p* is a state of its seeming to one that *p* is not dependent on inference from other beliefs and *that results from thinking about p*, as opposed to perceiving, remembering, or introspecting. An ethical intuition is an intuition whose content is an evaluative proposition (Huemer 2005, p. 102; emphasis added).

Note that Huemer does not say that *p* as the content of the intuition results from thinking. I read him as saying that what results from thinking about *p* is the in-

---

[7] Intuition is according to Descartes (1985, p. 14) "the indubitable conception of a clear and attentive mind which proceeds solely from the light of reason".

sight that *p* is not dependent on inference from other beliefs and does not need further justification. Moral φ-intuitions are ψ-intuitions that have passed through a process of reflection. Conscious reflection on the evaluative proposition *p* which is the content of an intuition is a System II process. Conscious reflection on *p* aims to establish two things. First, whether the person having that intuition is able to endorse, to identify with the proposition. One of Haidt's examples of an intuition is the judgement people express when asked for their opinion on voluntary sex between brother and sister. These people have probably never thought about that issue. Being asked for their opinion they "discover" how they think about sex between siblings. This "discovery" may cause them to ask whether this is what they really think about that issue. Do they really, e.g., condemn sex between siblings? If the answer is positive, they identify with the judgement. The judgement becomes then really theirs. The answer might also be negative. The second thing that reflection on an intuitive ψ-judgement aims to establish is the epistemic status of the judgement: Is the judgement in need of further justification or not?[8]

Intuitionists in philosophy are primarily interested in the specific epistemological function of intuitions. The intuition that *p* provides reasons or evidence for believing that *p* – the intuition's propositional content. Psychologists are also interested in the epistemological value of intuitions when they study the reliability of judgements resulting from intuitive processes. However, what is the relation between justification and reliability? In the next section, I argue that moral intuitions only have (prima facie) justificatory force if it can be shown that they result from *generally reliable* processes. Thus, if moral φ-intuitions result, although indirectly, from the same psychological processes as ψ-intuitions, psychological studies on the reliability of intuitive processes may also be relevant for examining the claim of philosophical intuitionists that moral (φ-)intuitions have (prima facie) justificatory force.

6 Justification and Reliability

Why should moral φ-intuitionism incorporate findings about the reliability of intuition generating processes that are provided by psychological studies? The core of seeming-state intuitionism is that seemings confer *prima facie* justification on certain beliefs. Some beliefs seem to be true in a non-inferential way.

---

[8] My view on φ-intuitions aligns with Audi's (2004, p. 46) view when he says that an intuition can be a conclusion of reflection, although it cannot be a conclusion of an inference.

If it seems to me that burning animals is wrong, I am *prima facie* justified in believing that burning animals is wrong. What role can empirical data have in such a theory? According to Huemer (2007, p. 30): "If it seems to you that *p*, then, in the absence of defeaters, you thereby have at least some degree of justification for believing *p*".

If we do need reasons for believing our moral intuitions, Huemer says, we also need reasons for trusting sense perception, memory, introspection, even reason itself. The result is global scepticism, which is not his concern (Huemer 2005, p. 107). For Huemer, the fact that seemings provide *prima facie* justification to beliefs implies that we are justified in believing them *unless countervailing evidence should arise that is strong enough to defeat the initial presumption in their favour*. Empirical data consisting either of evidence directly against the proposition that intuitively seemed true, or of evidence that our initial intuition was unreliable, can defeat an initial presumption (Huemer 2005, p. 105). This is what Huemer means by "phenomenal conservatism".[9] This view is the opposite to that of, e. g., John Symons, who wonders why a proposition's having the property of being favoured by intuition should count as a reason to believe that it is true; "we could only reasonably believe that this property is a guide to truth by virtue of some additional set of propositions concerning the reliability and nature of the faculty of intuition or common sense" (Symons 2008, p. 71).

Symons' epistemological position is akin to that of process reliabilism. Process reliabilists claim that what makes beliefs probably true is the dependability of the process or procedure by which the belief comes to be held or is (causally) sustained.[10] Contrary to an intuitionist theory that embraces phenomenal conservatism, a reliabilist moral intuitionism must answer the question why (and when) we ought to heed intuition. Therefore, a reliabilist moral intuitionism is dependent on empirical data that enable answering that question. A reliabilist moral intuitionism *needs* to be empirically informed. Empirical findings are, as we have seen, of limited relevance within Huemer's theory. Such findings could, according to Huemer, either provide evidence that defeats the initial presumption in favour of the justification of an intuition, or it could corroborate this presumption. But only a reliabilist moral φ-intuitionism has a theory-internal need to connect to empirical findings. Process reliabilism is able to connect moral φ-intuitionism to moral ψ-intuitionism. Since my aim in this chapter is not to prove that moral intuitionism needs to be empirically informed, but

---

[9] For a recent discussion on phenomenal conservatism, see Tucker (2013).
[10] According to Alvin Goldman (1979), all beliefs produced by reliable processes (of the sort that require no beliefs as input) are justified. A belief-forming process is reliable to the extent that it tends to produce true beliefs.

only to investigate whether empirically informed moral intuitionism makes sense, I do not need to argue that process reliabilism is superior to phenomenal conservatism. It suffices here to point out that process reliabilism is not a marginal, but a widely accepted theory.[11]

7 The Reliability of Automatic Processes

In section 5, I said that if moral φ-intuitions result, although indirectly, from the same psychological processes as ψ-intuitions, psychological studies on the reliability of intuitive processes may also be relevant for examining the claim of philosophical intuitionists that moral (φ-)intuitions have (prima facie) justificatory force. Before turning to empirical data on the reliability of intuitive processes, we need to clarify how the reliability of these processes should be understood and can be established. It is clear what is meant by the reliability of observations or memories. To establish the reliability of the processes leading to an observation or a diagnosis one needs substantial criteria of truth or, weaker, of correctness. Intuitive judgements are reliable if they track truth or correctness. I can claim reliability for my observations of birds if I have a track record showing that the majority of my observations in the past were correct. A medical diagnosis can also be said to be reliable if the doctor has a good track record in making diagnoses.

Psychologists, however, do not study the *absolute* reliability of intuitive judgements, but only their *relative* reliability in comparison to reasoned judgements. This kind of studies also require criteria for assessing reliability. Most psychological authors confine themselves to rather general statements about the relative (un-)reliability of intuitive or automatic thinking versus analysis or deliberation. According to Keith Hammond (1996), both types of processes produce errors, although the kind of errors produced tends to be different. In analytical thinking, errors can be quite spectacular. He states that an intuition rarely results in responses that are precisely correct, because it involves the tacit aggregation of different informational cues. Errors are not likely to be large, because of the absence of systematic biases. Systematic biases occur in deliberate thought. A small error, e.g., a minor mistake in a calculation, can lead to huge errors in the final result. Errors in deliberate thought tend to have an "all or nothing"

---

[11] Proponents of process reliabilism not only include Goldman, but also Alvin Plantinga (1993). Critics of process reliabilism argue that the reliable production of beliefs is not sufficient to justify them, and that it is very difficult to specify what types of belief-generating processes are reliable (see Audi 1988, p. 20).

quality. There are typically either no errors or only large ones (Hammond 1996). Robin Hogarth states that one has to consider (1) the trade-off and error implicit in tacit, automatic thinking and (2) the probability that a person will know the appropriate deliberate "formula". He assumes that the greater the complexity a task exhibits in analytical terms (as measured, e.g., by number of variables, types of functions, weighting schemes, and so on) the less likely it is that a person will both know the appropriate formula and apply it correctly (Hogarth 2002, p. 32, 2005, p. 76). His conclusion is that deliberate thought should be preferred to intuitive thinking when analytical complexity is easy. However, as analytical complexity increases, tacit processes become more accurate in a relative sense, which means that the increasing probability of making errors in analysis eventually outweighs the bias and error in tacit responses.[12] Bias in tacit judgements will reflect the conditions in which response tendencies have been learned: Were they acquired in *kind* or in *wicked* learning environments? To what extent is the partial information on which tacit responses are based unbiased (Hogarth 2002, p. 32, 2005, p. 76)?[13]

The major problem in assessing the evidence on the advantages and disadvantages of intuitive and deliberate systems is that few studies have been conducted with this issue specifically in mind. Hogarth (2002, pp. 25 ff.) believes that eight different kinds of studies are relevant: those on (1) remarkable cognitive performance, (2) naïve understanding of natural phenomena, (3) expertise, (4) clinical judgements, (5) deductive reasoning, (6) probabilistic thinking, (7) choice problems, and (8) specific tests of dual modes of thinking. Most relevant are the studies on expertise.

---

[12] A similar conclusion can be found in Woodward and Allman (2007). According to them, one role of social emotions and of moral intuitions is to help overcome the limitations of purely analytical or rule-based decision-making procedures such as cost-benefit analysis. The problem with trying to make moral decisions on a purely analytical basis is that we will quite likely leave out (or fail to pay sufficient attention to or to be motivated by) considerations that are important even from a cost-benefit perspective. They state that the number of different dimensions or different kinds of considerations that human beings are able to fully take into account in explicit conscious rule-guided decision making, is fairly small (Woodward and Allman 2007, pp. 194 ff.).

[13] In *kind* learning environments, people receive accurate and timely feedback that allows the tacit system to shape accurate responses. In *wicked* learning environments, feedback is lacking or misleading and people can learn to have confidence in responses that are quite inaccurate. The key point is, according to Hogarth (2002, pp. 19 f.), that the accuracy and timeliness of feedback affect the quality of the intuitions we acquire through tacit learning processes. You can not learn from feedback you do not receive, and some feedback may simply act to increase confidence in erroneous beliefs.

Judgements of experts are usually not the product of deliberate reasoning but of unconscious and automatic processes. Behavioural studies of skill acquisition have demonstrated that automaticity is central to the development of expertise, and practice is the means to automaticity (Posner and Snyder 1975). Through practice the speed and the smoothness of cognitive operations improve, which leads to a reduction of the cognitive demands of the situations, thus releasing cognitive resources (such as attention) for other, usually higher cognitive functions (such as planning and self-monitoring) (Feltovich, Prietula, and Ericsson 2006, p. 53). Studies within cognitive psychology have shown the superiority of experts over novices in nearly every aspect of cognitive functioning, from memory and learning to problem-solving and reasoning (Anderson 1981). Chess masters, for instance, have been found to perceive patterns of play more effectively (de Groot 1965) and to have a better memory for chess positions. Neill Charness (1976) showed that expert chess players do not rely on a transient short-time memory for storage of briefly presented chess positions; they are able to recall positions even after the contents of their short-term memory have been completely disrupted by an interfering activity. Subsequent research has shown that chess experts have acquired memory skills that enable them to encode chess positions in long-term memory (Ericsson and Kintsch 1995). Experts in physics, mathematics, and computer programming reveal similar superior skills (Mayer 1983).

The expertise studies show that expertise is limited to domains and is only acquired through exposure to and activity within specific domains. Thus, someone being an expert in one domain (e.g., chess) does not mean that she will be an expert in another domain (e.g., medicine) unless she has also had considerable experience in the latter. The studies also show that outstanding performance in any domain takes years of dedication. Moreover, high performers have typically followed demanding regimes of deliberate practice and benefited from good teachers (Hogarth 2002, p. 26).

These are, as I already noted, statements about the reliability of judgements resulting from automatic processes in general. The only serious research into the reliability of a specific kind of intuitive process I know of regards intuitive judgements flowing from goal-dependent automatic processes. Dutch psychologist Ap Dijksterhuis (2004) and his colleagues (Dijksterhuis et al. 2006) studied the reliability of judgements resulting from what they call "unconscious thinking". Unconscious thinking is what we do when we say that we are going to "sleep over" a difficult issue before making a decision. The characteristics of conscious and unconscious thought led Dijksterhuis and his colleagues to postulate the deliberation-without-attention hypothesis regarding the relation between mode of thought or deliberation (conscious versus unconscious) and the complexity and quality of choice. Complexity is defined as the amount of information a choice involves. A choice between objects for which one or two attributes are important (such as oven mitts or toothpastes) is simple, whereas a choice between objects for which many attributes are important (such as cars or houses) is complex. They hypothesised that conscious thought, due to its precision, leads to good choices in simple cases. However, because of its low capacity, conscious thought leads to progressively worse choices when things are more complex. Because of its relative lack of precision, unconscious thought (i.e., deliberation without attention) is expected to lead to choices of lower quality. However, the quality of choice does not deteriorate with increased complexity, allowing unconscious thought to lead to better choices than conscious thought under complex circumstances, this latter idea being the kernel of the deliberation-without-attention hypothesis.[14]

8 The Reliability of Moral ψ-Intuitions

As we have seen in the previous section, processes leading to judgements are reliable if they lead, at least in the majority of cases, to judgements that answer to pre-given substantive criteria of truth or correctness. As soon as we have established that certain processes predominantly result in judgements that accord with such criteria, we may label all the judgements flowing from these processes as reliable. Thus, to determine whether the processes resulting in intuitive moral ψ-intuitions are reliable we need pre-given substantive criteria of moral truth or correctness. But what is the source of these criteria? Moral judgements are in certain respects similar to legal judgements. Both are normative judgements. In the case of legal judgements, the source for finding criteria of legal truth or correctness is the law. Law as positive law consists of written rules.[15] Establishing the reliability of processes resulting in intuitive moral ψ-intuitions is more complicated. I distinguish between positive and personal morality. *Positive morality* re-

---

[14] Dijksterhuis and colleagues investigated this hypothesis in a number of experiments in which they compared the quality of choices between alternatives under different conditions. In a first experiment (Dijksterhuis 2004) participants were given information about four hypothetical apartments in their home city, Amsterdam. In a subsequent experiment, Dijksterhuis and colleagues (2006) presented subjects with a choice among different car models.

[15] Research by Chris Guthrie, Andrew Wistrich, and Jeffrey Rachlinski (n.d.) showed that judges often rely on intuitive judgements. They believe that deliberative decision making is more likely than intuitive decision making to lead to just outcomes, though intuitive judgements are frequently "good enough".

fers to the values, principles, and rules that are endorsed by (the majority of) *a social group* and that are used as the basis for moral (dis-)approval and moral praise and blame within that group. *Personal morality* refers to the values, principles, and rules that are endorsed by a *particular person*. Positive morality is a more appropriate source than personal morality when looking for pre-given substantive criteria of moral truth or correctness that can be used in determining whether the processes resulting in intuitive moral ψ-intuitions are reliable. Criteria derived from positive morality have a greater chance of being shared than criteria based on an individual's personal morality. Besides positive morality containing very general rules, there are contexts in which morality is institutionalised in codes or other authoritative statements. Such contexts might be a source for expert moral judgements. I return to the possibility of studies on the reliability of moral expertise later on, and start with studies on the reliability of intuitive judgements outside specialised professional contexts.

The only research on the reliability of such moral ψ-intuitions in particular I know of is that by Ham, van den Bos, and van Doorn (2009). They conducted two studies on the possible merits of unconscious thinking for people's justice judgements. Before starting their actual research, they set up a pretest in which they asked participants whether they shared the views of the researchers on which elements of an application procedure were unfair. Thus, the criteria for comparing the reliability of the judgements were known in advance. It is reasonable to assume that the views of the researchers which were endorsed by the participants, were based upon their shared positive morality. In both studies, participants were presented with complex and extensive information about four application procedures that job applicants had experienced. One of these descriptions of an application procedure implied a predominantly fair application procedure, and one implied a mostly unfair application procedure. The two remaining descriptions implied neither very fair nor very unfair application procedures. After the information on the application procedures had been presented, some participants (the conscious thought condition) could think about their justice judgements for three minutes and then were asked to indicate their justice judgements. Other participants (the unconscious thought condition) performed a distracter task for three minutes which prevented conscious thought about the justice judgements they had to make, after which they were asked to indicate their justice judgements. The remainder of the participants were asked to make justice judgements immediately (immediate judgement condition).

In experiment 1, participants were asked to directly compare the justice levels of the four application procedures and to indicate which procedure was the most just. In experiment 2, participants made their justice judgements comparable to the assessment of justice judgements in earlier justice research. They indicated their justice judgements on rating scales for each application procedure separately. The dependent variable the researchers constructed in all experiments was the accuracy of participants' justice judgements. They constructed accuracy scores that indicated whether participants correctly indicated the appropriate application procedure to be the fairest application procedure, the appropriate application procedure to be the most unjust procedure, and the appropriate two other ones as of intermediate justice levels. The results provide evidence for the merits of unconscious thought for justice judgements as these findings are the first to reveal that the accuracy of justice judgements increases under conditions that allow for unconscious thought relative to conditions of conscious thought or immediate judgement. Importantly, the findings indicate that unconscious thought leads to more accurate justice judgements than both conscious thought and immediate judgement can do.

I now turn to the reliability of expert moral judgements. Although the concept of moral expertise is highly contested,[16] I am convinced that moral expertise exists in specific domains.[17] A moral expert is someone who, in virtue of his knowledge, training, experience, and other "skills of ethical judgement and ethical sensitivity" (Lapsley and Narvaez 2005, p. 156 f.), is competent to make justifiable judgements on issues in a particular moral domain. Part of his expertise is also that he is able to defend his judgement in a convincing manner. Moral experts are better equipped to make authoritative and convincing judgements on issues in a particular domain than novices and outsiders, but only on issues in that particular domain. Moral experts are in important respects similar to legal experts. Both presuppose institutionalised contexts with an accepted body of theoretical and practical knowledge, of documents, policies, laws, protocols, and precedents. Both have expertise in a particular domain, of law, respectively morals. An important similarity is also that neither the legal nor the moral experts themselves create the policies and documents that are part of their expertise. Legal experts do not make laws. In democratic countries that is the prerogative of legislative bodies such as parliaments. For moral experts, the ultimate source of the moral beliefs and values that guide their judgements and decisions are not their own moral views, but the views of society at large which are embodied in the relevant documents and policies. Potential moral experts are, e.g.,

---

[16] In the last two decades there has been a continuous debate, mainly within medical ethics, on the existence and the nature of moral expertise. The central question in that debate seems to be whether knowledge of, and training in ethics (ethical theories and moral argumentation) makes one into a moral expert. For an overview of the discussion on moral or ethical expertise, see Weinstein (1994).

[17] I discuss the concept of moral expertise in more detail in Musschenga (2010, 2013).

members of ethical committees that evaluate protocols for research on humans or research with animals. The reliability of the judgements of such moral experts has never been the subject of empirical research. Empirical studies into the reliability of these experts in animal ethics or in clinical medical ethics are, at least in principle, possible. Substantive criteria of moral truth or correctness can be derived from authoritative moral codes and reports. These codes and statements constitute the normative base for determining the reliability of expert judgements.

9 Conclusion – Sense and Feasibility of an Empirically Informed Moral Intuitionism

My aim in this chapter was to investigate whether empirically informed moral intuitionism makes sense and what it requires. After examining the concepts of φ- and ψ-intuitions and relevant psychological and philosophical theories, I argued that φ-intuitions *indirectly* result from intuitive processes. Philosophical intuitions differ from ψ-intuitions in that they passed through a process of reflection. This reflection aims to find answers to two questions. The first is whether ψ-intuitions express what a person really thinks about an issue. If the answer is positive, she can be said to identify with the intuition. The second is what the epistemic status of the intuition is: Does the intuition that *p* provide immediate justification that *p*?

An empirically informed φ-moral intuitionism not only integrates findings of psychological studies on the origin of intuitions, but also findings on the reliability of intuitions. Empirical data only have limited relevance for moral φ-intuitionism in Huemer's theory. According to him, empirical data consisting either of evidence directly against the proposition that intuitively seemed true, or of evidence that our initial intuition was unreliable can only defeat an initial presumption. An empirically informed moral φ-intuitionism needs to answer the question why we should believe that moral intuitions can claim non-inferential credibility or justifying force. This requires accepting that the epistemological theory of process reliabilism needs empirical data to answer this question. Process reliabilism is, though well-established, still a controversial theory.

The feasibility of an empirically informed moral intuitionism depends not only on the plausibility of process reliabilism, but also on the availability of empirical studies on the reliability of unconscious processes generating moral ψ-intuitions. Until now, such studies are rare. They are also complicated because they presuppose agreement on substantive criteria of moral truth or correctness. The only relevant study I found, the research by Ham and colleagues (2009), showed the superiority of judgements resulting from unconscious thinking over the justice of an application procedure over as well fast and automatic judgements as reasoned judgements. Another finding that is relevant for empirically informed φ-moral intuitionism is that the ψ-intuitions that result from what Bargh (1989, p. 11) calls preconscious automaticity are the least reliable among the automatic judgements, even though they are surrounded with strong feelings of certainty. The reason that these gut-feeling type of ψ-intuitions are trusted by a subject as accurate and valid is just that they are generated preconsciously, without awareness of inferential activity or cognitive effort. Although confidence is a phenomenological feature of moral intuitions, it is reasonable to assume that reflection on these gut-feeling type of ψ-intuitions will not lead to the insight that no further justification is needed. However, it is difficult and perhaps impossible to determine which intuitive moral ψ-intuition judgements result from preconscious automatic processes. For this reason, empirical research that could confirm this assumption is not possible.

Empirical studies have shown that there is a positive correlation between the level of one's expertise and the reliability of one's ψ-intuitions on issues in one's domain of expertise. Although these studies did not focus on moral ψ-intuitions in particular, it is plausible to assume that their findings also apply to these intuitions. However, moral expert judgements are, as I argued in section 8, only possible within highly institutionalised and codified domains of morality. If competence and experience matter for the reliability of moral ψ-intuitions, not only should intuitions of experts on issues in their domain of expertise be assigned a greater justificatory force than that of laypeople and novices, it should also be recognised that moral intuitions of fully morally maturated individuals have a greater justificatory force than that of youngsters.

These ideas suggested by a still embryonal empirically informed moral φ-intuitionism are very tentative. They need to be corroborated by empirical studies focussing on the reliability of moral ψ-intuitions.

Bibliography

Anderson, John (1981): *Cognitive Skills and Their Acquisition*. Hillsdale: Erlbaum.
Audi, Robert (2004): *The Good in the Right. A Theory of Intuition and Intrinsic Value*. Princeton: Princeton University Press.
Audi, Robert (2015): "Intuition and Its Place in Ethics". In: *Journal of the American Philosophical Association* 1 (1), pp. 57–77.

Bargh, John (1989): "Conditional Automaticity. Varieties of Automatic Influence in Social Perception and Cognition". In: Uleman, James and Bargh, John (eds.): *Unintended Thought*. New York: Guilford, pp. 3–51.

Bargh, John (1990): "Auto-Motives. Preconscious Determinants of Social Interaction". In: Higgins, Edward and Sorrentino, Richard (eds.): *Handbook of Motivation and Cognition*. Vol. 2. New York: Guilford, pp. 93–130.

Bargh, John (1996): "Automaticity in Social Psychology". In: Higgins, Edward and Kruglanski, Arie (eds.): *Social Psychology. Handbook of Basic Principles*. New York: Guilford, pp. 169–183.

Bargh, John and Chartrand, Tanya (1999): "The Unbearable Automaticity of Being". In: *American Psychologist* 54 (7), pp. 462–479.

Bealer, George (2002): "Modal Epistemology and the Rationalist Renaissance". In: Gendler, Tamara and Hawthorne, John (eds.): *Conceivability and Possibility*. Oxford: Oxford University Press, pp. 71–125.

Bedke, Michael (2008): "Ethical Intuitions. What They Are, What They Are Not, and How They Justify". In: *American Philosophical Quarterly* 45 (3), pp. 253–269.

Charness, Neil (1976): "Memory for Chess Positions. Resistance to Interference". In: *Journal of Experimental Psychology, Human Learning and Memory* 2 (6), pp. 641–653.

de Groot, Adriaan (1965): *Thought and Choice in Chess*. The Hague: Mouton.

Descartes, René. (1985): "Rules for the Direction of the Mind". In: Cottingham, John; Stoothoff, Robert, and Murdoch, Dugald (eds.): *The Philosophical Writings of Descartes*. Cambridge: Cambridge University Press, pp. 7–78.

Dijksterhuis, Ab (2004): "Think Different. The Merits of Unconscious Thought in Preference Development and Decision Making". In: *Journal of Personality and Social Psychology* 87 (5), pp. 586–598.

Dijksterhuis, Ab; Bos, Maarten; Nordgren, Loren, and van Baaren, Rick (2006): "On Making the Right Choice. The Deliberation-Without-Attention Effect". In: *Science* 311 (5763), pp. 1005–1007.

Doris, John and Stich, Steven (2005): "As a Matter of Fact. Empirical Perspectives on Ethics". In: Jackson, Frank and Smith, Michael (eds.): *The Oxford Handbook of Contemporary Philosophy*. Oxford: Oxford University Press, pp. 114–155.

Ericsson, Anders and Charness, Neil (1994): "Expert Performance. Its Structure and Acquisition". In: *American Psychologist* 49 (8), pp. 725–747.

Ericsson, Anders and Kintsch, Walter (1995): "Long Term Working Memory". In: *Psychological Review* 102 (2), pp. 211–245.

Feltovich, Paul; Prietula, Michael, and Ericsson, Anders (2006): "Studies of Expertise from Psychological Perspectives". In: Ericsson, Anders (ed.): *Handbook of Expertise and Expert Performance*. Cambridge: Cambridge University Press, pp. 41–67.

Goldman, Alvin (1979): "What Is Justified Belief?". In: Pappas, George (ed.): *Justification and Knowledge*. Dordrecht: Reidel, pp. 1–23. Reprinted in: Goldman, Alvin (1992): *Liaisons. Philosophy Meets the Cognitive and Social Sciences*. Cambridge: MIT Press, pp. 105–126.

Gopnik, Alison and Schwitzgebel, Eric (1998): "Whose Concepts Are They, Anyway? The Role of Philosophical Intuition in Empirical Psychology". In: DePaul, Michael and Ramsey, William (eds.): *Rethinking Intuition*. Lanham: Rowman & Littlefield, pp. 75–91.

Guthrie, Chris; Wistrich, Jeffrey, and Rachlinski, Andrew (n.d.): "Judicial Intuition". In: *Vanderbilt Law School*. https://law.vanderbilt.edu/files/archive/Judicial_Intuition.pdf, retrieved on November 14, 2018.

Haidt, John (2001): "The Emotional Dog and Its Rational Tail. A Social Intuitionist Approach to Moral Judgment". In: *Psychological Review* 108 (4), pp. 814–834.

Haidt, John (2007): "The New Synthesis in Moral Psychology". In: *Science* 316 (5827), pp. 998–1002.

Haidt, John (2012): *The Righteous Mind*. New York: Pantheon.

Haidt, John and Bjorklund, Fredrik (2008): "Social Intuitionists Answer Six Questions About Moral Psychology". In: Sinnott-Armstrong, Walter (ed.): *Moral Psychology. Vol. 2. The Cognitive Science of Morality. Intuition and Diversity*. Cambridge: MIT Press, pp. 181–219.

Ham, Jaap; van den Bos, Kees, and van Doorn, Erik (2009): "Lady Justice Thinks Unconsciously. Unconscious Thought Can Lead to More Accurate Justice Judgments". In: *Social Cognition* 27 (4), pp. 509–521.

Hammond, Keith (1996): *Human Judgment and Social Policy*. New York: Oxford University Press.

Hodgkinson, Gerald; Langan-Fox, Janice, and Sadler-Smith, Eugene (2008): "Intuition. A Fundamental Bridging Construct in the Behavioural Sciences". In: *British Journal of Psychology* 99 (1), pp. 1–27.

Hoffman, Martin (2000): *Empathy and Moral Development*. Cambridge: Cambridge University Press.

Hogarth, Robin (2002): "Deciding Analytically or Trusting Your Intuition? The Advantages and Disadvantages of Analytic and Intuitive Thought". In: *Departament d'Economia i Empresa, Universitat Pompeu Fabra Barcelona*. http://www.econ.upf.edu/docs/papers/downloads/654.pdf, retrieved on November 14, 2018. A shorter version is published in: Betsch, Tilmann and Haberstroh, Susanne (2005) (eds.): *The Routines of Decision Making*. Mahwah: Erlbaum, pp. 67–82.

Huemer, Michael (2005): *Ethical Intuitionism*. New York: Palgrave Macmillan.

Huemer, Michael (2007): "Compassionate Phenomenal Conservatism". In: *Philosophy and Phenomenological Research* 74 (1), pp. 30–55.

Huemer, Michael (2008): "Revisionary Intuitionism". In: *Social Philosophy and Policy* 25 (1), pp. 368–392.

Kahneman, Daniel (2003): "Maps of Bounded Rationality. Psychology for Behavioral Economics". In: *The American Economic Review* 93 (5), pp. 1449–1475.

Kauppinen, Antti (2013): "A Humean Theory of Moral Intuition". In: *Canadian Journal of Philosophy* 43 (3), pp. 360–381.

Kauppinen, Antti (2015): "Intuition and Belief in Moral Motivation". In: Björnsson, Gunnar; Strandberg, Caj; Olinder, Ragnar; Eriksson, Jonnie, and Björklund, Fredrik (eds.): *Motivational Internalism*. Oxford: Oxford University Press, pp. 235–259.

Kohlberg, Lawrence (1976): "Moral Stages and Moralization. The Cognitive-Developmental Approach". In: Lickona, Thomas (ed.): *Moral Development and Behavior. Theory, Research and Social Issues*. New York: Holt, Rinehart and Winston, pp. 31–53.

Mayer, Richard (1983): *Thinking, Problem Solving, Cognition*. New York: Freeman.

Musschenga, Bert (2010): "Empirical Ethics and the Special Place of the Practitioner's Moral Judgements". In: *Ethical Perspectives* 17 (2), pp. 231–258.

Musschenga, Bert (2013): "Moral Expertise. The Role of Expert Judgments and Expert Intuitions in the Construction of (Local) Ethical Theories". In: Christen, Markus; Fischer, Jens; Huppenbauer, Markus; Tanner, Claudia, and van Schaik, Carel (eds.): *Empirically Informed Ethics. Morality Between Facts and Norms.* Berlin: Springer, pp. 195–209.

Narvaez, Darcia and Lapsley, Daniel (2005): "The Psychological Foundations of Everyday Morality and Moral Expertise". In: Lapsley, Daniel and Power, Clark (eds.): *Character Psychology and Character Education.* Notre Dame: University of Notre Dame Press, pp. 140–165.

Nisbett, Robert and Wilson, Timothy (1977): "Telling More Than We Know. Verbal Reports on Mental Processes". In: *Psychological Review* 84 (3), pp. 231–259.

Plantinga, Alvin (1993): *Warrant and Proper Function.* Oxford: Oxford University Press.

Posner, Michael and Snyder, Charles (1975): "Attention and Cognitive Control". In: Solso, Robert (ed.): *Information Processing and Cognition. The Loyola Symposium.* Hillsdale: Erlbaum, pp. 205–223.

Rest, James (1986): *Moral Development. Advances in Research and Theory.* New York: Praeger.

Russell, Daniel (2009): *Practical Intelligence and the Virtues.* Oxford: Clarendon Press.

Sinnott-Armstrong, Walter (2008): "Framing Moral Intuitions". In: Sinnott-Armstrong, Walter (ed.): *Moral Psychology. Vol. 2. The Cognitive Science of Morality. Intuition and Diversity.* Cambridge: MIT Press, pp. 47–77.

Sloman, Steven (1996): "The Empirical Case for Two Systems of Reasoning". In: *Psychological Bulletin* 119 (1), pp. 3–22.

Snow, Nancy (2010): *Virtue as Social Intelligence. An Empirically Grounded Theory.* New York: Routledge.

Stanovich, Keith and West, Richard (2000): "Individual Differences in Reasoning. Implications for the Rationality Debate?". In: *Behavioral and Brain Sciences* 23 (5), pp. 645–665.

Symons, John (2008): "Intuition and Philosophical Methodology". In: *Axiomathes* 18 (1), pp. 67–89.

Tucker, Chris (2013): *Seemings and Justification. New Essays on Dogmatism and Phenomenal Conservatism.* Oxford: Oxford University Press.

Weinstein, Bruce (1990): "The Possibility of Ethical Expertise". In: *Theoretical Medicine* 15 (1), pp. 61–75.

Woodward, John and Allman, Jim (2007): "Moral Intuition. Its Neural Substrates and Normative Significance". In: *Journal of Physiology* 101 (4–6), pp. 179–202.

Norbert Paulo
A Principle of Psychological Realism for Moral Epistemology

Abstract: This chapter starts from Owen Flanagan's Principle of Minimal Psychological Realism for first-order moral theory. The author argues that a similar principle of psychological realism also applies to (second-order) moral epistemic decision procedures which are used to determine the proper contents of first-order morality. He calls it the Principle of Minimal Psychological Realism for Moral Epistemic Decision Procedures (PRDP): "Make sure when constructing a moral epistemic decision procedure that the character and decision processing prescribed are possible, or are perceived to be possible, for creatures like us". Just as consequentialists implicitly endorse PMPR in first-order morality, so do proponents of Rawlsian moral epistemology implicitly endorse PRDP. Applying PRDP to different elements of Rawls' moral epistemic decision procedure, the author shows that his requirements concerning considered judgements do not violate the PRDP. Things are more complicated when it comes to the epistemic requirements concerning competent judges though. Some of them – particularly openness for belief revision and bias avoidance – are very demanding and might even violate the ought-implies-can principle. However, they do not violate the more flexible PRDP. There is one requirement in Rawls that does violate PRDP though, namely the requirement to imagine a social deliberation among a group of competent judges. PRDP does not apply to epistemic ideals that are not meant to be actually carried out. If proponents of such moral epistemic views were to develop decision procedures, PRDP would apply to these, too, the author argues.

1 Introduction

Almost three decades ago, in his pioneering *Varieties of Moral Personality*, Owen Flanagan has proposed the Principle of Minimal Psychological Realism (PMPR): "Make sure when constructing a moral theory or projecting a moral ideal that the character, decision processing, and behaviour prescribed are possible, or are perceived to be possible, for creatures like us" (Flanagan 1991, p. 32). This principle overlaps with certain interpretations of the better-known ought-implies-can principle. But where the latter is generally understood to apply to particular acts required of particular individuals, PMPR is meant to apply to persons in general, hence the "creatures like us" formulation (Flanagan 1991, p. 340, note 1).[1] This formulation, together with the qualification "or are perceived to be possible", makes the PMPR less restrictive than "ought implies can". The qualification allows for the prescription of characters, decision processing, or behaviour that are not possible right here and now, but which are realistically regarded as being possible for our descendants. So unlike "ought implies can", PMPR is not necessarily violated if a single person lacks the ability to do what she ought to do, not even when all currently existing humans lack this ability. PMPR is only violated if what ought to be done exceeds the ability of persons in general, including those descendants of ours with enhanced abilities.[2] PMPR is meant to apply to first-order questions of moral theory, i.e., questions about which character traits are good, which acts ought to be done, and so forth. To questions of first-order morality, moral precepts such as Kant's categorical imperative or the utilitarian calculus and moral theories such as virtue ethics or contractualism provide answers. The question I am interested in belongs to the realm of second-order morality, i.e., the part of meta-ethics that is concerned with the problem of how to decide which of the various moral theories and precepts is the right one. So my question is this: Does a similar principle of psychological realism also apply to (second-order) moral epistemic decision procedures such as Rawls' reflective equilibrium which are used to determine the proper contents of first-order morality?

For the purposes of this chapter I take it for granted that Flanagan's PMPR (or something very similar to it) – understood as applying to first-order morality – is by and large correct (Appiah 2009, chapter 3, Wong 2006, chapter 6, Rini 2014). The principle seems to capture the commonsensical main idea behind "ought implies can" and avoids the latter principle's strictness and narrowness. But even if we assume, *arguendo*, that PMPR is by and large correct, a note is in order concerning its reach and relevance: As has been pointed out regarding the ought-implies-can principle, PMPR, too, works primarily in a negative way: "Ought implies can" is normally not invoked to establish an *ought* and then to

---

[1] On "ought implies can" in general, and on the strange use of the word "ought" in the debate in particular, see Mackie (1977, chapter 3).
[2] It is hard to determine precisely which expectations for enhanced abilities are to be considered realistic enough from the point of view of the PMPR. It is not unreasonable to expect some kind of progressive change in human dispositions, no matter if they evolve naturally, are enabled by societal changes, or if they are triggered by non-traditional means such as biochemical or technological "enhancements" (Savulescu and Bostrom 2009, Buchanan and Powell 2018). The idea is simply to allow for meaningful regulative ideals but to exclude far-fetched ideals that appear to be impossible to achieve.

derive logically what we *can* do. Rather, from the fact that, empirically, humans cannot do something, it is normally inferred that it is not true that they ought to do it (Kahane 2016, p. 287). Similarly, for the PMPR, when science shows that something – such as acquiring a certain combination of character traits or behaving in certain ways – is not possible, or perceived to be possible, even for the best of humankind, then there is no point in prescribing it.

Consider consequentialism. It has often been argued that act consequentialism, as a moral theory, is flawed because it is too demanding (for an overview, see Sinnott-Armstrong 2015, section 6). If one understands the theory roughly as holding that one ought to always act so as to produce the best possible consequences, this clearly demands a lot from the agent: She ought to be very attentive of all the action opportunities open to her, to investigate the consequences of each opportunity, and then to act on the one with the best consequences (Kagan 1984). Moreover, most forms of consequentialism ask the agent to do all of this from an impersonal point of view (see Williams 1973, pp. 108 ff.). Against such demandingness objections, proponents of utilitarianism have pointed out that

> teleological theories [such as act consequentialism] can be construed as *standards or criteria of rightness* or as *decision procedures*. A standard or criterion of rightness explains what makes an action or motive right or justified; a decision procedure provides a method of deliberation. Teleological theories do provide criteria of rightness, but need not provide decision procedures (Brink 1986, p. 421; emphasis in original).

So the idea is that even if it were clear that act consequentialism is in fact too demanding as a method of deliberation about what to do, this would not speak against act consequentialism as a standard of rightness.[3] So moral theory

---

[3] Of course, things are more complicated than that. It has been argued that at least some of the demandingness objections do not fall under the "ought implies can" principle, because what they really object is not that something cannot be done, but that it cannot be willed. However, unlike "ought implies can", "ought implies *can will*" does not hold. The latter principle would be violated if some demand is beyond what people can motivate themselves to do, although they could do it nonetheless. Estlund (2011, 2014) believes that it is this principle that people have in mind when they find some requirements in Marxism, socialism, egalitarianism, or utilitarianism too unrealistic, unfeasible, or demanding (against this view in the realm of political philosophy, see Enoch 2018, for an overview, see Erman and Möller 2015). Perhaps Williams' point that utilitarianism is too demanding because people normally cannot motivate themselves to take an impersonal point of view is best understood as invoking "ought implies can will", whereas only the other objection that people really cannot be attentive of all the action opportunities open to them, investigate the consequences of each opportunity, and act on the one with the best consequences falls under "ought implies can". Be that as it may, in this chapter my interest is in the

might be autonomous in the sense that empirical considerations, as articulated in PMPR, are irrelevant for its adequacy (see, e.g., Schmidt 2011); moral theory simply is concerned with ideals of agency (and not with actual psychological states of humans), and with how humans ought to be (and not with how they actually are). In other words, it is normative and not descriptive.

Prima facie PMPR does not seem to apply when moral theory merely aspires to provide standards of rightness; it seems to be relevant only when moral theory also aspires to provide a decision procedure. However, Flanagan emphasises that this way of looking at moral theory misses an important point: A moral theory is deficient when it "fails to pass the test of its being shown how persons could conceivably live in accordance with it" (Flanagan 1991, p. 38). The theory is not deficient because its respective standards of rightness are inadequate, but because what is required of actual agents is not (clearly enough) determined by those standards. In acknowledging that a particular moral theory such as act consequentialism would be too demanding as a decision procedure, its proponents implicitly accept PMPR or something very similar to it. Again, this does not say that the theory is wrong as a standard of rightness; neither does it say that it is right. It merely says that it is deficient because it does not offer any guidance in figuring out what one ought to do from the point of view of this particular moral theory (see the discussion in Driver 2012, chapter 6).

One might think that the described deficiency is one of act consequentialism only, and that rule consequentialism circumvents the problem. The main idea of rule consequentialism is this: Particular acts are judged by reference to moral rules; the rules are judged by reference to the consequentialist moral principle (I discuss rule consequentialism at some length in Paulo 2016, chapter 8). This principle can be somewhat complex. Take, as an example, Brad Hooker's version of such a principle:

> An act is wrong if and only if it is forbidden by the code of rules whose internalization by the overwhelming majority of everyone everywhere in each new generation has maximum expected value in terms of well-being (with some priority for the worst off). The calculation of a code's expected value includes all costs of getting the code internalized. If in terms of expected value two or more codes are better than the rest but equal to one another, the one closest to conventional morality determines what acts are wrong (Hooker 2001, p. 32).

PMPR and not in demands that violate something like the "ought implies can will" principle. Put differently, Estlund argues against *maximal* psychological realism, but I merely defend *minimal* psychological realism.

Hooker is very much concerned with empirical questions, with what is possible, or perceived to be possible, for creatures like us, to use the wording of the PMPR. Importantly, this concern has implications not only for rule consequentialism as a decision procedure but also for the formulation of the very consequentialist principle as a standard of rightness. As the standard of rightness, the principle demands the maximisation of expected value, and the expected value depends on what people can, in fact, internalise.[4] So in Hooker's version of rule consequentialism, something like PMPR is recognised on the level of standards of rightness in that the feasibility of the more specific rules to be followed in everyday life – the decision procedure – is an integral element of the standard of rightness. In recognising a connection between decision procedure and standard of rightness, Hooker and other proponents of rule consequentialism implicitly endorse PMPR.[5]

2 Psychological Realism in Rawls

So far I introduced the PMPR as applied to first-order questions of moral theory, i.e., questions about which character traits are good, which acts ought to be done, and so forth.[6] The problem I am ultimately interested in in this chapter does not concern PMPR as proposed by Flanagan. Rather, I am interested in psychological realism beyond first-order morality, namely in the question whether a similar principle holds in decision procedures in moral epistemology. Flanagan hints at a parallel between moral theory and epistemology as a normative enterprise: both are often seen as being autonomous because they are not meant to reflect how humans actually behave or reason, but to set standards for how humans ought to behave or reason (Flanagan 1991, p. 24). But he does not develop the idea of a principle like PMPR for moral epistemology.

Let us call this the **Pr**inciple of Minimal Psychological **R**ealism for Moral Epistemic **D**ecision **P**rocedures (PRDP): *Make sure when constructing a moral epistemic decision procedure that the character and decision processing prescribed are possible, or are perceived to be possible, for creatures like us.*

---

[4] For Hooker (2001, pp. 76f.), "internalisation" roughly is the comprehension and acceptance of a moral rule. It is possible not to comply with a moral rule one has internalised.
[5] Some commentators argue that consequentialists cannot meaningfully distinguish between decision procedure and standard of rightness (Griffin 1992, Birnbacher 2007, pp. 211ff.). If this is true, rule consequentialists endorse PMPR even more clearly.
[6] For reasons of simplicity I focus on consequentialism. Flanagan (1991, part 1) makes similar points for deontological moral theory as well as for virtue ethics; see also Flanagan (2016).

In the previous section, I mentioned Hooker's rule consequentialist principle. How is this principle justified? What is the standard to judge such first-order moral theories or principles? How is one to decide which one to adhere to? This is the kind of moral epistemological question I am interested in. Hooker explicitly uses a certain moral epistemic device, namely John Rawls' well-known reflective equilibrium. As Rawls (1974, p. 8) put it, the main idea of reflective equilibrium is this:

> People have considered judgments at all levels of generality, from those about particular situations and institutions up through broad standards and first principles to formal and abstract conditions on moral conceptions. One tries to see how people would fit their various convictions into one coherent scheme, each considered judgment whatever its level having a certain initial credibility. By dropping and revising some, by reformulating and expanding others, one supposes that a systematic organization can be found.

In other words, to engage in the *method of reflective equilibrium* is to start from intuitions about certain problems or cases and to try to systematise those with principles. In that process of systemisation, intuitions and principles are reconsidered and revised until the set of intuitions and principles is coherent. Pretty much the same idea is already to be found in Rawls' (1951) earlier *Outline of a Decision Procedure for Ethics* (henceforth *Outline*), on which reflective equilibrium is modelled (for a comparison between reflective equilibrium and *Outline*, see Greenspan 2015, section 1). In *Outline*, Rawls holds that "a judgment in a particular case is evidenced to be rational by showing that, given the facts and the conflicting interests of the case, the judgment is capable of being explicated by a justifiable principle" (Rawls 1951, p. 187). If successful, the method of reflective equilibrium – or the procedure as described in *Outline* – leads to a *state of reflective equilibrium*. In this state of reflective equilibrium, a set of beliefs is considered to be justified *if and only if* it is coherent. In contrast to this "narrow" reflective equilibrium, where only intuitions about particular moral problems and cases as well as more general principles have to be brought into coherence, "wide" reflective equilibrium also requires coherence with a range of relevant background theories in order for a set of moral beliefs to be justified (on "wide" reflective equilibrium, see Daniels 1979, for recent overviews of the debate concerning reflective equilibrium more generally, see Cath 2016, Tersman 2018).

The distinction between decision procedure and standard of rightness is unclear in Rawls' moral epistemology. On the one hand, one can say that the method of reflective equilibrium describes a decision procedure which, if successfully carried out, leads to a state of reflective equilibrium, and that the state of reflective equilibrium cannot be achieved without carrying out the process described in the method of reflective equilibrium. In recognising this connection between decision procedure and standard of rightness, Rawlsian moral epistemology implicitly endorses PRDP. On the other hand, one can say that the state of reflective equilibrium can be reached without carrying out the method of reflective equilibrium first. It might be achieved by another decision procedure; or it might just magically occur. In distinguishing between decision procedure and standard of rightness in this way, Rawlsian moral epistemology would also implicitly endorse PRDP. No matter what the method that brings about the state of reflective equilibrium looks like, it must be distinct from the state of reflective equilibrium. As said above, act consequentialism would arguably be overly demanding and therefore defective when understood as a decision procedure, but it arguably can be defended as a standard of rightness. The state of reflective equilibrium alone – without a method of reflective equilibrium – would be similarly defective as a decision procedure, because it would merely provide the ideal to be achieved without providing any hints how to reach it. As Flanagan argued in the context of first-order morality, a moral theory is not only deficient because its respective standards of rightness are inadequate; it can also be defective because what is required of actual agents is not (clearly enough) determined by those standards. The same arguably holds in moral epistemology: In acknowledging that a particular moral epistemic theory would not be sufficiently action-guiding – or rather reason guiding – when understood as a decision procedure, one implicitly accepts PRDP or something very similar to it. The state of reflective equilibrium alone might be the right moral epistemic standard of rightness; but it would be deficient as a decision procedure because it does not offer any guidance in figuring out how to reach it. So, no matter if one views the state of reflective equilibrium as dependent or as independent from the method of reflective equilibrium, something like the PRDP holds for decision procedures in moral epistemology either way.

3 Minimal Psychological Realism in Rawls' Moral Epistemology

Now take a closer look at how PRDP would apply to Rawls' *Outline* and to reflective equilibrium. The procedure developed in *Outline* has roughly two parts, the first of which determines the *relevant judgements* about cases to be taken into account; the second part is the *justification of the principles* invoked in rationalising these judgements. It starts from intuitive judgements about particular cases. These judgements are intuitive in the sense that they are not consciously derived from principles, although there might be implicit principles at work (Rawls 1951, p. 183).[7] Rawls is not interested in all moral judgements, but in *considered judgements* by *competent judges* only.[8] In the procedure's second part, the thus preselected judgements get rationalised by various means. The judgements must be explicable by simple moral rules, which are the result of "moral insight", determined without "strong emotional or physical duress" (Rawls 1951, p. 187). The rules must, in turn, justify the judgements; they must further be action-guiding in non-trivial future cases and stand trial against alternative rules and other judgements.[9] Let us focus on the procedure's first part, which is about considered judgements by competent judges.

3.1 Considered Judgements

For Rawls (2005, pp. 47 f.), *considered judgements* are

> those judgments in which our moral capacities are most likely to be displayed without distortion. [...] For example, we can discard those judgments made with hesitation, or in which we have little confidence. Similarly, those given when we are upset or frightened, or when we stand to gain one way or the other can be left aside. All these judgments are likely to be erroneous or to be influenced by an excessive attention to our own interests. Considered judgments are simply those rendered under conditions favorable to the exercise of the sense of justice, and therefore in circumstances where the more common excuses and explanations for making a mistake do not obtain.

---

[7] Note that the proposition that some implicit principles might be driving the judgments does not entail anything about the innateness of a certain moral faculty by proponents of the so-called "linguistic analogy", see, e.g., Hauser, Young, and Cushman (2008), Mikhail (2011).

[8] It has been pointed out that this narrowing element is in tension with the coherence-oriented epistemology of the model. The question is this: When it is coherence that ultimately justifies, how is it rational to exclude certain judgments from entering the search process for the most coherent set of judgments (see van Thiel and van Delden 2009, Sayre-McCord 1996)?

[9] As I describe them here, both the procedure in *Outline* and reflective equilibrium are best understood as belonging to "narrow" reflective equilibrium, where "only" intuitions about particular moral problems and cases and more general principles have to be brought into coherence. In contrast, "wide" reflective equilibrium also requires coherence with a range of relevant background theories in order for a set of moral beliefs to be justified. I limit the discussion in this chapter to "narrow" reflective equilibrium, because "wide" reflective equilibrium does not seem to raise further problems for PRDP. "Wide" reflective equilibrium might be even more idealised than "narrow" reflective equilibrium, but this only seems to be true for the respective state of reflective equilibrium (i.e., for reflective equilibrium as a standard of rightness) and not for the respective method of reflective equilibrium (i.e., for reflective equilibrium as a moral epistemic decision procedure).

Basically, considered judgements are not systematically derived from moral principles, but can be reflective; they are made under favourable conditions; and they concern moral cases and problems with which the judge is familiar. Just as Rawls would advise, Hooker (2001, p. 12) starts his reasoning from moral intuitions – "beliefs that come with independent credibility". As he describes the moral epistemic procedure, "we search for a coherent set of moral beliefs and are willing to make many revisions so as to reach coherence. But we should start with moral beliefs that are attractive in their own right, i.e., independently of how they mesh with our other moral beliefs" (Hooker 2001, p. 13). He argues that some kind of common morality provides the moral beliefs about which most people confidently agree. Rules of this common morality are, e.g., "Help the needy", "Do not steal", "Do not lie", "Keep promises", and so on. But there are many more such intuitions Hooker (2001, p. 28) explicitly relies on, e.g.: "Any moral theory will be terribly counterintuitive if it requires you to make every decision on the basis of an equal concern for everyone. To be plausible, a moral theory must leave room for some considerable degree of bias (a) towards yourself and (b) towards your family, friends, benefactors, etc." These moral intuitions seem commonsensical, but note that some of them – especially those allowing for partiality – are controversial among ethicists, especially among consequentialists. Nevertheless, from the point of view of Rawls' procedure as developed in *Outline*, they are good candidates for considered judgements.[10] There is no apparent reason to think that Rawls' requirements concerning considered judgements would violate the PRDP.

3.2 Competent Judges

In *Outline* Rawls advises taking into account considered judgements by *competent judges* only. Competent moral judges are supposed to have "a certain requisite degree of intelligence, which may be thought of as that ability which intelligence tests are designed to measure". They are also "required to know those things concerning the world about [them] and those consequences of frequently performed actions, which it is reasonable to expect the average intelligent man to know. Further, a competent judge is expected to know, in all cases whereupon he is called to express his opinion, the peculiar facts of those cases". Moreover, a

---

10 Remember that Hooker invokes these intuitions in order to reason toward a rule consequentialist principle as a standard of rightness; he is not merely concerned with a decision procedure or method of deliberation as discussed above.

competent moral judge is required to be a "reasonable man", who "shows a willingness, if not a desire, to use the criteria of inductive logic in order to determine what is proper for him to believe"; who "whenever he is confronted with a moral question, shows a disposition to find reasons for and against the possible lines of conduct which are open to him"; who "exhibits a desire to consider questions with an open mind"; and who "knows, or tries to know, his own emotional, intellectual, and moral predilections and makes a conscientious effort to take them into account in weighing the merits of any question. He is not unaware of the influences of prejudice and bias even in his most sincere efforts to annul them". Finally, to be a competent judge, one is further required to have "sympathetic knowledge of those human interests which, by conflicting in particular cases, give rise to the need to make a moral decision" (Rawls 1951, pp. 178 f.). To sum up, Rawls conceives of a competent moral judge as someone with logical competence, conceptual understanding, empirical competence, empathetic understanding, openness to belief revision, and a willingness for bias avoidance (Schaefer and Savulescu 2016, see also Paulo 2018).

I have no doubt that Hooker has logical competence, conceptual understanding, empirical competence, empathetic understanding, openness to revision, and that he tries to avoid biases. What I doubt, though, is that the criteria for moral competency are actually helpful for the purposes of the moral epistemic procedure. I suspect that hardly anyone – and most certainly hardly any moral philosopher – would seriously question herself in these respects. But this is not just a mocking of people's general self-confidence.

Take openness to revision: First, it is not obvious that this openness is generally epistemically valuable. Recently, Jeremy Fantl has forcefully argued – against common sense – that there is often good epistemic reason not to be open-minded (where open-mindedness means that one is not psychologically disposed against being persuaded by an argument, to unreasonably violate any procedural norms in one's response to the argument, and that one is willing to be persuaded when one finds the argument compelling and is unable to locate a flaw; see Fantl 2018, p. 12). Second, and more importantly, there is ample evidence that moral convictions are generally very stable and hard to revise. It is in fact really difficult to be as open-minded as a competent moral judge is expected to be, and rationally warranted belief revision might require the use of certain rather strict procedures (Skitka 2010). After all, just as all humans, philosophers are "motivated reasoners", i.e., they use their rational and critical thinking capacities primarily to rationalise the beliefs they already have, to find weak spots in the arguments of others, and so forth. However, they are very bad in recognising weak spots in their own arguments, and only rarely weigh evidence against their beliefs appropriately (Mercier and Sperber 2011, 2017). This should not come as a big surprise. Self-criticism requires taking a detached view on one's own self. If there is a blind spot concerning the question of how we, as humans, form our moral beliefs, it is: oneself (Batson 2015, Paulo and Bublitz 2017). Of course, this does not mean that humans in general, and philosophers in particular, only rationalise and cannot escape their contingent psychological dispositions. They can learn constructive self-criticism, especially if others mirror their behaviour. Just think about the means widely used to explore oneself, primarily for psychotherapeutic treatments, mostly to cure depression, anxiety, or personality disorder. Given appropriate setting and supervision, such means could also be used to improve the self-understanding, self-criticism, and openness of perfectly healthy people, including philosophers. I should note that the effectiveness of psychotherapies is hard to measure (Lilienfeld et al. 2014), and they might have side-effects (Schermuly-Haupt, Linden, and Rush 2018). This is, of course, all the more important when it comes to psychedelic means, which might complement forms of psychotherapy. The neologism "psychedelia" (which roughly translates as "mind manifesting" or "mind revealing") is meant to capture the substances' alleged potential to do just that, to reveal or manifest one's own mind, and thereby to promote self-understanding, self-criticism, and openness (for a narrative of the new developments in research concerning psychedelia, see Pollan 2018). What is important for my point here is that psychotherapeutic means, and perhaps even psychedelic ones, might be helpful to promote openness to revision. Further research into the effectiveness and safety of such means is necessary to show whether or not they are conducive to moral epistemic aims. This is an important respect in which the PRDP differs significantly from the ought-implies-can principle. In some of the respects just mentioned "ought implies can" would yield the conclusion that a particular person who cannot do what reflective equilibrium demands of her would not have to follow Rawls' demands. The PRDP, in contrast, does not yield such a conclusion. It rather points to realistic means to enhance human abilities. Unlike proponents of "ought implies can" in moral epistemology, proponents of PRDP thus can account for the aspirational nature of moral epistemic methods and standards such as reflective equilibrium while also setting limits to its degree of ideality.

Let us look at one more example in which PRDP accounts for reflective equilibrium's aspirational nature before I show an instance in which the limits set by PRDP are violated. Consider again Rawls' (1951, p. 179) criterion that a "reasonable man" be one who "is not unaware of the influences of prejudice and bias even in his most sincere efforts to annul them; nor is he fatalistic about their effect so that he succumbs to them as being those factors which he thinks must sooner or later determine his decision". This criterion does not demand that a "reasonable man" be not prejudiced and biased. Rawls was well aware of the problem that all humans are likely to be biased, even if only implicitly so (on implicit bias, see Brownstein and Saul 2016a, 2016b, Brownstein 2018). So he assumes that the "reasonable man" would try his best to work around and counter his prejudices and biases. But Rawls goes even further. He seems to have realised – even before the heydays of rationality research since the 1980s (for an overview, see Kahneman 2012) – that, in many cases, even the best attempts to avoid prejudice and bias will not completely eliminate their effects (see Fricker 2007, also Anderson 2012, 2015). So he demands that the "reasonable man" is not "unaware of the influences of prejudice and bias even in his most sincere efforts to annul them". Yet this awareness should also not lead to fatalism about the effects of prejudices and biases. So Rawls basically says that it is sufficient for a "reasonable man" to counter his prejudices and biases as good as he can, and to continue from there – even if some effects of prejudice and bias remain. This prejudice and bias avoidance criterion strikes me as being very important – and as being very hard to fulfil. Although relatively simple means such as self-reflection and exposure might be good first steps towards less prejudice and bias (Monteith 1993, Monteith et al. 2002), many more demanding de-biasing methods have been empirically tested (for a general overview, see Brownstein 2017, subsection 4.2, for more details, see Lai, Hoffman, and Nosek 2013), none of which have (to my knowledge) been systematically used in moral epistemology. So if taken literally, Rawls' prejudice and bias avoidance criterion is rarely, if ever, fulfilled by moral philosophers.

Some of these doubts about the helpfulness of epistemic requirements such as the ones just discussed might even violate "ought implies can" in moral epistemology. However, they do not imply that the requirements formulated in reflective equilibrium violate the more flexible PRDP. After all, it is possible that moral philosophers take the efforts necessary to really be open for belief revision as well as those necessary to minimise the effects of prejudice and bias. That they do not reflect current – or historic – philosophical practice does not exclude the possibility of a future philosophical practice that actually follows Rawls' demands. From the point of view of Rawls' *Outline*, current philosophical practice is epistemically defective; but the procedure prescribed in *Outline* is generally possible for creatures like us.

3.3 Imagining Social Deliberation

However high Rawls' requirements for competent judges might be, being a competent judge and having singled out one's considered judgements is merely the first step in the procedure proposed in *Outline*. In its second part, the preselected judgements get rationalised by various means:

> once the class of considered judgments of competent judges has been selected, there remains to discover and formulate a satisfactory explication of the total range of these judgments. [...] Consider a group of competent judges making considered judgments in review of a set of cases which would be likely to arise in ordinary life. Then an explication of these judgments is defined to be a set of principles, such that, if any competent man were to apply them intelligently and consistently to the same cases under review, his judgments, made systematically nonintuitive by the explicit and conscious use of the principles, would be, nevertheless, identical, case by case, with the considered judgments of the group of competent judges (Rawls 1951, p. 184).

How these explications are meant to work in detail is very complicated (see Mikhail 2011, pp. 191 ff.). Here I want to focus on just one aspect of that form of rationalisation, namely on the social setting Rawls asks the reader to imagine: The reader is asked to imagine a social process in which one abstracts from hypothetical considered judgements of hypothetical competent judges. This arguably increases the aforementioned problems significantly. To fulfil the requirements set in *Outline*, any philosopher trying to reason about first-order moral theory and moral principles has to have immense imaginative capacities. It seems hard enough to pass the test of a competent judge and to determine one's own considered judgements. It is a totally different task to imagine how other competent judges would reason and what their considered judgements would be. I think it is fair to say that this is impossible for existing people as well as for creatures like us. It is one thing to ask for open-mindedness or to suggest perspective-taking, say, in order to increase epistemic value. But it is another matter to ask a person to imagine how others would think if they were open-minded and able to take different perspectives, especially when this is meant to extend to the process of refining and revising their initial moral convictions and background theories. It strikes me as being impossible to do this in a way that is epistemically valuable for my own second-order moral reasoning (which it is meant to be). I even feel unable to imagine a creature like us that could fulfil this Rawlsian task in an epistemically valuable way, because I would not even know what kind of ability this task would require.

So Rawls' requirement to imagine a social deliberation among a group of competent judges, as described in *Outline*, is not merely not helpful, it is impossible to fulfil for creatures like us and thus violates PRDP. Unlike the high demands on competent moral judges, the lack of the required imaginativeness does not point out a defect in current philosophical practice. It is because it violates PRDP that current practice is not defective in this respect (at least not for the reason that it does not live up to Rawls' demands). One might object that the imaginativeness requirement can be understood as a standard of rightness. I do not find this plausible because it is clearly introduced as part of the method of reflective equilibrium, not as part of the state of reflective equilibrium. But be this as it may, even if the requirement could be thus understood, this would support the PRDP. As demonstrated above for Flanagan's PMPR in the context of consequentialism, invoking the distinction between decision procedure and standard of rightness in moral epistemology is to implicitly acknowledge the PRDP.

I have spent much time and space on the procedure Rawls defended in *Outline*, because he was much more explicit in *Outline* than in the better-known reflective equilibrium. It is worth noting that the criteria for competent judges (including the imaginativeness requirement) I put so much emphasis on do not appear in reflective equilibrium as Rawls describes it in *A Theory of Justice* (2005, sections 4 and 9) and in *The Independence of Moral Theory* (1974). Due to the specific problems addressed in *A Theory of Justice*, some of the requirements for competent judges became elements of the "original position", especially of the idea of a "veil of ignorance" (Rawls 2005, pp. 118 ff.), which is explicitly not meant to work as a decision procedure but as a hypothetical ideal (for the specific role of reflective equilibrium in *A Theory of Justice*, see Hübner 2017). The imaginativeness required in *Outline* does not re-emerge here. Instead, Rawls talks in metaphorical terms about a hypothetical procedure in which different parties deliberate about conceptions of justice. This idea does make perfect sense as a moral epistemic ideal for it is clearly not meant to actually work in practice, nor are those who want to use reflective equilibrium meant to imagine the ideal working in practice.

4 Conclusion

In this chapter, I have argued that a principle of minimal psychological realism applies to moral epistemic decision procedures which are used to determine the proper contents of first-order morality. Building on Flanagan, I called it the Principle of Minimal Psychological Realism for Moral Epistemic Decision Procedures (PRDP): Make sure when constructing a moral epistemic decision procedure that the character and decision processing prescribed are possible, or are perceived to be possible, for creatures like us. I argued that proponents of Rawlsian reflective equilibrium implicitly endorse PRDP in moral epistemology. Applying PRDP to different elements of Rawls' moral epistemic decision procedure, I have argued that his requirements concerning considered judgements do not violate the PRDP. Things are more complicated when it comes to Rawls' epistemic requirements concerning competent judges. Some of them – particularly openness for belief revision and bias avoidance – are very demanding, maybe even impossible to fulfil for currently existing philosophers. So they might violate the ought-implies-can principle. However, they do not violate the more flexible PRDP. There is one requirement in Rawls that does violate PRDP though, namely the requirement to imagine a social deliberation among a group of competent judges as described in *Outline*. This requirement is impossible to fulfil for creatures like us and thus violates PRDP.

Note that, in this chapter, my focus is on the PRDP, which only applies to moral epistemic decision procedures. PRDP does not apply to epistemic ideals that are not meant to be actually carried out. E.g., when Rawls, in *A Theory of Justice*, talks in metaphorical terms about a hypothetical procedure in which different parties deliberate about conceptions of justice, this is clearly not meant to actually work in practice. The same seems to hold for Habermas' ideal discourse (Habermas 1983) and Dworkin's Herculean task to find the one right answer (Dworkin 1986, 2011, parts 1 and 2) as well as for many other rather idealistic theories in moral epistemology (on transcendental arguments as compared to reflective equilibrium, see de Maagt 2017). These are not moral epistemic decision procedures. However, if proponents of such moral epistemic views were to develop such decision procedures, PRDP would apply to these, or so I claim.

Acknowledgements

Thanks to Thomas Hurka and Christoph Lumer for helpful comments on earlier versions of this chapter.

Bibliography

Anderson, Elizabeth (2012): "Epistemic Justice as a Virtue of Social Institutions". In: *Social Epistemology* 26 (2), pp. 163–173.
Anderson, Elizabeth (2015): "Moral Bias and Corrective Practices. A Pragmatist Perspective". In: *Proceedings and Addresses of the American Philosophical Association* 89, pp. 21–47.
Appiah, Kwame (2009): *Experiments in Ethics*. Cambridge: Harvard University Press.
Batson, Daniel (2015): *What's Wrong with Morality? A Social-Psychological Perspective*. Oxford and New York: Oxford University Press.
Birnbacher, Dieter (2007): *Analytische Einführung in die Ethik*. Berlin: Walter de Gruyter.

Brink, David (1986): "Utilitarian Morality and the Personal Point of View". In: *Journal of Philosophy* 83 (8), pp. 417–438.
Brownstein, Michael (2017): "Implicit Bias". In: Zalta, Edward (ed.): *The Stanford Encyclopedia of Philosophy*.
https://plato.stanford.edu/archives/spr2017/entries/implicit-bias/, retrieved on November 14, 2018.
Brownstein, Michael (2018): *The Implicit Mind. Cognitive Architecture, the Self, and Ethics*. New York: Oxford University Press.
Brownstein, Michael and Saul, Jennifer (eds.) (2016a): *Implicit Bias and Philosophy. Vol. 1. Metaphysics and Epistemology*. Oxford and New York: Oxford University Press.
Brownstein, Michael and Saul, Jennifer (eds.) (2016b): *Implicit Bias and Philosophy. Vol. 2. Moral Responsibility, Structural Injustice, and Ethics*. Oxford and New York: Oxford University Press.
Buchanan, Allen and Powell, Russell (2018): *The Evolution of Moral Progress. A Biocultural Theory*. Oxford and New York: Oxford University Press.
Cath, Yuri (2016): "Reflective Equilibrium". In: Cappelen, Herman; Gendler, Tamar Szabo, and Hawthorne, John (eds.): *The Oxford Handbook of Philosophical Methodology*. Oxford and New York: Oxford University Press, pp. 213–230.
Daniels, Norman (1979): "Wide Reflective Equilibrium and Theory Acceptance in Ethics". In: *Journal of Philosophy* 76 (5), pp. 256–282.
de Maagt, Sem (2017): "Reflective Equilibrium and Moral Objectivity". In: *Inquiry* 60 (5), pp. 443–465.
Driver, Julia (2012): *Consequentialism*. New York: Routledge.
Dworkin, Ronald (1986): *Law's Empire*. Cambridge: Harvard University Press.
Dworkin, Ronald (2011): *Justice for Hedgehogs*. Cambridge: Harvard University Press.
Enoch, David (2018): "Against Utopianism. Noncompliance and Multiple Agents". In: *Philosopher's Imprint* 18 (16), pp. 1–20.
Erman, Eva and Möller, Niklas (2015): "Practices and Principles. On the Methodological Turn in Political Theory". In: *Philosophy Compass* 10 (8), pp. 533–546.
Estlund, David (2011): "Human Nature and the Limits (If Any) of Political Philosophy". In: *Philosophy & Public Affairs* 39 (3), pp. 207–237.
Estlund, David (2014): "Utopophobia". In: *Philosophy & Public Affairs* 42 (2), pp. 113–134.
Fantl, Jeremy (2018): *The Limitations of the Open Mind*. Oxford and New York: Oxford University Press.
Flanagan, Owen (1991): *Varieties of Moral Personality*. Cambridge: Harvard University Press.
Flanagan, Owen (2016): *The Geography of Morals. Varieties of Moral Possibility*. Oxford and New York: Oxford University Press.
Fricker, Miranda (2007): *Epistemic Injustice. Power and the Ethics of Knowing*. Oxford and New York: Oxford University Press.
Greenspan, Patricia (2015): "Confabulating the Truth. In Defense of 'Defensive' Moral Reasoning". In: *Journal of Ethics* 19 (2), pp. 105–123.
Griffin, James (1992): "The Human Good and the Ambitions of Consequentialism". In: *Social Philosophy and Policy* 9 (2), pp. 118–132.
Habermas, Jürgen (1983): "Diskursethik. Notizen zu einem Begründungsprogramm". In: id.: *Moralbewußtsein und kommunikatives Handeln*. Frankfurt am Main: Suhrkamp, pp. 53–125.

Hauser, Marc; Young, Liane, and Cushman, Fiery (2008): "Reviving Rawls' Linguistic Analogy. Operative Principles and the Causal Structure of Moral Actions". In: Sinnott-Armstrong, Walter (ed.): *Moral Psychology. The Neuroscience of Morality.* Vol. 2. Cambridge: MIT Press, pp. 107–143.

Hooker, Brad (2001): *Ideal Code, Real World. A Rule-Consequentialist Theory of Morality.* Oxford and New York: Clarendon Press.

Hübner, Dietmar (2017): "Three Remarks on 'Reflective Equilibrium'". In: *Philosophical Inquiry* 41 (1), pp. 11–40.

Kagan, Shelly (1984): "Does Consequentialism Demand Too Much? Recent Work on the Limits of Obligation". In: *Philosophy and Public Affairs* 13 (3), pp. 239–254.

Kahane, Guy (2016): "Is, Ought, and the Brain". In: Liao, Matthew (ed.): *Moral Brains. The Neuroscience of Morality.* Oxford and New York: Oxford University Press, pp. 281–311.

Kahneman, Daniel (2012): *Thinking, Fast and Slow.* London: Penguin.

Lai, Calvin; Hoffman, Kelly, and Nosek, Brian (2013): "Reducing Implicit Prejudice". In: *Social and Personality Psychology Compass* 7 (5), pp. 315–330.

Lilienfeld, Scott; Ritschel, Lorie; Lynn, Steven Jay; Cautin, Robin, and Latzman, Robert (2014): "Why Ineffective Psychotherapies Appear to Work. A Taxonomy of Causes of Spurious Therapeutic Effectiveness". In: *Perspectives on Psychological Science* 9 (4), pp. 355–387.

Mackie, John (1977): *Ethics. Inventing Right and Wrong.* Harmondsworth: Penguin.

Mercier, Hugo and Sperber, Dan (2011): "Why Do Humans Reason? Arguments for an Argumentative Theory". In: *The Behavioral and Brain Sciences* 34 (2), pp. 57–74.

Mercier, Hugo and Sperber, Dan (2017): *The Enigma of Reason. A New Theory of Human Understanding.* Cambridge: Allen Lane.

Mikhail, John (2011): *Elements of Moral Cognition.* Cambridge: Cambridge University Press.

Monteith, Margo (1993): "Self-Regulation of Prejudiced Responses. Implications for Progress in Prejudice-Reduction Efforts". In: *Journal of Personality and Social Psychology* 65 (3), pp. 469–485.

Monteith, Margo; Ashburn-Nardo, Leslie; Voils, Corrine, and Czopp, Alexander (2002): "Putting the Brakes on Prejudice. On the Development and Operation of Cues for Control". In: *Journal of Personality and Social Psychology* 83 (5), pp. 1029–1050.

Paulo, Norbert (2016): *The Confluence of Philosophy and Law in Applied Ethics.* Basingstoke: Palgrave Macmillan.

Paulo, Norbert (2018): "Moral-Epistemic Enhancement". In: Hauskeller, Michael and Coyne, Lewis (eds.): *Moral Enhancement. Critical Perspectives.* Cambridge: Cambridge University Press, pp. 165–188.

Paulo, Norbert and Bublitz, Jan Christoph (2017): "How (Not) to Argue for Moral Enhancement. Reflections on a Decade of Debate". In: *Topoi* 38 (1), 95–109.

Pollan, Michael (2018): *How to Change Your Mind. What the New Science of Psychedelics Teaches Us About Consciousness, Dying, Addiction, Depression, and Transcendence.* New York: Penguin.

Rawls, John (1951): "Outline of a Decision Procedure for Ethics". In: *Philosophical Review* 60 (2), pp. 177–197.

Rawls, John (1974): "The Independence of Moral Theory". In: *Proceedings and Addresses of the American Philosophical Association* 48, pp. 5–22.

Rawls, John (2005): *A Theory of Justice.* Cambridge: Belknap Press.

Rini, Regina (2014): "Psychology and the Aims of Normative Ethics". In: Clausen, Jens and Levy, Neil (eds.): *Springer Handbook of Neuroethics*. Dordrecht: Springer, pp. 149–168.

Savulescu, Julian and Bostrom, Nick (eds.) (2009): *Human Enhancement*. Oxford and New York: Oxford University Press.

Sayre-McCord, Geoffrey (1996): "Coherentist Epistemology and Moral Theory". In: Sinnott-Armstrong, Walter and Timmons, Mark (eds.): *Moral Knowledge? New Readings in Moral Epistemology*. New York: Oxford University Press, pp. 137–189.

Schaefer, Owen and Savulescu, Julian (2016): "Procedural Moral Enhancement". In: *Neuroethics* 12 (1), pp. 73–84.

Schermuly-Haupt, Marie-Luise; Linden, Michael, and Rush, John (2018): "Unwanted Events and Side Effects in Cognitive Behavior Therapy". In: *Cognitive Therapy and Research* 42 (3), pp. 219–229.

Schmidt, Thomas (2011): "Evolutionäre Erklärungen von Moral und die Autonomie der Ethik". In: Tarkian, Tatjana and Schmidt, Thomas (eds.): *Naturalismus in der Ethik. Perspektiven und Grenzen*. Paderborn: Mentis, pp. 87–107.

Sinnott-Armstrong, Walter (2015): "Consequentialism". In: Zalta, Edward (ed.): *The Stanford Encyclopedia of Philosophy*. https://plato.stanford.edu/archives/win2015/entries/consequentialism/, retrieved on November 14, 2018.

Skitka, Linda (2010): "The Psychology of Moral Conviction". In: *Social and Personality Psychology Compass* 4 (4), pp. 267–281.

Tersman, Folke (2018): "Recent Work on Reflective Equilibrium and Method in Ethics". In: *Philosophy Compass* 13 (6), e12493.

van Thiel, Ghislaine and van Delden, Hans (2009): "The Justificatory Power of Moral Experience". In: *Journal of Medical Ethics* 35 (4), pp. 234–237.

Williams, Bernard (1973): "A Critique of Utilitarianism". In: Smart, John and Williams, Bernard (eds.): *Utilitarianism. For and Against*. Cambridge: Cambridge University Press, pp. 77–150.

Wong, David (2006): *Natural Moralities. A Defense of Pluralistic Relativism*. Oxford: Oxford University Press.

Stephen J. Sullivan
Moral Epistemology Naturalised
Theory Justification in Ethics and Science

Abstract: In this chapter the "methodological naturalist" thesis that the justification of normative ethical theories employs roughly the same empirical method as the justification of scientific theories will be presented. More precisely, the author argues that ethical inquiry into the nature of moral properties such as rightness and wrongness, goodness and badness closely parallels scientific inquiry into the nature of the natural kinds studied in the natural sciences. A corollary is that ethical theories can be subjected to observational testing in much the same way as their scientific counterparts. Also, the limits of this parallel and some objections to the thesis are addressed.

1 Introduction

Moral beliefs are very often contrasted unfavourably with scientific beliefs with respect to empirical justifiability. Indeed, most philosophers and scientists may regard it as almost a truism that moral beliefs are incapable of empirical justification. But the philosophical field of metaethics (which consists roughly of moral epistemology and moral semantics) does include an empirical or "naturalistic" approach to the question of moral knowledge and justified moral belief according to which scientific and moral epistemology have much more in common than is generally believed.[1] On one version of this approach, some moral beliefs are indeed justifiable by means of the same empirical method by which many scientific beliefs are justifiable. That, at any rate, is a first approximation of the "methodological naturalist" view that I wish to defend.

Though probably never a popular view in philosophy, methodological naturalism – sometimes known as epistemic naturalism (Lutz and Lenman 2018) – has had some distinguished proponents, including John Dewey and arguably Aristotle, David Hume, William Kingdon Clifford, and Moritz Schlick. Important contemporary defenders include Sturgeon (1984, 2006), Miller (1992), Boyd (1988, 1995), Railton (1989, 2003), and Brink (1989). But the accounts that meth-

---

[1] The same goes for the semantics of scientific and moral discourse, a parallel to which I shall briefly be returning when I touch on the causal theory of reference in sections 1 and 2.

odological naturalists have given of the parallel between ethics and science are in general not detailed enough to persuade many philosophers that the parallel sheds much light on the justification of ethical theories. Moreover, in current metaethical discussions, methodological naturalism is closely linked to the debate over moral realism: roughly the view that there are objective moral facts about which we have some knowledge or justified moral belief. Current naturalists are typically concerned to defend realism against critics, such as John Leslie Mackie (1978, pp. 38f.), who argue that if there were objective moral facts, we would have no way of knowing them. My aim is to provide an account of the methodological parallel between ethics and science that is both detailed enough to be illuminating and (though I am a moral realist myself) clearly open to acceptance by anti-realists who both believe that moral judgements have truth values and deny that there are objective moral facts.[2]

Let me begin by formulating somewhat more precisely the version of methodological naturalism I want to defend. On this view, ethical inquiry into the nature of rightness and wrongness, goodness and badness, justice and injustice, and so on closely parallels scientific inquiry into the nature of the "natural kinds" studied in the natural sciences (and for that matter the social and psychological kinds studied in the social sciences). In particular, (non-moral) observation, inductive generalisation, explanation, and even intuition play essentially the same methodological or justificatory roles in these two forms of inquiry. (The grounds for this bold claim will be explained in section 2.) It is in this sense, I believe that the justification of normative ethical theories proceeds by the same empirical method as the justification of scientific ones.[3] A corollary is that ethical theories can be subjected to observational testing in much the same way as can their scientific counterparts.

To clarify and support these claims I will focus in section 2 on one specific scientific theory, the well-known and generally accepted H_2O theory of water,

---

[2] The account may be of interest even to noncognitivist anti-realists who reject this belief, holding as they do that the primary use of moral language is not to state facts but to express feelings, attitudes, or practical commitments. For a standard argument for noncognitivism starts from the premise that moral judgments are neither verifiable nor falsifiable (especially not empirically); and the thesis I defend contradicts that premise.

[3] My conflation of methodology and justification may initially be troubling, but in this chapter, I am talking about *methods of justification* rather than methods of discovery. As a metaethical aside especially for philosophers, let me note, too, that in ethics the method I describe is meant to be an empirical or "naturalistic" reconstruction of John Rawls' (1971) famous method of "wide reflective equilibrium". On the distinction between wide and narrow reflective equilibrium, see especially Daniels (1979). On the possibility of naturalising wide equilibrium, see Boyd (1988, pp. 185, 199–202, 206–209). Finally, see note 9, below.

and will consider the roles that observation, inductive generalisation, explanation, and intuition play in the justification of this theory. In section 3 I turn to a sample of normative ethical theories and argue that their evaluation likewise depends on these factors. In section 4 I return to the question of observational testing in ethics, emphasising the methodological point – quite familiar in the philosophy of science but virtually unnoticed until fairly recently in moral philosophy – that a theory is tested not in isolation but only in conjunction with auxiliary assumptions or hypotheses. In section 5 I acknowledge the limitations of the H_2O analogy and answer other problems and questions for my account. Finally, I will offer some brief concluding reflections in section 6.[4]

2 Theory Justification in Science

Let me begin by using the example of water to draw a distinction between *folk* and *deep* theories. Our folk theory of water is roughly our common-sense conception of it, a conception that describes the characteristics by which we ordinarily identify it (e.g., its being a clear, thirst-quenching fluid). A deep theory of water attempts to improve on the folk theory by specifying the "hidden nature" of the stuff: namely, characteristics of water (if any) that are essential to it but nevertheless are overlooked in the folk theory. The H_2O theory is, of course, a deep theory of water.

How is a deep theory such as the H_2O theory justified? The answer, I think, is that it meets – better, overall, than do alternative accounts – certain constraints we at least implicitly impose on theories when we assess their acceptability as accounts of the nature of a given kind.[5]

In the first place, samples of the stuff that the H_2O theory classifies as water are at least typically or frequently classified likewise by the folk theory. Furthermore, this substantial classificatory *overlap* is hardly coincidental: The characteristics by which the folk theory identifies water are non-accidentally correlated

---

[4] A fuller discussion of most of the issues raised in this chapter may be found in my Cornell University doctoral dissertation, *Moral Realism and Naturalized Metaethics* (Sullivan 1990).

[5] I will not try to argue for these constraints here. They can be given plausible rationales by means of the causal theory of reference (see note 6) and various accounts of ontological reduction, norm justification, scientific-hypothesis assessment, and objectivity. See Sullivan (1990, chapter 2 and 3); Boyd (1995, pp. 347–353) contains some useful though dense discussion of reduction in science and ethics. Also relevant are Willard Van Orman Quine's scientific extension of Rudolf Carnap's important notion of explication in Quine (1960, pp. 257–266), and Richard Brandt's related method of reforming definition (most helpfully discussed in Sturgeon 1982).

with – and hence *reliable* indicators of – the presence of H_2O molecules. Given such substantial, non-accidental overlap, the H_2O theory helps to explain how we could, in using the term "water", have all along been good detectors of H_2O – how we could actually have been referring to H_2O even before we came to accept the theory.[6] Thus we have some assurance that the H_2O and folk theories of "water" are indeed *referentially continuous* theories, i.e., accounts of the nature of the same stuff. In the second place, the H_2O theory offers additional explanatory gains or bonuses. It explains why the stuff classified as water by the folk theory has certain characteristics: both some of the observable features by which the folk theory identifies it, such as liquidity at moderate temperatures, and less obvious features, such as its ways of interacting with other substances. In the third place, the H_2O theory is neither *incompatible* with nor implausible in the light of relevant, well-supported background beliefs, such as the atomic theory of matter.

Note that it could (epistemologically speaking) have turned out that water had no "hidden nature", and that the best account of its nature was the folk theory itself. According to Hilary Putnam (1982, p. 241), certain diseases are in fact like this: after scientific investigation, it is discovered that there is nothing more to them than a cluster of unhidden "symptoms" with a diversity of causes.[7] But of course, we cannot assume in advance that this will be so concerning any particular natural kind.

Now observation, inductive generalisation, and explanation figure fairly straightforwardly in the foregoing treatment of the justification of the H_2O theory. Observation plays its most obvious role in giving us knowledge of what the folk theory says are samples or characteristics of water, and knowledge of the correlation between those instances and H_2O molecules. And it is partly through observation, too, that we learn about the less obvious characteristics which the H_2O theory helps to explain, and that the relevant background beliefs gain acceptance. Inductive generalisation plays its most obvious role when we move from ob-

---

[6] A specific theory of reference underlies this statement: the "epistemic access" version of the causal theory of reference. It is implicit in the writings of Hilary Putnam (1982) in his realist phase, among others, but is most clearly and fully worked out by Richard Boyd (1979). I explore, motivate, and elaborate this account of natural-kind term reference in Sullivan (1990, subsection 2.1), and apply it to ethical terms in Sullivan (1990, subsection 2.2). Perhaps this is the place to mention Mark Timmons' and Terry Horgan's important critique of what they call "new wave moral realist" efforts to apply the causal theory of reference to ethical terms. The main source here is Timmons' (1999) book *Morality Without Foundations*. The Timmons and Horgan challenge has received many responses; I am working out one of my own in a paper in progress called *Moral Twin Earth Revisited*.

[7] In Sullivan (1994) I explore a comparable possibility in relation to the divine command theory of morality.

served to unobserved samples of what the folk theory tells us is water: When, e.g., we infer a general tendency to interact in certain ways with other substances and a general correlation with H_2O molecules. Explanation figures prominently in a number of ways. First, I use the H_2O theory to explain our successful use of the term "water" to refer. Second, I explain the correlation with H_2O molecules as non-accidental or law-like rather than coincidental. Third, I explain this non-accidentalness itself in terms of the identity of water and H_2O. Finally, I use the H_2O theory to explain additional facts about the substance that the folk theory says is water.

What I have left entirely unclear so far is the role that intuition has to play. To understand this role we must consider again the folk theory of water with which scientific inquiry into the nature of the stuff began – a theory without which scientists would have been unable to identify samples of water to investigate in the first place.

Presumably, the folk theory of water goes something like this: Water is a clear, thirst-quenching liquid (at moderate temperatures) which falls from the clouds, is found in rivers, lakes, and so forth. If scientists had needed to justify this common-sense conception at the outset of their inquiry into the nature of water, they could only have appealed to widely accepted, *intuitive* judgements about water – judgements captured and systematised by the folk theory. (We do something similar even nowadays in talking to young children or non-native speakers.) To be sure, if the folk theory were *analytically* true – true a priori and solely in virtue of the meaning of the term "water" – then we could think of these judgements as purely linguistic or semantic (and perhaps stop talking of a folk theory). But Putnam (1982), Kripke (1980), Devitt (1981), and other causal or historical theorists of reference have argued persuasively that natural-kind terms lack analytic definitions.[8] The upshot is that substantive "intuitions" or common-sense judgements play an important, though much-neglected role in the justification of scientific theories of the nature of particular natural kinds.

3 Theory Justification in Ethics

Now there are folk (or common-sense) and deep theories of morality, too. To be sure, many normative ethical theorists are content with folk-theoretical or com-

---

[8] And note that dictionaries commonly go beyond analytic definitions of natural-kind terms when doing more than just giving brief synonyms; they provide empirical information about the relevant kinds.

mon-sense accounts of right and wrong, good and bad, and so forth – accounts that are supposed to capture widely shared moral intuitions or considered moral judgements.[9] The pluralistic deontological theory of William David Ross (1930, chapter 2) is a classic example. But other philosophers take more seriously the possibility that significant *revisions* of moral common sense may be necessary – in my parlance, that deep ethical theories may be superior. In this section, I want to consider several such theories.

Let's start with act utilitarianism, a theory often criticised for its "counterintuitive" implications or departures from common-sense morality. What might justify the act-utilitarian account of morality in terms of the promotion of the general happiness? Its defenders can argue that this account meets – better than its rivals – the same constraints we considered in connection with the H_2O theory. Indeed, some utilitarian arguments can be reconstructed in just this way.[10]

Take the "continuity constraint", with its overlap and reliability requirements. Act utilitarians often emphasise that obeying common-sense moral rules is typically or frequently the most effective way to promote the general happiness; in their view, the theory coincides significantly in its concrete moral implications with our folk theory (or theories) of rightness (Sidgwick 1963, pp. 85 ff., 423–426, 457, 461–468, 475 f., 493–497). And many act utilitarians likewise maintain that this correlation between the maximisation of the general happiness (for short: optimificity) and common-sense rightness is no accident, and that the happiness-promoting tendencies of common-sense moral rules help to explain our successful use of moral terms to refer. The appeal here – seldom made explicit – is to a "functionalist" account of popular moralities according to which they arise, persist, and change at least partly because of their effects on human happiness (Sidgwick 1963, pp. 455 ff., 465, 481, Toulmin 1986, chapter 10, Railton 2003, chapter 1).[11] And the law-like correlation itself is of course explained by identifying rightness with optimificity.

Consider, next, the "bonus constraint". Two additional explanatory gains might be these. First, it is arguably a feature of moral common sense that serious social injustice has the power to generate social unrest, movements for reform,

---

9 In Rawlsian terms, they are using the method of *narrow* reflective equilibrium; see Sullivan (1990, especially subsection 2.22).
10 In general, I intend my account of justification in ethics to be a rational reconstruction of our actual *practice* of normative ethical and metaethical debate, and thus to be plausible as a *description* of that practice.
11 There may be traces of the same line of thought in Hume (2000, pp. 319 ff., 335 ff., 339 f., 354 ff., 364 ff., and especially 369 f., 394), Sidgwick (1963, pp. 455 ff., 465, 481), Mill (1979, chapters 2 and 5), MacBeath (1952), Hare (1981, e.g., pp. 188, 202, 208, 211).

even revolution (Railton 2003, pp. 23 f.). And act utilitarians can and do explain this power by pointing out that it is just what we would expect if serious, lasting social injustice is understood in utilitarian terms as involving the unhappiness of large numbers of people (Mill 1979, chapter 5, Railton 2003, chapter 1, Brink 1989, pp. 245 f.). Second, they can and sometimes do explain standard examples of moral progress – such as changing social attitudes toward slavery, torture, cruelty to animals, and treatment of minorities (racial, religious, and sexual) and women – in terms of increasing appreciation of utilitarian considerations, brought about in part by enlargements of sympathy and by corrections of mistaken non-moral beliefs (Mill 1979, chapter 5, Sidgwick 1963, pp. 455 ff., 464, Hobhouse 1951, Singer 2011).

Of course, if act utilitarianism is defended in these ways – i.e., by means of its supposed superiority in fulfilling the first two constraints – then it will also need to meet the "compatibility constraint" as well. If, e.g., well-supported background beliefs give us good reason to deny that there is a law-like correlation (or any strong correlation at all) between common-sense rightness and optimificity, or that something like sociological functionalism concerning popular moralities is true, then the act-utilitarian case will be in grave jeopardy. And notice how *empirical* these issues are.

I will be somewhat briefer in my treatment of the other two "deep" ethical theories I promised to consider. A more thorough discussion would also extend my methodological-naturalist account to cover a variety of other ethical theories.[12]

The divine command theory is a second important theory of morality that has been thought to have counterintuitive implications, but that can be – and in effect has been – defended as meeting my three constraints. In Robert Adams' formulation of the theory, rightness and wrongness consist respectively in agreement and disagreement with the commands of a loving God. Adams (1979, p. 76) emphasises that intuitively or commonsensically wrong actions typically violate the commands of the loving God in whom he believes, and that this is no accident "in so far as God has created our moral faculties to reflect his commands". He explains this law-like correlation by identifying wrongness with the property of being contrary to the commands of a loving God (Adams 1979, especially pp. 74–77). Other divine command theorists have claimed an explanatory

---

[12] In Sullivan (1990, subsection 3.25), I briefly discuss the ideal-observer theory and the Kantian principle of respect for persons; and in *Moral Twin Earth Revisited* (see note 6) I apply my account to ethical egoism and Marxist social-class relativism. Boyd (1995, pp. 354 f.) includes some related points about the latter two theories. I think my account may also fit some forms of contractarianism, natural-law ethics, and rule utilitarianism, among other ethical theories.

bonus: Only their theory can explain how morality – right and wrong, good and bad, and so forth – can coexist with the all-powerful, absolutely sovereign creator of the universe (Idziak 1989). Of course, all these arguments are subject to the compatibility constraint; if, e.g., we have good reason to doubt the existence of an all-powerful God then the foregoing case for the divine command theory obviously will not get off the ground. And most standard arguments for atheism – e.g., the argument from evil – are clearly empirical.[13]

To round out our small but diverse sample of deep ethical theories, I will take a quick look at conventionalist relativism. Relativists of this kind stress that our intuitive moral convictions tend to coincide with those that prevail within our own culture or social group, and that this is, of course, no accident: in the process of socialisation or enculturation we get these convictions from that culture or social group. And they explain this correlation by identifying the moral rightness of an action with conformity to the dominant moral values of the relevant culture.[14] Typically they argue as well that relativism is the ethical theory most capable of helping to explain the cross-cultural diversity of moral beliefs (e.g., Harman 1994 contrast Drebushenko and Sullivan 1998). The operation of the three constraints in these arguments should be clear.

My discussion of act utilitarianism, the divine command theory, and relativism is intended to support the claim that observation, induction, explanation, and intuition play the same methodological roles in ethical inquiry into the nature of right and wrong, good and bad, and so forth, as they do in scientific inquiry into the nature of natural kinds such as water. I will take a closer look at these four methodological components one at a time.

(a) Observation: We observe what the folk theory says are morally right actions (perhaps ordinary cases of promise-keeping, for instance). Partly through observation, we learn about further features of these particular actions, such as their success or failure in promoting the general happiness, or in conforming to divine commands, or in following the prevailing moral beliefs of the relevant culture. And we make use of background beliefs, such as sociological functionalism, Judeo-Christian theism, or the anthropological thesis of cross-cultural diversity, that are themselves based in part on observation.

---

[13] It might seem question-begging to suppose that the premise that there is evil is empirical. But in fact, that premise is typically based on clearly empirical grounds, such as that innocent people *suffer*.

[14] Perhaps something like this is what Edward Westermarck (1960, pp. 262f.) is getting at, though he seems to defend an individualist relativism according to which your action is right if and only if you are following your own ethical values.

(b) Induction: We generalise about these further features or facts, moving from observed to unobserved cases of commonsensically right action in order to establish a general correlation between common-sense rightness and utilitarian, divine command, or relativist rightness.
(c) Explanation: We explain the general correlation by appeal to some mechanism or law that makes it non-accidental; and we explain this non-accidentalness by appeal to the identity between rightness and optimificity, or conformity to divine commands, or consistency with culturally dominant moral values. We thereby account for our successful use of "morally right" to refer. Finally, we give a utilitarian, divine command, or relativist explanation of other facts.
(d) Intuition: We rely on widely shared, "intuitive" moral judgements or common-sense moral convictions in formulating and utilising the folk theory of rightness.

4 Observational Testing in Ethics

In recent years a number of moral philosophers have noted the metaethical relevance of a widely accepted thesis (originating with Pierre Duhem and revived by Willard Van Orman Quine) in the philosophy of science. In Nicholas Sturgeon's words:

> [I]t is by now a familiar point about scientific principles [...] that they are entirely devoid of [observational] implications when considered in isolation. We do of course base observational predictions on such theories and so test then against experience, but that is because we do *not* consider them in isolation. For we can derive these predictions only by relying at the same time on a large background of additional assumptions, many of which are equally theoretical and equally incapable of being tested in isolation (Sturgeon 1984, p. 51, following Duhem 1952, chapter 6, Quine 1963, chapter 2).

And Sturgeon and David Collingridge have pointed out – followed by many others – that it is easy to derive observational consequences from ethical principles when they are conjoined to other principles or judgements (Sturgeon 1984, pp. 51f., Collingridge 1984, p. 235).

One of Sturgeon's examples is especially useful for my purposes. Take the act-utilitarian principle that an action is wrong if and only if it fails to maximise the general happiness; and conjoin it to the auxiliary assumption that it is always wrong to kill an innocent person deliberately. Clearly, we can deduce the general prediction or observational consequence that deliberately killing an innocent person always fails to maximise the general happiness. If we have sufficient confidence in our auxiliary assumption, we can treat the verification or falsification of this prediction as an empirical test of the utilitarian principle of wrongness (Sturgeon 1984, p. 51).[15]

Now in my methodological-naturalist account of theory justification in ethics, this example illustrates the following point: To try to meet the *overlap* requirement of the continuity constraint is in effect to subject a deep ethical theory to empirical testing by conjoining it with (components of) the common-sense theory and deducing observational consequences from them. Much normative-ethical debate can be reconstructed in precisely this way. We appeal to what we take to be an intuitively or commonsensically compelling moral principle or judgement, i.e., to what seems to be a central component or important application of our common-sense theory of morality. Then we criticise a proponent of a deep theory – such as utilitarianism, the divine command theory, or relativism – on the ground that its conjunction with that common-sense principle or judgement has false or improbable observational consequences.

Thus, to take a different example, Michael Slote (1977, p. 745) invokes his allegedly commonsensical "principle of morality and ignorance", according to which a principle of moral obligation is valid "only if it is [psychologically] possible for people to be committed to it as one of their basic principles of moral obligation without that commitment being due to [...] their being ignorant [...] of various [non-moral] facts". And he would have us use his principle to test theories of obligation empirically (Slote 1977, especially pp. 745, 764). We can do so only by conjoining it to such a theory and deducing the prediction that human beings have the psychological capacity to be committed to living up to the theory while remaining free of the ignorance in question.

The *reliability* requirement of the continuity constraint figures in a second way in which my account incorporates the Duhemian thesis. A deep theorist's attempt to meet this requirement will typically require specifying the causal mechanism(s) in virtue of which her deep theory, she claims, overlaps non-accidentally as well substantially with common-sense morality. In particular, as we have seen, the functionalist utilitarian points to the social function of common-sense moral codes in promoting social harmony and thereby human happiness; the divine command theorist may appeal to God's design of a properly working human conscience; and the relativist invokes the genesis of common-sense moral convictions in processes of socialisation. Now the postulation of such a mechanism allows us to use the deep theory to generate predictions about the

---

[15] Nick Zangwill (2008) offers a clever challenge to Sturgeon's position. I hope to work out a rebuttal in the near future.

social evolution of common-sense moral beliefs. E.g., functionalist utilitarianism, as Peter Railton (2003, p. 24) points out, leads us to expect certain patterns or tendencies in that evolution: broadly speaking, pressures from subordinated groups "to push the resolution of conflict further in the direction" of "giving fuller weight to [their] interests". But of course act utilitarianism by itself implies no such predictions; it does so only in conjunction with sociological functionalism and no doubt other (equally empirical) auxiliary assumptions.

Finally, the *bonus* constraint provides a third way that my account can utilise the Duhemian thesis, as an example from section 2 illustrates. Recall the common-sense view that serious, enduring social injustice causes social unrest and reformist or revolutionary movements. Now conjoin that view with the utilitarian principle that such social injustice consists in the unhappiness of a substantial portion of society with the way they are treated. We can then deduce the prediction that when large numbers of people are unhappy with the way their society treats them they will (other things being equal) contribute to social unrest and support movements for social change. This conclusion is arguably both independently plausible and well-confirmed.

5 Problems and Questions

5.1 Some Limitations to the H₂O Analogy

5.1.1 Error Accommodation

The folk and deep theories of water apparently agree completely about which actual samples are water samples (concerns about purity aside). In other words, the H₂O theory seems to supplement without genuinely revising common sense. But deep theories in ethics typically agree only in part – albeit significantly – with moral common sense, and thus are truly revisionist.

This may indeed be a real disanalogy; but if so, it is an artefact of my (no doubt debatable) choice of the H₂O theory, not an inherent defect in my comparison of scientific and ethical theories. Many other scientific theories of the nature of particular natural kinds are genuinely revisionist. E.g., the Au chemical theory of gold tells us that gold is a white rather than a yellow metal (the apparent yellowness of familiar samples being due to impurities).[16] What the disanalogy does suggest is that my account needs to include an *accommodation* constraint:

---

[16] I borrow this example from Kripke (1980, pp. 119, 124, 157).

A deep theory in ethics should help to explain or "accommodate" any *errors* it attributes to moral common sense, just as the chemical theory of gold does for our folk theory of gold.[17] And it is striking that ethical theorists – especially utilitarians – frequently do offer such explanations (MacBeath 1952, pp. 377f., Sidgwick 1963, pp. 455f., 464f., Mill 1979, chapters 2 and 5, Ross 1939, p. 69, Harman 1979, pp. 155f.).

5.1.2 Intuition in Ethics Versus Intuition in Science

"Intuition" probably does play a more prominent role in ethics than it does in science. In ethics it is usually less obvious – and often far less obvious – what the relevant folk theories are, with the result that much (perhaps most) normative-ethical debate is conducted at or near the level of common sense. Such debate consists primarily in appeals to intuitions about real or hypothetical cases – intuitions that are believed or hoped to be widely shared. It thus amounts either to argument about the contents of folk theories in ethics or to argument about the ability of a given deep theory to meet the overlap requirement. In natural science, by contrast, the contents of the relevant folk theories are typically pretty clear from the start, so that they may be taken for granted and the common-sense level virtually ignored (Sullivan 1990, pp. 150ff.).

I think this disanalogy is genuine, but I do not see why it ruins the methodological parallel I have drawn between ethics and science. What it may indicate is that normative ethical theorising, unlike, e.g., chemistry, is not a *science* – a conclusion with which very few moral philosophers, naturalists or not, are likely to disagree.[18]

5.1.3 Cultural Variability

Common-sense conceptions of water do not seem to differ significantly across culture. But is not moral common sense culturally variable, so that different cultures accept different folk theories of, e.g., moral rightness?

---

[17] Paul Thagard (1982, especially p. 38) makes a similar point in the philosophy of science, and I borrow the term "accommodation" from him. I prefer to treat this accommodation constraint not as a separate constraint but as a requirement of the continuity constraint; see Sullivan (1990, subsections 3.23 and 3.24).

[18] This point about pre-scientific status is developed a little further in subsection 5.1.4, below.

I do not know whether common sense about water is culturally invariant at the present time; but suppose for the sake of argument that it is, and that the same holds true of other natural kinds. I concede that moral common sense does appear to be culturally variable, especially if we do not look too hard for shared, underlying principles or values. But the naturalist who accepts my account has no reason to panic, I think, in the face of this apparent disanalogy.

For one thing, it is worth noting that even folk theories of specific natural kinds are not without a form of cultural variability: they differ across time. E.g., water was once widely believed in Western culture to be an element; this is no longer the case (Railton 1989, p. 157).

For another thing, and more importantly, several normative-ethical options are open to the methodological naturalist who concedes the disanalogy. Conventionalist relativism is, of course, a serious option in my account: perhaps moral truth is subjective and relative to culture, as truth in etiquette and fashion seems to be. Even a realist relativism is possible here: there might turn out to be different but still objective *kinds* of moral rightness, as there are different kinds of jade and as there may be different kinds of physical mass.[19] Finally, ethical universalism (sometimes called absolutism) remains an option: even radical cross-cultural diversity in common-sense morals may be reconcilable with a *uniquely correct* morality. For there may be substantial underlying moral agreement, and a well-developed *error theory* – a theory of *distorting factors* – may plausibly account for all or most of the residual disagreement.[20]

5.1.4 Possible Misconceptions About the H_2O Analogy

The analogy might be thought to have the following implications, though I do *not* intend them: (1) moral rightness, wrongness, and so forth are *observable*; (2) folk theories in ethics must be accurately expressible in general *principles* rather than

---

[19] On jade, see Putnam (1982, p. 241); on mass, see Field (1973); on the possibility of a realist relativism in ethics, see, e.g., Tolhurst (1986), Boyd (1988, pp. 224ff., 1995, pp. 352ff.).
[20] In reply to the relativist argument from moral diversity, universalists have often stressed not only the possibility of underlying moral agreement but also the operation of distorting factors such as self-interest, ideology, and religion that help to explain the errors that universalism ascribes to some individuals and cultures; see, e.g., Johnson (1986, especially p. 131), Gilbert (1986, especially p. 131), Boyd (1988, pp. 219–222, who speaks explicitly of the need for an error theory), Brink (1989, pp. 202–209). Some have noted, too, the usefulness of the causal theory of reference in rebuttals of arguments from diversity; see, e.g., Gilbert (1984, p. 177), Boyd (1988, pp. 199, 210f., 213), Sullivan (1990, subsection 4.3).

in terms of prototypes (also known as paradigm cases) or family-resemblance concepts; (3) *emotions*, such as sympathy and respect, play no role in moral knowledge; (4) there are moral *experts*; and (5) some normative ethical theory is (or will in the foreseeable future become) as *well-supported* as the H_2O theory. Each of these claims deserves an extended treatment that I cannot give here. But I do want to make some brief comments about them from the standpoint of my methodological naturalism.

Claim (1) is especially noteworthy because the methodological naturalism I am defending might mistakenly be considered to depend on the intuitionist view – criticised by John Leslie Mackie, among others, as epistemologically strange – that we possess a special faculty of moral perception or intuition by which we directly apprehend some moral facts or truths.[21] But as I indicated in section 3, the metaethical analogue of observation in science is *non-moral* observation in ethics. Although I am open to the possibility that there are instances of theory-laden moral observation that parallel theory-laden instances of scientific observation, my methodological naturalism does not depend on that possibility (see Sturgeon 1984, for some very helpful discussion).

I note concerning claim (2) that the prototype theory of concepts has become popular in cognitive psychology in recent decades, and that some moral philosophers, such as Mark Johnson (1993), have plausibly extended it to moral semantics.

As for claim (3), many moral philosophers, especially empiricists, have for centuries granted an important role to emotions in shaping our moral judgements. David Hume (2000, pp. 368–377, 393f.) is the classic example.

Claim (4), that there are moral experts, has been questioned by moral philosophers at least as far back as Aristotle, who is well-known for stressing the primary role of upbringing in creating virtuous people with good ethical judgement. And indeed, if ethical inquiry fails to qualify as a science, as I suggested earlier, then we should probably not expect formal ethical study to generate moral knowledge in the way that formal scientific study generates scientific knowledge (Brink 1989, p. 96, makes a closely related point). None of this, however, is to deny that formal ethical inquiry can deepen one's understanding of theoretical and practical issues in normative ethics.

Finally, regarding claim (5), we have good reasons to deny any normative ethical theory to be as well-supported as the H_2O theory of water. Some reasons are familiar by now: ethics is not a science and there are no moral experts com-

---

[21] For Mackie's criticism, see Mackie (1978, pp. 38f.), Sullivan (1990, subsection 3.1; I discuss (3) in subsection 3.25).

parable to experts in chemistry. David Brink (1989, pp. 205 f.) adds the important point (influenced by Parfit 1984, pp. 453 f.) that secular ethical inquiry is relatively underdeveloped compared to scientific inquiry due religious constraints and influences that science largely shed centuries ago.

5.2 The Status of Moral Common Sense

How, if at all, are we justified in relying on moral common sense in the first place? Well, in the absence of special reason to distrust them we are no less entitled to appeal to folk theories in ethics as we are in science; the burden of proof here is surely on anyone who wishes to contrast ethics with science, as moral sceptics so often do.[22] Admittedly, common-sense moral beliefs are neither self-evident nor in any other way self-justifying, nor are they logically derivable – given the is-ought gap – from exclusively non-moral beliefs. But neither are common-sense beliefs about a particular natural kind self-justifying, and I cannot see how they may be derived from other beliefs that are not explicitly about that kind.[23]

Of course, this comparison does not show that any moral beliefs *are* justified, nor does my overall methodological-naturalist account. For one thing, positive arguments for moral scepticism – such as John Leslie Mackie's argument from metaphysical strangeness – must be met (Mackie 1978, pp. 40 f.).[24] For another, a general theory of epistemic justification is needed to deal with the negative sort of moral scepticism that simply demands over and over again – typically in foundationalist fashion – a justification for each moral belief. And I cannot in this limited space begin to do justice to these sceptical challenges.

But I will close this section with a brief comment on each. First, moral nihilism, or eliminativism concerning morality, is indeed an anti-realist option for a methodological naturalist. If moral common sense really is riddled with errors, and no satisfactory deep theory is available, then nihilism is worth taking very seriously. Moral rightness and wrongness, goodness and badness, and so

---

[22] Indeed, folk physics, astronomy, and so forth are easy to ridicule; see, e.g., Shermer (2006).
[23] Closely related points about logical derivability are made in Post (2003, pp. 240 f.), Baggini and Fosl (2003, p. 99). For an excellent discussion of the role of common sense in ethics, see Singer (1986); it includes an important contrast between common sense and folklore (Singer 1986, pp. 235–238).
[24] For important rebuttals, see, e.g., Brink (1989, pp. 171–179), Sturgeon (2006, pp. 110 ff.); also relevant is Sullivan (1990, subsection 4.1).

forth, could turn out to be analogous to ghosts and phlogiston.[25] But I do not myself see much plausibility to this option as things stand.

Second, I think the proper response to negative moral scepticism is to defend a *contextualist* theory of justification according to which a belief is justified only against the background of other beliefs at least temporarily taken for granted and not in need of justification, and from which it is legitimately inferable. In a context in which all moral beliefs are in question, and given the is-ought gap, the negative moral sceptic is right to insist that they are unjustified. But this hardly shows that none possess justification *in ordinary contexts* in which many common-sense moral beliefs are taken for granted. And in this respect – assuming now the failure of *positive* moral scepticism – moral common sense is once again no worse off than common-sense conceptions of natural kinds.[26]

6 Conclusion

According to the version of methodological naturalism I have defended, the method for justifying normative ethical theories is roughly the same as the method for justifying scientific theories of the nature of natural, social, and psychological kinds.[27] I certainly cannot claim to have shown that this metaethical theory is correct or that it is superior to its rivals. But I hope I have made a reasonable

---

25 Alisdair MacIntyre (1984, pp. 69f.) compares belief in moral *rights*, though not moral beliefs generally, to belief in witches and unicorns; so his approach is partly eliminativist. Michael Slote develops a more systematically but still selectively eliminativist approach, using virtue ethics, in Slote (1992, parts III and IV).

26 On contextualist justification, see Sullivan (1990, subsection 3.52). This account is indebted to the work of Michael Williams; see especially his important book *Unnatural Doubts* (Williams 1991). I apply contextualism to moral beliefs in Sullivan (1990, subsection 3.52). Closely related forms of metaethical contextualism may be found in Bambrough (1979, especially pp. 22f., 25f., 32, 101f., 127–130, 136f.), Hook (1963, especially pp. 52f., 60f.), Williams (1983, pp. 113–117), Larmore (1987, pp. 28ff., 131, 149f., 158, note 14), and most helpfully, Thomas (2006, part III).

27 I must admit that a more precise formulation of what I have actually done would replace "scientific theories" with "at least one scientific theory". (Besides water, theories of disease and gold are mentioned in passing.) There is clearly much work to do, especially in connection with social science and psychology (theories of psychiatric disorders already seem to be apt cases). But the water and morality parallel I have elaborated seems to me sufficient to make this research program a promising one. Moreover, even if it turned out that my account worked only for natural kinds such as water and gold, it would still have great metaethical significance in providing major parallels between the justification of some scientific theories and that of ethical theories.

case that it deserves to be taken seriously by everyone who ponders the epistemological status of moral beliefs or the relationship between science and ethics.

Bibliography

Adams, Robert (1979): "Divine Command Metaethics Modified Again". In: *Journal of Religious Ethics* 7 (1), pp. 66–79.
Baggini, Julian and Fosl, Peter (2003): *The Philosopher's Toolkit*. Oxford: Blackwell.
Bambrough, Renford (1979): *Moral Scepticism and Moral Knowledge*. New York: Humanities Press.
Boyd, Richard (1979): "Metaphor and Theory Change. What Is 'Metaphor' a Metaphor For?". In: Ortony, Andrew (ed.): *Metaphor and Thought*. New York: Cambridge University Press, pp. 356–408.
Boyd, Richard (1988): "How to Be a Moral Realist". In: Sayre-McCord, Geoffrey (ed.): *Essays on Moral Realism*. Ithaca and New York: Cornell University Press, pp. 181–228.
Boyd, Richard (1995): "Postscript to 'How to Be a Moral Realist'". In: Moser, Paul and Trout, John (eds.): *Contemporary Materialism. A Reader*. New York: Routledge, pp. 343–356.
Brink, David (1989): *Moral Realism and the Foundations of Ethics*. Cambridge: Cambridge University Press.
Collingridge, David (1984): "Criticizing Preferences". In: *Philosophy* 59 (228), pp. 231–241.
Daniels, Norman (1979): "Wide Reflective Equilibrium and Theory Acceptance in Ethics". In: *Journal of Philosophy* 76 (5), pp. 256–282.
Devitt, Michael (1981): *Designation*. New York: Columbia University Press.
Drebushenko, David and Sullivan, Stephen (1998): "Harman on Relativism and Moral Diversity". In: *Critica* 30 (89), pp. 95–104.
Duhem, Pierre (1952): *The Aim and Structure of Physical Theory*. Princeton: Princeton University Press.
Field, Hartry (1973): "Theory Change and the Indeterminacy of Reference". In: *Journal of Philosophy* 70 (14), pp. 462–481.
Gilbert, Alan (1984): "Marx's Moral Realism". In: Ball, Terence and Farr, James (eds.): *After Marx*. Cambridge: Cambridge University Press, pp. 154–183.
Gilbert, Alan (1986): "Moral Realism, Individuality, and Justice in War". In: *Political Theory* 14 (1), pp. 105–135.
Hare, Richard (1981): *Moral Thinking. Its Levels, Methods and Point*. Oxford: Oxford University Press.
Harman, Gilbert (1977): *The Nature of Morality. An Introduction to Ethics*. Oxford: Oxford University Press.
Harman, Gilbert (1994): "Moral Diversity as an Argument for Moral Relativism". In: Odegard, Douglas and Stewart, Carole (eds.): *Perspectives on Moral Relativism*. Milliken: Agathon, pp. 13–31.
Hobhouse, Leonard Trelawny (1951): *Morals in Evolution*. London: Chapman & Hall.
Hook, Sidney (1963): *The Quest for Being and Other Studies in Naturalism and Humanism*. New York: Delta Books.
Hume, David (2000): *A Treatise of Human Nature*. Oxford: Oxford University Press.

Idziak, Janine (1989): "In Search of 'Good Positive Reasons' for an Ethics of Divine Commands. A Catalogue of Arguments". In: *Faith and Philosophy* 6 (1), pp. 47–64.

Johnson, Mark (1993): *Moral Imagination. Implications of Cognitive Science for Ethics.* Chicago: The University of Chicago Press.

Johnson, Wayne (1986): "Explaining Diversity in Moral Thought". In: *Southern Journal of Philosophy* 26 (1), pp. 115–133.

Kripke, Saul (1980): *Naming and Necessity.* Cambridge: Harvard University Press.

Larmore, Charles (1987): *Patterns of Moral Complexity.* Cambridge: Cambridge University Press.

Lutz, Matthew and Lenman, James (2018): "Moral Naturalism". In: Zalta, Edward (ed.): *The Stanford Encyclopedia of Philosophy.* https://plato.stanford.edu/archives/sum2018/entries/naturalism-moral/, retrieved on November 14, 2018.

MacBeath, Alexander (1952): *Experiments in Living. A Study of the Nature and Foundation of Ethics in the Light of Recent Work in Social Anthropology.* New York: Macmillan.

MacIntyre, Alisdair (1984): *After Virtue.* Notre Dame: University of Notre Dame Press.

Mackie, John Leslie (1978): *Ethics. Inventing Right and Wrong.* London: Penguin.

Mill, John Stuart (1979): *Utilitarianism.* Indianapolis: Hackett.

Parfit, Derek (1984): *Reasons and Persons.* New York: Oxford University Press.

Post, John (2003): "Method, Madness, and Normativity". In: *Philo* 6 (2), pp. 235–248.

Putnam, Hilary (1982): *Philosophical Papers. Vol. 2. Mind, Language and Reality.* Cambridge: Cambridge University Press.

Quine, Willard Van Orman (1960): *Word and Object.* Cambridge: MIT Press.

Quine, Willard Van Orman (1963): *From a Logical Point of View. Logico-Philosophical Essays.* New York: Harper Torchbooks.

Railton, Peter (1989): "Naturalism and Prescriptivity". In: *Social Policy and Philosophy* 7 (1), pp. 151–174.

Railton, Peter (2003): *Facts, Values, and Norms. Essays Toward a Morality of Consequence.* New York: Cambridge University Press.

Rawls, John (1971): *A Theory of Justice.* Cambridge: Harvard University Press.

Ross, William David (1930): *The Right and the Good.* Oxford: Oxford University Press.

Ross, William David (1939): *Foundations of Ethics.* Oxford: Oxford University Press.

Shermer, Michael (2006): "Folk Science. Why Our Intuitions About How the World Works Are Often Wrong". In: *Scientific American.* https://www.scientificamerican.com/article/folk-science/, retrieved on November 14, 2018.

Sidgwick, Henry (1963): *The Methods of Ethics.* London: Macmillan.

Singer, Marcus (1986): "Ethics and Common Sense". In: *Revue Internationale de Philosophie* 40 (158), pp. 221–258.

Singer, Peter (2011): *The Expanding Circle. Ethics, Evolution, and Moral Progress.* Princeton: Princeton University Press.

Slote, Michael (1977): "Morality and Ignorance". In: *Journal of Philosophy* 74 (12), pp. 745–767.

Sturgeon, Nicholas (1982): "Brandt's Moral Empiricism". In: *Philosophical Review* 91 (3), pp. 389–422.

Sturgeon, Nicholas (1984): "Moral Explanations". In: Copp, David and Zimmerman, David (eds.): *Morality, Reason and Truth*. Totowa: Rowman & Allanheld, pp. 19–78.

Sturgeon, Nicholas (2006): "Ethical Naturalism". In: Copp, David (ed.): *The Oxford Handbook of Ethical Theory*. New York: Oxford University Press, pp. 91–121.

Sullivan, Stephen (1990): *Moral Realism and Naturalized Metaethics*. Doctoral Dissertation. Ann Arbor: University Microfilms.

Sullivan, Stephen (1994): "Why Adams Needs to Modify His Divine-Command Theory One More Time". In: *Faith and Philosophy* 11 (1), pp. 72–81.

Thagard, Paul (1982): "From the Descriptive to the Normative in Psychology and Logic". In: *Philosophy of Science* 49 (1), pp. 24–42.

Thomas, Alan (2006): *Value and Context. The Nature of Moral and Political Knowledge*. Oxford: Clarendon Press.

Timmons, Mark (1999): *Morality Without Foundations. A Defense of Ethical Contextualism*. New York: Oxford University Press.

Tolhurst, William (1986): "Supervenience, Externalism and Moral Knowledge". In: *Southern Journal of Philosophy* 24 (1), pp. 43–55.

Toulmin, Stephen (1986): *The Place of Reason in Ethics*. Chicago: The University of Chicago Press.

Westermarck, Edward (1960): *Ethical Relativity*. Paterson: Littlefield, Adams & Co.

Williams, Bernard (1983): *Ethics and the Limits of Philosophy*. Cambridge: Harvard University Press.

Williams, Michael (1991): *Unnatural Doubts. Epistemological Realism and the Basis of Scepticism*. Oxford: Blackwell.

Zangwill, Nick (2008): "Science and Ethics. Demarcation, Holism and Logical Consequences". In: *European Journal of Philosophy* 18 (1), pp. 126–138.

Marcel Mertz
Empirical Incursions[1]
Or How Empirical Information May Influence the Validity of a Moral Norm

Abstract: On the basis of the assumption that moral norms are central both to lived morality and professional ethical reflection, the present chapter, rooted in empirical bioethics, aims to identify empirical incursions into normative theory by showing how empirical information from social-scientific research in particular may influence various dimensions of the validity of moral norms. To this end, the author first provides a definition and analysis of the structure of a moral norm. He then establishes a number of dimensions of the validity of moral norms that correspond to specific elements of this structure (including philosophical or social justification and legitimacy, applicability to specific situations, social implementation, and the effects of norms), while also discussing how these dimensions may be influenced by empirical information. He concludes with a critical consideration of the significance of these dimensions of validity and the empirical influences on them for different ways of "doing ethics".

1 Introduction

1.1 Empirical Information and Ethics

In philosophical ethics – or philosophy as such – empirical information (in the form of the results of (social-scientific) research)[2] has traditionally been regarded

---
[1] The present chapter consists mainly of modified and translated material that originally formed part of the author's Ph.D. thesis (Mertz 2015; only available in German), particularly its chapters 10 and 12, and to a lesser extent its chapters 1 and 16.
[2] Though there are other possible meanings of "empirical information" or "empirical data" (such as subjective sense experience, accumulated life experience, or "experienceable reality"), these terms are primarily used in the following to refer to the results of (social-)scientific studies using empirical research methods. Accordingly, they are understood as beliefs that have been (theoretically or critically) interpreted and that correspond to (empirical) statements (that may function as descriptive premises in arguments), rather than as "raw sense data" or similar entities. In addition, scientific theories that are based on empirical research findings may also constitute "empirical information" in this context, even if one acknowledges that any theory will also contain non-empirical elements.

https://doi.org/10.1515/9783110613797-012

with suspicion. Even though clear trends to the contrary have emerged in recent decades, such as "experimental philosophy" and "experimental ethics" (see, e.g., Knobe and Nichols 2008, Luetge, Rusch, and Uhl 2014), pragmatist ethics (see, e.g., Kitcher 2011), and "empirical (bio-)ethics" (see subsection 1.2, below), a tendency to shield ethics and its normative theory from empirical incursions has remained. This has often been based on the enduring suspicion that the use of empirical data in ethics would necessarily lead to an is-ought fallacy or a naturalistic fallacy (see, e.g., de Vries and Gordijn 2009).

It is nonetheless interesting to note that possible aversion to or scepticism toward empirical research is particularly prevalent within *normative* or *general ethics*. In the historically more recent field of *applied ethics*, empirical knowledge and empirical research are generally more acknowledged to be indispensable. This is illustrated, e.g., by the frequent calls for interdisciplinarity within applied ethics. Yet it may also simply be due to the fact that, in the complex subsystems characteristic of modern societies, viable ethical judgements – and *a fortiori* implementable ethical problem-solving strategies – are hardly possible without detailed empirical knowledge of these systems, their operative logics, and the convictions and motivations of their key actors (cf. Kaminsky 1999).

This divergence may also be due to the potentially significant differences between the aims of normative or general ethics and those of applied ethics. While the former is at least primarily concerned with formulating general moral principles, clarifying central ethical concepts, and ultimately with ethical *theory building*, the latter is concerned primarily with concrete ethical judgements and problem-solving in specific fields, such as our relationship to the environment, technology, and animals, or to patients and health systems as a whole.

1.2 Empirical (Bio-)Ethics

This difference in aims is particularly evident in the interdisciplinary activities of medical ethics and/or bioethics. Bioethics is not concerned with the development, critique, and modification of general moral theories, but rather with reflection, judgement formation, and often with practical problem-solving. There are historical reasons for this, including the exigency of the moral challenges that have emerged since the 1960s (in part due to the increasingly technical character of medicine, e.g., assisted ventilation, defibrillation, cardiopulmonary bypass, generally advanced life support in the intensive care unit), which has pushed ethicists to turn back to "practical questions" rather than concentrating exclusively on meta-ethics (cf. Toulmin 1982). Within the field of bioethics itself, the relationship between empirical research and ethics has also been discussed at length. This is no doubt partly due to the field's proximity to medicine, which has been heavily oriented toward empirical knowledge since the modern era (cf. the contemporary paradigm of evidence-based medicine; see, e.g., Kunz et al. 2007, Howick 2011). The disciplinary independence of bioethics from philosophical ethics, as manifested in some institutionalised forms of bioethics that are frequently engaged in by doctors and other health professionals rather than philosophers (see, e.g., Borry, Schotsmans, and Dierickx 2005) may also play an important role here.

What has been particularly decisive for the relationship between empirical research or empirical information and (bio-)ethics in the last twenty years, however, is the development of a research approach termed *empirical (bio-)ethics* (see, e.g., Ives, Dunn, and Cribb 2017, Mertz et al. 2014, Widdershoven, Abma, and Molewijk 2009, McMillan and Hope 2008), or in some variants *evidence-based (bio-)ethics* (see, e.g., Salloch 2012, Strech 2008, Goldenberg 2005). Contrary to what one might initially assume, "empirical ethics" is not a synonym for descriptive ethics. Most forms of empirical ethics are rather characterised by a rule-governed (i.e., methodologically substantiated) interdisciplinary combination of (socio-)empirical research and normative-ethical analysis (Ives et al. 2018, Mertz et al. 2014, McMillan and Hope 2008). Empirical ethics therefore primarily designates various methodological variations of an interdisciplinary bioethics that addresses normativity on the one hand and specific questions concerning methodological practices and the use of empirical research (such as quantitative or qualitative social-scientific research) on the other. It does not address meta-ethical questions such as the *is-ought gap* in detail, which are sometimes only considered to have limited significance for empirical ethics discourses (de Vries and Gordijn 2009, p. 201).

Meta-ethical considerations nevertheless inevitably arise when it comes to the philosophical and above all methodological question of the relationship between normative theory and empirical information. This is true even when "theory" only refers to a "mid-level theory" such as the principlism widespread in bioethics (see especially Beauchamp and Childress 2009)[3] or to a not uncommon, pragmatic "syncretism" of a range of values, norms, principles, and virtues that are all considered important (e.g., thinking about what values et cetera could be important for ethically analysing the use of robots in the care of the elderly (see,

---

[3] Principlism is an approach that, instead of using a philosophical "full-blown" moral theory, identifies mid-level principles that are important for a specific practice, such as "respect for patient autonomy", "beneficence", "non-maleficence", and "justice" for medical ethics (Beauchamp and Childress 2009); for other examples, see Emanuel, Wendler, and Grady (2008) on clinical research ethics, and Strech, Neitzke, and Marckmann (2012) on public health ethics.

e.g., Sharkey and Sharkey 2012), irrespective of their origin and without referring to a sole moral theory or ethical approach). Understanding how such a relationship is possible is not only important from a purely philosophical or general theoretical perspective, but also for the concrete design of ethical studies or empirico-ethical studies.[4]

1.3 The Functions of Empirical Information

The way in which empirical research may relate to normative theory is bound up with the functions that empirical information may serve within (bio-)ethics. Here one might distinguish between an *epistemic function* (such as knowledge of empirical reality that is relevant for an ethical judgement), an *implementation function* (such as the selection and assessment of suitable and successful behavioural change strategies in existing social praxis), and an *evaluative function* (such as assessing whether actors follow moral norms or the extent to which they live up to a particular ideal).[5] Particularly interesting from a philosophical perspective is a *justificatory function*, i.e., the evaluation of those aspects of principles, norms, values, and normative theories with direct justificatory relevance. This may involve identifying descriptive presuppositions in justificatory normative arguments or demonstrating that norms can be implemented or followed (the principle of *ought implies can*; see, e.g., Schleidgen, Jungert, and Bauer 2010, Kohl 2015, van Ackeren and Kühler 2016).

In the following, the justificatory function will play a particularly important role, though the implementation function and evaluative function will also be addressed. This is because the same empirical information can in principle serve a number of different functions; empirical information is not tied to any specific function *per se*. Exactly which function will be served in any given empirico-ethical research project or ethics study depends on the aim and questions of this research, on the normative theory that underlies it, and on the methodology used to link the empirical information to normative theory, which may favour some functions while excluding others (cf., e.g., *pragmatic hermeneutical empirical ethics*; Widdershoven and van der Scheer 2008; and *evidence-based*

---

[4] I.e., empirical studies that, against the backdrop of specific research interests and concepts (including theories), explicitly attempt to link empirical data collection and analysis to normative ethical analysis (empirical ethics).
[5] For a more detailed elaboration, see Mertz (2015, pp. 12f).

or *information-critical ethics*; Strech 2008).⁶ What is also crucial are the particular elements of normative theory to which empirical information is related, which may include (basic) concepts, (formal) moral principles, values, virtues – and indeed moral norms.

1.4 Moral Norms as Core Entities in Lived Morality and Ethical Reflection

As generalised guidance and thus as rules for action (Ott 2002, p. 458), moral norms can be regarded as key elements of normative theory to which empirical information can be meaningfully related. This will be the guiding assumption in what follows. A particular normative theory (such as Kantianism or utilitarianism), however, will not be presupposed.

These assumptions do not exclude the fact that the values from which norms are derived, as well as virtues, may nevertheless be relevant to ethical judgement formation and moral orientation. Some normative theories, such as virtue ethics and casuistry, make very little reference to norms. Focussing on moral norms is therefore a conscious choice and only *one* possible means of addressing the relationship between empirical information (or empirical research) and theory (or ethics) – and one that cannot necessarily be applied (to the same extent) to every normative theory.

However, using "moral norm" as a central concept is still not unproblematic, as there are several discipline-depending definitions of the term "moral norm" as well as of the related term "social norm" (e.g., from philosophical ethics, sociology, or psychology). Although the understanding of "moral norm" in this chapter should be clearer at the end of section 2, a short characterisation at the start might thus be helpful.

Generally, "moral norm" is understood as a specific kind of a social norm, and is therefore a "descriptive norm". It mainly describes what groups or societies *regard* as morally prohibited, required, or permitted. Whether it also is or can be a "prescriptive norm" that (rationally) *should* guide our thinking and acting – i.e., whether a moral norm can actually be "moral" from an ethical, not just sociological point of view – is object to ethical reflection, justification, and critique. Thereby, "(normative) ethics" is understood as the rational and normative

---

6 These various possible functions can also be restricted by the normative theory applied to any given case. Deontological moral theories, e.g., attribute less importance to the implementation function than some consequentialist theories (e.g., Birnbacher 2016).

reflection on and investigation of morality. So, moral norms could exist that, as extreme example, entail lynching all foreigners (e.g., because they are deemed harmful to society). What makes them "moral" *prima facie* is just that they are part of the moral thinking or, if sufficiently institutionalised, also acting of a group. But of course, ethically, it has to be discussed whether such a moral norm is actually *valid* (e.g., intersubjectively well-defendable) and thus should be accepted as a prescriptive norm. Thus, it is *not* part of the definition of the term "moral norm" that a norm actually is ethically defendable, as this may presuppose certain normative theories or standpoints about what "makes" a norm moral from an ethical point of view.

One factor that speaks in favour of focussing on moral norms then is that, in the sphere of lived morality, they exert a strong influence (on people's actions and judgements) in the form of social norms and are regularly made the subject of public discourses. Even if individual ethical judgement formation is not (just) based on norms, norms still play an important orienting role here. Furthermore, as proposed or hypothetical norms, they are deeply rooted in the history of philosophical ethics and its systems, and therefore belong to the basic concepts of ethics as a discipline. Last but not least, moral norms are often appealed to in order to justify ethical judgements or actions, both in daily life and in ethics as a discipline. Norms can therefore be regarded as core entities in lived morality, as in everyday and professional ethical reflection, which is a further reason why it may be particularly worthwhile to examine the functions of empirical information in relation to these elements of normative theory.

One important and obvious function of empirical information is to make norms more specific or concrete (e.g., Richardson 1990, Dietrich 2009, Strech 2008). Such specification consists in enriching a general norm for a particular area of application by means of additional clauses and information derived from context-specific facts and details, so that the norm becomes more effective at regulating action in concrete cases.

Where both general and specific norms are concerned, however, the question always arises of whether they are sufficiently justified or legitimated, i.e., why, ultimately, one should follow a norm and not another competing norm. In the following, I shall therefore consider the extent to which empirical information can exert an influence on various dimensions of the *validity* (in German *Geltung*) of a moral norm, or is even essential for a norm to acquire validity at all – and thus can be a "prescriptive norm".

To this end, I first present an analysis of the (deep) structure of moral norms, since in order to determine the potential influence of empirical information on a norm's validity, one first of all has to understand "where" in the structure of a norm empirical information can play a role. Second, I establish various dimensions of validity that correspond to specific elements of the structure of moral norms (such as philosophical or social justification and legitimacy, applicability to particular situations, implementation in social practice, and the (social) effects of an implemented norm). On the basis of examples, I discuss how these dimensions of validity – and therefore the corresponding elements of a norm's structure – can be influenced by empirical information. The chapter nonetheless does not discuss whether the influence of empirical information on a norm's validity is (always) justified, since this depends on the normative theory (e. g., Kantianism, utilitarianism, contractualism, virtue ethics, discourse ethics, et cetera; see, e. g., Copp 2006) and methodological position (e. g., foundationalism, coherentism, reflective equilibrium; see, e. g., Steup 2018, Arras 2007), but also different strands of empirical ethics (see, e. g., Ives, Dunn, and Cribb 2017), such as pragmatic hermeneutic empirical ethics (Widdershoven and van der Scheer 2008) or symbiotic empirical ethics (Frith 2012) to which one subscribes; it rather only aims to discuss how empirical information *may* play a role in influencing the validity of a moral norm.

2 The Definition and Structure of Moral Norms

2.1 Definition

In the context of this chapter it is not possible to present and defend in detail a possible definition of a moral norm (for such a treatment, see Mertz 2015, chapters 10 to 12). I will therefore have to adopt a stipulative definition.

This definition is based on the hypothesis that reducing the term "norm" to "normative statement" – as often takes place in (analytic) philosophical ethics – systematically prevents us from identifying aspects of norms whose validity is most strongly influenced by empirical information. While moral norms can be *expressed* by norm statements (Ott 2002, p. 458), then, norm statements are not *identical* to norms.[7] A norm statement is only the (written or verbal) linguistic and thereby public (i.e., intersubjectively exchangeable) formulation of, say, a private mental output (such as a subjective idea or imagination) (Rohwer 2008, p. 9). Another premise for the definition is that the *definiens* "moral norm" must not have a *definiendum* that already entails that the moral norm is "valid" (i.e., legitimate, justified). This is, as already mentioned in subsection

---

[7] This distinction is somewhat analogous to that between *laws of nature* and *scientific laws* (i.e., statements about presumed laws of nature that are based on research).

1.4, because it is up to normative-ethical reasoning and debate to determine whether a moral norm actually has validity (in whatever dimensions).

Against this backdrop, the following definition of a "moral norm" can be offered (following Mertz 2015, p. 87): A moral norm is defined as a *social norm*, i.e., a formal or largely non-formal normative rule (a rule of action, an imperative for action, or an objective) that determines how the members of a social group, community, or society are to act or behave in particular situations in view of the (possible) actions or (possible) forms of behaviour (reactions) of other members of the group (community, society), and that also exhibits the following feature *in addition* to those essentially shared by all social norms:[8] with respect to its content, the norm is concerned with care, preventing harm, safeguarding (granted and recognised) rights, or establishing justice, and may exhibit a greater or lesser degree of specificity (cf. more general and abstract basic norms and more specific norms).

Two further precisions are also necessary here: An *institutionalised moral norm* is defined as a moral norm in which the action/behaviour demanded by the rule and the associated internal and external sanctions and behavioural regularities can be empirically observed in the relevant group (e.g., a community or society). And a *potential moral norm* is defined as a moral norm (whether general or specific) that only exists as an idea or as an intersubjectively exchangeable proposal (in the form of a normative statement) and in which many of the general characteristics of a social norm are only potentially or hypothetically contained.

The distinction between an institutionalised and a potential norm is important insofar as ethical reflection (e.g., as carried out by professional ethicists) does not simply consist in discussing existing (i.e., institutionalised) norms, but also in constructing norms that do not (yet) express any existing social norms or only contain their key properties *in potentia*. A potential moral norm should therefore be understood as a proposal stipulating a rule that (some or all) individuals in (some or all) areas of life should follow or orient themselves by. One might of course also make the stronger claim that, for rational reasons,

---

[8] These include: (1) that most members of the group advocate the rule as a normative conviction and thereby acknowledge its binding character (which is why non-conformist behaviour can justifiably be regarded as censurable); (2) that in recognising the rule, members of the group cultivate normative and empirical or anticipatory expectations concerning other members' behaviour and expectations; and (3) that the (recognised) rule may fulfil various psychological and social functions within the group, such as enabling needs to be satisfied, removing cognitive and normative burdens from individuals, and improving cooperative efficiency and conflict regulation (e.g., Müller and Müller-Andritzky 1993, Bicchieri, Muldoon, and Sontuoso 2018).

we are required to act in such and such a way. Nevertheless, in such cases we can only speak of a moral norm *as though* it already exhibited many (or all) of the characteristics of a social norm. Whether the potential moral norm may in fact be fully realised as a social norm, however, is an empirical question (which we shall address later).

As a final remark on the definition of moral norms, it is important to distinguish between more general or abstract moral norms or mid-level principles (such as "one shall not murder", "the diversity of species is to be protected", and "the autonomy of patients is to be respected") and more specific (or "specified") norms (such as "where the offspring of giraffes in zoos cannot be given to other zoos due to a lack of need or a lack of means, these offspring shall be used as feed for the zoo's predators, and this decision is to be publicly communicated in a transparent way").

Specific or specified moral norms will be particularly important in what follows, since it is with these norms that bioethics generally engages. Bioethics, as "applied ethics" (in contrast to general normative ethics), is rarely concerned with the most general norms or even with formal moral principles such as the categorical imperative ("theory"), but rather with what should be done in particular (yet typical) cases ("choices", "decisions") (e.g., Kaminsky 1999, p. 157, Smith Iltis 2000, p. 272, Eriksson, Helgesson, and Segerdahl 2006, p. 390). Those who are interested in the relation between empirical information and moral norms in bioethics in particular would therefore do best to orient themselves by such specified norms than by general or abstract norms.

2.2 Structure

Because of the already mentioned tendency to think of moral norms prominently as explicit norm statements (thus as verbalisations of "prescriptive norms"), one should distinguish between a *surface structure* and a *deep structure* when reconstructing the structure of a moral norm.[9] The surface structure expresses the norm in the form of a norm statement, which therefore mainly reflects the semantic structure of a statement. In contrast, the *deep structure* consists of ontological or epistemological presuppositions underlying the (explicit) elements of the norm statement (e.g., whether the norm is recognised as a moral norm by group members, whether the norm is followed by group members, whether the

---

[9] This structural analysis can potentially also be applied to other norms, such as legal norms. Here, however, I only claim that it applies to *moral* norms.

norm has the intended effects, or whether it is, in a given social context, possible to act the way the norm prescribes). The deep structure thus primarily relates to the moral norm as a *social* norm. In analysing such structures, it is helpful to explain a norm statement in a way that already reveals the surface structure (based on, i.a., Ott 2002, Lachmayer 1977, Hopf 1987):

Norm N states that, as norm kind NK in activity/object domain (type) T and with intention I: "For all norm addressees NA (except $NA_{1, 2, ..., n}$), on account of norm authority NAT, it holds that, for the benefit of norm beneficiary NB, in all cases C of situation S (except $C_{1, 2, ..., n}$), action A [which ensures the establishment/persistence of situation SZ] is x'ed, or sanctions $SA_{1, 2, ..., n}$ shall follow", which brings about effect E.

To give an example, this structure *could* look like the following for a moral norm about obtaining informed consent in clinical studies:

Paragraph 26 about *"Informed Consent"* of the World Medical Association's Declaration of Helsinki (World Medical Association 2013) [N]
states as a *specified moral norm* [NK]
for *medical research with human subjects* [T]
with the intention of *safeguarding that researchers obtain valid informed consent when conducting a clinical study* [I]:
"For all *physicians or others who are (also) involved in medical research involving human subjects*[10] (except *physicians or others only involved in medical care*) [NA],
on account of the *World Medical Association as the main international organization representing physicians* [NAT],
it holds that, for the benefit of *human subjects involved in medical research (e.g., patients or healthy subjects)* [NB],
in all cases where *human subjects are capable of giving informed consent for participating in a clinical study* (except in cases *involving minors where the capability of giving informed consent is controversial*),[11] *informing potential subjects adequately 'of the aims, methods, sources of funding, any possible conflicts of interest, institutional affiliations of the researcher, the anticipated benefits and potential risks of the study and the discomfort it may entail, post-study provisions and any other relevant aspects of the study'* (World Medical Association 2013) [A][12]
(for ensuring that *human subjects can decide in an informed and voluntary way whether they want to participate in the study* [SZ])

---

[10] See paragraph 2 of the *Declaration of Helsinki* (World Medical Association 2013).
[11] This is because of different standards – also legally – regarding the capabilities and rights of minors to make decisions about their own involvement in medical research.
[12] Paragraph 26 of the *Declaration of Helsinki* is actually longer than this excerpt; further actions mentioned such as the right to refuse to participate in a study are omitted here for simplicity's sake.

is required [is x'ed],[13]
or else *the study may not be approved or, when already being conducted, be discontinued, and the researchers barred from conducting further research or, as physicians, may even lose their medical license* [SA]",
which brings about *that researchers in medical research obtain valid informed consent of potential human subjects, but also increases bureaucratic and legal requirements when planning and conducting a study* [E].

Strictly speaking, however, only the section in quotation marks is the norm statement (in the example above: "For all physicians or others who are (also) involved [...]" to "[...] or, as physicians, may even lose their medical license"). The other sections represent additional elements of the surrounding surface structure of a norm. In the following, the twelve elements of the norm statement are presented and their meaning as elements of the norm's surface structure (SS) and its deep structure (DS)[14] are briefly discussed step by step (following Mertz 2015, p. 94 f.; for an overview of the surface structure, deep structure, and the various dimensions of validity, see table 2, p. 227 f.):

Norm N states [...]
> **Subject (SS):** The subject that contains all of the following elements (e.g., paragraph 26 of the *Declaration of Helsinki*).
> **The norm's mode of existence (DS):** Information specifying whether the norm exists as, say, a subjective idea or as a social fact (e.g., as a social fact, as it is written in a declaration of an international organisation).

[...] as norm kind NK [...]
> **Norm kind (SS):** E.g., a general norm, a specified norm, a meta-norm (such as a rule prescribing which material norm should be prioritised when norms conflict).
> **Norm recognition (DS):** Information specifying whether the norm is already recognised or whether the conditions are in place for the recognition of a norm.

[...] in activity/object domain (type) T [...]
> **Type (SS):** The domain of activity (such as clinical practice or medical research) that the norm regulates, orients, or sanctions, or to whose ab-

---

[13] Original wording: "each potential subject must be adequately informed of" (World Medical Association 2013, par. 26).
[14] The following list of deep structural elements does not claim to be exhaustive.

stract/ontological objects the norm refers (e.g., moral, legal, aesthetic, or technological objects, et cetera).

Pertinence of the activity/object domain (DS): Information specifying whether the activity/object domain is applicable or appropriate to what follows in the norm statement (e.g., if some activities fall more into the category of organisational activity than that of individual activity, the "doctor-patient relationship" type would not be as suitable as the "institutional framework of the hospital institution" type).

[...] with intention I [...]

Pragmatic linguistic function (SS): Information concerning the effect that the speaker (or norm originator) intends the expression of the norm to have on the addressee, such as evoking certain feelings, eliciting certain values or decisions, encouraging the addressee to perform certain actions, or pushing his or her behaviour in a certain direction (e.g., ensuring that researchers obtain informed consent); the latter is most often the case where moral norms are concerned.

Context of the discussion of the norm (DS): Information specifying whether the norm is being discussed seriously – e.g., being proposed – or whether it is being discussed in relation to a fictitious context (such as a philosophical thought experiment, which is definitely not the case in the example above).

[...] "For all norm addressees NA (except $NA_{1, 2, ..., n}$) it holds that [...]

Norm addressee group, with exceptions (SS): The person or group of people to whom the norm is directed (e.g., physicians involved in research). Though proper names are usually not contained in norm statements, the norm addressee group can be restricted by specifying certain social roles or positions (such as "doctor", "care-givers in department XY", "clinical researchers", et cetera).

Existence/capability of the norm addressee group (DS): Information specifying whether the norm addressee group exists and whether its members are in principle capable of acting as norm addressees (someone may, for instance, not be obviously capable of acting as a norm addressee on account of their current or long-term psychological state).

[...] on account of norm authority NAT, [...]

Norm authority (SS): The person or institution that establishes or defends the norm or that has the authority to ensure it is observed (e.g., the World Medical Association in the example above).

Norm justification (DS): The identification of what (or potentially who) functions as the norm authority, i.e., the authority that "guarantees" that the norm is "right" (or "true" or "valid") (e.g., in the example above the power and legitimacy the World Medical Association may have as an international organisation of physicians for being a regulating entity, but also more general norms or values that may justify the specified norm).

Norm authority recognition (DS): Information specifying whether the norm authority (e.g., the World Medical Association) is recognised or whether it can be recognised (e.g., are the conditions for the recognition of a norm authority given?).

Norm motivation (DS): Information specifying whether the justification of the norm or the invocation of the norm authority can motivate the norm addressees to observe it.

[...] for the benefit of norm beneficiary NB [...]

Norm beneficiary group (SS): The group of entities (generally persons, yet potentially non-human animals) for whose benefit the norm is to be observed; as with the norm addressees, the beneficiary group can be restricted by specifying appropriate roles (such as "patients" or "other researchers").

Existence/capability of the norm beneficiaries (DS): Information specifying whether the designated norm beneficiary group exists or can in principle function as such (does the norm of prohibiting murder, e.g., also apply to embryos, i.e., are embryos here norm beneficiaries?).

[...] in all cases C of situation S (except in $C_{1, 2, ..., n}$) [...]

Situation types and exception clauses (SS): Common, generalisable (action) situations (such as decisions on whether or not to continue treatment at the end of someone's life, or including a patient in a clinical study) in which the norm holds with certain exception clauses, i.e., indications of legitimate exceptions to the rule in cases of norm conflicts or where the norm proves to be unreasonable.

Existence of the situation/state of affairs (DS): Information specifying whether the situation addressed by the norm can exist or how realistic/probable it is, and whether there are typical states of affairs that lead to exceptions.

[...] action A [which ensures the establishment/persistence of situation SZ] [...]

Action (SS): The action to which the substance of the norm (e.g., "is required") relates. The action may also be explicitly tied to the objective of establishing a certain situation or allowing it to persist, as exemplified by the example above (ensuring informed consent).

The possibility of action (DS): Information specifying whether the required action is possible or implementable in general or for the intended norm addressees.

[...] is x'ed, [...]

> **Substance, i.e., a normative predicate (SS):** E.g., "is required (ought)", "is permitted", "is forbidden", including further distinctions between various forms of permission, such as indifference (where something is neither required nor proscribed) or toleration (where something is at least not prohibited).
> **Exigency (DS):** Information specifying how urgently a norm should be followed, particularly where there are conflicting norms in play.
> **Norm compliance (DS):** Information specifying whether the substance of the norm is complied with, i.e., whether the relevant behavioural regularities and associated behavioural expectations can be observed among the relevant actors, including whether the norm is already regarded as normality by these actors.

[...] or sanctions $S_{1, 2, ..., n}$ shall follow", [...]

> **Sanction clauses (SS):** The consequences that are or should be incurred in case of norm violations (including penalties, social ostracism, et cetera, such as discontinuation of an already started clinical study).
> **Existence/effectiveness of sanctions (DS):** Information specifying whether the sanctions do indeed exist and whether they are applied and are effective, or whether it can at least be assumed that the sanctions will be applied and be effective.

[...] which brings about effect E.

> **Effects (SS):** The intended (e.g., no clinical study done without proper prior informed consent) and unintended (e.g., higher bureaucratic requirements) consequences of complying with the norm, including behavioural changes in individuals and changes in states of affairs in the world. The effects of norm compliance need not necessarily correspond to the intentions of the speaker or the norm originator.
> **Conditions of success (DS):** Information specifying whether the norm leads to the desired behaviour or desired situation (e.g., whether *in fact* no study is done without proper prior informed consent because of, i.a., paragraph 26 of the *Declaration of Helsinki*), and if so, how often and with what likelihood, or whether this can at least be assumed.
> **Function fulfilment (DS):** Information specifying whether the norm fulfils its social and possible psychological functions and how efficiently it does so, or which functions the norm can or should fulfil and how efficiently it is likely to do so.

It is important to note that not all of the (surface structure) elements are always required for a moral norm. Exception clauses, e.g., are not necessary. Some elements, however, are certainly indispensable, such as the norm addressee group, the norm beneficiary group, action, and substance – even if the norm beneficiary group, e.g., includes all living persons.

Any norm that actually exists in a society or a social group, i.e., that is in fact followed, will exhibit these elements – which by no means imply that the answers to the associated questions must be known to all. Furthermore, any norm that can potentially be followed by a society or social group will likewise contain these elements *in potentia*, or, when critically examined, will need to offer a possible answer to questions such as, "Why should this norm be institutionalised when it is unclear whether it will be able to elicit the required behaviour?" The fact that a particular moral norm is only a potential moral norm therefore does not relieve it of its deep structure.

In the next section, I shall consider the various dimensions of validity of moral norms, in order to assign these to the different structural elements of norms and thereby elucidate the extent to which empirical information can affect the validity of a norm.

3 Validity of Moral Norms

"Validity" here refers in general to a norm's intersubjectively binding character, or "the objective foundation for the recognition of statements, laws, norms, values, and so on (that first makes such a binding character possible)" (Thiel 2004, p. 729; own translation).[15]

In philosophical debates, this "objective foundation" has often been linked to (propositional) truth (see, e.g., Copp 2006, Morscher 2011): if a proposition accurately describes a given state of affairs, then the proposition is considered true (at least in the most common forms of the correspondence theory of truth). In meta-ethics, cognitivism assumes that even normative propositions such as norms or correct norm propositions can be true or false This view is contested both by non-cognitivists and by some cognitivists who deny that norms can be true, while still according them a truth-like validity, e.g., on the basis of speech act theory. As an alternative to the view that the relevant "objective foundation" has to involve truth, "validity" can also be identified with a justificatory procedure, so that a norm that has proved itself via the right procedure is considered valid (or right) (as, e.g., in discourse ethics, where a norm's validity is

---

[15] Original wording: "die (solche Verbindlichkeit allererst ermöglichende) objektive Grundlage des Anerkanntseins von Sätzen, Gesetzen, Normen, Werten etc."

given by a discourse that upholds openness, ignores power relations, ensures that all those affected by the norm can contribute to the discourse, or are at least virtually considered, et cetera).

Here is not the place to enter into meta-ethical questions such as whether a norm can be true or false (see again, e.g., Copp 2006, Morscher 2011). Rather, it is assumed that a rational demonstration of the validity of a norm in the form of a justification or a (methodological) procedure is sufficient as a concept of (philosophical) validity. Whether this justification or procedure serves to establish a norm's truth or merely demonstrates its validity in another manner is not relevant for the present purposes, as cognitivists and (most) non-cognitivist both can work with moral norms, even though they differ on their reasons for validity and the respective theoretical implications (e.g., how "strong" a justification of a norm possibly can be).

What is relevant, by contrast, is that a group consensus that a rule is in force and that all members should observe it is also considered as a *kind* of validity (Thiel 2004, p. 729), as is the empirical recognition and observance of norms ("social validity") (Lumer 1999, p. 450). Both of these kinds of validity involve truth insofar as they rest on an empirically observable state of affairs (such as the actual recognition of a norm).

"Validity" should therefore not be restricted to a rational demonstration in the form of a justification or a (methodological) procedure that shows why a norm is valid – though this kind of validity ("philosophical validity") should by no means be neglected (as will be discussed in subsection 4.1, below). It may well be a false trichotomy to claim that a norm has either social validity, legal validity, or philosophical validity, since a norm may well possess all of these kinds of validity (or, as I shall put it below, these dimensions of validity).

In the following, "validity" is therefore understood to provide an answer to the question *why a norm should in general or in a particular context be binding for an actor, and/or why it in fact is*. One might then ask why or on what basis a norm is valid and seek an intersubjective justification for it. This is perhaps the most usual way of enquiring after a norm's validity. Yet we might also ask for whom, when, or in which cases a norm is valid. When it comes to the validity of norms in specific, real situations, these questions are often no less important than those concerning justification, which is why it is also crucial to distinguish between validity in general or *prima facie* validity (analogous to *prima facie* duties; cf. Beauchamp and Childress 2009, pp. 14f.) and context-specific or actual validity (analogous to actual duties; cf. Rehmann-Sutter, Porz, and Scully 2012, p. 442). In the following, I shall therefore also discuss aspects of validity that are significant for such context-specific validity. Furthermore, where each dimension of validity is concerned, it is important to think in a continuum, since (the) validity (of a dimension of validity) may be more or less given. Also, it has to be noted that because there are several dimensions of validity, a norm may have validity in one dimension but not in another dimension.

On the basis of the above considerations, as well as the definition of a moral norm and analysis of the deep structure of moral norms, now, four main dimensions of validity can be presented:
- *The dimension of rightfulness* (the norm is regarded as "right" or "true");
- *The dimension of applicability* (the norm is applicable to/fits the relevant cases);
- *The dimension of realisability* (the norm can be implemented and complied with/is complied with);
- *The dimension of impact* (the norm leads to the intended consequences).

In the subsequent sections, this categorisation will be elucidated through the discussion of fourteen sub-dimensions of validity (for an overview, see table 1, below).[16]

Table 1: Overview of validity dimensions

Dimension of Rightfulness	Dimension of Applicability	Dimension of Realisability	Dimension of Impact
Intersubjective Justifiability	Relevance	Acceptance	Effectiveness (of Sanctions)
Generalisability/ Transferability	Attributability	Observability/ Reasonableness	Functionality
Weight	Extent of Protection	Practicability	Reliability of Consequences
Legitimacy			
Institutionalisation			

---

[16] This list of validity dimensions likewise does not claim to be exhaustive; in the following, I only assume that it is possible to capture the central dimensions of validity. A number of validity dimensions that are considered less important by the author but that were originally identified in Mertz (2015, pp. 98f., overview on pp. 100f.), are omitted for reasons of space and readability. For this reason, the structural elements do not all have corresponding validity dimensions, and some of the validity dimensions that may correspond to structural elements are not presented. Finally, a few validity dimensions were also merged.

4 Dimensions of Validity, Moral Norms, and Empirical Information

In this final stage, the various dimensions of validity that moral norms possess (or at least could possess) in view of their superficial structure and deep structure are presented. This means that now the two separate results of identifying the structure of a moral norm (section 2) and of identifying dimensions of validity of a moral norm (section 3) are combined. For this, first, a main dimension of validity is shortly introduced, and then, various sub-dimensions of this main dimension are presented, along with the corresponding part of the structure of a moral norm.[17] The latter, together with their corresponding validity dimensions, are illustrated in table 2. In addition, considerations on the extent to which empirical information can influence these dimensions of validity (and thus also the respective structural elements of a moral norm) are included, thereby combining dimensions of validity and structure of moral norms with the question of how empirical information can influence a moral norm, i.e., where "empirical incursions" can be found.

4.1 The Dimensions of Rightfulness

When a norm possesses the following dimensions of validity, it is regarded as *prima facie* "right" (or even "true") – either in general or in a specific context – and is therefore binding for the relevant actors.

---

[17] A certain correspondence between structural elements of a moral norm and (sub-)dimensions of validity is given by the way both were initially researched: Having identified specific structural elements, it was possible to think about whether an already identified main dimension of validity is "applicable" to this structural element, and if so, what kind of sub-dimension it might correspond to. Conversely, but to a lesser degree, having identified specific dimensions of validity allowed questioning whether a structural element of a moral norm that plays a role regarding validity is still missing, especially concerning elements of the deep structure of a norm. Thus, the assumption of a correspondence between dimensions of validity and structural elements of norms is mainly justified by coherence, but also by deductive reasoning, i.e., starting from a structural element and reflecting on what would be required to justify this particular part of a moral norm (e.g., what kind of empirical information), which included thinking about respective dimensions of validity.

4.1.1 The Dimension of (Intersubjective) Justifiability

Traditionally, norms have acquired their general validity through their (intersubjective) justification or justifiability and thus ultimately via their rationality (e.g., Ott 2002). Such a justification aims to show that a norm is "right". This "justified acceptability" should not be confused with the actual acceptance of a norm (Ott 2002, p. 458), which is important for the dimension of institutionalisation and rests on the concept of social validity (as discussed in subsection 4.1.5). Neither should it be confused with the norm's fitness for certain purposes, which rather falls within the dimensions of impact and that of practicability.

In order to describe the factors that are supposed to make (moral) norms objectively valid, Gorecki speaks of "normmaking facts". These may include human nature and its needs, rationality, moral facts, and intuitions. For Gorecki, the presence or absence of such normmaking facts in part determines the validity of a norm (Gorecki 1991, p. 350f.). Yet even if we can speak of "normmaking facts" of various kinds, concrete validity claims always refer to the human beings who present them (Rohwer 2008, p. 12) and who may introduce them into a discourse or even implement them.

In attempting to justify a moral norm in a discourse, one might set out either from an "internal" justification that is immanent to an (already accepted) value and norm system, or from an "external" justification. A norm is considered "internally" justified when its validity can be derived from other higher norms (including principles) or by appeal to values. Many norms are directly or indirectly related to (widely recognised) values, and where these values are generalisable (i.e., can claim intersubjective validity), then norms can be justified through them (following Ott 2002, p. 458). E.g., paragraph 26 of the *Declaration of Helsinki* about obtaining valid informed consent (see section 2) can be justified by referring to paragraph 4, a paragraph that is part of the section "General Principles", and which states: "It is the duty of the physician to promote and safeguard the health, well-being and rights of patients, including those who are involved in medical research. The physician's knowledge and conscience are dedicated to the fulfilment of this duty" (World Medical Association 2013, par. 4). An "external" justification, by contrast, has to appeal to something outside the existing or accepted value and norm system in order to claim validity for a norm. This may be a "normmaking fact" or a "rule of recognition" (Gorecki 1991, pp. 350, 353), i.e., a meta-norm that is used to refer to another norm system. E.g., paragraph 26 of the *Declaration of Helsinki* can be justified by referring to deontological or "rights-based" normative theories that emphasise the right of persons to decide freely on matters that concerns them, or by referring to consequentialist theories that argue that well-being and future willingness of potential subjects to participate in research may be reduced when research participants are included without being able to give informed consent.

Here it is important to note two things that "justification" need not necessarily imply. Firstly, it need not mean "non-empirical". The acceptance of a (moral) norm can be regarded as rational and thus as justified if it has been critically examined in light of the relevant empirical facts and argumentative theory, i.e., if it is accepted in the face of *all* the relevant information. Empirical information can also play a role in arguments in the field of discourse ethics, and in consequentialist theories, it is precisely the (expected) empirical consequences of a norm that serve to justify it (insofar as they lead, e.g., to less pain and greater happiness). Secondly, justification need not only imply validity in a philosophical sense. Although it is common to draw an (interdisciplinary) distinction between philosophical validity, legal validity, and social validity, and to understand philosophical validity as "validity based on justification" (Lübbe 1990, p. 599; own translation),[18] it is difficult to see why the validity of positive statutes (law) should not (also) require justification, in order to ensure both the effectiveness and the legitimacy of legal norms.

It should also be noted that the reasons why a norm is valid (right) are not necessarily the same as the reasons why a particular actor should observe it. The dimension of (intersubjective) justification, however, generally presumes ideal actors – and perhaps has to do so for theoretical reasons –, yet real actors have various motivational and cognitive limitations (Schleidgen, Jungert, and Bauer 2009, p. 61). This highlights the need to also take into account dimensions of validity that relate to factors such as actors' motivations and norm observance. A norm justification can then be used to show that a norm fulfils certain moral criteria, but it is not identical to the establishment of social validity or of other forms of validity, even if the norm justification may be relevant where motivational questions are concerned.

This is why a (norm) justification is understood here as providing justificatory reasons as to why a norm is valid (right) or – according to some meta-ethical positions – true. At issue here is not simply an instrumental rationality (as when the subjective reason for complying with a norm is the potential sanction that may otherwise be incurred, e.g., a clinical researcher complying with the norm of obtaining informed consent only because if she or he would not, her or his research could be discontinued, which is contrary to her or his interests), but rather a reflective, evaluative, and sometimes normative form of rationality that is not (only) bound to one's own interests, but on "good reasons" in an

---

[18] Original wording: "Geltung kraft Begründung".

open, intersubjective and argumentative discourse. The latter is one form of norm authority, if not the only form.

The structural elements of a moral norm: Unsurprisingly, this dimension of validity corresponds to the following structural elements: norm authority (SS), and particularly norm justification (DS) and norm authority recognition (DS). It bears little or no relation to norm motivation (DS).

Empirical information: In comparison with the following dimensions of validity, this dimension is the one in which we might most critically question the extent to which empirical information can influence validity, with the possible exception to the assessment of empirical consequences as part of the justification of a norm, which is more unproblematic. Such assessment need by no means be confined to consequentialist theories, though in other normative theories it will often have a different status – potentially one that has little to do with a "justification" as understood here, and more with what later is subsumed under the dimensions of impact.

Where the above-mentioned "normmaking facts" are concerned, however, empirical research inevitably comes into the frame, since such facts are often based on (sometimes insufficiently informed or considered) anthropological, sociological, or psychological background assumptions concerning "human nature", individual and group behaviour, the functioning of institutions and organisations, human society, and the relation between society and the individual (see, e.g., Haimes 2002, Graumann and Lindemann 2009). Empirical data can either confirm or correct such assumptions concerning human nature and other subjects (e.g., Singer 1998), and can thereby play a role in determining the validity of the norm. Justifications based strongly on the existence of (a specific understanding of) free will could be challenged by empirical investigations of, e.g., experimental psychology or neuroscience denying such a capacity. Where the "internal" justification of norms is concerned, it is also possible to empirically investigate whether the underlying values or superordinate norms are sufficiently acknowledged in the relevant society. The emphasis on autonomy of patients that is most often part of modern Western medical ethics may be contrasted with empirical results that some patients actually do not want this high amount of autonomy when it comes to medical decision-making, e.g., they may want to rely more on the physician's expertise and recommendation because they feel overburdened by making autonomous decisions according to medical ethics' ideals. Such enquiries can also bear on the dimension of acceptance (see below), even though this dimension is concerned with the acceptance of the norm itself, rather than its potential underlying values.

4.1.2 The Dimension of Generalisability/Transferability

This dimension is concerned with whether, as a result of social, political, and cultural conditions, a norm is only valid for a particular institution or country, or whether it may retain its validity in another institution or country.[19] Regardless of its intersubjective justification, a norm that "works" in the particular social and political conditions of one cultural setting may not work in another cultural setting. If we were to accept for the sake of argument that the justification for euthanasia were wholly uncontroversial in the Netherlands, this does not mean that the relevant norms could be applied, say, to Germany, i.e., that they would be valid in this new context. It is likewise questionable whether the moral norms of a contemporary veganism adapted to the way of life of industrialised nations could be transferred to a society in which every possible food source needs to be utilised to prevent starvation. Contexts therefore need to exhibit sufficient structural and/or functional similarity in order for a norm to be generalised or transferred in this sense.

The structural elements of a moral norm: Where this dimension is concerned, the following structural elements are also particularly important: norm authority (SS), norm justification (DS), and norm authority recognition (DS).

Empirical information: This dimension reflects a rather pragmatic conception of the validity of moral norms, since these cannot be evaluated here without reference to the relevant context and social circumstances. If one accepts, however, that the possibility of transferring norms from one specific social context to another depends on the associated conditions and the similarity of the contexts, then quantitative studies are required to confirm this generalisability. It must be empirically shown that the conditions, living circumstances, and contexts in which people act are sufficiently similar as a whole and not just in certain individual cases. Empirical data (of a qualitative nature) can also contradict the generalisability of norms when it shows that the contexts in which the norm is supposed to apply in fact differ too greatly from one another to be adequately addressed by the norm. Last but not least, assumptions concerning the universality of values and principles in philosophical reflection can be confirmed, cor-

---

[19] This is why "generalisability" does not mean universalisability; it is not the question of whether one can convincingly argue that person A should observe a norm as much as person B insofar as the conditions for the two are the same, or whether the norm is just as valid for the one who expresses it as the one to whom it is directed. In accordance with the terminology used here, the question of the universality of norms is a question of (intersubjective) justification, i.e., of whether a norm can be intersubjectively accepted on a rational basis, and not one of its generalisability to different social and cultural settings.

rected, or even rejected by means of empirical studies (Alvarez 2001, pp. 510f.), which can also influence the generalisability of a (specific) norm.

4.1.3 The Dimension of Weight

If a norm is not especially weighty (or exigent) in a given situation, its validity or binding character, i.e., the reason for observing it in this situation, is diminished. This is particularly significant when two or more norms or principles are competing or conflicting with one another (as in a dilemma situation where two actions are required that cannot both be carried out) and so cannot both (or all) be valid at the same time, e.g., respecting a patient's wish not to treat a potentially deadly infection, but being also compelled to treat the infection by a principle of beneficence or by the physician's duty to provide medical care. At this point, if not before, a further criterion is needed to evaluate the validity of the norms in question (following Reßing 2009, p. 31). This criterion is the absolute or relative weight of a norm in relation to a competing norm. Where a norm carries absolute weight in relation to other norms, it will enjoy greater (general and context-specific) validity in any situation. If it only carries relative weight in relation to other norms, the situation in question will determine whether it enjoys greater (general or context-specific) validity. This is often referred to as the weighing and balancing of norms (see, e.g., Beauchamp and Childress 2009, pp. 19f.), which generally consists in weighing up the goods that the norm is intended to safeguard or promote, i.e., in determining which goods are most important.

The structural elements of a moral norm: The structural elements that correspond to this dimension of validity are the substance (SS) and exigency (DS) of the norm, and norm compliance (DS).

Empirical information: In order to analyse a specific, empirically given situation (such as a "case" in bioethics) and to understand what is "at stake" within it, social-scientific research is not initially required, even if the relevant information is empirical in nature (such as the wishes of the patient, or who is affected by a decision and how). Social-scientific research can nevertheless provide information on the kinds of goods that are to be taken into account in "typical" cases or situations, through analyses of prior cases, e.g., or interviews and surveys with relevant stakeholders. For exactly what is relevant and important in any given situation, and in what way it is so, can often only be conveyed by those who are experiencing it (Rehman-Sutter, Porz, and Scully 2012, p. 440). This can help to reduce the risk of aspects of the empirical situation being falsely presented or understood, and thereby prevent false normative conclusions from being drawn as to which norm to follow (Dunn et al. 2012, p. 469).

Social-scientific research can also provide insights into the decisions that actors tend to make in such situations and the arguments on which they base them. Population and preference surveys might be used, e.g., to determine which goods should be considered important (or more important in cases of conflict) and/or why. Although such surveys should not be used uncritically on pain of committing an *ad populum* fallacy, empirical information can influence this dimension of validity either by indicating what is most important to protect or by providing arguments as to why a norm is or should be considered more important than another.

4.1.4 The Dimension of Legitimacy

This dimension is concerned with whether the norm-giving authority or the norm authority is recognised by the norm addressees or the broader population in a society (or community). The question may arise, e.g., of whether ethicists *qua* ethicists can be considered legitimate norm-giving authorities in a democratic society, or whether politically legitimated authorities or other similar bodies are needed to perform this function. Validity through legitimacy may amount to either general validity or context-specific validity. Where the latter is concerned, one might ask why, in research ethics committees (REC), health technology assessment (HTA), or clinical ethics consultation (CEC) projects,[20] the recommendations of ethicists should be considered binding for others.

This validity dimension is of course not easy to determine. Nevertheless, social-scientific studies on institutions, discourses, and the contexts in which actors operate may nonetheless provide indications as to which norm-giving authorities are (or may be) recognised (in each case) and which are not.[21]

---

[20] In CECs, ethicists may enjoy a certain level of authority, yet here too this authority is rarely all-encompassing, due to the oft-held view that ethicists should primarily function as facilitators or moderators, rather than as philosophers who attempt to determine what is morally right on the basis of moral theories (see, e.g., Reiter-Theil 2005, Haltaufderheide et al. 2016).

[21] One might object that this validity dimension involves confusion between genesis and validity, i.e. that what is important is not *whence* the norm originates but rather whether it can be shown to be valid. Two responses can be given to this objection. Firstly, one cannot say in principle that genesis can never influence validity. This is due to the fact that the genetic fallacy is an informal rather than a formal fallacy, and therefore admits of exceptions. If there are reasons to think that, in a particular case, the genesis of a norm can exert an influence on its validity, it is not fallacious to draw certain conclusions concerning the conditions of a norm's val-

The structural elements of a moral norm: The decisive structural elements in the dimension of legitimacy are the norm authority (SS), norm justification (DS), and norm authority recognition (DS).

Empirical information: Empirical information can be important in at least two respects in establishing or rejecting the validity of a norm through its legitimacy. Examples here would include (sociological) studies on what constitutes legitimacy in societies and groups and how it is produced, and on which norm-giving authorities are recognised in a society or group and why. Alongside such general investigations, more specific studies involving interviews or observation may also investigate whether a particular norm authority is recognised in a particular setting (such as a hospital or research institution). Where such studies cast doubt on whether a norm-giving authority is recognised and thus enjoys legitimacy, the validity of this validity dimension may be reduced.

4.1.5 The Dimension of Institutionalisation

The dimension of institutionalisation is largely concerned with what is termed "social validity". This usually denotes a kind of empirical (and general) validity that differs theoretically from the justificatory and legal validity discussed in section 3. To deny a norm's empirical validity (by stating, e.g., that it "only exists on paper") is clearly not to deny its legal or moral validity. As a form of empirical validity, social validity means that the norm is actually observed and/or recognised, or that socially valid norms are generally observed, whereas infringements are usually met with sanctions (Lumer 1999, p. 451); they therefore enjoy validity "through their influence on action" (Lübbe 1990, p. 599; own translation).[22]

The fact that norms are seldom followed by all, i.e., that there are deviations from the norm, constitutes a problem for the concept of social validity. Do such deviations not show that the norm clearly is not (sufficiently) valid? One potential probabilistic response to such a question would be to point out that those who act contrary to the norm run the risk of incurring sanctions (Lübbe 1990, p. 587). On this approach, the reality of a norm lies in its "impact prospects",

---

idity from those of its genesis. Indeed, this is generally how questions of legitimacy are in fact addressed: for the intended addressee group, what is important is precisely who or what originated the norm (such as a medical society) or how it was developed (e.g., via a formal voting procedure). Secondly, one might note that a lack of validity in this dimension does not necessarily mean a lack of validity in the dimension of justification; in the latter, the genesis of the norm may often be (largely) irrelevant.

22 Original wording: "kraft Einfluss auf das Handeln".

i.e., the risk run by those who violate it of being sanctioned (Lübbe 1990, p. 587; own translation).[23] While cases where norm contraventions go unsanctioned serve to reduce the norm's validity, then, they do not neutralise it entirely. This approach for measuring of the actual validity of the norm would seem more convincing than that of so-called effectiveness quotas, i.e., "the probability that in a particular situation that is relevant to the implementation of the norm (a norm-typical situation), the norm will either be observed or [...] will be enforced via sanctions", since this is more difficult to assess than, say, the sanctions imposed when legal norms are contravened (Hopf 1987, p. 242; own translation).[24]

Alongside the susceptibility of norm violations to sanctions, the fact that actors are aware of norms also ensures that they have social validity. To tie the social validity of norms purely to their actual observance or to the sanctioning of violations thus ultimately misses an important aspect of validity, whereby a norm can remain relevant for action even when it is contravened (Hopf 1987, p. 244). Accordingly, a norm has social validity or institutional validity when it is followed by most people and when contraventions are generally sanctioned, which also implies that norm contraventions are regarded as such in the relevant social group – i.e., that there is a consensus that the norm is valid and that violations have to be sanctioned.

The structural elements of a moral norm: This dimension of validity is reflected in the subject (SS) of the norm and the norm's mode of existence (DS), though is likely also related to the norm as a whole. The link to the mode of existence is due to the fact that a moral norm has to at least exist as a logical construct in order to be institutionalised.

Empirical information: On the one hand, the empirical information in question here relates to whether a norm is in fact followed and/or recognised (as "right"), as well as the parts of the population in which this is (generally) the case and in which it is not. On the other hand, empirical information derived from general socio-empirical research on the institutionalisation of norms and the conditions under which they lose their validity can also be drawn upon in evaluating this dimension of a norm's validity. Here one might then assess whether current conditions are propitious for the institutionalisation of a potential norm, using methods such as discourse analyses and surveys.

---

23 Original wording: "Wirkungs-Chance der Norm".
24 Original wording: "die Wahrscheinlichkeit, mit der in einer bestimmten, für die Umsetzung der Norm einschlägigen (normtypischen) Situation diese entweder befolgt wird oder [...] durch Sanktionen bekräftigt wird".

4.2 The Dimensions of Applicability

The following dimensions of validity are concerned with whether, in all cases x to n, the norm is (*prima facie*) applicable or suitable in a specific manner, i.e., whether it exhibits context-specific validity. They generally address the conditions that need to be fulfilled for a norm to be applicable to a situation and thus to be binding in a specific case – such as that an actor belongs to the norm addressee group and that there are no special rules or exceptions for this situation or this group of people.

4.2.1 The Dimension of Relevance

Whether a specific situation in fact belongs to a type that ought to be regulated by the norm is a question of relevance (cf. Lachmeyer 1977, p. 60). What underlies debates on, e.g., whether post-trial access (PTA) of new drugs tested in Third World countries, i.e., the free-of-charge or at least low-cost access to a drug for all study participants after trial completion, is obligatory (a) because it prevents exploitation or (b) because it may improve the health of the relevant community, is the question of which norms are most pertinent to this type of situation: those that prevent people being exploited or those that promote health.

A further important factor is the generality or specificity of the norm, i.e. the number of situations or cases that can be subsumed under the norm, as well as those that cannot be subsumed under it on account of the relevant exception clauses. This is important for the context-specific validity of a norm, since it may be crucial to know whether a norm is both applicable in general to a certain type of situation (such as "passive assisted dying in neonatology where the prognosis is infaust") and to specific cases with their own particular conditions (such as "a case of passive assisted dying in neonatology where the prognosis is infaust, and which is requested by the appropriate legal guardians contrary to medical advice").

The structural elements of a moral norm: This dimension is primarily concerned with the norm type (SS) and the pertinence (DS) of the norm, as well as the situation type (SS), exception clauses (SS), and the existence of the situation/circumstances (DS).

Empirical information: Empirical information is required to ascertain whether the particular situation we are faced with corresponds to the ostensible situation type for this norm. This may not be a trivial matter, since the task of understanding and recognising a situation that calls for the application of a norm may be aggravated by existing social practices and organisations. In some cases, it may be necessary to empirically investigate existing social practices in order to make clear the relevance of a norm to the (potential) norm addressees, by demonstrating that the situation in question (which may include or generate a moral problem) corresponds to the situation type: "Without data to prove that the problem is local – 'here, in our own institution' – it is too easy to dismiss the problems as not relevant to 'us'" (Solomon 2005, p. 43). E.g., discussions about norms regarding explicit rationing of health care may not be recognised as relevant for a health care system or individual health care providers as long as it is not shown that implicit rationing is already a reality, and thus such norms are needed to improve ethically the way rationing is done.

Empirical information can also show that a norm is not relevant because it is too unspecific. In order to assess which (further) specifications may be appropriate or expedient, it may likewise be necessary to carry out empirical studies based, e.g., on cases where the norm's application was complicated by a high level of context-specificity (Spranzi 2012, p. 482). Empirical studies can also demonstrate that exceptions are necessary, by showing that a norm is not permissible in a given context or would have undesirable consequences. This may be due to the particular situational circumstances, the unsuitability of the means available for the intended ends, or the presence of other norms that apply to the specific context. The evidence may also show that, in certain situations, a norm is applicable to a particular addressee group but not to another. Prioritising resources on the basis of cost-effectiveness studies may be a relevant norm for those who have to implement social policies (e.g., those who have to determine institutional regulations), but not in "bedside decisions from patient to physicians" (Pearlman, Miles, and Arnold 1993, p. 201). If such information does not by itself lead to a change in the norm addressee group, either the situation type will need to be described more precisely or an exception clause will need to be introduced into the norm stipulating that it does not hold for certain people.

Finally, the relevance of a norm is also problematic where empirical evidence demonstrates that what the norm is supposed to regulate – the situation type or the individual situation to be subsumed under it – is rarely the case, and probably will also in (near) future be rarely the case. The situation type implied by the norm is then in a certain sense "exotic" (think, e.g., of the moral norms that are intended to regulate our initial contact with extra-terrestrials), which is why the norm is only seldom relevant and therefore very rarely applied. Possible exceptions, however, are cases where it is empirically to be expected that they might *become* more prevalent in the near future, e.g., artificial intelligence and autonomous cars.

4.2.2 The Dimension of Attributability

Validity in the form of attributability is concerned with whether there are specific "competent" individuals among the intended norm addressees, or whether these are at all part of the "moral universe" (general validity) – particularly when the norm has already been more specifically formulated to state who should perform certain actions (a specified norm). A norm that calls for addressees who do not exist or who do not fulfil the conditions specified in the norm cannot be binding on anyone in a specific situation.[25]

The structural elements of a moral norm: This dimension of validity is linked to the structural elements of the norm addressee group (SS) and thus the existence/capability of the addressee group (DS).

Empirical information: At a general level, empirical information here may simply concern the preconditions that have to be fulfilled for an entity to be a moral agent – or, in other words, which entities can act morally at all and whether a particular entity adequately fulfils these conditions in a particular case.

While the basic capacity for moral agency is very widespread, it is clear that more specific conditions may need to be fulfilled in order to function as the norm addressee of a specific moral norm. These conditions might include, e.g., being sufficiently informed to make a particular decision or being a legitimate representative of a non-responsive patient. In such cases, empirical research can help to elucidate the conditions in which individuals are able to serve as norm addressees for a given norm (such as the experience they require in order to act in accordance with the norm or the extreme psychological conditions in which they can no longer function as a norm addressee or moral agent for the norm).

4.2.3 The Dimension of the Extent of Protection

In a similar manner to the dimension of attributability, this dimension determines whether specific individuals are to be considered among the norm beneficiaries (or are at all part of the "moral universe"). If there are simply no individuals who can function as norm beneficiaries in a given situation, the norm understandably loses its binding character. However, this might be seldom the

---

25 The difference between the dimensions of attributability and relevance is that attributability refers to the capacity of "moral agents" (persons), not to the prevalence or probability of a moral situation occurring and to the relevance of regulating a certain type of situation, et cetera.

case when it comes to more general or abstract norm beneficiaries (such as "all living persons"). It can be of more importance regarding specific norm beneficiaries, such as certain patient groups, e.g., for norms that intent to protect especially vulnerable persons (e.g., persons suffering from dementia). Then, it might sometimes be more difficult to decide whether a person is among the norm beneficiaries or not (e.g., is the person already suffering dementia, or is she or he just suffering mild cognitive impairment, thus may – reasonably – be not covered by a norm trying to protect persons with especially severe cases of dementia).

The structural elements of a moral norm: The most important structural elements here are those of the norm beneficiary group (SS) and the existence/capability of the norm beneficiaries (DS).

Empirical information: Empirical information can be decisive in determining the extent of the moral universe (i.e., who is protected by morality). Where the justification of the criteria determining who is morally deserving of protection or a moral patient is conceptual or simply stipulative in nature (like the criteria of moral agency), then it is still necessary to consider whether and to what extent an empirical object fulfils these criteria. In other words, in order "to decide whether regarding to creature X it is required to act according to [norm] N we have to validate empirically whether X is actually sentient" (Schleidgen, Jungert, and Bauer 2009, p. 67).

Whether someone or something (such as a severely cerebrally damaged person, an embryo, or an animal) is a moral patient and thus part of the moral universe is therefore an empirical question – at least insofar as the normative criterion determining when someone or something belongs to this universe has been established. Sometimes, however, even this criterion rests on empirical knowledge. In discussions on the capacity for autonomy among the mentally ill, e.g., an important role may be played by theoretical presuppositions that are susceptible to being undermined by empirical data.

In concrete cases, it may then be necessary to assess whether particular individuals can be classified as norm beneficiaries (i.e., "those affected"), in order also to avoid any bias in determining the extent of protection (see, e.g., Schicktanz 2009).

4.3 The Dimensions of Realisability

The dimensions of validity falling under this category are concerned with whether a norm is (*prima facie*) implementable and capable of being observed, or whether it has already been implemented and is observed and therefore binding.

It is not enough, then, for a norm merely to have a *potentially* binding character (see the above validity dimensions); it must also be *possible* for this binding character to be heeded – at least in theory. For this, aspects of the (social) acceptance of a norm, its observability in a given institutional context and its practicality as a means of implementation in a social praxis may play an important role.

4.3.1 The Dimension of Acceptance

The fact that a norm is formulated or justified does not necessarily mean that it will be implemented. In order to ensure that norms are complied with, "strategies that appeal to reason" may well be used alongside "sanction and power-oriented strategies" (Hopf 1987, p. 247; own translation).[26] Dunn et al. (2012, p. 473) argue, e. g., that norms have to be both convincingly (philosophically) justified (which here implies the dimension of justification) *and* convincing for the (relevant) norm addressees – otherwise they will not be accepted or complied with. A norm that receives little or no acceptance (in the relevant social groups) will lose its (potentially) binding character, which will reduce the likelihood that it will be complied with and render its institutionalisation more difficult (see, e. g., Birnbacher 2016).

The dimension of acceptance should be distinguished from that of institutionalisation, since norms may (still) be institutionalised even if their acceptance level is low or non-existent. Conversely, norms may be accepted that have not yet been institutionalised (on a broad scale) – someone might believe that a norm is right, for instance, without this norm being followed (yet) by the social group as a whole. The dimension of institutionalisation accordingly only registers *that* a norm is followed by a group, but not *why* the group members *de facto* orient themselves by it, i. e., why they (ought to) feel bound by the "ought" of the norm.

The reasons why actors in fact abide by a norm (or ought to) must therefore also include the reasons that the actors themselves have for orienting themselves by it or being motivated to do so. Even if these reasons will necessarily include instrumental, prudential, and egoistic motives (e. g., avoiding sanctions), actors may also be swayed by their understanding of what is "valid" (Lübbe 1990, p. 600).

The structural elements of a moral norm: Acceptance is reflected in a number of structural elements, including the norm kind (SS) and thus norm rec-

---

[26] Original wording: "an die Vernunft appellierende Strategien" and "sanktions- und machtorientierten Strategien".

ognition (DS). It is also found in the norm authority (SS) and the norm motivation (DS), and in part in the sanction clauses (SS) and thus the existence/effectiveness of the sanction (DS).

Empirical information: Empirical research is clearly required to determine a norm's level of acceptance. If we identify acceptance with, say, (broad) consensus within a group or society, empirical research using representative surveys might show that there is no (broad) consensus in a given case, or that there is indeed a broader consensus than had previously been thought, and this will influence the validity of this dimension of validity. Furthermore, empirical research is needed to identify the reasons why a norm is accepted or not. It can determine, for instance, which norms most strongly correspond to actors' preferences, intuitions, and views (Wendler 2006, p. 547), and which therefore have the highest validity in this dimension. In addition, such research can help to empirically determine what actors find helpful and effective (Lawrence and Curlin 2011, p. 213), which can in turn help modify a norm so as to increase its acceptability. In such cases, empirical findings not only reveal a norm's level of acceptance but can also indicate ways to increase this acceptance and thus the validity of the (modified) norm.

4.3.2 The Dimension of Observability/Reasonableness

Ethical thinking in philosophy sometimes tends to neglect the social and institutional contexts (e. g., involving group behaviour) that shape individuals' possibilities for action (see Solomon 2005, p. 43). The dimension of observability/reasonableness is therefore concerned with whether actors in a (given) social setting can follow a norm and whether such compliance is reasonable (e. g., does not lead to serious moral conflicts or involve illegal activity). The dimension is linked to the principle of *ought implies can:* briefly put, a norm whose observance would significantly disadvantage the relevant actors or that is simply unreasonable may lose its validity for these actors – regardless of whether the norm is justified or accepted by them. Here, also questions concerning the (psychological and emotional) overburdening of individuals that pertain to norm observability have to be subsumed. What is decisive for validity in the form of observability is that the actions required by the norm are in principle possible, i.e., implementable (this is what distinguishes this dimension from the last dimension in this category – that of practicability –, even though they are somehow related).

The structural elements of a moral norm: The most relevant structural elements with respect to observability and reasonableness are action (SS), norm addressee group (SS), and therefore also the possibility of action (DS), as well as to a certain extent the conditions of success (DS) and the existence/capability of the norm addressees (DS).

Empirical information: Empirical research is necessary to assess actors' potential psychological and sociological limitations. Empirical research using interviews, surveys, and analyses of written accounts may show that observing a norm would serve to disadvantage the relevant addressees, leading to overloading or overwork, psychological difficulties, or conflicts with institutional norms that cannot simply be annulled. Empirical research can also provide insights into why actors may act contrary to an existing norm – perhaps even one that they accept in principle. These insights may then reveal possibilities for modifying the norm. Empirical research can nevertheless also be important in verifying the presence or absence of *alleged* limitations – in assessing, e.g., whether the "practical constraints" mentioned by actors do indeed exist and hinder the observance of the norm.

4.3.3 The Dimension of Observability/Practicability

By themselves, norms by no means determine "how that which they require can be realised" (Rohwer 2008, p. 4; own translation).[27] The question of how the behaviour required by the norm or how the state of the world that it aims to promote can in fact be realised is not answered by the norm itself; a norm does not even have to entail that the required behaviour or desired state of the world is (fully) empirically realisable.

In light of the *ought-implies-can* principle, however, one can nonetheless demand that at least some means of approximating the desired ideal can be indicated, so that the norm does not merely retain a dubious hypothetical significance or risk being reduced to a "paper tiger". This implies that what the norm requires must in principle be possible, i.e., (physically and above all institutionally) implementable. In order to be recognised as a norm, to acquire context-specific validity, and to orient action and instigate the desired behaviour, a norm must therefore (also) exhibit a certain degree of validity in the form of practicability; a norm requiring transplanting organs (e.g., kidneys) to all who actually need one would be impossible in this regard (because available organs are scarce), even when individuals would, in principle, be able to observe the norm from a mere psychological or sociological point of view (i.e., it would not a lead to a disadvantage for the individual, or to psychological difficulties,

---

[27] Original wording: "wie das, was durch sie gefordert wird, realisiert werden kann".

et cetera). Such a norm would thus describe an ideal, but what it requires could not be implemented. Similarly, implementing physician assisted suicide in a hospital in Germany, based on an according moral norm, would currently be probably institutionally impossible, given the position of the German Federal Medical Association.[28] Nevertheless, a norm that has no practical validity, i.e., a norm that cannot be implemented or can only be implemented with great difficulty, can still have justificatory validity and thus a form of "ideal" validity in a broad sense.

The structural elements of a moral norm: This dimension of validity finds its structural counterparts in action (SS), the possibilities of action (SS), and in part in the conditions of success (DS).

Empirical information: The actual possibilities for and limits on individuals' or group actions that are crucial to the realisability of a norm can in principle only be empirically identified. The implementation of a norm is always accompanied by an "at least implicit image of the potential or actual norm observer or decision-maker" (Irrgang 2008, p. 384; own translation).[29] This image includes assumptions about what the actors or norm addressees are capable of, what they have difficulties with, and where their limits lie. It may be confirmed or corrected by empirical research, particularly where actors' motivational possibilities and limits are concerned (Schleidgen, Jungert, and Bauer 2009, p. 63).

A further potential task of empirical (psychological) research is to show how behaviour may be influenced (Suhler and Churchland 2009, p. 81). Accordingly, if such research shows that, as currently formulated or institutionalised, a norm fails to change behaviour, then the norm is not suitable for implementation in such a form and therefore loses this form of validity. Finally, research can also show why it may be difficult to implement a moral norm (Pearlman, Miles, and Arnold 1993, p. 198), which can help to show how the norm (and therefore its validity) may be enhanced.

4.4 The Dimensions of Impact

The dimensions of validity that fall under this category are concerned with whether and how a norm reaches its objectives and/or fulfils its function, or

---

28 The professional order of the *Federal Medical Association* states clearly that physicians are not allowed to assist in a suicide attempt ["Sie dürfen keine Hilfe zur Selbsttötung leisten"] (see § 16 in German Federal Medical Association 2018, p. A 5).
29 Original wording: "zumindest implizites Bild des potentiellen oder tatsächlichen Anwenders oder Entscheiders".

whether it is likely to do so (i.e., "its prospects for success"), and therefore whether it can claim to be binding. These dimensions ideally presuppose that the norm in question has already been implemented, or that similar norms have been implemented that allow us to draw appropriate analogies. In other cases, however, probability-based estimates may still be generated. Since the impact of a norm depends on its particular social setting, these dimensions are primarily concerned with context-specific validity.

4.4.1 The Dimension of Effectiveness (of Sanctions)

This dimension is concerned with whether actual behaviour sufficiently corresponds to the behaviour required by the (implemented) norm, or whether this correspondence can be achieved through sanctions. A norm can therefore be considered effective if there is a significant correspondence between the required behaviour and actual behaviour, leaving open whether a significant correlation is sufficient here or whether a causal connection also needs to be demonstrated (i.e., that it is indeed the norm that results in the observability of the required behaviour, rather than this behaviour (also) being generated by other causes). If it can be shown that the correspondence is due to the sanctions in particular, we can speak of *sanctions-specific* effectiveness.

A norm that has not yet been institutionalised, however, can still possess some degree of validity in this dimension as long as good reasons can be provided as to why it is likely to be effective. A norm that is effective should, *ceteris paribus*, be considered more binding than one that is not or may not be.

The structural elements of a moral norm: This dimension of validity corresponds to the following structural elements: the effects of the norm (SS), its conditions of success (DS), sanction clauses (SS), and the existence/effectiveness of sanctions (DS).

Empirical information: Studies on whether (ethical and legal) regulatory measures have achieved their goals or whether the implementation of a norm (in the form of institutional guidelines, procedures, documentation requirements, and so on) has been successful are relatively rare (McMillan and Hope 2008, p. 17). Likewise, research that evaluates implemented norms et cetera and that might lead also to improvements are rarely undertaken (though see, e.g., Wieschowski et al. 2018, Bossert et al. 2017).

It would clearly be inadmissible to suggest that what is empirically better (here: more effective) is for that reason alone morally good. Nevertheless, a norm that can retrospectively be shown – e.g., through surveys, observation, or document analysis (of, e.g., educational material) – not to generate the required behaviour to a sufficient extent is of questionable value, even if the norm is clearly justified and relevant. At the very least, a lack of validity in this dimension would make it more difficult to argue that someone should comply with a norm. Studies on the impact of norms, however, are always beset by the problem that such assessments are only possible if the norm or a similar norm has already been institutionalised for some time, even if only tentatively.

Empirical research can also assess the effectiveness of the sanctions accompanying the norm. Where potential norms are concerned, general insights into the effects of particular sanctions in particular situations can help to estimate the effectiveness of the prospective sanctions for the norm in question.

4.4.2 The Dimension of Functionality

If an (implemented) norm fulfils its intended psychological or sociological functions, it exhibits functional validity. Some of the important functions of moral norms include relieving cognitive and normative pressure on actors by providing orientation and justification (thus reducing moral distress and similar phenomena), promoting cooperative action, and conflict-regulation (e.g., Müller and Müller-Andritzky 1993, Bicchieri, Muldoon, and Sontuoso 2018).

As with the category of effectiveness, a norm that can be shown to fulfil its function or that can reasonably be expected to do so is likely to be more binding on actors (for instrumental reasons) than a norm that fails to fulfil its function. We might also consider a norm efficient if it meets its objectives and/or fulfils its function better than an alternative norm or a modification of the same norm. Now it is of course necessary to specify in more detail what exactly is meant by "better" here, i.e., whether it means the norm can (or was) implemented with less effort, whether its implementation requires fewer resources, whether it can better reduce moral distress among the relevant actors than other norms, and so on. Despite this need for further specification of the meaning of functional validity, however, it should be clear that a norm that is more efficient is also more binding than one that is less efficient.

The structural elements of a moral norm: The dimension of functionality tends to relate to the norm as a whole. In structural terms, however, an important role is played here by the effects of the norm (SS) and the conditions of success (DS).

Empirical information: Empirically assessing whether a norm fulfils its functions is similar to assessing the effectiveness of a norm. What is essential in the former, however, is not whether the required behaviour has been brought about but whether, e.g., the relevant actors feel better informed or better oriented, whether they feel less pressure in making decisions, and so on. This could be the case even if the actual behaviour was not sufficiently aligned with the requirements of the norm.

4.4.3 The Dimension of the Reliability of the Norm's Consequences

In this final dimension, validity results from the fact that a norm not only brings about the desired consequences but also does not lead to unintended and undesirable consequences, i.e. does not give rise to new (moral) conflicts that in turn have to be regulated (e.g., Irrgang 2008, p. 364, Mertz et al. 2014, p. 10). Since any action has consequences, and since action in complex situations and complex environments can also have equally complex consequences that are potentially difficult (for individuals) to understand, norms whose observance can be shown or predicted to lead to no or very few unintended consequences may acquire greater validity.[30]

While it is not unimportant to determine the consequences of actions of the norm addressees that act in accordance with a norm, this dimension is also concerned with the further consequences that may result from the implementation of a norm in social praxis, or from the fact that it is already part of such praxis. Here, too, a norm can have both desirable and undesirable consequences, even when the (direct) consequences of individuals acting in accordance with it are positive. A norm may help to improve patients' well-being through the actions it requires, e.g., while at the same time overburdening care-givers on account of the manner in which it has been integrated into their daily praxis.

The structural elements of a moral norm: This dimension of validity is related particularly to the effects of the norm (SS), its conditions of success (DS), and, with respect to the norm as a whole, to function fulfilment (DS).

Empirical information: The kinds of consequences that are relevant to this dimension of validity need to be recognisable or foreseeable, which may not always be easy, particularly when it comes to potential norms and norms whose effects are hypothetical. Examples here include the moral norm, proposed in the context of the Feminist Sex Wars, of banning the production and consumption of pornography on the grounds that both lead to violence against women, or moral norms involving the outlawing of first-person shooter games on the

---

[30] In consequentialist normative theories, the consequences of the norm can also serve as part of its justification, because consequentialism bases justification (solely) on consequences, often including unintended consequences.

grounds that they increase players' willingness to use violence or even create incentives for shooting rampages.

The extent to which particular consequences are demonstrable (and how) is one that has to be answered by the social sciences, (health) technology assessment, or in general by disciplines concerned with "outcome" research. It may also be possible, however, to estimate these consequences by drawing analogies from similar historical cases. Likewise, surveys with actors and other affected individuals can provide indications of the (possible) consequences and side-effects of norms that ethicists may not have considered. Nevertheless, a distinction should be made here between the mere possibility of an undesired consequence (as often is customary in ELSI – Ethical, Legal, and Social Issues – research) and empirically substantiated evidence that this consequence has a certain likelihood of occurring.

5 Conclusion

On the approach adopted here, moral norms are understood as part of normative (ethical) theory, which is why empirical influences on a given norm also have an influence on a given normative theory. Nevertheless, on this conception, moral norms are not understood *only* as part of normative theory; as social norms, they can also reflect lived moral praxis. Insofar as they are logical constructs, however (i.e., do not as norm statements refer directly to an observable object), they always remain theory-bound, even if they are not part of an *explicit* theory.

In order to assess the extent to which empirical research, particularly in the social sciences, may influence moral norms (and *a fortiori* normative theory), the present chapter considered the potential influence of such research on the *validity* of moral norms. On the basis of the above definitions and analyses of moral norms, I first of all argued that a moral norm does not simply has validity *as such*. Its overall validity is rather a product of various different dimensions of validity that relate to its rightfulness, applicability, realisability, and impact. A norm can therefore enjoy a significant level of validity in one dimension (e.g., in terms of its acceptance and institutionalisation) and a lower level in others (such as justification, or context-specific relevance or weight).[31]

---

[31] It can also be assumed here that different dimensions of validity may be dependent on one another (such as generalisability on justification, institutionalisation on acceptance, and so on). It is nonetheless unclear whether these dependencies are necessary or contingent, i.e., whether a particular dimension of validity always depends on another or only does so in specific cases.

Table 2: Elements of a moral norm and corresponding validity dimensions

Expl. Norm	N	states as NK	in T	with I:	"for all NA (except NA₁,₂,...)."	on account of NAT, it holds that,		for the benefit of NB,
Surface Structure	Subject	Norm kind	Type	Pragmatic linguistic function	Norm addressee group (with exceptions)	Norm authority		Norm beneficiary group
Deep Structure	Mode of existence	Norm recognition	Pertinence	Context	Existence/capability of the norm addressee group	Norm justification *(Norm authority recognition)*	Norm motivation	Existence/capability of the norm beneficiary group
Validity Dimensions	Institutional-isation (especially the norm as a whole)	Acceptance	Relevance	Authenticity [not addressed in this contribution]	Attributability; observability/reasonableness	Justifiability; generalisability/ transferability; legitimacy	Acceptance (justifiability)	Extent of protection
	Compatibility with the law [not addressed in this chapter]							

Expl. Norm	in all cases C of S (except in)	A [ensuring establishment/persistence of]		is x'ed,		or sanctions SA$_{1,2,...n}$ shall follow",	which brings about effect E
Surface Structure	Situation types and exception clauses	Action		Substance		Sanction clauses	Effects
Deep Structure	Existence of the situation/circumstances	Possibility of action		Exigency		Existence/effectiveness of sanctions	Conditions of success; (function fulfilment – especially the norm as a whole)
			(Conditions of success)		Norm compliance		
Validity Dimensions	Relevance	Observability/reasonableness; practicability		Weight		Acceptance; effectiveness (of sanctions)	Effectiveness (of sanctions); reliability of consequences; (functionality – especially the norm as a whole)
	Compatibleness with the law [not depicted in this contribution]						

Table 2: Elements of a moral norm and corresponding validity dimensions (*Continued*)

Empirical incursions into normative theory or into the norm itself can then be located in these different dimensions of validity and the corresponding structural elements of norms. One might find incursions, e.g., in those dimensions of applicability where relevance is determined using empirical specifications, or when empirically assessing who meets the criteria for a norm beneficiary. Where the dimensions of rightfulness are concerned, however, incursions may take place at the level of the psychological and sociological background assumptions (concerning, say, psychological egoism or the relationship between individual and society) that form the descriptive premises for the justification of a norm. Likewise, incursions may be observed in empirical assessments of the legitimacy of a norm-giving authority. Other important incursions may occur in the dimensions of realisability – when assessing, say, the reasonableness of a norm using psychological research – and in the dimensions of the impact of a norm, when investigating whether a norm does in fact lead to the desired behaviour or state of the world.

Though such empirical incursions may result in a norm exhibiting different levels of validity in different dimensions, this is unproblematic insofar as it would be too idealistic to demand that a moral norm should exhibit the highest level of validity in *all* validity dimensions in order to be considered binding. If we acknowledge a range of dimensions of validity, we can accept that "impracticality alone" is no "refutation" of a norm (Singer 1998, p. 485, see also Weaver and Trevino 1994) while nonetheless granting that the practicability of a norm may be an important factor in assessing whether to advocate it, and one that should not be excluded from our ethical reflection.

What remains to be discussed is the level of validity that should be considered decisive and the dimensions of validity that are to be regarded as most important (at least in any given discourse). Some dimensions of validity, e.g., are likely to be attributed greater significance in academic moral philosophy than in interdisciplinary bioethics or lived moral praxis. This analysis does not intend to address the level of validity required by a norm, nor how one might convincingly "grade" validity (on the basis, say, of "harder" or "softer" empirical evidence), nor which dimensions of validity should be regarded as particularly important. It rather provides a theoretical basis for discussing such questions. The value of the foregoing analysis of the structure of moral norms and their corresponding dimensions of validity therefore lies less in its revelation of something completely new than in its systematic ordering of various questions concerning the validity of moral norms and the potential influence of empirical information upon them.

Whether or not empirical information should or "should be allowed to" influence the validity of a particular dimension also cannot be addressed here; the aim of the chapter was rather simply to show where it may do so. Which empirical incursions into the validity of moral norms are to be considered permissible depends heavily on the normative theory to which one subscribes and one's methodological views on the relationship between empirical research and ethics (or in this case, moral norms). There are nevertheless very few *explicit* methodologies that address this link between normative theory, empirical information, and justificatory or explanatory relationships from a perspective beyond that of the basic models of classical deontology and consequentialism (e. g., Birnbacher 2016, Salloch, Schildmann, and Vollmann 2012, Widdershoven and van der Scheer 2008).

Any attempt to develop a methodology that would clarify which empirical incursions should be considered permissible in the different validity dimensions might be met with the objection that we do not need to take into account so many dimensions of validity in ethics – and particularly not those in which the importance of empirical information is relatively uncontroversial. On this view, even if we accept that "validity" cannot simply be identified with "justifiability", we can still question whether ethicists should have to address such dimensions of validity, which are perhaps better left to social scientists in any case. Should it not precisely be the task of ethicists to focus *solely* on the dimension of justifiability?

The response one gives to this question will ultimately depend on what one associates with "ethics" as an academic and practical undertaking, or what "kind" of ethics one engages in. Whether one is more heavily oriented toward classical philosophical ethics in the form of general normative ethics or toward a strongly interdisciplinary and practical applied ethics, as is often the case in bioethics, will of course make a difference here.[32] The closer one comes to praxis and to working *with* practitioners, the more strongly one should bear in mind other dimensions of validity alongside justifiability, especially since the difficulties encountered in such areas do not usually revolve around a "mid-level principle" such as "respect for patient autonomy" (including the duty of obtaining informed consent) requiring extensive justification in order to acquire validity. The challenges encountered in these areas consist rather in how to specify such a principle as a norm in order to ensure that it is relevant and effective in practice, and therefore (more) binding, or how to ensure that what should

---

[32] Incidentally, nothing in principle speaks against a division of labour whereby primarily philosophical ethicists on the one hand and primarily interdisciplinary ethicists on the other would address different ethical questions, topics, and problems – including, in this case, different dimensions of a moral norm's validity.

be achieved is in fact achieved by means of suitable "tools" (such as handouts, guidelines, decision-making models, processual changes, and so on).

Where this last point in particular is concerned, empirical research is crucial in ensuring that we (continue to) argue and act on a rigorous basis and therefore maintain quality standards that – above all – should protect those who are affected by a norm (such as patients or their relatives). Establishing or maintaining links with empirical research when constructing, modifying, and evaluating moral norms or ensuring their validity is then itself an ethical requirement that ethicists working in practically oriented domains should not seek to evade.

Bibliography

Alvarez, Allen (2001): "How Rational Should Bioethics Be? The Value of Empirical Approaches". In: *Bioethics* 15 (5–6), pp. 501–519.

Arras, John (2007): "The Way We Reason Now. Reflective Equilibrium in Bioethics". In: Steinbock, Bonnie (ed.): *The Oxford Handbook of Bioethics*. Oxford and New York: Oxford University Press, pp. 46–71.

Beauchamp, Tom and Childress, James (2009): *Principles of Biomedical Ethics*. New York: Oxford University Press.

Bicchieri, Cristina; Muldoon, Ryan, and Sontuoso, Alessandro (2018): "Social Norms". In: Zalta, Edward (ed.): *The Stanford Encyclopedia of Philosophy*. https://plato.stanford.edu/archives/win2018/entries/social-norms/, retrieved on November 14, 2018.

Birnbacher, Dieter (2016): "Where and When Ethics Needs Empirical Facts". In: Brand, Cordula (ed.): *Dual-Process Theories in Moral Psychology. Interdisciplinary Approaches to Theoretical, Empirical and Practical Considerations*. Wiesbaden: Springer VS, pp. 41–55.

Borry, Pascal; Schotsmans, Paul, and Dierickx, Kris (2005): "The Birth of the Empirical Turn in Bioethics". In: *Bioethics* 19 (1), pp. 49–71.

Bossert, Sabine; Kahrass, Hannes; Heinemeyer, Ulrike; Prokein, Jana, and Strech, Daniel (2017): "Participatory Improvement of a Template for Informed Consent Documents in Biobank Research. Study Results and Methodological Reflections". In: *BMC Medical Ethics* 18 (78).

Copp, David (2006): "Introduction. Metaethics and Normative Ethics". In: id. (ed.): *The Oxford Handbook of Ethical Theory*. Oxford and New York: Oxford University Press, pp. 3–35.

Copp, David (ed.) (2006): *The Oxford Handbook of Ethical Theory*. Oxford and New York: Oxford University Press.

de Vries, Rob and Gordijn, Bert (2009): "Empirical Ethics and Its Alleged Meta-Ethical Fallacies". In: *Bioethics* 23 (4), pp. 193–201.

Dietrich, Julia (2009): "Die Kraft der Konkretion oder Die Rolle deskriptiver Annahmen für die Anwendung und Kontextsensitivität ethischer Theorie". In: *Ethik in der Medizin* 21 (3), pp. 213–221.

Dunn, Michael; Sheehan, Mark; Hope, Tony, and Parker, Michael (2012): "Toward Methodological Innovation in Empirical Ethics Research". In: *Cambridge Quarterly of Healthcare Ethics* 21 (4), pp. 466–480.
Emanuel, Ezekiel; Grady, Christine, and Wendler, David (2008): "An Ethical Framework for Biomedical Research". In: Emanuel, Ezekiel; Grady, Christine; Crouch, Robert; Lie, Reidar; Miller, Franklin, and Wendler, David (eds.): *The Oxford Textbook of Clinical Research Ethics*. New York: Oxford University Press, pp. 123–135.
Eriksson, Stefan; Helgesson, Gert, and Segerdahl, Pär (2006): "Provide Expertise or Facilitate Ethical Reflection? A Comment in the Debate Between Cowley and Crosthwaite". In: *Medicine, Healthcare and Philosophy* 9 (3), pp. 389–392.
Frith, Lucy (2012): "Symbiotic Empirical Ethics. A Practical Methodology". In: *Bioethics* 26 (4), pp. 198–206.
German Federal Medical Association (2018): "(Muster-)Berufsordnung für die in Deutschland tätigen Ärztinnen und Ärzte". In: *Deutsches Ärzteblatt* 115 (24), pp. A 1–9.
Goldenberg, Maja (2005): "Evidence-Based Ethics? On Evidence-Based Practice and the 'Empirical Turn' from Normative Bioethics". In: *BMC Medical Ethics* 6 (11).
Gorecki, Jan (1991): "Moral Norms. The Problem of Justification Reconsidered". In: *The Journal of Value Inquiry* 25 (4), pp. 349–359.
Graumann, Sigrid and Lindemann, Gesa (2009): "Medizin als gesellschaftliche Praxis, sozialwissenschaftliche Empirie und ethische Reflexion. Ein Vorschlag für eine soziologisch aufgeklärte Medizinethik". In: *Ethik in der Medizin* 21 (3), pp. 235–245.
Haimes, Erica (2002): "What Can the Social Sciences Contribute to the Study of Ethics? Theoretical, Empirical and Substantive Considerations". In: *Bioethics* 16 (2), pp. 89–113.
Haltaufderheide, Joschka; Mertz, Marcel; Vollmann, Jochen, and Schildmann, Jan (2016): "Open Peer Commentary. Do Not Try to Run Before You Can Walk. Empirical and Meta-Ethical Presuppositions of Using Ethical Theory in Clinical Ethics Consultation". In: *The American Journal of Bioethics* 16 (9), pp. 51–53.
Hopf, Christel (1987): "Normen in formalen Organisationen. Theoretische und methodische Probleme der empirischen Analyse". In: *Zeitschrift für Soziologie* 16 (4), pp. 239–253.
Howick, Jeremy (2011): *The Philosophy of Evidence-Based Medicine*. Chichester: John Wiley & Sons.
Irrgang, Bernhard (2008): "Realisierbarkeit sittlicher Urteile als ethisches Kriterium. Implikationen für Theorien angewandter Ethik". In: Zichy, Michael and Grimm, Herwig (eds.): *Praxis in der Ethik. Zur Methodenreflexion in der anwendungsorientierten Moralphilosophie*. Berlin: Walter de Gruyter, pp. 359–386.
Ives, Jonathan; Dunn, Michael, and Cribb, Alan (eds.) (2017): *Empirical Bioethics. Theoretical and Practical Perspectives*. Cambridge: Cambridge University Press.
Ives, Jonathan; Dunn, Michael; Molewijk, Bert; Schildmann, Jan; Baeroe, Kristine; Frith, Lucy; Huxtable, Richard; Landeweer, Elleke; Mertz, Marcel; Provoost, Veerle; Rid, Annette; Salloch, Sabine; Sheehan, Mark; Strech, Daniel; de Vries, Martine, and Widdershoven, Guy (2018): "Standards of Practice in Empirical Bioethics Research. Towards a Consensus". In: *BMC Medical Ethics* 19 (68).
Kaminsky, Carmen (1999): "'Angewandte Ethik' zwischen Moralphilosophie und Politik". In: Rippe, Klaus (ed.): *Angewandte Ethik in der pluralistischen Gesellschaft*. Freiburg im Üechtland: Universitätsverlag Freiburg, pp. 143–159.
Kitcher, Philipp (2011): *The Ethical Project*. Cambridge: Harvard University Press.

Knobe, Joshua and Nichols, Shaun (eds.) (2008): *Experimental Philosophy*. Oxford: Oxford University Press.
Kohl, Markus (2015): "Kant and 'Ought Implies Can'". In: *The Philosophical Quarterly* 65 (261), pp. 690–710.
Kunz, Regina; Ollenschläger, Günter; Raspe, Heiner, and Jonitz, Günther (eds.) (2007): *Lehrbuch Evidenzbasierte Medizin in Klinik und Praxis*. Cologne: Deutscher Ärzte-Verlag.
Lachmeyer, Friedrich (1977): *Grundzüge einer Normentheorie. Zur Struktur der Normen dargestellt am Beispiel des Rechtes*. Berlin: Duncker & Humblot.
Lawrence, Ray and Curlin, Farr (2011): "The Rise of Empirical Research in Medical Ethics. A MacIntyrean Critique and Proposal". In: *Journal of Medicine and Philosophy* 36 (2), pp. 206–216.
Lübbe, Weyma (1990): "Der Normgeltungsbegriff als probabilistischer Begriff. Zur Logik des soziologischen Normbegriffs". In: *Zeitschrift für philosophische Forschung* 44 (4), pp. 583–602.
Luetge, Christoph; Rusch, Hannes, and Uhl, Matthias (eds.) (2014): *Experimental Ethics. Towards an Empirical Moral Philosophy*. New York: Palgrave Macmillan.
Lumer, Christoph (1999): "Geltung, Gültigkeit". In: Sandkühler, Hans (ed.): *Enzyklopädie Philosophie*. Vol. 1. Hamburg: Felix Meiner, pp. 450–455.
McMillan, John and Hope, Tony (2008): "The Possibility of Empirical Psychiatric Ethics". In: Widdershoven, Guy; McMillan, John; Hope, Tony, and van der Scheer, Lieke (eds.): *Empirical Ethics in Psychiatry*. New York: Oxford University Press, pp. 9–22.
Mertz, Marcel (2015): *Kriteriologische Unterdetermination von Ethik durch Empirie. Normgeltungskriterien für die Verwendung empirischer Evidenz bei moralischen Normen*. Doctoral Dissertation. In: *MADOC, Publikationsserver der Universität Mannheim*. https://ub-madoc.bib.uni-mannheim.de/37477/1/Dissertation_Mertz.pdf, retrieved on November 14, 2018.
Mertz, Marcel; Inthorn, Julia; Renz, Günter; Rothenberger, Geza; Salloch, Sabine; Schildmann, Jan; Wöhlke, Sabine, and Schicktanz, Silke (2014): "Research Across the Disciplines. A Road Map for Quality Criteria in Empirical Ethics Research". In: *BMC Medical Ethics* 15 (17).
Morscher, Edgar (2011): "Kognitivismus/Nonkognitivismus". In: Düwell, Marcus; Hübenthal, Christopher, and Werner, Micha (eds.): *Handbuch Ethik*. Stuttgart and Weimar: J.B. Metzler, pp. 36–48.
Müller, Günter and Müller-Andritzky, Maria (1997): "Norm, Rolle, Status". In: Frey, Dieter and Greif, Siegfried (eds.): *Sozialpsychologie. Ein Handbuch in Schlüsselbegriffen*. Weinheim: Psychologie Verlags Union, pp. 250–254.
Ott, Konrad (2002): "Prinzip/Maxime/Norm/Regel". In: Düwell, Marcus; Hübenthal, Christoph, and Werner, Micha (eds.): *Handbuch Ethik*. Stuttgart and Weimar: J.B. Metzler, pp. 457–463.
Pearlman, Robert; Miles, Steven, and Arnold, Robert (1993): "Contributions of Empirical Research to Medical Ethics". In: *Theoretical Medicine* 14 (3), pp. 197–210.
Rehmann-Sutter, Christoph; Porz, Rouven, and Scully, Jackie (2012): "How to Relate the Empirical to the Normative. Toward a Phenomenologically Informed Hermeneutic Approach to Bioethics". In: *Cambridge Quarterly of Healthcare Ethics* 21 (4), pp. 436–447.

Reiter-Theil, Stella (2005): "Klinische Ethikkonsultation. Eine methodische Orientierung zur ethischen Beratung am Krankenbett". In: *Schweizerische Ärztezeitung* 86 (6), pp. 346–351.

Reßing, Maximilian (2009): "Prinzipien als Normen mit zwei Geltungsebenen. Zur Unterscheidung von Regeln und Prinzipien". In: *Archiv für Rechts- und Sozialphilosophie* 95 (1), pp. 28–48.

Richardson, Henry (1990): "Specifying Norms as a Way to Resolve Concrete Ethical Problems". In: *Philosophy & Public Affairs* 19 (4), pp. 279–310.

Roberts, Laura (2000): "Evidence-Based Ethics and Informed Consent in Mental Illness Research. Commentary". In: *Archives of General Psychiatry* 57 (6), pp. 540–542.

Rohwer, Götz (2008): "Regeln und Regelmäßigkeiten". Working Paper. In: *Statistical Concepts and Models for Social Research, Ruhr-Universität Bochum.* http://www.stat.rub.de/papers/drn.pdf, retrieved on November 14, 2018.

Salloch, Sabine (2012): "'Evidenzbasierte Ethik'? Über hypothetische und kategorische Handlungsnormen in der Medizin". In: *Ethik in der Medizin* 24, pp. 5–17.

Salloch, Sabine; Schildmann, Jan, and Vollmann, Jochen (2012): "Empirical Research in Medical Ethics. How Conceptual Accounts on Normative-Empirical Collaboration May Improve Research Practice". In: *BMC Medical Ethics* 13 (5).

Schicktanz, Silke (2009): "Zum Stellenwert von Betroffenheit, Öffentlichkeit und Deliberation im empirical turn der Medizinethik". In: *Ethik in der Medizin* 21 (3), pp. 223–234.

Schleidgen, Sebastian; Jungert, Michael, and Bauer, Robert (2010): "Mission: Impossible? On Empirical-Normative Collaboration in Ethical Reasoning". In: *Ethical Theory and Moral Practice* 13 (1), pp. 59–71.

Sharkey, Amanda and Sharkey, Noel (2012): "Granny and the Robots. Ethical Issues in Robot Care for the Elderly". In: *Ethics and Information Technology* 14 (1), pp. 27–40.

Singer, Ming (1998): "Paradigms Linked. A Normative-Empirical Dialogue About Business Ethics". In: *Business Ethics Quarterly* 8 (3), pp. 481–496.

Smith Iltis, Ana (2000): "Bioethics as Methodological Case Resolution. Specification, Specified Principlism and Casuistry". In: *Journal of Medicine and Philosophy* 25 (3), pp. 271–284.

Solomon, Mildred (2005): "Realizing Bioethics' Goals in Practice. Ten Ways 'Is' Can Help 'Ought'". In: *Hastings Center Report* 35 (4), pp. 40–47.

Spranzi, Marta (2012): "The Normative Relevance of Cases. Rhetoric and Empirical Ethics". In: *Cambridge Quarterly of Healthcare Ethics* 21 (4), pp. 481–492.

Steup, Matthias (2018): "Epistemology". In: Zalta, Edward (ed.): *The Stanford Encyclopedia of Philosophy.* https://plato.stanford.edu/archives/win2018/entries/epistemology/, retrieved on November 14, 2018.

Strech, Daniel (2008): "Evidence-Based Ethics. What It Should Be and What It Shouldn't". In: *BMC Medical Ethics* 9 (16).

Strech, Daniel; Neitzke, Gerald, and Marckmann, Georg (2012): "Public-Health-Ethik. Normative Grundlagen und methodisches Vorgehen". In: Schwartz, Friedrich; Walter, Ulla; Siegrist, Johannes; Kolip, Petra; Leidl, Reiner; Dierks, Marie-Luise; Busse, Reinhard, and Schneider, Nils (eds.): *Public Health. Gesundheit und Gesundheitswesen.* Munich: Urban & Fischer, pp. 137–142.

Suhler, Christopher and Churchland, Patricia (2009): "Psychology and Medical Decision-Making". In: *The American Journal of Bioethics* 9 (6–7), pp. 79–81.

Thiel, Christian (2004): "Geltung". In: Mittelstrass, Jürgen (ed.): *Enzyklopädie Philosophie und Wissenschaftstheorie*. Vol. 1. Stuttgart and Weimar: J.B. Metzler, p. 729.

Toulmin, Stephen (1982): "How Medicine Saved the Life of Ethics". In: *Perspectives in Biology and Medicine* 25 (4), pp. 736–750.

van Ackeren, Marcel and Kühler, Michael (eds.) (2016): *The Limits of Moral Obligation. Moral Demandingness and Ought Implies Can*. New York: Routledge.

Weaver, Gary and Trevino, Linda (1994): "Normative and Empirical Business Ethics. Separation, Marriage of Convenience, or Marriage of Necessity?". In: *Business Ethics Quarterly* 4 (2), pp. 129–143.

Wendler, David (2006): "One-Time General Consent for Research on Biological Samples". In: *British Journal of Medicine* 332 (7540), pp. 544–547.

Widdershoven, Guy; Abma, Tineke, and Molewijk, Bert (2009): "Empirical Ethics as Dialogical Practice". In: *Bioethics* 23 (4), pp. 236–248.

Widdershoven, Guy and van der Scheer, Lieke (2008): "Theory and Methodology of Empirical Ethics. A Pragmatic Hermeneutic Perspective". In: Widdershoven, Guy; McMillan, John; Hope, Tony, and van der Scheer, Lieke (eds.): *Empirical Ethics in Psychiatry*. New York: Oxford University Press, pp. 23–36.

Wieschowski, Susanne; Chin, William; Federico, Carole; Sievers, Sören; Kimmelman, Jonathan, and Strech, Daniel (2018): "Preclinical Efficacy Studies in Investigator Brochures. Do They Enable Risk-Benefit Assessment?". In: *PLoS Biology* 16 (4), e2004879.

World Medical Association (2013): *Declaration of Helsinki. Ethical Principles for Medical Research Involving Human Subjects*.
https://www.wma.net/policies-post/wma-declaration-of-helsinki-ethical-principles-for-medical-research-involving-human-subjects/, retrieved on November 14, 2018.

James Konow
Is Fairness in the Eye of the Beholder?[1]
An Impartial Spectator Analysis of Justice

Abstract: A popular sentiment is that fairness is inexorably subjective and incapable of being determined by objective standards. This chapter, on the other hand, seeks to establish evidence on unbiased justice and to propose and demonstrate a general approach for measuring impartial views empirically. Most normative justice theories associate impartiality with limited information and consensus. In both the normative and positive literature, information is usually seen as the raw material for self-serving bias and disagreement. In contrast, this chapter proposes a type of impartiality that is associated with a high level of information and that results in consensus. The crucial distinction is the emphasis here on the views of impartial spectators, rather than implicated stakeholders. I describe the quasi-spectator method, i.e., an empirical means to approximate the views of impartial spectators. Results of a questionnaire provide evidence on quasi-spectator views and support this approach as a means to elicit moral preferences. By establishing a relationship between consensus and impartiality, this chapter helps lay an empirical foundation for welfare analysis, social choice theory, and practical policy applications.

1 Introduction

> There is no objective standard of "fairness."
> "Fairness" is strictly in the eye of the beholder.
> [...] To a producer or seller, a "fair" price is a
> high price. To the buyer or consumer, a "fair"
> price is a low price. How is the conflict to be
> adjudicated? (Friedman 1977, p. 70)

The central concern of most normative economics is the distribution of benefits and burdens among members of society, i.e., distributive justice. The large volume of relatively recent empirical research on justice (or fairness) has demonstrated the importance of this value for economic decision-making in both the laboratory and the field, e.g., Corneo and Fong (2008), Ellingsen and Johannes-

---

[1] This chapter was originally published as Konow (2009).

https://doi.org/10.1515/9783110613797-013

son (2004, 2005), and Faravelli (2007). Attempts to apply lessons from such research must, however, confront sceptical challenges that, at best, views of fairness are inexorably biased, or that, at worst, fairness is a vacuous construct employed opportunistically. The popular belief expressed in the quote above that "fairness is in the eye of the beholder" is one that justice researchers frequently encounter in dealing both with the general public and with some academic colleagues. The abandon with which people wield fairness arguments, often on opposite sides of the same issue, contributes, no doubt, to the impression reflected in this refrain. Indeed, researchers have also documented that biased views of fairness significantly impact not only words but decisions about the allocation of real economic resources, e.g., Babcock and Loewenstein (1997). Nevertheless, this sentiment typically fails to distinguish the fairness of the implicated stakeholder from that of the impartial spectator. Moreover, fairness bias implies its complement: unbiased fairness. If an impartial standard exists, the crucial question, which is both theoretical and at least potentially empirical, is how one can identify what is just and the principles, if any, that guide unbiased justice. This chapter proposes an empirical approach to this question inspired by Adam Smith's (1759) impartial spectator model. The evidence presented here indicates the relevance of distributive preferences for economic policy across a wide range of real world contexts. It is also consistent with the conclusion that there exists an empirical means for identifying unbiased views that can inform social choice theory, welfare analysis, and public policy.

This study employs a simple method to explore Smithian impartiality in the context of justice. The method of investigation is the one used in most studies of empirical social choice, viz., attitude surveys consisting of vignettes (i.e., hypothetical scenarios) that elicit preferences over the distribution of benefits or burdens. Nevertheless, no previous study, to my knowledge, has addressed the particular problem raised here. Different research questions require different methods, and there are advantages and disadvantages with any choice. Given the goals of this study, a survey method was chosen, because, among other reasons, it allows one better to target impartial preferences and to do so over allocations in a wide range of contextually rich circumstances like those encountered with real policy analysis.

The terms "justice" and "fairness" refer, in this chapter, to impartial distributive preferences. Thus, the subject matter is defined quite generally, although it does not include certain considerations such as procedural issues and reciprocal preferences. Much justice research has focussed on equality, but an important and growing empirical literature reveals widespread preferences for unequal allocations, e.g., Cappelen et al. (2007), Ellingsen and Johannesson (2005), Frohlich and Oppenheimer (1992), Gächter and Riedl (2005), and Schokkaert, Capeau, and Devooght (2003). The current study is in this vein, and the eight distinct vignettes in the questionnaire prompt more complex distributive preferences that usually produce unequal allocations. They describe a wide variety of real world ethical concerns, including environmental protection, fair wages, welfare, job security, tort law, bioethics, globalisation, and media ethics. Four scenarios are not informed by any specific theory but rather concern issues in applied ethics, whereas the other four are designed with certain distributive concepts in mind, namely, efficiency, equity, need, and rectificatory justice. These cases represent an uncharacteristically broad set of real world applications for studies in this literature.

Another distinctive feature of this study concerns how "impartiality" is conceptualised. Rawls authored the most widely known approach to impartiality and justice: the ideal state for forming judgements about justice is an "original position" in which stakeholders are placed behind a veil of ignorance of any specifics associated with their roles or stakes. This normative approach suggests that information is associated with divergence of views, which is seemingly supported by studies indicating increased information contributes to biased moral views and higher rates of dispute. The current study explores an alternate approach to impartiality inspired by Adam Smith that seeks to elicit the judgements of impartial spectators, rather than implicated stakeholders, whom information is liberally provided, rather than denied. Actually, this is an incomplete description of the contrasting informational assumptions: Rawls also envisions plentiful information in order to enable moral judgement, as long as it is consistent with the veil of ignorance. But the version of Smith considered here does not restrict even personal information: agents are invited to reference their personal knowledge and experience-based intuitions, and impartiality is achieved instead through the absence of stakes. Nevertheless, this comparison serves primarily to provide background, since the purpose here is not to test Rawlsian impartiality or to evaluate empirically its merits relative to an alternative approach. Rather, the focus of this study is on properties of Smithian impartiality.

The hypothesis tested in this chapter is that the impartial spectator can be approximated empirically. But if spectator views can be empirically derived, this provides a means for justice scholars to identify general principles of justice, a foundation for social choice theory, and a practical guide for evaluating policy and implementing the exigencies of justice in real situations. An empirically informed theory of unbiased justice offers an attractive basis for both normative and positive analysis. In particular, an impartial spectator theory of justice is a promising approach to the kinds of issues addressed by normative theorists and political economists. For instance, it can inform questions of voting, income distribution, wealth distribution, and taxation. An understanding of "unbiased justice" can assist political discourse by helping to identify biased claims that are erroneously justified by manipulation of justice principles to unjust ends. It can also serve as a guide for economic policy in a variety of contexts, including in resolving labour-management conflicts, in the regulation of industries, and in the allocation of costs and benefits of public programs.

This chapter considers evidence on properties that are commonly considered desirable for impartiality. The results of the study indicate that, for spectators, information results in a convergence of views, i.e., it significantly reduces variance, and that the effects of personal characteristics, which can be associated with personal bias, are neither large nor systematically significant. These patterns are favourable to the claim that the impartial spectator can be approximated in the real world and provide a different perspective from much previous theoretical and empirical work. The results additionally illuminate factors that affect distributive preferences in a set of real world contexts.

Section 2 of this chapter discusses different theories of impartiality and summarises the "quasi-spectator" method for investigating impartiality. Section 3 motivates and presents the survey design chosen for the study. Section 4 summarises the results on means and variances and presents the results of regression analyses of the possible effects of personal bias. Section 5 concludes.

2 Impartiality

This section describes different theoretical concepts of impartiality and the general empirical approach to impartiality proposed here, which is inspired by Smith.

2.1 Theoretical Background

How should one conceptualise impartiality? Philosophers and social scientists have proposed various approaches, but two notions of impartiality have dominated most normative discourse in economics: the Rawlsian *original position* and the *impartial spectator* (or *impartial observer*) model. In *A Theory of Justice*, John Rawls (1971) explicated a thought experiment called "the original position". This is a hypothetical state in which self-interested individuals initially choose the principles that guide the basic structure of society behind a "veil of ignorance" of any particulars related to themselves, including information about their future position in that society. Rawls maintained that, under such conditions, there would be a high level of agreement regarding the principles of justice, which, he claimed, would protect the interests of the least well off member of society. A different approach is the impartial spectator model, which can be traced to David Hume (1983) and, especially, to Adam Smith in his *The Theory of Moral Sentiments* (1809). Heirs to Smith's legacy have stressed different aspects of his writings and have interpreted them in different ways. Many readers have focussed on sympathy, whereby the impartial spectator assumes the positions of affected parties, both cognitively and affectively. Common to both Rawls and Smith, however, is the notion that impartiality creates consensus. Indeed, Rawls explicitly asserts that, behind a veil of ignorance, people would reach unanimous agreement on the principles of justice. The relationship between impartiality and consensus is an extremely important, but largely ignored, aspect of both normative and positive justice research. Consensus provides a compelling foundation for prescriptive claims of the superiority of one set of outcomes, principles or ethical theories over another. In addition, some degree of consensus is usually critical to the formulation and implementation of policies in most social and political institutions. This, therefore, is the primary focus of attention in this chapter.

The chief impartial observer models known to economists are two that Harsanyi proposed (although Harsanyi rarely made any connection to Smith). Amiel, Cowell, and Gaertner (2009) present an interesting empirical investigation of these two models. In the one model, Harsanyi (1978) proposes that individuals have internalised moral preferences, which they might express as third parties (indeed, he suggests they might even express these as stakeholders trying to remain impartial). Nevertheless, Harsanyi allows that these moral preferences could differ across individuals. In the other model (Harsanyi 1953, 1955), he proposes that the impartial observer engages in a thought experiment. The observer considers the objective and subjective circumstances of every person and imagines himself having an equal probability of being each of those persons, ignoring his own actual station. This latter model entails judgements from a hypothetical state and, in this respect, resembles Rawls' original position. Both of Harsanyi's two models are formulated in terms of lotteries with von Neumann-Morgenstern utility, and in both cases he argues for utilitarian ethics.

The models of Rawls and Harsanyi are extremely important contributions to this literature. This study, however, is neither an empirical test of them nor a comparative empirical analysis of their strengths, important as that endeavour is.[2] Rather, it proposes and tests empirically a new interpretation of Smith's im-

---

2 Traub et al. (2005) report an interesting experiment that examines different types of impartial-

partial spectator model that differs in several respects from these other models. Harsanyi considers choice under risk, and the observers have potentially conflicting moral preferences in the one model or engage in reasoning behind a veil of ignorance in the other, as with Rawls. In contrast, I propose and investigate the impartial spectator as one who exists contemporaneously, is present in real people, is informed of the relevant circumstances, embraces a common value system, and whose judgements do not necessarily (and, in Smith's examples, usually do not explicitly) involve choice under risk. Some parts of this characterisation are consistent with Rawls or one of the Harsanyi models, but none incorporates this particular configuration. Specifically, this impartial spectator is not now and has no expectation of ever being implicated in the situation being evaluated, that is, he has no stake, real or imagined, that might bias judgements of right and wrong. Moreover, the spectator seeks to be fully informed of the relevant particulars and processes this information rationally with respect to internalised values. Smith believes that sympathetic identification can help one to understand better the objective and subjective circumstances of others, so the spectator also engages in this exercise. This chapter will focus on the incremental impact of information, an aspect of impartiality that has not only been largely neglected but that is often considered anathema to impartiality. Nevertheless, it is crucial to exploring the proposed concept of impartiality given the relationship it posits between impartiality, information, and stakes.

Obviously, as with all models of impartiality, the impartial spectator is stated in idealised form. Nevertheless, I believe what is promising about this approach is not only its appeal to moral intuition but also its practical implications for empirical ethics research. Veil of ignorance approaches have extremely stringent informational requirements: agents must reason from self-interest but ignore any and every fact that could introduce a self-interested bias into their judgements. The impartial spectator, on the other hand, is not denied any information, including about his own station in life. Indeed, the spectator is encouraged to acquire all information that might be relevant to reaching moral decisions, including possibly from his own experiences and circumstances. Impartiality in this model is achieved by considering only evaluations of individuals who have no stake in the situation they are judging.

Some critics have argued that the veil of ignorance is problematic on theoretical grounds: how much information is enough to evaluate allocations or institutions but not too much to bias judgements? Can such conditions exist even

---

ity, including versions of Rawls and Harsanyi, which focuses on choice behind different types of veils of ignorance.

hypothetically? Rawls would disallow even information about risk preference, but it is difficult to imagine the thought experiment that obtains under such conditions. Nevertheless, one objection is that it is even more problematic to actualise the veil of ignorance in the real world. Frohlich and Oppenheimer (1992) have simulated Rawlsian conditions in the laboratory using subjects who in groups reason about and vote on redistribution prior to being informed about their individual income classes. Their studies generate fascinating and compelling results about group decision making and distributive preferences, which mostly contradict Rawls' claims about those preferences. Nevertheless, it is difficult to believe that people really leave their personal interests and experiences at the laboratory door, as the veil of ignorance would require them to do, or to imagine how this thought experiment could be extended to real world situations where stakes are high and knowledge of one's position cannot be denied. In contrast, the impartial spectator is an informed party situated in the real world, even as an ideal, so one can more readily conceive of empirical tests of this model.

Although this study is not a comparative empirical analysis of the veil of ignorance and spectator concepts of impartiality, the review of these concepts in this section provides background to the current study and highlights some potential theoretical and practical advantages of the spectator approach. The next section builds on the *spectator model* of this section, which is stated in theoretical terms, to formulate the *quasi-spectator method*, which represents an empirical means for testing the model.

2.2 Quasi-Spectator Method

One can recognise the ideal of the impartial spectator in many real social institutions. For example, judges, juries, independent arbitrators, and regulators are all supposed to be third parties who seek all relevant information on the issues they are deciding without being tainted by any claim related to those same issues. Violations to this impartiality are often prohibited by law. In matters of jurisprudence, the rules of evidence are largely designed with the aim of liberally providing relevant information. Nevertheless, the ideal conditions of impartial spectatorship are probably never realised in the real world. For example, spectators with no material claim might still interject their interests into a situation by vicarious identification with the one stakeholder or the other. Even if self-interest plays no real or imagined role, spectator judgements can be biased by limited information or unrepresentative experiences. Given these facts, is there a means to identify to some degree of certainty spectator judgements under the less than ideal conditions that exist in the real world?

I propose to take seriously the sometimes implicit and other times explicit claim of most normative theory that impartiality results in unanimity. Since the conditions of perfect impartiality are presumably never obtained, however, one can at best observe the judgements of a "quasi-spectator". This is an observer who has no salient stakes in the matter at hand and possesses some, if not all, information relevant to his internalised moral values. The quasi-spectator method proposed here, therefore, refers to any empirical method that elicits the moral judgements of such agents. Given incomplete information, quasi-spectators might still disagree based on their differing beliefs about the unknowns. The notion that "true" spectator views can at best be approximated is in keeping with the kind of statistical uncertainty with which empirical researchers routinely deal and with a distribution of measured views that is not degenerate. But what evidence is there that spectator judgements can even be approximated? The critical property that I propose to address this question is *consensus*. This is a convergent trend of opinion by quasi-spectators that accompanies the addition of relevant information. This approach operates from the assumption that spectators share a common set of values such that, as information related to their values is added, their views of what is just will, on average, converge. Thus, complete impartiality and, therefore, unanimity are probably never observed in the real world given the difficulties of both eradicating all stakes and providing all relevant information. But convergence, on average, toward a particular view by quasi-spectators as information is added is taken as favourable evidence of the impartial spectator. Consistent with normative theory (and empirical method), then, consensus is seen as central to an analysis of impartiality.

Against this background, the current study focuses on consensus as a test of spectator impartiality: the prediction is that increasing relevant information will, on average, increase convergence (i.e., reduce dispersion) of the moral views of quasi-spectators. Considering conflicting empirical findings as well as alternate theoretical considerations, the relationship between information and convergence is an open question. Babcock and Loewenstein (1997) report a series of experimental and field studies of bargaining with plentiful information. They find that informing subjects of their positions increases rates of bargaining disputes and impasse, which they trace to biased processing of information. Their claim finds support in the psychology literature indicating that biases increase with the number of criteria at one's disposal (Dunning, Meyerowitz, and Holzberg 1989). Nevertheless, these studies involve stakeholders, i.e., implicated parties whose judgements are impacted by self-interest. It is not-surprising that, when interests diverge, views are biased and disperse.

Other experimental evidence, however, suggests that information promotes consensus. Konow (2005) analyses a series of studies, including bargaining experiments by Alvin Roth and his colleagues, in which information was varied. High information was generally found to decrease the variance of expected payoffs. Nevertheless, those experiments were not designed to address the question at hand and, therefore, limit the conclusions one can draw in this regard for at least two reasons. First, those experiments involved stakeholders bargaining over their own payoffs rather than spectators expressing unbiased preferences. Second, the procedures of the experiments provided little or no context for moral judgement, even in the high information conditions.

In contrast to these studies, the current one is concerned with the moral claims of third parties. Even with quasi-spectators, however, it is not clear on a priori grounds whether or how information would affect convergence. On the one hand, additional information could complicate moral reasoning, resulting in increased noise. Also, if individuals do not agree on moral principles or on their relative importance or residual interests corrupt their judgement, information could introduce elements that feed these tendencies toward divergent views. On the other hand, the quasi-spectator approach outlined above postulates that people operate from a common set of principles. If agents entertain multiple principles, then this model posits that, at least as impartial spectators, they share a common sense of how to weigh the principles, i.e., there is a high level of agreement on trade-offs. Relevant information allows quasi-spectators to reduce the role of potentially differing implicit assumptions and to evaluate more accurately the implications of their principles, resulting in greater consensus. Thus, whether information contributes to convergent or divergent moral judgements by spectators is also an open question on theoretical grounds. Since the evidence and arguments on consensus seemingly cut both ways, the null hypothesis that is tested in the analysis that follows is that information has no effect on convergence.

Some experimental studies have compared the decisions of quasi-spectators and stakeholders: Konow (2000), Croson and Konow (2009), and Konow, Saijo, and Akai (forthcoming) find that the decisions of the former are significantly less disperse than those of the latter. Although these results are consistent with the impartial spectator approach, these studies do not vary information to subjects and do not, therefore, address the central prediction of spectatorship raised here. In addition, studies relating information and stakeholder consensus, while interesting, do not bear on the matter at hand: the quasi-spectator method has nothing to say about whether stakeholder views converge more or less than those of spectators. Moreover, the self-interested bias of stakeholder views renders their judgements inferior to those of spectators for purposes of inferring impartial views (Konow 2008). Some survey studies, on the other hand, have elicited moral views of quasi-spectators under different information conditions, e.g., the important and seminal survey study of fairness by Kahneman, Knetsch, and Thaler (1986) presents alternate passages in different versions of scenarios. These interesting and informative results stimulated an impressive volume of subsequent research, but they are based on variation in informational content using contrasting versions. Similarly, Yaari and Bar-Hillel (1984) present contrasting versions of a question where information is stated as facts or as beliefs, but the basic information is not manipulated. In order to test the quasi-spectator method, however, contrasting versions do not suffice: one must observe the marginal effect of information, i.e., information must be varied incrementally.

Of the extant research, Faravelli (2007) is closest in several ways to the current project. In his study, students read two questions about a scenario involving Robinson and Friday and select the "just" distribution of a resource from among three or four choices. Different versions of the second question include additional information about the responsibility or need of the parties, which is often found to increase the frequency of certain choices. Faravelli's design is clever and well suited to his purposes, which include studying the effects of economics training and adherence to specific theoretical principles. His findings are generally consistent with the quasi-spectator method proposed here. The current study, though, differs in several ways in its goals and, therefore, also in its method: subjects face eight different scenarios, they choose allocations that "should be" implemented from a continuous interval rather than discrete set, different versions of the same question are never presented to the same subjects, the scenarios reflect commonly confronted contexts that require policy decisions, and the subject pool includes a broad cross section of college majors and years. The following section describes the specific design, procedures, and questions employed here.

3 Description of the Questionnaire

3.1 Design and Procedures

The quasi-spectator method can be applied using different empirical tools, e.g., one can elicit the decisions of informed third parties in experiments or the moral views of respondents to surveys. This study employs a written questionnaire consisting of vignettes administered to subjects who are university students. This approach has been widely employed in justice research, and, especially, in the empirical social choice literature, e.g., Gaertner, Jungeilges, and Neck (2001) and

Schokkaert and Capeau (1991). Specifically, this chapter reports results for two versions of each question, the high information and low information treatments, involving different groups of subjects (i.e., a between-subjects-design). I begin by reviewing some reasons for these choices below.[3]

Experiments allow stricter controls, but we are interested here in judgements embedded in real social institutions, and vignettes provide a contextual richness that is better suited to that end. On the matter of the degree of realism, more abstract scenarios could perhaps be more directly related to theories of justice, but in this study that point was secondary to questions of consensus in real world contexts. Also, more hypothetical content might seem more general, but specific context has actually been shown to aid reasoning about abstract concepts. Moreover, generality is addressed here by the use of eight very different scenarios, a number that is large by the standards of such research. A survey was also a more practical choice, given the comparatively large number of scenarios, the between-subjects-design for the low and high information treatments, and the more than 100 observations that were collected for each information condition of each scenario.[4] Material stakes have the advantage that subject decisions affect real outcomes, and the presence of stakes has sometimes been shown to produce significant differences in behaviour (Forsythe et al. 1994). On the other hand, Rubinstein (1999) compares numerous studies with and without pay and concludes that the results are qualitatively the same. Moreover, for the purpose at hand, the justice concepts that inform four of the scenarios have been corroborated in experiments with monetary stakes, as summarised in the following section. In addition, stakes risk introducing a different bias that is troubling for this particular study, namely, a self-interested bias.

As just stated, the results reported here are based on two information conditions. In the *low information* treatment, one set of respondents reads a scenario involving the distribution of some variable of social or economic value, e.g., how much to reduce the discharge of a pulp mill's pollutants into a river given the environmental impact and the effect on employment at the mill. The participants are not cast in any stakeholder role in the scenario, indeed, the text of some scenarios in this study explicitly promotes a third party view, e.g., the pulp mill is

---

[3] This review draws on Konow (2003), where the reader can find a more detailed discussion of the pros and cons of using different subject pools and empirical methods to investigate justice preferences.

[4] This concern was amplified by the fact that the results analysed in this chapter were part of a larger study that involved not only the two versions of each question reported here but a total of twelve versions per scenario. Thus, it would have been prohibitively costly to investigate this many variations in paid experiments or in the field.

portrayed as being located in a different part of the country so as to minimise any imagined concern by respondents for their own employment or hardship from the pollution. The response format is continuous on a closed interval, e.g., the pollutants can be reduced by any amount between 0 and 100 percent. In the *high information* treatment, a different group of respondents reads a scenario that is identical to the low information one, save the addition of a passage that contains supplemental information that was a priori considered relevant. Relevance was verified by an empirical criterion, namely, based on whether the information generated a statistically significant shift in the mean response of participants. In the case of two of the eight scenarios, content was revised to increase mean differences. In the pollution scenario, the additional passage provided more information about the consequences of different levels of pollution reduction for workers and neighbours of the mill. The between-subjects-design was chosen in order to avoid any tendency on the part of participants consciously to over-respond or under-respond to the different versions.

The questionnaire asked respondents to select how resources "should" be allocated. This might sometimes differ, however, from what they call "just", e.g., they might think taxes should be lowered but believe higher taxes are more just.[5] This issue arises from the subtle fact that justice terminology is commonly used in different senses, i.e., with different levels of specificity. As evidence in Konow (2001) suggests, survey respondents, on average, interpret the words "fair" and "just" in a manner that is intermediate to a quite specific sense (viz., accountability) and a very general sense, which encompasses all distributive preferences, including those that respect efficiency and need. Both the specific and intermediate senses are important to investigate, but in the current study I deliberately chose this phrasing with the aim of eliciting the more general distributive preferences that typically inform policy, as in the tax example above.

The content of the scenarios was informed by a stylised fact from various experiments. The highly controlled conditions of the laboratory can prove a powerful means of investigation, and it is often appropriate to restrict information about many variables, including subject contributions, abilities, choices, needs, and identity. The results of a number of experiments suggest, however, that subject decisions under such conditions are not always representative of the more complex distributive justice preferences typically encountered in real life. In particular, when the context is very lean, decisions appear to be made more frequently based on heuristics than is the case in more complex high stake situations in real life. For example, in many experiments there is no jus-

---

5 I thank a referee for this example and for pointing out the need to clarify this point.

tice-relevant information and equal splits often emerge as a modal choice, including in simple versions of the ultimatum game, the dictator game, and the trust game. Equal splits appear to arise here by default, not because of any general preference for equality.[6] Under such conditions, increasing information about individuals and variables of interest might very well increase variance, ostensibly contrary to the claim of the quasi-spectator model. But the object of the current study, and the domain of the quasi-spectator model that motivates it, is moral judgement under conditions approximating the usually richer information set found in the real world. That is, this method proceeds from a base (the low information condition) in which decisions at least potentially reflect some degree of moral reflection and do not just reduce by default to equal splits, and it then explores the effect on variance of additional information (in the high information condition). For this reason, it employs surveys applied to a number of real allocation problems in a wide range of situations with some moral context, even in the low information conditions.

Consensus consistent with the spectator model is seen here as a reduction in the variance around the respective means in the high information versus the low information treatments. Since an empirical criterion was used to define and corroborate the relevance of the incremental information in the high information condition, statistically testing differences between the two treatments might seem circular. This, however, is not the case: a test of difference in means helped establish the independent variable (relevant information), but the dependent variable of interest is variance, which was not used as a criterion for selecting or verifying the relevance of any survey content. Moreover, as previously discussed, other studies on the effects of information suggest that it is an open question whether and how information might affect variance in spectator views. Demographic information was also collected and employed to evaluate the possible effects of bias in spectator judgements that might be related to personal characteristics.

The method described above is very simple, but, to my knowledge, no previous study has addressed this question or possessed a design consisting of these particular elements. Although it is a prominent feature of normative theory, consensus has remained relatively neglected in the empirical analysis of justice. In most research, treatment effects have focussed on differences in means or cat-

---

[6] Konow (2003) argues that equality of allocations is not a general principle of justice, i.e., one that most agents value in general terms under the ideal conditions of perfect information. Rather, it surfaces for a variety of other reasons, including as a special case of other general principles, due to negotiation or cognitive costs, or as a kind of "default" when no information is available about the variables needed for more careful justice evaluation.

egorical choices, rather than differences in variance. Thus, most survey studies in this area have employed categorical choice formats, e.g., as with Faravelli (2007) or the seminal contribution of Yaari and Bar-Hillel (1984) to empirical social choice (although Gaertner 1994 is one exception). There are advantages to the discrete choice format (including potentially simplifying the cognitive task), but given the interest here not only in means but variance, the continuous response format is a more natural choice.

Given the large number of total observations needed, a convenience sample of students was used. Specifically, 1,383 undergraduate students from a wide range of majors signed up to participate in the survey to satisfy a course requirement for general psychology and economics classes at Loyola Marymount University from 2003 to 2006. Usually, most students in these classes complete the requirement by selecting several studies based on their schedules and nondescript summaries of the studies, minimising possible selection biases. A comparison of student and non-student populations across a number of studies of fairness and moral judgement sometimes reveals differences but indicates no remarkable pattern of subject pool effects. Indeed, the findings reported in Alatas et al. (2006) suggest that any social preferences displayed by students are expressed even more strongly in a non-student population. Various measures were undertaken consistent with good survey design. In order not to tax respondent attention, no subject answered more than six questions, and on each questionnaire form, long versions of scenarios were balanced with short versions of other scenarios so that the questionnaires could be completed in about 20 minutes. Simple and clear instructions prompted respondents to choose a single allocation for each question (instructions and the demographic questionnaire can be found in the Appendix). To deal with possible order effects, a randomised Latin square design was employed. That is, scenarios were randomly assigned to a variety of different orders. To facilitate comparison of results across scenarios, the response interval for all questions was from zero to a power of ten (i.e., 10, 100, 1,000, et cetera). The author read the instructions and answered any questions for all sessions. Participants were seated at a distance from one another and turned in their forms so that no one, including the author, could trace a form to a given subject.

3.2 The Vignettes

The complete questionnaire consists of eight vignettes (or hypothetical scenarios) that cover a wide range of social institutions and policy areas. Four are inspired by four different concepts of justice, viz., efficiency, need, accountability, and rectificatory justice. In order both to examine the robustness of any findings to a wider range of contexts, and not just to theoretically informed scenarios, four additional questions are framed in the context of four different fields of applied ethics, viz., environmental ethics, media ethics, bioethics, and business ethics. A word about the first three concepts of justice (efficiency, need, and accountability) is in order: these are three principles that have previously been proposed as a part of a general theory of distributive justice, e.g., Konow (2003). In that theory, context (i.e., the set of salient variables and individuals) determines the relative importance of principles and the trade-offs among them. Actually, any set of principles or values that is associated with a significant shift in responses when information is added would have sufficed, but I chose ones that have been found in other studies to have substantial explanatory power. Here the principles are applied to new contexts, which permits additional tests of their generality.

Table 1 summarises the eight questions according to which of the four justice concepts or four applied-ethics fields they belong, the social institution in which they are framed and the specific policy area that is addressed. Tables 2 and 3 present the content of the vignettes. The passages in both brackets and italic did not appear in the low information condition but were added to the text in the high information condition. I will now briefly discuss each of the questions.

Table 1: Summary of questions

	Social institution	Policy area
Justice concept		
1. Efficiency principle	Firm	Resource allocation
2. Need principle	Government	Welfare
3. Accountability principle	Labor market	Wage setting
4. Rectificatory justice	Judiciary	Tort law
Applied ethics		
5. Environmental ethics	Regulatory agency	Environmental regulation
6. Media ethics	Media/entertainment industry	Mergers
7. Bioethics	Health care industry	Resource allocation
8. Business ethics	Firm	Globalization

Question 1 is motivated by the efficiency principle, which advocates the maximisation of aggregate surplus. A number of studies have found support for this goal, e.g., Charness and Rabin (2002), Kritikos and Bolle (2001), and Oxoby (2013). Specifically, this question addresses the matter of allocating firm resources to maximise consumer satisfaction and shareholder value in the context of an actual technological change we have observed in recent years.

Question 2 addresses the need principle, which simply requires that allocations be sufficient to meet each individual's basic requirements for life, including for food, shelter, and clothing. In this example, needs are met through state support. Evidence of a concern for needs is apparent, for example, in the studies of Gaertner, Jungeilges, and Neck (2001) and Kravitz and Gunto (1992).

Question 3 reflects the accountability principle. Whereas the efficiency and need principles deal with the absolute level of allocations, the accountability principle addresses the relative size of allocations across individuals. This principle allocates in proportion to the factors that affect contributions and that individuals can control. For example, a worker who is twice as productive as another should be paid twice as much, if his greater productivity is due entirely to factors he can control (e.g., hours worked) but not if it is due to factors outside his control (e.g., a physical disability). This principle finds support in the results of surveys and experiments (see Konow 2000, 2003). Since the only difference between the workers in question 3 is hours worked, one would expect a fair distribution of earnings to be in proportion to their fraction of total hours.

Question 4 is about rectificatory, or corrective, justice. Whereas the three principles outlined above deal with *distribution*, this concept has to do with *redistribution*. Rectificatory justice, which can be traced to Aristotle's *Nicomachean Ethics* (1925), addresses an initial injustice that must be rectified by the redistribution of benefits or burdens between individuals in order to establish or re-establish equity according to the reigning justice principle or principles in the particular context. In the case in which one party is wronged by another, Aristotle's claim is simply that the one should compensate the other for losses. The scenario in this question is inspired by a tort case based on a real trial that was employed in a series of studies of fairness bias reported in Babcock and Loewenstein (1997).[7]

Table 2: Justice concept questions

---

1. A large company has two divisions. The one division produces film for traditional cameras, which is the business the company was founded on. The other, newer division is focused on technologies for digital photography and printing. Due to changing consumer demand, the traditional film division is on the decline and its share of company revenues is falling. The company's budget for plant, machinery and equipment in the coming year totals $10 billion, and its board must decide how much of this to devote to the film division and how much to the

---

7 I wish to thank Linda Babcock for kindly sharing the materials they used in those studies.

digital division. [*Company finance analysts expect revenues from the film division to fall from 60% currently to only 10% in five years. In order to protect the company's financial health and survival, they recommend focusing expenditures for plant, machinery and equipment on the digital division and devoting $9 billion of next year's budget to the digital division and only $1 billion to the film division.*] How much of this $10 billion do you think the board should budget for the *film* division of the company (Enter a number in billions of dollars from 0 to 10)?

$ _____ billion

2. The state provides support to those in need for a limited period of time. For example, John, who needs one year to complete a high school diploma, is eligible to receive such support. [*The state has determined that the basic needs of a person living in this area for food, housing and clothing equal $800 per month.*] How much do you think the state should provide in total support for John per month (Enter a number from $0 to $1000)?

$ _____ per month

3. Suppose Adam and Bill worked last weekend stuffing envelopes for a mass mailing. This job took a total of 11 man hours, but Adam worked more hours than Bill. [*Specifically, Adam worked 8 hours whereas Bill worked 3 hours.*] The total pay for this 11 hour job is $100. How much of this $100 do you think Adam and Bill should each receive (Enter amounts for each person below and make sure the two amounts total $100)?

Adam $ _____
Bill $ _____
Total $100

4. You are the judge deciding the outcome of a civil suit brought by a motorcyclist against the driver of a car that hit him. The suit demands $100,000 in damages for medical expenses, loss of earnings and pain and suffering (vehicle repairs were covered by insurance), but the actual award could be anything between $0 and $100,000. In court testimony, the facts have been presented as follows. The motorcyclist pulled out of a parking lot into a street a few feet from a stop sign and was thrown from his motorcycle when the car struck him. [*As a result of the accident, the motorcyclist has lost earnings of about $3,000 due to missed work time and has incurred medical expenses of around $12,000.*] How much do you think the court should require driver of the car to pay the motorcyclist (Enter a number from $0 to $100,000)?

$ _____

The first four questions are informed by justice concepts. The next four questions, on the other hand, address distributive justice more generally, without any theoretical presuppositions about the underlying preferences for the distribution of benefits and burdens. These scenarios draw from applied-ethics fields and help to establish that any pattern that emerges is not specific to the theoretical framework, while extending the analysis to a larger set of contemporary problems.

Question 5 involves a classic case of a negative externality in which the benefits of pollution reduction must be weighed against the costs in terms of lost jobs. Question 6 portrays a scenario inspired by a widely publicised 1989 merger, where the private interests of corporations were balanced against the public good of providing information on matters of public interest. In many communities, emergency care has been threatened in recent years and is viewed by some as being at critically low levels. Question 7 addresses the provision of emergency care versus preventative services at a hospital that has insufficient resources to fund both fully. One of the important transformations associated with globalisation is the movement of many manufacturing operations from developed countries to developing countries. Question 8 describes the situation of a US company that must decide how much of its operations to locate in a developing country.

Table 3: Applied-ethics questions

---

5. The Environmental Protection Agency (or EPA) is responsible for regulating the discharge of degradable waste by a pulp mill into a river. The pulp mill involved is located in a different region of the country. The EPA must decide whether to require the pulp mill to reduce its waste discharges into the river and, if so, by how much. Doing so would reduce various adverse effects of the discharge, but complying with EPA requirements would also require the pulp mill to cut its labor force of 400 workers and, perhaps, to close down altogether. [*Cutting the waste by 30% would eliminate the noxious odors coming from the river but would result in the unemployment of 10 workers at the pulp mill. Cutting the waste by 60% would also make the river safe for drinking, swimming and fishing, but would cause a total of 20 workers to be laid off. Eliminating the waste altogether (that is, reducing it by 100%) would allow the return of an additional type of fish valued by some sports fishermen but would make the pulp mill unprofitable so that it would have to close down and lay off all 400 of its workers.*] By how much, if any, do you think the EPA should require the pulp mill to *reduce* its discharges (Enter a number from 0% for "no reduction" to 100% for "complete elimination" in the space below)?
_____ %

6. Newstime, Inc. is a financially sound corporation that publishes several long established and respected magazines. These magazines provide the sole source of its $30 billion in annual revenue and represent about one-tenth of the magazine market nationwide. There are numerous smaller magazine publishers, but they generally specialize in niche markets and do not have sufficient resources or expertise to support general news reporting. Several companies in the movie industry are interested in merging with Newstime in order to take advantage of mutually beneficial business opportunities. The largest and most profitable merger would be with Entertainment Studios, which would generate estimated total annual revenues of $100 billion from the combined magazine and movie operations. [*Opponents of this merger argue that similar mergers have resulted in higher magazine prices and have seriously compromised journalistic integrity. They give many examples, such as the case in which, after such a merger, a once venerable news magazine ignored news of wars and humanitarian disasters in favor of sensationalized coverage aimed at promoting second rate movies produced within its entertainment division.*] The possibilities for Newstime, then, are 1) to break

up and become smaller and more specialized, 2) to maintain its operations at their current size ($30 billion annual revenue), or 3) to become a larger corporation by merging with a film and TV corporation. In terms of annual revenue, how large a corporation do you think Newstime should be (Enter a number in billions of dollars from 0 to 100 in the space below)?
$ _____ billion

7. A hospital budget committee must decide how much of the budget it controls to allocate to the hospital's emergency services versus to its preventive services for the community. [*At present, many patients in the community go to the emergency room for their non-emergency needs because they are uninsured. By increasing the budget to preventative services to 60%, the needs of these patients would be covered, and the reduced burden on emergency services would allow it to provide almost the same level of services as previously.*] What percentage of the budget do you think should be allocated to *preventative services* (Enter a number from 0% to 100% in the space below)?
_____ %

8. A medium sized manufacturing company has already moved 20% of its operations from the US to a developing country because of cost considerations. [*The company's Chief Financial Officer (CFO) has commissioned several studies and reports that the company must move 60% of its operations to the developing country or it will go bankrupt.*] What percentage of its operations do you think this company should locate in the *developing country*, whereby any remaining operations remain in the US (Enter a number from 0% to 100% in the space below)?
_____ %

Seeing the actual questions, the reader might have a sense of the direction in which the additional information could carry responses. Indeed, that is exactly what is hoped for, if the premise behind the quasi-spectator model is correct: the interpretation of any convergence in the high versus low information conditions is precisely that the additional information allows respondents to evaluate the fairness of allocations more accurately based on their common values, which readers presumably also share, on average. Nevertheless, this could also raise the suspicion that convergence is specific to the wording of the questions. In particular, it is possible that the information produces responses that are chosen for their cognitive salience (i.e., as focal points) rather than their moral relevance. The following section presents the results of the survey as well as evidence on this question.

4 Results and Analysis

Section 4.1 presents the results on means and variances for the high and low information conditions of each scenario, tests of differences in means and variances between the two treatments, and analysis of possible focal point effects. Section 4.2 uses multivariate regression analysis to examine potential effects of personal bias.

4.1 Analysis of Means and Variances

The mean, variance, and number of observations are summarised by question and information condition in table 4. Tests of differences in means and variances are also presented in this table. Note that the highly significant differences in mean views between high and low information treatments confirm the relevance of the information employed for all eight scenarios. Regarding the mean differences, no predictions were made for the four applied-ethics questions. For the first four questions, however, the incremental information shifts judgements in the direction consistent with the proposed justice concepts. The additional information in question 1 on the consequences for consumers and stakeholders in the company results in a significant decrease in funding for the film division, in line with a concern for efficiency. In question 2, information on the high cost of meeting basic needs is associated with an increase in support for the needy individual. Explicit information about the larger than expected discrepancy in hours between the two workers in question 3 results in increase in pay to the one who worked longer and a proportional distribution of pay consistent with the accountability principle: Adam worked 72.7 percent of the total hours (8 out of 11), and respondents gave him, on average, 73.4 percent of the total pay, an insignificant difference ($t = 1.19$, two-tailed $p = 0.23$). In question 4, information about the costs associated with the accident causes a significant reduction in judgements in the direction of compensating that loss (perhaps with some compensation for pain and suffering). All of these results, therefore, tend to support roles for the three principles of distributive justice and rectificatory justice.

Table 4: Effects of information on means and variances

Question	Information condition		Hypothesis tests	
	High	Low	Difference in means (t-statistic)	Difference in variances (F-statistic)
	Mean Variance Obervs.	Mean Variance Obervs.		
Justice concept				
1. Efficiency principle	2.53 2.32 111	3.81 3.96 114	−1.32** (−4.70)	−1.64** (1.71)
2. Need principle	771 43.759 105	444 68.736 102	327** (9.89)	−24.977* (1.57)
3. Accountability principle	73.4 36.8 112	60.2 44.9 112	13.2** (15.43)	−8.1 (1.22)
4. Rectificatory justice	33.245 0.41E9 108	55.157 1.19E9 122	−21.912** (−5.96)	−0.78E9** (2.90)
Applied ethics				
5. Environmental ethics	60.1 245.1 104	42.1 620.7 103	18.0** (6.23)	−375.5** (2.53)
6. Media ethics	46.4 515.9 121	58.6 1018.1 122	−12.2** (−3.44)	−502.2** (1.97)
7. Bioethics	57.6 78.7 108	44.8 286.8 103	12.8** (6.86)	−208.1** (3.64)
8. Business ethics	54.9 405.4 129	35.1 603.2 123	19.8** (6.97)	−197.8* (1.49)

Notes: *$p<0.05$, **$p<0.01$. The tests of difference in means are based on two-tail t-tests. For question 4, variance is expressed in billions of dollars (i.e., E9).

A comparison of variances across information conditions in table 4 is striking: high information is associated with reduced variance in every instance. In addition, we can reject the null hypothesis of no change in variance at the 5 percent level of significance for seven of eight questions. The quasi-spectator approach predicts that increased relevant information will, *on average*, reduce variance, and these results are very supportive of this prediction.

The quasi-spectator approach posits that variance falls with increased relevant information due to the improved capacity of agents to reason from a common set of values. As mentioned in the previous section, however, an alternate possibility is that the information is merely creating a focal point, i.e., respondents are cognitively attracted to a specific value provided. I call this the "focal point hypothesis" and address it first with some general observations about the method used in this study and then with more formal analysis.[8] I note that one stylised fact that emerged from this study and the larger project of which it was a part (Konow 2008) is that irrelevant information (i.e., information that does not significantly shift the mean) can be specific or general, but relevant (i.e., mean shifting) information is more specific. Actually, it is probably unsurprising on reflection that information that aids moral reasoning (i.e., is relevant) must also contain details. But if relevant information is necessarily specific, this does complicate the process of determining whether reduced variance results from the kind of consensus predicted by the quasi-spectator method or merely from a focal point.

One approach is to include multiple pieces of information that might serve as focal points, as done in questions 4 and 5. A more direct and compelling approach, however, uses that fact that the focal point hypothesis, by its very definition, implies a higher proportion of responses at a particular value in the high information than the low information condition. That is, the modal response with high information should systematically occur with a greater frequency than the modal response under low information. Another possible interpretation of the focal point is that the median response in the high information condition occurs with greater frequency than the median response in the low information condition. The former version probably has more intuitive appeal, but I include both in order to give this hypothesis its best shot. Note, however, that the focal point hypothesis implies systematically more frequent responses with high information but does not *necessarily* imply reduced variance, e.g., variance could be higher if there are multiple focal points or if non-focal point responses become more disperse. The quasi-spectator method, on the other hand, predicts system-

---

[8] I wish to thank a referee for motivating a more detailed examination of this issue.

atically reduced variance, but is consistent with more or less frequent modal and median responses. In fact, given the overall tendency of respondents to make choices at discrete intervals, one might expect more frequent modal and median responses with any kind of reduced variance, but the quasi-spectator method does not systematically predict this outcome.

Table 5: Proportions of modal and median responses

Question	Mode			Median		
	High info	Low info	Difference (High–Low)	High info	Low info	Difference (High–Low)
1	0.31	0.25	0.06	0.31	0.25	0.06
2	0.31	0.25	0.06	0.31	0.25	0.06
3	0.32	0.66	−0.34**	0.09	0.66	−0.57**
4	0.15	0.20	−0.05	0.14	0.20	−0.06
5	0.62	0.26	0.36**	0.62	0.01	0.61**
6	0.40	0.30	0.10	0.07	0.09	−0.02
7	0.60	0.19	0.41**	0.60	0.19	0.41**
8	0.31	0.18	0.13*	0.31	0.12	0.19**

*$p<0.05$, **$p<0.01$, two-tail t-tests of differences in proportions.

Table 5 reports the fraction of modal and median responses under the high and low information conditions for the eight scenarios. The focal point hypothesis implies that the difference between these values for high minus low should be positive, indicating a greater proportion of responses at certain values in the high information treatment. Nevertheless, we see that this difference is positive at conventional levels of significance according to a test of differences in proportions in only three of the eight scenarios (questions 5, 7, and 8). This difference is insignificant for four other scenarios and is even significantly negative for one (question 3). These results hold using both modal and median responses. Thus, there is some evidence consistent with focal points for three questions, but the results of table 5 do not reveal a *systematic* pattern of focal points that would explain the *systematic* reduction in variance reported in table 4. Moreover, if it is the presence of specific information rather than its moral relevance that attracts responses, scenarios that introduce multiple potential focal points in the high information condition, such as questions 4 and 5, might be expected to increase variance and/or decrease modal or median responses, but there is no significant evidence of any of that.

Table 6: Determinants of dispersion in responses (std. dev.)

Regressors	(1)	(2)
Information	−6.34**	−6.56**
	(1.56)	(1.47)
Frequency of mode	−6.98	
	(6.57)	
Frequency of median		−4.92
		(4.34)
Constant	22.70**	22.23**
	(2.66)	(2.38)
Question 2 dummy	6.03	6.02
	(2.88)	(2.85)
Question 3 dummy	−9.72*	−10.72
	(3.20)	(2.88)
Question 4 dummy	9.04*	9.23*
	(2.96)	(2.89)
Question 5 dummy	3.85	2.89
	(3.08)	(2.86)
Question 6 dummy	10.25*	8.74*
	(2.92)	(2.98)
Question 7 dummy	−3.85	−4.09
	(2.99)	(2.90)
Question 8 dummy	4.53	4.46
	(2.89)	(2.87)
R-squared	0.95	0.95

Notes: The dependent variable is the standard deviation of responses in the question/information conditions; standard errors are in parentheses; *p<0.05, **p<0.01.

Multivariate regression analysis permits a more formal comparison of the consensus versus focal point interpretations of the results. I normalised the responses to all questions to a 100-point scale and regressed the variance of responses in each of the sixteen question/information conditions on a dummy for high information (1 for High, 0 for Low), the frequency of the potential focal point (in two separate OLS regressions for the mode and median) in that condition, and dummies for the questions (with question 1 as the omitted category). I carried out the same two regressions with the standard deviation in each condition as the dependent variable and came to qualitatively the same conclusions regarding the significance of the variables of interest. Using the standard deviation as the measure of dispersion produced an overall better fit, however, so these results are reported in table 6. The coefficients on the Information dummy indicate that, controlling for potential focal points and scenarios, the additional information produces a highly significant decrease in dispersion ($t = -4.07$, $p = 0.007$ for the mode, and $t = -4.46$, $p = 0.004$ for the median). The coefficients on the frequencies of potential focal points are negative but not significant, even at the 25 percent level ($t = -1.06$, $p = 0.329$ for the mode, and $t = -1.13$, $p = 0.301$ for the median). Thus, these results strongly support relevant information, and not focal points, as the reason for reduced variance.

4.2 Personal Bias

The results reported above are consistent with the quasi-spectator approach to impartiality. Nevertheless, quasi-spectators are not ideal spectators, a fact that raises the question of whether they are, to some degree, subject to personal bias and, if so, what the magnitude of that bias is. In this section, therefore, we consider personal bias through the effects on responses of various personal characteristics, which might plausibly serve as proxies for self-interested influences on moral judgement. For example, low income respondents might support more redistribution in the welfare scenario because of a self-interested identification with that group (and, conversely, high income might support less redistribution). These results are also potentially interesting because of the possibility that justice evaluation varies systematically across gender, race, major, income class, et cetera.

Table 7 reports the results of OLS regressions of the pooled responses from the high and low information conditions on a set of explanatory variables for each of the eight questions. The first six regressors are dummy variables. The Information dummy equals 1 for the High Information condition and 0 for the Low Information condition. The Gender dummy equals 1 for female and 0 for male. The Nonwhite dummy equals 0 for white and 1 for all other categories – Nonwhite was collapsed into a single variable due to the low number of observations in certain more specific categories and because of the mostly similar patterns for nonwhites. The college dummies (Business, Communications/Fine Arts, Science/Engineering) identify which of the four colleges at this university the respondent's major is in, where Liberal Arts is the omitted category. Class is the year in school, followed by Age, Expenditures on all categories during the school year, Parents' annual income (estimated to intervals of $25,000), Hours worked by the respondent per week and annual Earnings over the past year. The personal characteristic variables mostly had low or insignificant correlations with one another. Two exceptions were the relatively high Class/Age and Hours worked/ Earnings correlations, respectively. Therefore, I ran four separate regressions for each question using only two variables from each of these categories (i.e., Class/Hours, Class/Earnings, Age/Hours, Age/Earnings). These revealed no differences in the signs of significant variables and almost no differences in levels of significance, so the regressions reported here use the complete set of explanatory variables.[9]

In table 7, the Information dummy controls for the effect of relevant information, and the signs and even the magnitudes of the information effects in table 7 are very close to the differences in means in table 4. Of the 88 remaining coefficients on the personal characteristic variables, only 8 percent (i.e., 7) are significant at the 5 percent level. Moreover, an F-test fails to reject the null hypothesis of no systematic variation in moral views due to personal characteristics for all eight questions. I will discuss the personal characteristic variables and suggest interpretations of the individually significant results.

Gender is not significantly related to moral judgements in these scenarios, contrary to some studies of social preferences, although probably consistent with most. The significant coefficient on the Nonwhite dummy in question 2 indicates that this group supports $82 more welfare support per month than whites. This might reflect a stronger belief on their part in the value of government support for education and for addressing basic needs. Three results on major are significant, whereby no coefficient on Science and Engineering is significant. Business students support about $2 less than the proportional pay (and less than Liberal Arts students) in question 3. One conjecture about this is that, as future managers, these students are more committed to equal treatment of workers within firms than to unequal rewards, consistent with Frank's (1988) story about greater wage equality within firms than across them. These future managers also back moving about 9 percent more of the company's operations overseas than Liberal Arts students in order to protect the company's finances. Communications students strongly support keeping Newstime smaller, against the forces of merging. The most plausible explanation seems to be that, by virtue of their professionally oriented training, they are more sensitive than other ma-

---

9 In the few cases where significance changes, most involve significant variables being more so using the complete set, contrary to expectations, which should allay any concern that the impact of any personal characteristic is being understated in the reported regressions. The one exception is question 6, where Expenditures generates a p-value slightly greater than 0.05 in the regression with all regressors and a p-value slightly less than 0.05 in three of the four regressions using only two of the four variables in question.

Table 7: Regression analysis of responses

Regressors	Question							
	1. Efficiency	2. Need	3. Account.	4. Rectific.	5. Environ.	6. Media	7. Bioeths.	8. Busns.
Information	-1.174***	333.4***	13.35***	-21925***	19.07***	-12.58***	13.84***	18.67***
	(0.239)	(33.4)	(0.81)	(3907)	(2.97)	(3.58)	(1.90)	(2.85)
Gender	0.057	-4.7	-0.50	4999	4.47	1.54	1.25	-4.17
	(0.249)	(35.8)	(0.86)	(4155)	(3.18)	(3.74)	(2.02)	(3.00)
Nonwhite	0.364	82.1*	-1.71	5018	-2.12	2.73	-0.21	-3.70
	(0.262)	(37.3)	(0.90)	(4130)	(3.33)	(3.75)	(2.05)	(3.00)
Business	-0.277	-23.5	-1.98*	-565	0.94	0.92	-2.75	8.74*
	(0.288)	(42.1)	(0.97)	(4532)	(3.71)	(4.29)	(2.27)	(3.41)
Communications/Fine Arts	0.590	-2.7	-1.67	-2110	-1.78	-16.61**	-1.65	5.92
	(0.358)	(55.8)	(1.29)	(6295)	(4.94)	(6.22)	(2.65)	(4.43)
Science/Engineering	0.690	-4.95	0.07	-14888	-2.81	3.66	-4.57	9.21
	(0.424)	(56.2)	(1.42)	(8042)	(5.13)	(6.84)	(3.97)	(5.47)
Class	0.055	-19.4	-0.34	4536	1.44	2.94	1.36	2.44
	(0.247)	(30.1)	(1.01)	(3457)	(2.63)	(3.57)	(1.31)	(2.84)
Age	-0.203	18.7*	-0.46	-573	0.30	-2.09	0.63	-2.54
	(0.169)	(7.7)	(0.82)	(2811)	(0.68)	(2.72)	(0.41)	(2.10)
Expenditures ($1000/year)	-0.011	-1.3	0.00	275*	-0.11	0.22*	0.03	0.13
	(0.009)	(1.4)	(0.02)	(113)	(0.13)	(0.10)	(0.05)	(0.08)
Parents income	0.005	9.1	-0.25	-738	-0.35	1.50	-0.44	-0.42
	(0.068)	(9.7)	(0.23)	(1101)	(0.85)	(1.02)	(0.54)	(0.80)

Table 7: Regression analysis of responses (Continued)

Regressors	Question							
	1. Efficiency	2. Need	3. Account.	4. Rectific.	5. Environ.	6. Media	7. Bioeths.	8. Busns.
Hours worked (per week)	-0.006	-0.9	0.00	-289	-0.16	-0.05	0.08	-0.08
	(0.013)	(1.8)	(0.05)	(225)	(0.16)	(0.20)	(0.11)	(0.18)
Earnings ($1000/year)	0.034	1.7	-0.06	67	-0.59	-0.36	-0.10	0.12
	(0.025)	(7.3)	(0.14)	(415)	(0.63)	(0.45)	(0.24)	(0.37)
Observations	217	204	217	222	203	238	202	247
R-squared	0.18	0.37	0.60	0.18	0.20	0.12	0.25	0.22

Notes: */**/*** denotes a p-value less than .05/.01/.001. Standard errors are in parentheses. The omitted categories for the dummy variables are White, Male, and Liberal Arts College.

jors to the adverse impact on the journalistic mission of the magazine of merging with an entertainment company.

Class has no significant impact, but Age has one that seems reasonable. Older respondents appear to be more generous in supporting the completion of the student's education in question 2 (by about $19 per year of age). Respondents in question 4 want to award the damaged party $275 more for every $1,000 more they spend each year, or $4,599 for a one standard deviation difference in expenditures ($16,722). The reason for this last result is unclear, but perhaps "big spenders" identify with the damaged party, which they otherwise see as being on the low end of possible settlements. Higher expenditures are also associated with a small preference for merging a news magazine with a movie company in question 6. Parents' income, Hours worked and Earnings have no significant effects.

These results suggest that personal characteristics might occasionally insinuate themselves into the moral decisions of quasi-spectators, but the evidence does not support them as systematic predictors of distributive preferences. A separate question, however, is how important a variable is, i.e., how much of the variance in the dependent variable a regressor explains. That is, a marginally significant variable might still explain a high fraction of the variance. The typical approach to this is to examine semi-partial correlations, i.e., the percentage of the variance in the dependent variable that a given regressor uniquely explains, and to compare these for different regressors. This is equivalent to the change in the value of the R-squared when a variable is added to the regression.[10] Based on this, tests reported in table 8 show that all personal characteristics combined account for only 3 to 8 percent of the variance in distributive preferences, compared to 13 to 60 percent for all regressors. Since the information in the questions was designed to produce differences, comparisons of the effects of information and personal characteristics must be taken with a grain of salt. But it is interesting to report that no single personal characteristic accounts for as much variance as information, indeed, all of the personal characteristics combined explain less variance than information for seven of the eight questions, according to table 8.

---

10 The sum of these semi-partial correlations will not, however, usually add up to the R-squared for the regression with all regressors because of correlations between the regressors and for the practical reason that the R-squared sometimes differs due to different numbers of observations in the regressions caused by missing data (as is the case with these data).

Table 8: Importance of information versus personal characteristics

	Regressors (R-squared)	
Question	All personal characteristics	Information dummy
Justice concept		
1. Efficiency principle	0.08	0.09
2. Need principle	0.04	0.32
3. Accountability principle	0.07	0.52
4. Rectificatory justice	0.05	0.13
Applied ethics		
5. Environmental ethics	0.03	0.16
6. Media ethics	0.08	0.05
7. Bioethics	0.04	0.19
8. Business ethics	0.05	0.16

5 Conclusion

This chapter presents an empirical approach to impartiality inspired by the impartial spectator model of Adam Smith. The proposed quasi-spectator method postulates a direct relationship between relevant information and consensus, i.e., reduced variance in moral judgements. This is, in fact, opposed to important theoretical claims and empirical findings. First, normative approaches to impartiality, like Rawls', typically associate impartiality with restrictions on certain kinds of information, whereas the spectator approach places no such limits on information. Second, some empirical studies of fairness bias suggest that information feeds self-serving biases and disagreements. Of course, the important distinction in the spectator model in comparison to these others is the focus on informed spectators, rather than informed stakeholders. But a third point is that it is not obvious on a priori grounds that increased information will favourably affect spectator convergence given practical considerations, e.g., information could complicate moral reasoning. In fact, a related study (Konow 2008) finds that irrelevant information does not reliably affect spectator consensus: variance might increase or decrease, but it is usually not significantly affected.

The current study finds that relevant information is reliably related to convergence of moral views, in support of the quasi-spectator method. The contextually rich scenarios were designed to reflect a wide range of real world situations. The analysis of the pooled data indicates that convergence is driven by the increased ability of agents to reason from common moral principles, rather than by focal point effects. Evidence from personal characteristics suggests that the impact of personal bias on the moral judgements of spectators is neither systematically significant nor large in magnitude.

Normative work in economics and philosophy involves judgement under some conditions of impartiality, which, in turn, is usually associated with consensus. By establishing a relationship between consensus and conditions of impartiality, it is hoped that this chapter helps to lay an empirical foundation for welfare analysis and social choice theory. That is, the aim is to identify views using a method that has normative appeal, which then establishes its validity for evaluating, and perhaps even informing, prescriptive theories. Empirical social choice has contributed in a significant way to the critical analysis of important normative theories. As this field moves ahead, perhaps the current of work running from empirical analysis to theory will also strengthen. In this study, the results for the first four questions, which are based on justice concepts, also add to the evidence in support of the efficiency, need, and accountability principles of distributive justice and of rectificatory justice.

By embedding the empirical analysis in real world issues, I hope that this approach will ultimately also lead to practical policy applications, including to contexts such as those described in the scenarios here. These include questions of the fair restructuring of industries impacted by changing technology and demand, state support of the indigent, compensation for labour, the settlement of civil suits, environmental regulation, resources for the press, support for health care, and relocation of jobs in a globalised world. Developing and refining means for identifying impartial views about such contentious issues could prove helpful in designing solutions and resolving conflicts to important problems.

Acknowledgements

I thank an editor and two referees of *Social Choice and Welfare*, Kjell Arne Brekke, Joseph Earley, Marco Faravelli, Christel Fricke, Wulf Gaertner, Andrew Healy, Astri Hole, Bertil Tungodden, participants at the Workshop on Social and Moral Norms in Intentional Action at the University of Oslo and at the plenary session on experimental philosophy at the 2007 North American meetings of the Economic Science Association for their helpful comments and suggestions. I retain sole responsibility, of course, for any shortcomings.

Bibliography

Alatas, Vivi; Cameron, Lisa; Chaudhuri, Ananish; Erkal, Nisvan, and Gangadharan, Lata (2009): "Subject Pool Effects in a Corruption Experiment. A Comparison of Indonesian Public Servants and Indonesian Students". In: *Experimental Economics* 12 (1), pp. 113–132.

Amiel, Yoram; Cowell, Frank, and Gaertner, Wulf (2009): "To Be Involved or Not to Be Involved. A Questionnaire-Experimental View on Harsanyi's Utilitarian Ethics". In: *Social Choice and Welfare* 32 (2), pp. 299–316.

Aristotle (1925): *Ethica Nicomachea*. London: Oxford University Press.

Babcock, Linda and Loewenstein, George (1997): "Explaining Bargaining Impasse. The Role of Self-Serving Biases". In: *Journal of Economic Perspectives* 11 (1), pp. 109–126.

Cappelen, Alexander; Hole, Astri; Sørensen, Erik, and Tungodden, Bertil (2007): "The Pluralism of Fairness Ideals. An Experimental Approach". In: *The American Economic Review* 97 (3), pp. 818–827.

Charness, Gary and Rabin, Matthew (2002): "Understanding Social Preferences with Simple Tests". In: *The Quarterly Journal of Economics* 117 (3), pp. 817–869.

Corneo, Giacomo and Fong, Christina (2008): "What's the Monetary Value of Distributive Justice?". In: *Journal of Public Economics* 92 (1), pp. 289–308.

Croson, Rachel and Konow, James (2009): "Social Preferences and Moral Biases". In: *Journal of Economic Behavior & Organization* 69 (3), pp. 201–212.

Dunning, David; Meyerowitz, Judith, and Holzberg, Amy (1989): "Ambiguity and Self-Evaluation. The Role of Idiosyncratic Trait Definitions in Self-Serving Assessments of Ability". In: *Journal of Personality and Social Psychology* 57 (6), pp. 1082–1090.

Ellingsen, Tore and Johannesson, Magnus (2004): "Promises, Threats and Fairness". In: *The Economic Journal* 114 (495), pp. 397–420.

Ellingsen, Tore and Johannesson, Magnus (2005): "Does Impartial Deliberation Breed Fair Behavior?". In: *Rationality and Society* 17 (1), pp. 116–136.

Faravelli, Marco (2007): "How Context Matters. A Survey Based Experiment on Distributive Justice". In: *Journal of Public Economics* 91 (7–8), pp. 1399–1422.

Forsythe, Robert; Horowitz, Joel; Savin, Eugene, and Sefton, Martin (1994): "Fairness in Simple Bargaining Experiments". In: *Games and Economic Behavior* 6 (3), pp. 347–369.

Frank, Robert (1988): *Passions Within Reason. The Strategic Role of the Emotions*. New York: Norton.

Friedman, Milton (1977): "Fair Versus Free". In: *Newsweek*, July 4, p. 70.

Frohlich, Norman and Oppenheimer, Joe (1992): *Choosing Justice. An Experimental Approach to Ethical Theory*. Berkeley: University of California Press.

Gächter, Simon and Riedl, Arno (2005): "Moral Property Rights in Bargaining with Infeasible Claims". In: *Management Science* 51 (2), pp. 249–263.

Gaertner, Wulf (1994): "Distributive Justice. Theoretical Foundations and Empirical Claims". In: *European Economic Review* 38 (3–4), pp. 711–720.

Gaertner, Wulf; Jungeilges, Jochen, and Neck, Reinhard (2001): "Cross-Cultural Equity Evaluations. A Questionnaire-Experimental Approach". In: *European Economic Review* 45 (4–6), pp. 953–963.

Harsanyi, John (1953): "Cardinal Utility in Welfare Economics and in the Theory of Risk-Taking". In: *Journal of Political Economy* 61 (5), pp. 434–435.

Harsanyi, John (1955): "Cardinal Welfare, Individualistic Ethics, and Interpersonal Comparisons of Utility". In: *Journal of Political Economy* 63 (4), pp. 309–321.

Harsanyi, John (1978): "Bayesian Decision Theory and Utilitarian Ethics". In: *The American Economic Review* 68 (2), pp. 223–228.

Hume, David (1983): *An Enquiry Concerning the Principles of Morals.* Indianapolis: Hackett.

Kahneman, Daniel; Knetsch, Jack, and Thaler, Richard (1986): "Fairness as a Constraint on Profit Seeking. Entitlements in the Market". In: *The American Economic Review* 76 (4), pp. 728–741.

Konow, James (2000): "Fair Shares. Accountability and Cognitive Dissonance in Allocation Decisions". In: *The American Economic Review* 90 (4), pp. 1072–1091.

Konow, James (2001): "Fair and Square. The Four Sides of Distributive Justice". In: *Journal of Economic Behavior & Organization* 46 (2), pp. 137–164.

Konow, James (2003): "Which Is the Fairest One of All? A Positive Analysis of Justice Theories". In: *Journal of Economic Literature* 41 (4), pp. 1188–1239.

Konow, James (2005): "Blind Spots. The Effects of Information and Stakes on Fairness Bias and Dispersion". In: *Social Justice Research* 18 (4), pp. 349–390.

Konow, James (2008): "The Moral High Ground. An Experimental Study of Spectator Impartiality". Manuscript, Loyola Marymount University.

Konow, James (2009): "Is Fairness in the Eye of the Beholder? An Impartial Spectator Analysis of Justice". In: *Social Choice and Welfare* 33 (1), pp. 101–127.

Konow, James; Saijo, Tatsuyoshi, and Akai, Kenju (forthcoming): "Equity Versus Equality. Spectators, Stakeholders, and Groups". In: *Journal of Economic Psychology.*

Kravitz, David and Gunto, Samuel (1992): "Decisions and Perceptions of Recipients in Ultimatum Bargaining Games". In: *The Journal of Socio-Economics* 21 (1), pp. 65–84.

Kritikos, Alexander and Bolle, Friedel (2001): "Distributional Concerns. Equity- or Efficiency-Oriented?". In: *Economics Letters* 73 (3), pp. 333–338.

Oxoby, Robert (2013): "Paretian Dictators. Constraining Choice in a Voluntary Contribution Game". In: *Constitutional Political Economy* 24 (2), pp. 125–138.

Rawls, John (1971): *A Theory of Justice.* Cambridge: Belknap Press.

Rubinstein, Ariel (1999): "Experience from a Course in Game Theory. Pre- and Postclass Problem Sets as a Didactic Device". In: *Games and Economic Behavior* 28 (1), pp. 155–170.

Schokkaert, Erik and Capeau, Bart (1991): "Interindividual Differences in Opinions About Distributive Justice". In: *Kyklos* 44 (3), pp. 325–345.

Schokkaert, Erik and Devooght, Kurt (2003): "Responsibility-Sensitive Fair Compensation in Different Cultures". In: *Social Choice and Welfare* 21 (2), pp. 207–242.

Smith, Adam (1809): *The Theory of Moral Sentiments.* Glasgow: Chapman.

Traub, Stefan; Seidl, Christian; Schmidt, Ulrich, and Levati, Maria (2005): "Friedman, Harsanyi, Rawls, Boulding – or Somebody Else? An Experimental Investigation of Distributive Justice". In: *Social Choice and Welfare* 24 (2), pp. 283–309.

Yaari, Menahem and Bar-Hillel, Maya (1984): "On Dividing Justly". In: *Social Choice and Welfare* 1 (1), pp. 1–24.

Appendix

Instructions

This questionnaire consists of several questions each describing a different scenario. Please read each question carefully, and then supply a numerical answer in the space provided. Please give exactly one answer to every question, as we cannot use forms with multiple or incomplete answers. This is not a test of knowledge or ability. Instead, we are interested in what you think should be done in each scenario given the information provided.

After you complete the questions, there is a final page requesting subject information. When you are finished, please put your form and pencil down and wait quietly. When everyone is finished you will individually and confidentially deposit your forms in the box in the front.

Demographic Questionnaire

Please answer all questions, indicating just one answer per question, as we cannot use forms with incomplete or multiple answers.

1. What is your college?

    1 Business   3 Liberal Arts
    2 Communications and Fine Arts   4 Science and Engineering

2. What is your first major (if undeclared, write UD)?

    _____

3. What year in college are you?

    1 Freshman   3 Junior
    2 Sophomore   4 Senior
                     5 Graduate

4. What is your age?

    _____ years

5. What is your gender?

   1 Male
   2 Female

6. What is your ethnicity (if several apply, please choose the one that you consider most accurate)?

   1 Asian/Pacific-Islander   4 Latino/Hispanic
   2 Black/African-American   5 Middle-Eastern
   3 Caucasian   6 Native-American/American Indian

7. What is your best estimate of your total expenditures this school year (September through May)? Please consider all expenses including tuition, housing, food, clothing, transportation, entertainment, etc., even if some are covered by financial aid or grants.

   $ _____ for the current school year (September through May)

8. What is the total (gross) income last year of your parents or guardians (or spouse, if married)? Exclude your own earnings. Please choose a single response, even if it is a guess.

   1 $0 to less than $25,000   5 $100,000 to less than $125,000
   2 $25,000 to less than $50,000   6 $125,000 to less than $150,000
   3 $50,000 to less than $75,000   7 $150,000 or more
   4 $75,000 to less than $100,000

9. How many hours per week do you usually work (Enter 0 if none)?

   _____ hours per week

10. Approximately how much money have you earned total through your work over the past year (the past twelve months)?

    $ _____

David Miller
Needs-Based Justice
Theory and Evidence

Abstract: The aim of this chapter is to use both philosophical analysis and empirical evidence to map the way in which claims of need feature in our thinking about distributive justice. The first question is whether a clear line can be drawn between needs and other demands that can be described as interests or preferences, and if so how? Where needs can be identified, what role do they play in decisions over resource allocation? In particular, does justice require that those whose needs are greatest should always have first claim on the resources available, or should resources be distributed more widely and evenly, for example in proportion to relative degrees of need? Might there even be cases in which triage is considered to be a just practice, with priority given to those whose needs can be fulfilled with least expenditure of resources? What difference, if any, does it make if recipients are responsible for having unsatisfied needs as a result of their past behaviour? Does this diminish their claim to be helped, or maybe eliminate it entirely? By reviewing experimental and other work on relevant aspects of justice, the author explores how far philosophical theories of needs-based justice capture the role that needs play in lay thinking about just distribution.

1 Introduction

In this chapter, I examine the relationship between empirical research and normative theory through the lens of a particular problem: what justice demands of us in response to claims of individual need. That justice is sometimes, though not always, need-based in this sense is now widely recognised. "To each according to their needs" was first introduced as a principle of distributive justice by Marx and his communist predecessors and successors, and has since passed into the political mainstream as a guiding maxim for the welfare state.[1] What exactly the principle means is much less clear, however, as I will demonstrate in the course of the chapter. Where resources are plentiful, and everyone's needs can be met in full, it is easy to see what it requires. But in cases of relative scarcity – unfortu-

---

[1] Whether Marx himself saw the maxim as a principle of *justice* remains a contentious topic. For different views, see Wood (1980), Buchanan (1982), Lukes (1985, chapter 4).

nately very often the situation we face in practice – applying it is not straightforward at all. Whose needs should be granted priority? Should we try to meet as many needs as possible, or should we attend first to those who are currently the worst-off? Does it matter if two equally needy people – say two people suffering from the same ailment – get different treatment? And so on.

To answer these and other questions, it is illuminating to examine the evidence about how people at large think such dilemmas should be resolved. There is now a quite considerable body of experimental and other research on what people take justice to require when needs are at issue. But philosophers may still be inclined to doubt whether this evidence is really relevant to their own normative enquiries. Why, they may ask, should a philosophical investigation of needs-based justice take account of what is after all mere opinion, delivered by people who are in no sense moral experts? To this question I offer two replies.[2]

First, presumably, the final aim of normative theorising as carried out by philosophers is to provide practical guidance on matters of moral or political concern. When such a theory is presented, the principles it contains must, therefore, be ones that people might actually come to embrace and act upon. But if so, they must be accessible to the relevant agents, which means that there must at least be a bridge between these principles and the beliefs (about justice and so forth) that people already hold. The theory may hold out the promise of making prevailing beliefs more internally coherent, better grounded in evidence, and so forth, but it cannot dispense with them altogether. So, it is important to find out, at least as a starting point, what these beliefs actually are.

Second, attending to empirical evidence about how non-philosophers think can help philosophers to guard against deficiencies in their own reasoning processes. The latter ought to be more self-reflective than they usually are about the status of the intuitions or "considered judgements" that they deploy in order to justify their conceptual or normative claims. One reason is that (in Western democracies anyway) their social position biases them in favour of certain views and against others: like other university faculties in the humanities, their political convictions are overwhelmingly liberal when measured against the views of the population at large.[3] This means that they will often regard as self-evidently

---

[2] See also Miller (2018), on which I draw here.
[3] For some evidence about this in the case of American academics, see Rothman, Lichter, and Nevitte (2005). Among the general public 18 percent self-identified as liberal and 37 percent as conservative in 1999; for philosophers, the figures were 80 percent liberal and 5 percent conservative. For a study of Canadian professors that did not single out philosophers specifically but

true, and therefore as touchstones for normative reasoning, moral or political judgements that people in the wider society are likely to reject. Another is that philosophers are inevitably tempted to adjust what they take to be their "pre-theoretical" judgements to fit the theoretical positions they have already arrived at independently. To give one example, few philosophers seem willing to grant *desert* the central role that it plays (alongside need) in popular conceptions of distributive justice. A likely explanation is that they have already decided that the concept is problematic, perhaps because they are convinced on metaphysical grounds that individuals cannot be responsible for their decisions and actions in the way that they would need to be for the notion of personal desert to make sense. So, they conclude, a defensible theory of distributive justice must either dispense entirely with the idea of desert or at the very least reinterpret the concept so as to avoid this metaphysical problem. But even supposing that this conclusion is correct, the danger here is one of prematurely discarding intuitions about the practical force of desert claims, which are supposed to form part of the raw data out of which the theory of justice is to be constructed. Observing the role that desert plays in the thinking of people who have not yet been forced to confront the problem of determinism and free will can serve as a valuable corrective to this tendency.

There are of course many reasons to exercise caution when looking at the results of experiments or survey research. We need to be sure that the question the subjects thought they were answering was indeed the question to which the philosopher is seeking an answer. Interpreting empirical evidence in order to support normative conclusions is a potentially hazardous undertaking. But that does not imply that we should not make the attempt.

I begin the chapter by commenting on the relative neglect of needs-based justice at the hands of political philosophers over the last several decades. I then point out that, in contrast, claims of need appear to carry considerable weight when laypersons are asked what a fair distribution of some resource would require. Finally, I consider a number of different ways of formulating the principle of distribution according to need and examine which of these interpretations finds support in popular opinion. I conclude that, regrettably, no single formulation captures what people believe is fair in every case. Needs-based justice, both philosophical reflection and empirical research suggest, is deeply pluralistic in nature.

---

nonetheless identified teaching humanities as a main predictor of holding political views well to the left of the public's, see Nakhaie and Brym (2011).

2 Need in Liberal Theories of Distributive Justice

It is quite striking how little attention has been paid to claims of need in the most influential theories of justice to have emerged over the last several decades. This is not to say that needs have been entirely neglected by philosophers. Important conceptual discussions in the 1980s sought to establish that needs were indeed an independent source of normativity, rejecting the idea that needs claims are purely instrumental in nature (always taking the verbal form "A needs X in order to Y") and so always derived whatever force they had from the final end that the needed item served (see Braybrooke 1987, Thomson 1987, Wiggins 1987, chapter 1). Later authors offered further support to the claim that meeting needs was morally obligatory and a matter of justice (Brock 1998, Miller 1999, chapter 10, Reader 2007). In complete contrast, philosophers who adopted classical liberal or libertarian positions were deeply sceptical that needs as such had any relevance to justice (Minogue 1963, chapter 4, Nozick 1974, chapter 8). It might be charitable or benevolent to help a person in need, but justice was a matter of individual rights, and their corresponding obligations, and so need only became normatively relevant when it could be shown that a person's needy condition was the result of a prior rights-violation (say, because they had been robbed of their means of subsistence).

Most liberal philosophers, however, chose neither explicitly to endorse nor explicitly to reject need as a criterion of distributive justice. Instead, they argued that there was no reason to pay specific attention to needs, because they could be dealt with through being included under the aegis of some broader concept. Consider, e.g., utilitarian philosophers who advocate using overall welfare, understood either as happiness or as desire satisfaction, as the goal by which proposed policies should be evaluated. Meeting their needs is one important way to increase people's welfare, but not the only way, and in some cases, needs should carry less weight than strong desires, they argued. Griffin (1986, chapter 3) gives the example of a group of scholars choosing to spend resources on an extension to their library rather than on purchasing exercise equipment for the sake of their health. Since they get more welfare by satisfying their well-informed desire for more books than by meeting their need for bodily health, why should the latter be given precedence when a decision about expenditure is being made? From this perspective, needs drop out of the picture as a relevant criterion of distribution, because they can be subsumed under the broader category of welfare.

John Rawls' theory of justice is often presented as a corrective to the deficiencies of utilitarianism. But like his utilitarian rivals, Rawls pays no specific attention to needs. In the first full presentation of his theory, what Rawls refers to as "the precept of need" is given one paragraph in a book of 600 pages (Rawls 1971, pp. 276 f.). The reason for this neglect is fairly clear. According to Rawls, social justice concerns the distribution of "primary goods" – listed as "rights and liberties, opportunities and powers, income and wealth" – and he assesses that distribution by looking at how representative individuals occupying different social positions, like unskilled workers, fare. So, the need claims of particular individuals, such as those with disabilities or special health care requirements, never enter the picture (see further Sen 1980). Rawls speaks of needs only when discussing the transfer branch of government, which is supposed to correct the market distribution of income and wealth by giving resources to those who are worst off economically. In other words, need-based claims for income are subsumed under the general principle of controlling inequalities so as to maximise the living standard of the least advantaged group – the so-called "difference principle" (Rawls 1971, § 12–13). Rawls mentions in passing a different kind of justice that concerns the allocation of goods to particular persons, but at this stage, he simply excludes it from his theory as a potentially misleading distraction (Rawls 1971, pp. 88 f.).

In his later presentation of the theory (Rawls 2001), Rawls tried to respond to the charge that he had overlooked one important dimension of social justice by failing to notice how citizens who had the same share of primary goods might nonetheless have very different individual needs (for this criticism, see especially Sen 1980, 1992, chapter 5). He did so by arguing that access to medical care, specifically, should be regarded as one component of the basic bundle of goods whose size the difference principle aimed to maximise (Rawls 2001, § 51). Each citizen could anticipate that over the course of her lifetime she could expect to require some medical treatment, and so access to health care should be factored into the calculation of her life prospects. Rawls did not, however, have anything more specific to say about justice in health care – for instance about who among the needy had the strongest claims to be treated – nor about needs of other kinds, nor about the position of people with serious disabilities who could not aspire to be "fully co-operating members of society". Thus, what was almost certainly the most influential theory of social justice to have appeared in the last half-century virtually eliminated need as an independent criterion of distribution.

Another theory of distributive justice that has been influential over the same period is Ronald Dworkin's "equality of resources" view (Dworkin 1981). This might appear to give more scope to needs than Rawls' theory by virtue of the fact that it regards personal capacities and incapacities as among the resources that a theory of justice must take into account. Thus, insofar as need can be represented as an internal resource deficiency, we might expect Dworkin to count it as a feature that may entitle its bearer to receive additional resources by way of compensation. And he does indeed devote some attention both to the issue of people with handicaps and to the issue of health care in Dworkin (2000, especially chapters 2 and 8). However, in order to tackle this problem, he has to introduce a special conceptual device: hypothetical insurance. To explain this through the example of medical need: In order to decide what provision a state should make for health care – how much it should spend and what priorities it should adopt when resources are scarce – we should ask what health care insurance people would buy in advance if they did not know what their own medical needs were likely to be.[4] In reaching a decision, people would be expected to trade off buying different levels of insurance against other ways of using their money. So again, this is a case in which need considerations get subsumed under a wider principle, in this case compensating people for disadvantages that they would have insured against suffering in advance. Need claims are not allowed to have independent force. Dworkin's answer to the question "Is satisfying this particular need a matter of justice?" is "It depends on whether people generally would have chosen to purchase insurance against the chance of having it". The same principle is applied to other misfortunes, such as the chance of becoming unemployed.

Inspired partly by the work of Rawls and Dworkin, but moving beyond them in a more egalitarian direction, a number of philosophers have recently defended the so-called "luck egalitarian" theory of distributive justice (see, e.g., Temkin 1993, Knight 2009, Cohen 2011, part 1, Knight and Stemplowska 2011, Tan 2012). According to this theory, no-one should be worse off than anyone else unless they are responsible for being worse-off, e.g., by developing expensive tastes or gambling away their resources. Conversely, inequalities that can be attributed to brute luck – such as a storm that demolishes my house but not yours – should be compensated for by redistribution from the lucky to the unlucky. At first sight, it looks as though this principle will be sensitive to variations in need: being prone to disease or requiring more calories than average to stay healthy look like exactly the kind of involuntary misfortune that luck egalitarians will seek to rectify via resource transfers. But notice that special needs of this sort are treated no differently from other sources of disadvantage, like having meagre talents or being born into a poor family. Luck egalitarians use an undiscriminating, and often ill-defined, currency of advantage or disadvantage that can incor-

---

[4] Of course, this is likely to vary from one person to the next, depending on how averse they are to particular risks, so Dworkin has to stipulate that what justice requires the state to provide is the level of coverage that most people would choose to buy under these conditions.

porate being needier than others but without giving that condition any special weight. Notice also that a luck egalitarian will distinguish between needs that a person has as a result of her innate bodily features or of accidents that befall her, and needs that she has as a result of lifestyle or other choices for which she is personally responsible, and will mandate that she be compensated only for having special needs in the first category. So, on this view, justice does not require that we should respond to people's needs regardless of how they have arisen.

What explains this reluctance among recent philosophers to take needs seriously as an independent criterion of distributive justice? There is a long-standing concern about whether it is possible to identify needs in a suitably objective way: How does one separate a need from a strongly held desire, for instance? There is also a challenge, pressed especially by followers of Amartya Sen and his theory of capabilities (Sen 1992), that to use need-fulfilment as the currency of justice is implicitly paternalistic, because it overlooks the importance of allowing people to decide for themselves whether they wish to use the resources at their disposal to satisfy their needs, or to do something else with them (Sen 1984; for a more qualified assessment, see Alkire 2002, chapter 5). More important still, however, may be the understandable, but mistaken, tendency of philosophers to search for some single encompassing principle or formula to define distributive justice, such as Dworkin's "equality of resources" or Sen's "equal capabilities". Despite what Marx said, it seems unlikely that justice could be nothing other than a response to unmet need, so if needs are going to count at all under a single-principle definition, it must be through being subsumed under some wider, more abstract, concept such as disadvantage. The cost, however, is to lose the special imperative force that normally attaches to claims of need, as I shall demonstrate below by reference to evidence about public opinion. The moral we should draw here is that it's a mistake to try to reduce justice to any such simple formula. Justice is more like a department store than a specialist boutique.[5] Needs-based justice is an important department, but by no means the whole of the store. Moreover, as we will see later, it is equally problematic to try to reduce needs-based justice itself to a single all-encompassing principle.

---

5 I have mapped some of the main departments in Miller (2017).

3 Needs-Based Justice – Evidence About Public Opinion

As we have seen, philosophers sometimes doubt whether any real distinction can be drawn between people's needs and their desires. But we find that in popular understandings of justice, needs are indeed distinguished from preferences and desires, and given special weight. Here is one survey experiment designed to test whether people's distributive choices vary depending on whether they are confronting differences in need or differences in pleasure or satisfaction (Yaari and Bar-Hillel 1984). Respondents were invited to divide a shipment of grapefruit and avocados between two persons. In one version these individuals were described as being able to derive different amounts of vitamin from the two fruits; in the alternative version they were described as getting different amounts of pleasure from consuming the fruits, as revealed by the price they were willing to pay for them. The numerical values given in the two cases were the same. But the pattern of results was quite different. In the "needs" version, respondents overwhelmingly chose the distribution that gave the two individuals the same amount of vitamin. In the "tastes" version, there was more variety in the responses, but the most popular choice was the utility-maximising outcome, which was quite inegalitarian (one person got twice as much pleasure as the other). What the research shows, then, is first that people recognise a practically relevant difference between needs and tastes, and second that when faced with two individuals whose needs were assumed to be the same, they see justice as requiring the distribution of resources that satisfies those needs equally.

Other studies have explored how the introduction of needs-related information has the effect of shifting people away from efficiency concerns – maximising the satisfaction of preferences – towards solutions that ensure that everyone's basic needs are met. One such study explored how participants made different decisions over the allocation of educational resources depending on whether a basic subject that every student would be expected to need (such as mathematics) or an optional subject (such as theatre) was involved (Matania and Yaniv 2007). However, the shift appears to be partial rather than total, in the sense that although survey respondents tend to prioritise outcomes in which all needs are fulfilled, they are willing to balance this against other factors, such as large efficiency gains (see Konow 2001); as philosophers would put it, they do not attach strict lexical priority to fulfilling needs. As we will see shortly, it also makes a difference to their judgement how the needs have arisen – whether, e.g., as a result of profligate behaviour. Nevertheless, when asked to rate the relative importance they attached to different aspects of social justice – reducing large inequalities of income, recognising people's merits, and guaranteeing that basic needs are met – a large sample of European respondents gave their strongest endorsement to the third objective (Forsé and Parodi 2009).

The evidence presented thus far confirms that needs feature prominently in popular conceptions of distributive justice, but we would like to know more about the precise role that they play. In particular, what weight are they given when they compete with claims of other kinds, such as claims of desert or of efficiency? And how do people handle cases in which there are insufficient resources available to meet everyone's needs? What are their priorities in these circumstances?

The weight that is given to need claims will be affected by a number of factors. The first, and most obvious, is the nature of the good whose allocation is in question. It is widely recognised that what distributive justice demands depends on the kind of good being distributed – in philosophy this is a view associated with Michael Walzer (1983), and evidence about the various rules people apply to the allocation of resources of different kinds was presented in a classic paper by Foa and Foa (1976). In relation to needs, a simple partition is between goods whose only use is to meet needs – wheelchairs and medicines, for instance – goods that are irrelevant to need – prizes and badges of honour, for instance – and goods that can be used to meet need but are valued beyond that point, such as money, food and housing. It's hardly surprising that subjects should see need as a proper ground of allocation for goods in the first category, since in this case justice and efficiency tend to pull together rather than apart – at first sight, there seems to be no reason to allocate these goods on any ground other than relative need. What is surprising, therefore, is that when potential recipients are described as unequally deserving (as measured for instance by their respective contributions to a connected task), subjects want to give some weight to this factor even in the case of a good such as medicine (Scott and Bornstein 2009). In other words, they seem to think that unequal performance must be rewarded even where the recipient has no practical use for some part of what he is getting as a reward, and someone else is left with unsatisfied needs. Again, we discover that although claims of need weigh heavily when resource distributions are being made or recommended, they are not awarded strict priority over claims of other kinds, even in cases where the good being distributed is needs-specific – such as prescription medicine in the experiment just described.

How this weighing is carried out will depend on the context in which the distributive judgement is being made. "Context" can mean different things here. E.g., one study manipulated the degree to which need claims were regarded as urgent, by comparing distribution in an emergency caused by a flood, with distribution of the same resources under normal conditions (Scott and Bornstein

2009). Perhaps not surprisingly, people in the flood condition gave greater weight to the need principle. Another factor is the relationship that prevails between the parties to the distribution. When recipients are described as having a close personal relationship – one of friendship, say – this increases the likelihood of needs being used to govern the allocation of resources between them (Lamm and Schwinger 1980, Deutsch 1985, Sondak, Neale, and Pinkley 1999). There is a question here, however, about whether in such cases it is *justice* specifically that dictates distribution according to need. An alternative reading is that when people are involved in relationships of solidarity, justice is pushed aside and compassion, generosity, or the wish to preserve social harmony takes its place, which entails responding to need rather than to desert or entitlement. One experiment tried to test for this possibility by prompting one half of a rather small sample of subjects to allocate resources justly between two recipients, one with greater needs than the other, while the other half were not given the justice prompt (Lamm and Schwinger 1983). The justice prompt increased the weight given to need when the recipients were described as superficial acquaintances, but decreased it when the recipients were described as close friends. Here, then, it looks as though asking respondents to focus on justice had the effect of dampening down the generous idea that between friends, need is all that should count when relevant resources have to be distributed. Justice was once described by David Hume as a "cautious, jealous virtue" (Hume 1975, p. 184) and he argued that there were circumstances, including radical changes in human motivation, in which it would no longer be needed, being replaced by "much nobler virtues, and more valuable blessings" (Hume 1978, p. 495). He was wrong to think that claims of need could never be claims of justice, but right to think that justice might sometimes stand in the way of generosity, when the latter takes the form of attending *exclusively* to need at the expense of other factors such as desert and equality.

The importance that people attach to claims of need depends, then, on the context in which they are being asked to make or rule upon a distribution of goods – where contextual variables include the urgency of the situation being described, and the relationship between the parties to the distribution. It also depends on whether potential recipients are seen as being responsible for having the needs in question. In general, personal responsibility, whether it takes the form, e.g., of engaging in behaviour that damages future health, or wasting the resources that might be used to satisfy need by excessive consumption, has the effect of lessening the force of need claims: People asked to award resources will give preference to those who cannot be held responsible for their needy condition.⁶ However, this applies most forcefully in circumstances of scarcity where hard choices have to be made. To the extent that resources are relatively abundant and there are no competing claims, only those of a politically conservative disposition seem to want to punish those responsible for having needs by withholding resources (Skitka and Tetlock 1992). And there is also evidence that in friendship contexts, people may be willing to ignore responsibility issues and focus simply on relative need (Lamm and Schwinger 1980).

4 Distribution According to Need – What Does It Mean?

Having briefly sketched the general role that need considerations play in popular understandings of justice, I now want to focus on the question of how, more precisely, a needs-based principle of justice should be defined. When we say "to each according to their needs", what exactly do we mean? Which distribution of goods, in circumstances of scarcity, would satisfy this principle?⁷

We can begin by noting a point that is fairly obvious once stated, but still capable of being overlooked, namely that there is an important disanalogy between the needs principle just cited and the corresponding principle of desert. When justice requires that resources should be allocated so as to match the respective deserts of the recipients, it is in one way contingent which resources are used for that purpose. We usually assume that the right way to reward differences in productive performance is through inequalities of income, but as far as justice is concerned, we could equally well use gold stars or awards of the Order of Lenin.⁸ What matters at the bar of justice is the matching of performance and reward, not the currency in which reward is measured. When need

---

6 For the medical case, see Ubel et. al (2001). For a case involving access to winter fuel, see Schwettmann (2012). See also Skitka and Tetlock (1992) for an analysis that brings together scarcity of resources relative to need, and personal responsibility for need. For an experiment in which personal responsibility appears to have little effect, see Gaertner and Schwettmann (2007).
7 In the absence of scarcity, we can interpret the principle as simply requiring that everyone's needs should be satisfied. This is doubtless what Marx had in mind when he said that the principle came into its own when "all the springs of co-operative wealth flow more abundantly" and "the narrow horizon of bourgeois right [can] be crossed in its entirety" (Marx 1977, p. 569).
8 The latter may not be the best example, because it appears to have had only one grade (though it was possible for Soviet citizens to be awarded it repeatedly). So, imagine a fine-tuned version in which different grades correspond to different levels of merit.

is the basis of distributive justice, in contrast, the pertinent resources are of course those which can satisfy unmet needs. So, in the case of any given distribution of such resources, we can ask both about the *ex ante* schedule of (unsatisfied) needs to which it responds, and about the *ex post* schedule of (unsatisfied) needs that it produces. It is by no means clear what the focus of our attention should be: on the (absolute or relative) needs people have to begin with, or on the (absolute or relative) needs they are left with after the distribution has taken place?

We can expand on this point by observing that when somebody is in need, there are at least three pertinent questions to ask, setting aside now the issue of how they came to be in a needy condition. The first is how needy they are in absolute terms: how large the gap is between the resources available to them now, and the resources that would raise them to an acceptable level of provision. The second is how needy they are relative to others in the relevant group: are they better or worse off than others in the comparison class? The third is how many resources it would take for their position to be improved, in other words how capable they are of converting resources into diminished levels of need. Looking at how people set priorities when asked what would be the fairest allocation of goods among needy recipients, we find that they pay attention to each of these factors (see Hurley et al. 2017). In particular, they do not always prioritise the person with the greatest needs if it turns out that it would take a lot of resources to improve that person's condition significantly. The practice of triage, as carried out in medical emergencies, finds some resonance in the attitudes of the general public, though less so than with health professionals themselves.[9]

Is there any way of consolidating these potentially conflicting factors into a single principle that might then be used to define need-based justice normatively? Let me review some possible candidates. Consider first the principle of minimising total neediness. Assume that we can assign each person a need score, based on the size of the gap between what she now has and what she would have to have to satisfy her needs completely – the gap could be measured in terms of the calorific intake needed for a healthy diet, or the amount of pain medication that would bring full relief, for instance. The proposal is then that, given a fixed quantity of resources, justice requires that they should be allocated in such a way as to reduce the aggregate need score as far as possible. This would respond both to the depth of recipients' initial need, and to their differ-

---

[9] In the case of organ transplants, for example, medical professionals give greater weight than members of the public to longer-term chances of survival as opposed to the urgency of a patient's need. Non-medics divide fairly evenly on the question whether urgent cases should receive scarce organs even if their prospects are uncertain. See Umgelter et al. (2015).

ential capacities to convert resources into satisfied need. If Alice responds to pain medication more effectively than Bob, then the principle will favour allocating the medicine to her. A critic might argue that minimising total neediness is a principle of efficiency rather than a principle of justice, and therefore immediately ruled out as a candidate for needs-based justice. But this dismissal is too quick. It's plausible to say that unmet need in the presence of resources that could satisfy it is an injustice, and the bigger the gap the greater the injustice; it's also plausible that what we are required to do in the face of injustice is to minimise it. So minimising neediness is at least a prima facie candidate in our search.

Nonetheless, it should be rejected on the grounds that it pays no attention to how different people are treated relative to one another. It may skew the distribution of resources too far in favour of those who are easiest to help. It may recommend doing nothing for those who are in greatest need. Even if triage may sometimes be regarded as acceptable, the principle we are now looking at goes beyond this by attaching no special weight to having large unfulfilled needs except insofar as this may provide a bigger opportunity for lowering the overall need score. Moreover, in Alice and Bob type cases, we may also be concerned that the principle rewards Alice for her genetically-determined ability to respond well to paracetamol. Simply aiming to minimise neediness, in short, would involve setting aside several factors that seem important components of need-based justice.

With this in mind, consider a second candidate principle: strict priority for the neediest. Here, justice would require us to allocate resources to those with the highest need scores until they reach parity with the next highest group, then treat the two groups together until the next threshold is reached, and so forth. This principle responds to depth of need, but at the cost of paying no attention at all to capacity to benefit – so that it excludes triage even in cases where the position of those who are worst off can only be improved slightly despite their being assigned large quantities of resources. And although it responds to the inequality between the worst-off group and everyone else by decreasing the gaps between them, it pays no attention to other inequalities in need scores. So, if we think that justice is at least partly comparative in this context – it is concerned about how people fare relative to one another in general – then the strict priority principle will be found wanting.

In response to at least the first of these worries, some philosophers have advocated a weighted priority principle (see, e. g., Crisp 2002). Here, we measure an improvement by multiplying a reduction in someone's need score by a factor that captures how needy they were to begin with. E. g., we might use a simple arithmetic weighting, counting a reduction from 100 to 99 as 100, and a reduction from 10 to 9 as 10. This is intended to capture the intuition that it is more important to attend to those whose unmet needs are greater than to those whose unmet needs are smaller. Given the resources available, justice on this view requires us to allocate them so as to reduce neediness as far as possible, but with the chosen weighting factor built into that calculation.

It's implausible to believe that when people are asked to choose a fair allocation of necessary goods, they consciously employ such a weighted priority principle. Nevertheless, the principle might be recommended as a way of rationalising the choices they do make, and in some cases, it may well succeed in doing so – we may be able to assign an implicit weighting factor based on people's observed choices. However, it, too, faces some objections. One is that, despite its tilt in favour of the neediest, there are going to be cases in which it advocates helping a large number of less needy people instead. If enough people can have minor headaches relieved at the cost of denying someone a kidney transplant, the principle will advocate doing that.[10] Another problem is that it incorporates no inherent concern for how people are treated relative to one another. Of course, if two people start out with the same need scores and are equally responsive to treatment, then the principle dictates that they should be provided with the same resources. But this is a special case. Where people differ along either of these dimensions, the weighted priority principle provides no guarantee that horizontal equity between them will be preserved. But such comparative concerns seem to play an important role in popular understandings of distributive justice (see Cuadras-Morato, Pinto-Prades, and Abellan-Perpinan 2001).

What does "horizontal equity" mean in the case of people with unequal needs? One interpretation is that their need scores should be equalised as far as possible: if we cannot relieve everyone's pain or hunger completely, we should at least distribute resources so that they end up equally in pain or equally hungry. Cuadras-Morato, Pinto-Prades, and Abellan-Perpinan (2001) refer to this as the "equal loss solution" and they show that it is frequently preferred when people are asked to choose between different ways of allocating health care resources. I offered a qualified defence of this principle in an earlier discussion (Miller 1999, chapter 10). The principle's strength is that it responds to all cases in which one person's needs are more fully satisfied than another's, no matter how high or low their absolute need scores. But it has some corresponding disadvantages. It

---

[10] Crisp responds to this problem by introducing a needs threshold such that those with relatively trivial needs are excluded at the first stage of implementation and only come into consideration if there are surplus resources after the weighted priority principle is applied to those above the threshold. But, as he himself puts it, "where the threshold falls, of course, is the key question any proponent of this view must answer" (Crisp 2002, p. 140).

gives no special weight to improving the absolute position of the very needy. And it counsels against satisfying needs when this can only be done at the expense of increasing inequality between those who have them – so if there are two people needing the same operation and only one can be treated, it may recommend doing nothing. This seems counterintuitive. In my earlier discussion, I tried to mitigate these objections by pointing out that there are indeed cases in which justice demands that we forgo Pareto improvements – in other words, that justice and efficiency are not the same, and they may pull apart in some cases. But where needs are at stake, it seems that a comparative concern with how people are treated relative to one another faces competition from a rival non-comparative concern of justice that those in need should be aided as far as resources allow.

At this point, it might seem that any way of formalising needs-based justice that captures most of what people intuitively believe is going to involve two or more principles being traded off against one another. But before embracing pluralism in that form, I want to consider two attempts to develop combined accounts that give justice ratings by adding together different components according to some formula – in other words this is a bit like scoring an ice-dance competition where contestants get a technical mark and an artistry mark, and these are added together to produce a total mark. The first of these has been proposed by Nicole Hassoun (2009) in the form of what she calls the effectiveness principle. This works as follows: "First, rank the possible policies from best to worst according to how much weighted need they alleviate. Second, rank the possible policies from best to worst according to the number of people they help. Third, for each policy, combine its ranking in terms of how much weighted need it alleviates with its ranking for how many people it helps to yield its final score" (Hassoun 2009, pp. 259f.).

The weighted need component corresponds to what I earlier called a weighted priority principle – it assesses options by how effectively they reduce need overall, but with a weighting in favour of those whose initial need scores are higher. The new element is the proposal to rank policies according to the number of people helped, which is intended to offset the tendency of the weighted priority principle to give too much emphasis to the claims of the neediest.[11] It is meant to open the door to justified cases of triage. But how plausible is the

---

[11] By the same token, however, Hassoun's effectiveness principle makes matters worse in the kind of case that worries Crisp, where the weighted priority principle still allows a large quantity of relatively minor need claims to outweigh the more serious claims of a few badly-off people, since it adds in a component that gives credit simply for the number of people who are aided.

claim that the justice of an allocation should be conditioned by the sheer number of people whose needs are met?

Empirical studies have found some evidence that those surveyed favour allocations that are inclusive in the sense that each recipient gets *something* even though their claims are in other ways quite different (Pritzlaff-Scheele and Zauchner 2017). One might interpret this as showing a form of respect for persons – no-one is being simply ignored when the distribution of resources is made. Still, it is difficult to understand why sufficient respect is not being shown when everyone's claims are properly *considered* by whoever is performing an allocation, even if the end result is that some people get nothing because whatever claim they might have is justifiably outweighed by the stronger claims of other people. So, one might wonder whether the numbers being aided has the deeper significance that Hassoun's effectiveness principle implies, as opposed merely to being a way of signalling that no-one has been overlooked.

There is a second possibility, however, which emerges when we disambiguate one of Hassoun's formulations of the second half of the effectiveness principle: "institutions should try to help *as many people as possible* meet their needs" (Hassoun 2009, p. 258). The ambiguity is whether this should be read to mean "meet their needs in full". Special importance might be attached to getting people up the point where their needs are fully satisfied – where they have sufficient food, housing space, medical care, and so forth to live a decent life. There is evidence that justice evaluations are not linear as needs are progressively met, but jump sharply upwards when that threshold is crossed (Weiß, Bauer, and Traub 2017). This, then, might justify including a component that captures the number of people whose needs are fully satisfied by an allocation in our conception of needs-based justice.

But on further reflection, is the idea that special weight should be given to getting people up to the threshold where their needs are fully met defensible? Looking at the issue through welfarist spectacles, such a proposal can seem absurd. If, to use the example from Weiß, Bauer, and Traub (2017), we say that for a decent life a household needs 1,000 units of living space, why should we judge an increase from 800 to 1000 units as more significant than an increase from 600 to 800? Normally we would think that providing extra living space counts for more the more cramped you are to begin with. However, justice is not welfarist, so there is at least room to argue that achieving justice in full counts for more than reducing injustice below the threshold when the numerical gain is the same in each case. But I remain puzzled as to what form the argument here would have to take.[12]

I turn finally to a second composite principle of needs-based justice, proposed in Siebel (2017). This combines a measure of overall need-satisfaction with a second element that measures the comparative degree to which the needs of different people are satisfied. For technical reasons, this second element uses the *proportion* of each person's overall need claim that is met rather than the equal outcome measure discussed above.[13] Incorporating this element helps respond to one of the deficiencies we found in the simple injunction to maximise need-satisfaction, namely that principle's blindness to the way people are treated relative to one another – the fact, e. g., that some may end up much worse off than others simply because they are poor converters of need-satisfying resources. Siebel's combined principle also places a premium on changes that help people at the bottom end of the scale, because doing so will simultaneously promote both overall need-satisfaction and proportionate satisfaction. In this respect, it goes some way in the same direction as a weighted priority principle.

Yet there remain problems with Siebel's proposal. Although it is less vulnerable than the principle of equalising need scores to the charge that it may licence "levelling down", there are still circumstances in which it will recommend this. Helping someone whose unfulfilled needs are already small may reduce overall neediness but increase inequality between needy people, in which case Siebel's combined principle may rule against it, as he concedes. Whether this is a problem depends on whether you think levelling down in the name of fairness is ever justifiable when operating in the domain of needs.

Moreover, the combined principle requires a weighting factor in order to combine its two measures in a single formula. The question is whether that weighting factor is going to be a constant across all contexts in which meeting

---

[12] Suppose, by way of analogy, that I owe one person £200 and another person £400 and I have an indivisible lump sum of £200 to allocate. What would be the argument for paying off the smaller debt in full? I could, of course, say "well, at least I've paid off one of my debts", and that might be satisfying to know, but how could it be what justice requires? My intuition is rather that justice requires reducing the larger debt, or at most is neutral between the two options.

[13] I am not convinced, however, that this is an improvement. According to Siebel's second component, if your needs are two-third fulfilled and so are mine, fairness is entirely satisfied. But what if your needs are considerably greater than mine so that the extent of your unmet need is much bigger in absolute terms? It seems that you may have a fairness complaint against me. Cuadras-Morato, Pinto-Prades, and Abellan-Perpinan (2001) who test support for both the "proportional solution" and the "equal loss solution" find that people's choices vary according to the specific features of the case, but generally tend to favour the latter.

needs is at issue. We might, on the contrary, think that considerations of horizontal fairness are more important in some contexts than others. So, e.g., in cases where we believe triage is justified, we are willing to overlook the unfairness involved in sacrificing the very badly off in order to be able to restore many more people to functioning. If we think that this policy can still be just on balance, then it seems we are adjusting the weighting between the two parts of the formula when dealing with such a case. But if the weighting factor is allowed to vary in this way, it's not clear how the composite principle is going to improve upon straightforward pluralism where we concede openly that need-based justice may involve applying different principles of distribution depending on the context.

5 Conclusion

If a philosophical theory of justice aims among other things to systematise widely-shared beliefs about fair distribution, then it must pay considerably more attention to claims of need than recent liberal theory has done. Admittedly, lay people may not be attuned to the distinctions that philosophers wish to draw. E.g., if asked whether responding to need is a matter of justice or of compassion, they are likely to say that it is both at once. But we have surveyed evidence that shows that people treat need claims as special, and attach high importance to fulfilling them wherever possible, so if justice takes precedence over other values in our practical reasoning as philosophers such as Rawls claim,[14] then it must give these claims a central role. Needs-based justice is not the whole of justice, but it is certainly a key department.

When we begin to inquire into the content of needs-based justice, however, we find that it is a complex idea. It is one thing to add "to each according to their needs" to the list of distributive principles that includes "to each according to their rights", "to each according to their deserts", and so forth; it is another matter to say exactly what the principle mandates in conditions of scarcity. As we canvassed the evidence from experiments and surveys, we found that subjects responded positively to a number of different factors related to need: how badly-off people are, either absolutely or relative to others; whether available resources are being used effectively to meet needs; whether people with similar

---

14 "Justice is the first virtue of social institutions, as truth is of systems of thought [...] an injustice is tolerable only when it is necessary to avoid an even greater injustice" (Rawls 1971, pp. 3f.).

needs get treated in the same way; whether people are themselves responsible for being in need; whether people reach the point where their needs are fully met; whether everyone gets something, even if less than others. We looked to see whether there was any way of combining all of these factors into a single principle, and found there was not. Admittedly, some principles proposed by philosophers do a better job than others at capturing the entirety of needs-based justice. E.g., it seems clear that a weighted priority principle more accurately reflects the relative weights that lay people attach to the different factors than does a strict priority principle. But no principle – not even the two-part composites examined at the end of the last section – captures everything that seems to matter.

The question for philosophers, therefore, is whether they are willing to discard some of this evidence in their search for a (relatively simple) theory of needs-based justice. E.g., they might argue that no real significance should attach to the threshold factor – getting people to the point where they are completely free of pain or have exactly the calorific intake judged to be sufficient for a healthy life. Perhaps when people attach high justice ratings to outcomes that meet such conditions, the explanation has to do with *salience* rather than anything deeper than that. This is a question that further research might explore. So, a normative theory of justice can respond to empirical evidence selectively, provided good reasons are offered for setting some of it aside. Even so, it seems unlikely that the theory is going to be as simple in form as those discussed in the second section of the chapter. Needs-based justice turns out to be pluralistic at a fundamental level.

Acknowledgements

An earlier version of this chapter was presented to the conference on "Need-Based Justice and Distribution Procedures", DFG Research Group FOR2104, University of Vienna, March 1st to 3rd, 2018. I should like to thank the audience on that occasion for their suggestions, and Malte Meyerhuber for written comments on a previous draft. I am also very grateful to Clare Cai for providing valuable research assistance while the chapter was being written.

Bibliography

Alkire, Sabina (2002): *Valuing Freedoms. Sen's Capability Approach and Poverty Reduction.* Oxford: Oxford University Press.
Braybrooke, David (1987): *Meeting Needs.* Princeton: Princeton University Press.
Brock, Gillian (ed.) (1998): *Necessary Goods. Our Responsibilities to Meet Others' Needs.* Lanham: Rowman & Littlefield.
Buchanan, Allen (1982): *Marx and Justice.* Totowa: Rowman & Allanheld.
Cohen, Gerald (2011): *On the Currency of Egalitarian Justice, and Other Essays in Political Philosophy.* Princeton: Princeton University Press.
Crisp, Roger (2002): "Treatment According to Need. Justice and the British National Health Service". In: Rhodes, Rosamund; Battin, Pabst and Silvers, Anita (eds.): *Medicine and Social Justice. Essays on the Distribution of Health Care.* Oxford: Oxford University Press, pp. 134–143.
Cuadras-Morato, Xavier; Pinto-Prades, Jose-Luis, and Abellan-Perpinan, Jose-Maria (2001): "Equity Considerations in Health Care. The Relevance of Claims". In: *Health Economics* 10 (2), pp. 187–205.
Deutsch, Morton (1985): *Distributive Justice. A Social Psychological Perspective.* New Haven: Yale University Press.
Dworkin, Ronald (1981): "What Is Equality? Part 2. Equality of Resources". In: *Philosophy and Public Affairs* 10 (4), pp. 283–345.
Dworkin, Ronald (2000): *Sovereign Virtue. The Theory and Practice of Equality.* Cambridge: Harvard University Press.
Foa, Edna and Foa, Uriel (1976): "Resource Theory of Social Exchange". In: Thibaut, John, Spence, Janet, and Carson, Robert (eds.): *Contemporary Topics in Social Psychology.* Morristown: General Learning Press, pp. 99–131.
Forsé, Michel and Parodi, Maxime (2009): "Distributive Justice. An Ordering of Priorities. A Comparative Analysis of European Opinions". In: *International Review of Sociology* 19 (2), pp. 205–225.
Gaertner, Wulf and Schwettmann, Lars (2007): "Equity, Responsibility and the Cultural Dimension". In: *Economica* 74 (296), pp. 627–649.
Hassoun, Nicole (2009): "Meeting Needs". In: *Utilitas* 21 (3), pp. 250–275.
Hume, David (1975): "An Enquiry Concerning the Principles of Morals". In: Hume, David: *Enquiries Concerning Human Understanding and Concerning the Principles of Morals.* Oxford: Clarendon Press, pp. 169–284.
Hume, David (1978): *A Treatise of Human Nature.* Oxford: Clarendon Press.
Hurley, Jeremiah; Mentzakis, Emmanouil; Giacomini, Mita; DeJean, Deirdre, and Grignon, Michel (2017): "Non-Market Resource Allocation and the Public's Interpretation of Need. An Empirical Investigation in the Context of Health Care". In: *Social Choice and Welfare* 49 (1), pp. 117–143.
Knight, Carl (2009): *Luck Egalitarianism. Equality, Responsibility, and Justice.* Edinburgh: Edinburgh University Press.
Knight, Carl and Stemplowska, Zofia (eds.) (2011): *Responsibility and Distributive Justice.* Oxford: Oxford University Press.
Konow, James (2001): "Fair and Square. The Four Sides of Distributive Justice". In: *Journal of Economic Behavior and Organization* 46 (2), pp. 137–164.

Lamm, Helmut and Schwinger, Thomas (1980): "Norms Concerning Distributive Justice. Are Needs Taken into Consideration in Allocation Decisions?". In: *Social Psychology Quarterly* 43 (4), pp. 425–429.

Lamm, Helmut and Schwinger, Thomas (1983): "Need Consideration in Allocation Decisions. Is It Just?". In: *Journal of Social Psychology* 119 (2), pp. 205–209.

Lukes, Steven (1985): *Marxism and Morality*. Oxford: Clarendon Press.

Marx, Karl (1977): *Critique of the Gotha Programme*. In: McLellan, David (ed.): *Karl Marx. Selected Writings*. Oxford: Oxford University Press, pp. 610–616.

Matania, Eviathar and Yaniv, Ilan (2007): "Resource Priority, Fairness, and Equality-Efficiency Compromises". In: *Social Justice Research* 20 (4), pp. 497–510.

Miller, David (1999): *Principles of Social Justice*. Cambridge: Harvard University Press.

Miller, David (2017): "Justice". In: Zalta, Edward (ed.): *The Stanford Encyclopedia of Philosophy*. https://plato.stanford.edu/archives/fall2017/entries/justice/, retrieved on November 14, 2018.

Miller, David (2018): "Justice Beyond the Armchair". In: *Contemporary Political Theory* 17 (1), pp. 97–104.

Minogue, Kenneth (1963): *The Liberal Mind*. London: Methuen.

Nakhaie, Reza and Brym, Robert (2011): "The Ideological Orientations of Canadian University Professors". In: *The Canadian Journal of Higher Education* 41 (1), pp. 18–33.

Nozick, Robert (1974): *Anarchy, State, and Utopia*. Oxford: Blackwell.

Pritzlaff-Scheele, Tanja and Zauchner, Patricia (2017): "Meeting Needs. An Experimental Study on Needs-Based Justice and Inequality". In: *DFG Research Group 2104, Need-Based Justice and Distribution Procedures, Working Paper* 2017–17.

Rawls, John (1971): *A Theory of Justice*. Cambridge: Harvard University Press.

Rawls, John (2001): *Justice as Fairness. A Restatement*. Cambridge: Harvard University Press.

Reader, Soran (2007): *Needs and Moral Necessity*. London: Routledge.

Rothman, Stanley; Lichter, Robert, and Nevitte, Neil (2005): "Politics and Professional Advancement Among College Faculty". In: *The Forum* 3 (1), pp. 1–16.

Schwettmann, Lars (2012): "Competing Allocation Principles. Time for Compromise?". In: *Theory and Decision* 73 (3), pp. 357–380.

Scott, John and Bornstein, Brian (2009): "What's Fair in Foul Weather and Fair? Distributive Justice Across Different Allocation Contexts and Goods". In: *Journal of Politics* 71 (3), pp. 831–846.

Sen, Amartya (1980): "Equality of What?". In: *The Tanner Lectures on Human Values* 1, pp. 197–220.

Sen, Amartya (1984): "Goods and People". In: Sen, Amartya: *Resources, Values and Development*. Oxford: Blackwell, pp. 509–532.

Sen, Amartya (1992): *Inequality Reexamined*. Oxford: Clarendon Press.

Siebel, Mark (2017): "To Each According to His Needs. Measuring Need-Based Justice". In: *DFG Research Group 2104, Need-Based Justice and Distribution Procedures, Working Paper* 2017–14.

Skitka, Linda and Tetlock, Philip (1992): "Allocating Scarce Resources. A Contingency Model of Distributive Justice". In: *Journal of Experimental Social Psychology* 28 (6), pp. 491–522.

Sondak, Harris; Neale, Margaret, and Pinkley, Robin (1999): "Relationship, Contribution and Resource Constraints. Determinants of Distributive Justice in Individual Preferences and Negotiated Agreements". In: *Group Decision and Negotiation* 8 (6), pp. 489–510.

Tan, Kok-Chor (2012): *Justice, Institutions, and Luck. The Site, Ground and Scope of Equality*. Oxford: Oxford University Press.

Temkin, Larry (1993): *Inequality*. New York: Oxford University Press.

Thomson, Garrett (1987): *Needs*. London: Routledge and Kegan Paul.

Ubel, Peter; Jepson, Christopher; Baron, Jonathan; Mohr, Tara; McMorrow, Stacey, and Asch, David (2001): "Allocation of Transplantable Organs. Do People Want to Punish Patients for Causing Their Illness?". In: *Liver Transplantation* 7 (7), pp. 600–607.

Umgelter, Katrin; Tobiasch, Moritz; Anetsberger, Aida; Blobner, Manfred; Thorban, Stefan, and Umgelter, Andreas (2015): "Donor Organ Distribution According to Urgency of Need or Outcome Maximization in Liver Transplantation. A Questionnaire Survey Among Patients and Medical Staff". In: *Transplant International* 28 (4), pp. 448–454.

Walzer, Michael (1983): *Spheres of Justice. A Defence of Pluralism and Equality*. Oxford: Martin Robertson.

Weiß, Arne Robert; Bauer, Alexander Max, and Traub, Stefan (2017): "Needs as Reference Points. When Marginal Gains to the Poor Do Not Matter". In: *DFG Research Group 2104, Need-Based Justice and Distribution Procedures, Working Paper* 2017–13.

Wiggins, David (1987): *Needs, Values, Truth. Essays in the Philosophy of Value*. Oxford: Blackwell.

Wood, Allen (1980): "The Marxian Critique of Justice". In: Cohen, Marshall; Nagel, Thomas, and Scanlon, Thomas (eds.): *Marx, Justice, and History*. Princeton: Princeton University Press, pp. 244–282.

Yaari, Menahem and Bar-Hillel, Maya (1984): "On Dividing Justly". In: *Social Choice and Welfare* 1, pp. 1–24.

Lars Schwettmann
A Simple Vote Won't Do It
Empirical Social Choice and the Fair Allocation of Health Care Resources

Abstract: The author reflects on the potential interdependence between empirical and normative research in the context of allocating scarce health care resources. Relevant aspects are discussed with respect to an approach designated as empirical social choice (ESC), which intends to provide empirical evidence on the tenability of axioms characterising different arbitration schemes. Different roles for empirical work are distinguished. Scholars in the field of ESC claim that their studies reveal ethical judgements and, thereby, provide input to an interpersonal reflective equilibrium. Furthermore, it is argued that the roles ascribed determine answers on four central methodological question: First, should studies utilise hypothetical or real distribution problems? Second, who should be asked? Third, which perspective should be taken? Fourth, should quantitative or qualitative approaches be used?

1 Introduction

One of the most important duties of policy-makers nowadays concerns the provision and funding of health care. In practically all societies there is a public health care sector that is at least partly financed collectively. Thus, both the proportion of the governmental budget to be spent on the health system and the allocation within the system are – to some degree – the responsibilities of governments. However, health policy-makers worldwide must take their allocation decisions in a situation of growing financial pressure and increasing need for health care services caused by demographic shifts, epidemiological changes, and rapid medical-technical progress. Clearly, the decisions have severe consequences for the lives of the individuals concerned and are typically characterised as "hard ethical choices" (Daniels 1993), where norms of fairness are pivotal. Furthermore, they are demanding in terms of so-called "enlightened morals" of the alleged moral experts and even more so in terms of the moral convictions or mores of a society that provides some part of health care publicly. Finally, the specific political environment is characterised by highly involved stakeholder groups with self-interested aims and activities.

https://doi.org/10.1515/9783110613797-015

Therefore, health policy-makers are in need of tenable and sustainable decisions. In the present chapter, the potential interdependence between empirical and normative research in the context of allocating scarce health care resources will be discussed. This question has already attracted much attention in various scientific disciplines even leading to new notions such as "empirical ethics" (Borry, Schotsmans, and Dierickx 2004, Richardson 2002, Richardson and McKie 2005). I will present and discuss an approach from the field of economics designated as *empirical social choice* (ESC) by Gaertner (2009) as well as Gartner and Schokkaert (2012). It sets out to examine the *tenability* of axioms formulated to characterise allocation schemes (Yaari and Bar-Hillel 1984) and, thus, can be regarded as one systematic way to combine normative and empirical research.

From the perspective of economics, any governmental decision under scarcity constraints leads to opportunity costs; corresponding resources can be spent only once and lead to foregone alternative usages, which then reflect the cost of the alternative chosen. In our case, this may concern either non-health related projects or alternative health care, which remains unprovided. Corresponding questions mainly focus on the allocation or, synonymously, *rationing* of resources, which generally denotes "any method to determine who receives what quantity of a scarce good or service" (Breyer 2013, p. 8). More specifically, economists usually claim that the focus should be on *explicit non-price rationing*: First, society should transparently endorse precise (explicit) allocation rules rather than determine budgets for health care providers in which case final allocation decisions must be made at the local level (hence the term "bedside rationing"). Second, based on most real-world health care systems, such methods are considered that do not make use of the price mechanism and allocate scarce resources below the market price or even at no charge. E. g., scarce donated organs are not allocated via auctions but on the basis of other criteria such as urgency of need or prospects of success.

When it comes to the allocation of health care resources, health policy-makers usually aim at both improving total population health and reducing unfair health inequality. E. g., a new cancer screening program may be expected to increase population health on average, but also to worsen population health inequalities due to variable uptake of screening by different societal groups (Asaria et al. 2015). Health economic evaluation methods typically focus exclusively on the maximisation of total population health and, thereby, ignore health inequality impacts arising from the interventions assessed. Only recently, health economists have started to enhance their methods by incorporating health inequality impacts into their evaluation methods (Cookson et al. 2017). Nevertheless, survey research on the underlying trade-off between efficiency and equity concerns plays already an important role in the health economic literature for many years (see, e.g., discussions on the method of "person trade-off" by Nord 1995, Nord et al. 1999, Doctor, Miyamoto, and Bleichrodt 2009). However, as pointed out by Gaertner and Schokkaert (2012), many health economists seem to believe that corresponding ethical problems can be solved by survey work on preferences of those people who will be affected by the decisions. Consequently, one may ask why we do not just let citizens, (potential) patients, or payers vote on the rationing of health care resources.

Of course, information about what people want from their health system is an important input for politicians who seek re-election, health administrators who act as agents of their customers, and researchers who want to see their own ideas put into practice. However, allocation decisions may also conflict with the limits of what is thought to be "morally permissible" (Hausman 2000, p. 44). Even the acceptance of health policy measures by the majority of people in a society can be based on bad reasons (Miller 1994). One recent example could be the demand for limiting access to *basic health care* for refugees by larger parts of the population in some countries, today. Hence, the normative beliefs held by members of society should be subjected to critical scrutiny. According to the ESC approach, moral judgements collected from laypeople cannot substitute moral reflection and argumentation. But they could serve as input for a process, which aims at justifying allocative decisions and – ideally – reaching an *interpersonal reflective equilibrium* (Rawls 1971, 1974, Daniels 1979).

The present chapter will discuss this approach in the context of allocating health care resources. Taking parts of the book by Gaertner and Schokkaert (2012) as a starting point, the chapter is structured as follows: Section 2 provides a general classification of ESC. The focus of section 3 is on potential roles ascribed to empirical work in ESC. In section 4, I discuss major methodological consequences. Section 5 summarises the main characteristics of ESC and concludes.

2 Empirical Social Choice – A First Classification

Empirical research on distributive justice in economics can be divided into two branches, which have evolved rather independently over the last four decades (Schwettmann 2009, Konow and Schwettmann 2016). On the one hand, behavioural or *positive economics* applies descriptive strategies and regards what "is". Results of monetarily incentivised experiments have stimulated descriptive theories of social preferences, which inter alia include fairness concerns as well as related moral preferences, such as unconditional altruism or reciprocity which occasionally have also been labelled as fairness. On the other hand, *normative economics* uses prescriptive analyses and concerns itself with what "ought to be". In the corresponding empirical strand of the literature, mainly findings of self-reported surveys and vignette studies are used to investigate prescriptive theories of distributive justice (see Konow 2003, for a review). ESC is one such approach, which aims to impact normative theories about social choice applied to issues of distributive justice and related topics such as the measurement of inequalities (for applications to the health context, see Bleichrodt, Rohde, and van Ourti 2012, Tarroux 2015) or voting behaviour (Regenwetter et al. 2007). It must, yet, be noted that both the descriptive and the prescriptive branch have not only grown autonomously, but are often found to be strictly kept separated from each other. Some of the underlying reasons will be elicited in the following sections.

Welfare economics and social choice theory have a strong normative claim. Inter alia they intend to specify or even substantiate philosophical ideas by means of axioms and models, examine the consistency of philosophical theories, and establish standards to evaluate social outcomes (Miller 1994, Roemer 1996). The classical welfare-economic distinction between individual utilities and social values is of major relevance in the context of health care (see Sen 1970, Goodin 1986, for general introductions). Individual preferences are used to obtain a measure of individual well-being, e.g., in different health states, while distributional and other relational considerations are embodied in the shape of a social welfare function (SWF), which takes up an ethical position and can be characterised axiomatically.

In general, the axiomatic approach has gained momentum and is applied to game theory and resource allocation alike (see Thomson 2001, for an overview). However, Luce and Raiffa (1957) have already described the intentions and advantages of the axiomatic method when it comes to the determination of an *arbitration scheme*, i.e. a rule which assigns each person in a distribution conflict a unique payoff. Surprisingly, although the authors had no empirical programme in mind, their elaborations can be read as a preliminary description of the ESC approach, which set off about 25 years later with the seminal work by Yaari and Bar-Hillel (1984). According to Luce and Raiffa (1957, p. 121; emphasis added) "players are often willing to submit their conflict to an arbiter, an *impartial outsider* who will resolve the conflict by suggesting a solution". In fact, in normative approaches impartiality is a seminal precondition to avoid self-serving biases of moral preferences. The authors continue that we "may suppose that the arbiter sincerely envisages his mission to be 'fairness' to both players". They assume that the arbiter reports his or her own ethical standards if no obvious fairness criterion exists in a distributive situation. However, other motives rather than fairness may influence decisions.

Next, Luce and Raiffa (1957, pp. 121 ff.; emphasis added) elaborate the central advantage of the axiomatic method in the realm of distributive justice:

> Rather than dream up a multitude of arbitration schemes and determine whether or not each withstands the test of plausibility in a host of special cases, let us [...] examine *our subjective intuition* of "fairness" and formulate this as a set of precise desiderata that any acceptable arbitration scheme must fulfil [...]. By means of a (small) finite number of axioms we are able "to examine" the infinity of possible schemes, to throw away those which are unfair, and to characterize those which are *acceptable.*

According to Gaertner and Schokkaert (2012), two main research programmes are deducible from this description of the axiomatic approach. On the one hand, the logical connections between axioms proposed to characterise a unique (class of) arbitration schemes can be investigated solely with the help of applied mathematics. On the other hand, the (ethical) acceptance of axioms and, therefore, the fairness of arbitration schemes cannot be determined by applying mathematical tools. In this case, Luce and Raiffa (1957, p. 121) use the unspecific notion of "our subjective intuitions". Turning against a significant input of empirical studies on this question, some theorists have emphasised that "essential ingredients of a debate over normative issues are critical reflection and thorough assessment of the arguments being used" (Bossert 1998, p. 283). Hence, a "vote among uninformed individuals" should not suffice to settle an ethical issue satisfactorily. As the reader will surely know, such reservations are regularly articulated with respect to moral psychology, empirical ethics, experimental philosophy, and ESC.

Authors in the field of ESC claim that their empirical findings are of relevance for the reflective processes in philosophical ethics, normative economics, and policy. This is said to be due to the specific empirical method applied to elicit moral preferences. Here, the studies by Yaari and Bar-Hillel (1984) as well as Bar-Hillel and Yaari (1993) serve as the blueprint for subsequent questionnaire experiments. The authors confronted students with hypothetical allocation problems in different contexts, which were supposed to be easily accessible for laypeople. The students were asked to solve the problems *justly*. The questions were theory-based in the way that different arbitration schemes characterised by specific sets of axioms lead to distinct allocations in the given situation. Bar-Hillel and Yaari (1993) clarify that they intend to consider an increased number of introspecting individuals and, thereby, interpret Luce and Raiffa's (1957) notion of "our subjective intuitions" in a very broad way. Accordingly, empirical work may give useful insights into the ethical "acceptability" of axioms or allocation rules.

The ESC approach just sketched provokes fierce criticism from both normatively oriented researchers and descriptive analysts. Hence, we need to elaborate two central issues: First, it must be specified which role empirical work can play in social choice and distributive justice – and which not. Second, each role requires, but also excludes, certain empirical instruments. I will successively consider these aspects in the next two sections and, at the same time, relate corresponding answers to the context of allocating health care resources.

3 Which Role for Empirical Work in Empirical Social Choice?

Gaertner and Schokkaert (2012, subsection 2.1) mainly try to defend the ESC approach against objections of normatively oriented researchers. I partly follow their structure and begin with *seemingly* easy-to-digest roles for empirical work with a special focus on the health context. Afterwards, I elaborate on the application of the concept of an interpersonal reflective equilibrium in the ESC literature. Finally, I clarify which roles are usually *not* ascribed to empirical work in ESC.

3.1 Application, Prevention, Revelation, and Complementation – Easy-to-Digest Roles?

According to Gaertner and Schokkaert's (2012) first argument, any theory of justice finally aims to be *applied*. Therefore, empirical insights into the social and political environment are necessary to evaluate the acceptability of a presumably justified normative concept and to detect potential reservations. The authors claim that this role for empirical work should be most easily acknowledgeable by normative researchers as it solely concerns the explainability of a theory, but not its justification. Also, Klonschinski (2016, chapter 7) discusses the fear that decisions on priority setting are made by "philosopher kings" and counters that "when it comes to the implementation of health policy, the citizens have the last word anyway". Nevertheless, from my point of view, this first role does not reflect a real interdependence between empirical and normative research, but rather concerns aspects of public choice and the process of political decision-making. Furthermore, a considerable degree of paternalism is contained in Gaertner and Schokkaert's (2012, p. 10; emphasis added) statement that to "build a convincing case, a better insight into the structure of the uninformed opinions, that have 'to be *corrected*', may be extremely useful, even necessary".

The second potential role for empirical input concerns the possible *prevention* of different biases. In the context of allocating scarce health care resources especially two biases are of relevance. On the one hand, normative and empirical scholars may subliminally be influenced by their own characteristics such as age, health history, or social and cultural background. E.g., Klingler and colleagues (2013) as well as Gerber-Grote and colleagues (2014) explain that the public and academic discussion about health economic evaluation in Germany is influenced by experiences during the Nazi regime, where parts of the population were designated as "life unworthy of life" (*lebensunwertes Leben*, see also Schwettmann 2016, for a discussion). This influence differs from the obvious possibility of a self-serving bias, which can always affect researchers and participants in experiments. On the other hand, researchers often describe allocation problems by typical examples, which may limit their perspective. The allocation of donated organs, people lying on rail tracks or sitting shipwrecked in a boat are often regarded cases. However, many real-life situations of scarcity, such as the allocation of treatment time, are regularly less dramatic.

A third argument in favour of empirical work claims that corresponding studies may *reveal* an incompleteness of a theoretical concept in the way that it ignores important features of real-world cases. Yaari and Bar-Hillel (1984) identified a strong context-dependency of respondents' judgements in formally identical distribution problems, which was not stipulated in welfare economic approaches. In fact, some framing effects may also fall into this category. E.g., in the study by Ahlert, Funke, and Schwettmann (2013) the ordering in which participants faced decision problems had a strong impact on exclusion decisions from medical treatment. Such findings may be taken up by theoretical reasoning.

The fourth potential role for empirical studies is even more constructive. Gaertner and Schokkaert (2012) explain that some theoretical approaches explicitly demand empirical input as a *complement*. They refer to the example of Roemer's (1993, 1998) concept of equality of opportunity. The so-called "responsibility cut" (Schokkaert and Devooght 2003), i.e., the line between effort characteristics, for which individuals should be held responsible, and circumstances, for which they should receive compensation, is of major importance. Roemer (1993) argues that the determination is a societal question and may provoke different answers in different societies. In the realm of health care distribution, survey studies, such as Schokkaert and Devooght (2003) or Diederich, Schwettmann, and Winkelhage (2014), may provide additional input into the underlying normative debate about the location of this cut.

To summarise, the four positions described assign an increasingly prominent role to empirical work in social choice. However, many researchers in the field of ESC go one step further.

3.2 Interpersonal Reflective Equilibrium and Empirical Social Choice

Yaari and Bar-Hillel (1984) proposed a methodology which enables them to incorporate empirical findings into the model-building process. Here, they explicitly relate their own approach to the Rawlsian (1971) notion of a reflective equilibrium. In short, Rawls describes a process of moral deliberation, in which a person moves back and forth between "considered judgements", i.e., particular beliefs and intuitions about justice in a specific case, and "general principles of justice", e.g., the two principles that would according to Rawls be chosen in the "original position". In case of a conflict, the person may either specify, refine, or even discard the principle if it sharply contradicts the considered judgement, or may revise and correct his or her initially considered judgement if the arguments in favour of the principle are strong enough. If principles and considered judgements come into correspondence, a reflective equilibrium is achieved.

Before relating this notion to the ESC approach, let me elaborate a bit on Miller's (1994) view on the potential role for empirical work regarding the reflective equilibrium. His view may serve as a helpful link between ESC and empirical ethics. According to Miller, the notion of *considered judgements* is crucial for empirical work. Only those beliefs about justice are treated as considered judgements, which are free of emotions and personal interest, and of which the individual is confident about. Also, beliefs should be free of any contradictions and not be based on factual errors (see especially Daniels 1979, for further potential distortions). Hence, Miller asks how to evaluate whether beliefs in fact fulfil these requirements. He proposes to widen the focus of Rawls' individualistic perspective, to compare the relevant individual beliefs with those of others and, if there is disagreement, to elaborate underlying reasons. Thus, acceptance of judgements is important, but justification should be the focus of empirical inquiry.

A second argument of Miller in favour of empirical input concerns Rawls' (1993) notion of "public justifiability". Miller (1994, p. 181) explains that "a valid theory of justice must be one which the citizens of a well-ordered society can justify to one another using only commonly accepted modes of arguments". Hence, rather than focussing only on the implementation of a theory, justifiability is now an ethical precondition. This aspect can be related to Rawls' (1993,

p. 306) interpretation of the "original position", in which individuals are supposed to be guided not only by a "conception of rational choice as understood in economics or decision theory", but also by "norms of reasonableness" which make the individual propose only those principles that are acceptable to all people with a "sense of justice" once the veil of ignorance is lifted. Here, Miller (1994) argues that this *reasonableness* also leads to the interpretation of the reflective equilibrium as an *interpersonal equilibrium* with respect to the beliefs of distinct individuals.

Similarly, the basic intuition of the model-building process underlying the ESC approach can be described as a "dialogue between the theorist and the public" (Gaertner and Schokkaert 2012, p. 17). Yaari and Bar-Hillel (1984) start from the basic structure of the axiomatic approach to distributive justice described by Luce and Raiffa (1957) (see section 2) and propose an iterative procedure via self-corrections and revisions. More concretely, in a first step a set of axioms is formulated to express desired properties of any allocation mechanism. Next, with the help of applied mathematics or logic the questions of existence and characterisation of mechanisms satisfying these axioms must be answered. If no such mechanism exists, the initial set of axioms must be revised. If several mechanisms are identified, they must be compared in order to determine additional properties which help to finally distinguish between them.

These additional properties are then tested for their *tenability*. If they are found to be untenable, the set of axioms is revised again, whereas in the case of no further revisions a state of equilibrium is reached. The relation between the notion of a reflective equilibrium and this procedure is obvious. Loosely speaking, economic theories expressed by sets of axioms and corresponding distribution mechanisms take the role of Rawls' general principles, while answers by respondents in adequately structured questionnaires are said to be based on "ethical judgements", which then replace the "considered judgements" in Rawls' notion. However, it is an advantage of the axiomatic approach to disentangle complex normative conceptions and to focus on axioms reflecting their specific characteristics rather than on the entire theoretical notion.

It is the test of the *tenability* of these axioms and distribution mechanisms from which a demand for empirical work arises. Yaari and Bar-Hillel (1984) argue that any theory of justice must be evaluated by their performance when confronted with evidence. In the present case, evidence is provided by "moral intuitions" and "ethical judgements" usually made by thoughtful, impartial, and unemotional individuals. The similarity to Miller's (1994) interpretation of considered judgements is apparent. In their later work, Bar-Hillel and Yaari (1993, p. 59) also pronounce that their approach solely focuses on "ethical notions in people's minds – not their actual behaviour", which is usually biased by various other factors and considerations. Furthermore, although the authors do not state it explicitly, they obviously see the notion of a reflective equilibrium as an interpersonal conception. Nevertheless, even confirmed empiricists like Bar-Hillel and Yaari do not deny the central role for normative elaboration and philosophical reflection. Ethical judgements are seen as guides for evaluating the tenability of axioms or distribution mechanisms. But it is certainly possible – and often more reasonable – to keep to the general principle and discard the considered judgement in a specific context.

It seems that this thinking has also gained momentum in the field of health economics in recent years. E. g., Tsuchiya and Dolan (2009, p. 157) conclude from their study on the acceptance of different equality notions in the context of health care distribution that "robust violations of particular axioms in the SWF may lead to some of those axioms [...] being relaxed in certain contexts". This is a very careful statement compared to many others in this literature where researchers more often hold a positivistic view on issues of distributive justice and want to solve decision problems by empirical work. Thus, it is also advisable to point out the limits to empirical work for the ESC approach.

3.3 Limits to Empirical Work

To close this section, let me reconsider the view that questions about the fair allocation of scarce health care resources can finally be answered by the beliefs of the (majority) of the target population, being it citizens, (potential) patients, or premium payers. According to this position, which has also been expressed by several health economists (see, e.g., Dolan 1998 and Johannesson 1999), empirical work would not only be essential but decisive. However, from the elaborations in the previous subsection it should be clear that the ESC approach does not concur with such a view. Similarly, Miller (1994) explains that corresponding empirical work should be based on a normative justice theory. He argues that such a foundation is necessary to know whether distributive judgements are based on justice or on other motives. According to Miller, this knowledge may help researchers to make predictions in cases of changing circumstances or new information.

In subsection 17.3 of his remarkable book, Hausman (2015) summarises several of his main arguments against a rather extreme position of what he calls "empirical ethics". From my point of view, six points already raised in earlier contributions (Hausman 2000, 2002) are helpful to identify important limits of empirical work in the realm of allocating health care resources.

First, an ethical position is not right just because the majority of the target group agrees or because it displays a "social consensus". One may think of examples such as slavery, ethnic cleansing, or female infanticide to recognise the important distinction between acceptance and justification. Second, Hausman (2000) asks how to define which groups are decisive and how to settle disagreements between different decisive groups.

Third, it remains an open question regarding what happens if no consensus can be reached. In Miller's (1994) as well as Yaari and Bar-Hillel's (1984) interpretation of an interpersonal reflective equilibrium a reconsideration of either the justifications of each position or the set of axioms would be possible. Nevertheless, this demands insights into underlying reasons for individual judgements. Fourth, empirical ethics implies that a social consensus would always be right. However, each process towards a reflective equilibrium should enable the researcher to carefully investigate reasons for moral disagreement.

Fifth, social consensus on moral issues is based on today's accepted moral views, which in turn may depend on past arguments raised by reformers. Such an evolution would be hindered by a focus on majorities. Finally, Hausman (2002) asserts that concerns of the population should not be ignored when deciding on the health system. However, he points out that patients and premium payers are not better able to state what is morally right or wrong only because the outcome of the decision concerns them.

Hausman (2015, p. 238) concludes that the process towards a reflective equilibrium should "pay attention to accepted values", but it is a "misconceived hope [to resolve] moral questions by measurement rather than argument". This position is not at odds with the ESC approach. In contrast, it sets clear limits to the usage of empirical findings beyond the roles described in subsections 3.1 and 3.2. Furthermore, each of these roles has specific implications for the empirical methods applied to obtain the raw material needed. Section 4 provides answers to four important methodological questions.

4 Methodological Consequences

The empirical method applied by Yaari and Bar-Hillel (1984) has already been sketched in section 2: Participants in questionnaire experiments are confronted with abstract, hypothetical decision problems in different contexts. They are asked to take the position of an outside observer and to allocate a given resource justly between different (groups of) individuals. The given situations are structured in the way that distinct distribution mechanisms characterised by different sets of axioms lead to different allocation proposals. Yaari and Bar-Hillel claim that these methodological aspects follow from their interpretation of a reflective equilibrium to provoke ethical judgements of laypeople which are meaningful for the model-building process in social choice theory. In this section, I focus on methodological aspects partly discussed by Gaertner and Schokkaert (2012), which I assess as particularly relevant for respective studies on the fair allocation of scarce health care resources.

Some preliminary words on the general setting of corresponding studies might be helpful. According to Gaertner and Schokkaert (2012), ESC studies use a *quasi-experimental approach*. Rather than asking people directly which principle should be applied in a given context, respondents read specific stories describing hypothetical real-life problems and are asked to select from a given set of solutions the one they judge most fair or just. Additionally (or alternatively), they are given the option to make their own proposals. This fits perfectly to the discovery-role of empirical work described in subsection 3.1. Different randomly selected participants receive systematically varied problems so that distinct response patterns can be related to these manipulations. This specific approach is said to be able to reveal useful ethical judgements and intuitions to investigate the tenability of axioms and distribution mechanisms.

A related issue, also mentioned by Gaertner and Schokkaert (2012), concerns the distinction between *ethical intuitions* and *reasoned opinions*. The answering of a single decision problem primarily sheds light on intuitions. In contrast, facing a sequence of variants of a basic situation induces subjects to think about differences, reflect on their own reaction to these variations, and, thus, provide reasoned opinions. Of course, the latter proceeding carries the risk of manipulating the way a respondent thinks about a problem. However, reflected, thorough, and informed answers may be helpful, even necessary, if trade-offs between distribution mechanisms are regarded. Hence, the requirements for considered judgements mentioned in subsection 3.2 must be met. Respondents must take their tasks seriously and think intensively about the matters presented to them (see also Elster 1995). The study reported by Ahlert and Schwettmann (2017) provides an example for this setting. In their questionnaire investigation each respondent received a sequence of 16 systematically varied, hypothetical allocation problems where a limited amount of treatment time had to be allocated to patients who differed with respect to their initial health level and their ability to benefit from treatment time. Finally, participants were asked to verbally describe the allocation rule they had developed during the experiment. Answers revealed that subjects were clearly aware of the different features of the problems. They were able to describe and apply sophisticated rules which focussed on several characteristics of the situations simultaneously (i.e., conditional rules) or even utilised threshold values. Most remarkably, participants followed their respective intuitions very consistently. I turn now to four important methodological issues of ESC studies in the context of health and health care.

4.1 Hypothetical or Real Distribution Problems?

Bar-Hillel and Yaari (1993) put the distinction between expressed and revealed sentiments at the centre of their argumentation. Usually, economic laboratory experiments with subjects driven by self-interest are distinguished from questionnaire experiments focussing on the impartial spectator perspective. From my point of view this is misleading. On the one hand, questionnaire experiments on distributive justice may also create real decision problems. E.g., in the study by Ahlert, Funke, and Schwettmann (2013) a payment scheme was introduced to impose monetary costs for participants on departures from a utilitarian distribution mechanism in either a "health" or a "neutral" context. On the other hand, laboratory studies may induce subjects to act as "quasi-spectators", i.e. third parties whose decisions have actual consequences for others but not for themselves (Konow 2003, 2012). Hence, the focus should be on the distinction between hypothetical (non-incentivised) and real (incentivised) problems. They lead to preferences which are either stated by verbal answers or choices of different hypothetical distribution options or are revealed via distribution behaviour.

A helpful related categorisation of descriptive empirical studies comes from Elster (1995). His first dimension concerns the place of an investigation where he distinguishes between artificial and real-life settings. The second dimension regards the object of the study, being it attitudes or behaviour. In artificial settings, attitudes are studied via surveys or experiments (the study by Frohlich and Oppenheimer 1992 provides a classical example), while other experiments clearly focus on the actual behaviour of participants. In real-life settings, content analysis may help revealing justice attitudes, whereas (real-life) behavioural studies consider local justice such as processes of wage formation or donated kidney allocations. Güth and Kliemt (2010) subsume practices of the latter category under the notion of "normative facts". Furthermore, in Elster's (1995) classification, revealed preferences are usually observed from behavioural studies.

One challenge for monetarily incentivised experiments in health economics is the representation of different health states. Some researchers (e.g., Hennig-Schmidt, Selten, and Wiesen 2011, Godagar and Wiesen 2013, Hennig-Schmidt and Wiesen 2014) have connected benefits in the lab to payments for real patients outside to investigate effects of different payment systems for physicians or "other-regarding behaviour". Nevertheless, various further questions of distributive justice concerning people in urgent need for health care seem to be difficult to reflect by monetary equivalents.

A second problem already mentioned concerns the fact that actual behaviour is regularly determined by a combination of different motives including self-interest, various moral considerations, or other norms. Gaertner and Schokkaert (2012) argue that corresponding findings are certainly illuminating if the aim is to predict actual behaviour. However, as explained in subsection 3.2, this is explicitly not the case in ESC and its focus on ethical judgements.

Miller (1992) as well as Gaertner and Schokkaert (2012) list potential advantages and disadvantages of questionnaire studies, which use hypothetical distribution problems rather than real problems in the lab. Especially with respect to health, such studies enable the researcher to present contextually rich situations with clear links to real-life problems. Certainly, respondents are more sensitive to contextual and framing issues and may take distribution problems less seriously, since answers have no real consequences. The quote that "actions speak louder than words" of Bikhchandani, Hirshleifer, and Welch (1992, p. 996) nicely expresses this reservation about the credibility of stated preferences. Thus, Gaertner and Schokkaert (2012) suggest to carefully control for context and framing effects. They report from their experiments that respondents generally take non-incentivised questionnaire studies seriously if the task is not too complex.

4.2 Whom to Ask?

The choice of the "right" subjects to ask depends on the role ascribed to empirical findings. If one agrees with Yaari and Bar-Hillel's (1984) or Miller's (1994) interpretation of an interpersonal reflective equilibrium described in subsection 3.2, a sample being representative for the entire society should be the ultimate choice. The idea of a dialogue between the theorist and the public, but especially the ethical precondition that a theory of justice should be justifiable to the citizens, implies the need for surveys being representative of the general public. Furthermore, corresponding results are certainly also useful for the other roles of empirical work explained in subsection 3.1 including the identification of biases on the side of the researcher or cultural-dependent effects. Additionally, such findings can help evaluating the acceptance of normative concepts before their political implementation. In this case, the characteristic of representative surveys as an instrument of political decision-making becomes visible.

Nevertheless, a focus on specific groups may be a reasonable alternative especially at earlier stages of the process. Actual or future decision-makers in the healthcare sector are of interest if empirical findings are used to characterise real-life problems or to evaluate the acceptance of a theory of justice among those who should implement it, e.g., physicians.

Furthermore, several studies use student samples if they want to ask laypeople. Of course, compared to the general public, they are easier to approach, usually highly motivated, and better able to understand more complex situations. Hence, as argued by Gaertner and Schokkaert (2012), if the aim is to discover new features of real-world cases or to evaluate trade-offs between axioms, student samples may represent a reasonable alternative. However, the two authors also warn that students might see questionnaire studies – but of course also lab experiments – as a kind of exam if they either perceive or suspect a connection between the questions and the topics covered in their lectures. Also, they may be prone to a social desirability bias, especially if the study is conducted by their own teacher. Hence, it is vital to avoid such perceptions, e.g., by approaching students at an early stage in their course of studies or in a more neutral surrounding, e.g., in different lectures or in a computer lab.

4.3 Which Perspective Should Be Taken?

Luce and Raiffa's (1957) description of an impartial outsider cited in section 2, who is asked to solve a distribution conflict, already points towards the central role of this concept for justice theories. It has a long history in economic and philosophical research and is the working horse in the field of ESC. Yaari and Bar-Hillel (1984) create abstract hypothetical questionnaire situations to bring respondents into the position of a detached outside observer and to receive unbiased ethical judgements. In health contexts, this requirement seems to be both necessary and hard to achieve.

There exists by now a reasonable number of studies which have focussed on effects from the position of the decision-maker in a hypothetical situation. In ESC and health economic studies, this aspect is found to be of utmost importance. In their study on rankings of income distributions Bosmans and Schokkaert (2004) distinguish three types of preferences related to different positions: "direct ethical preferences" of an impartial and sympathetic observer (ISO); "preferences behind a veil of ignorance" (VOI), where a rational individual knows that he or she and all other members of society will end up in either income position with equal probability; and "purely individual risk preferences" (PIR), where the focus is entirely on personal income. While the first position is related to Smith's (1759) *impartial spectator*, the second case resembles the *veil of ignorance* scenario of Rawls (1971) or Harsanyi (1953, 1955). The main finding is that response patterns are different for all three positions, where the VOI case is between the other two.

The usage of distinct perspectives when eliciting preferences over allocations of health care resources is also prominent in the health economic literature (Dolan et al. 2003, Tsuchiya and Watson 2017). E. g., in their study on social values assigned to different health states, Pinto-Prades and Abellán-Perpiñán (2005) inter alia construct positions similar to those used by Bosmans and Schokkaert (2004). One of their findings is that their VOI treatment yields results almost identical to a self-concerned position under risk which is similar to the PIR perspective. However, the results of the person trade-off method that applies the position of an impartial sympathetic observer clearly depart from these results. Hence, both streams of literature seem to reach surprisingly similar results: Judgements of an impartial outside observer depart from preferences of rational individuals behind a veil of ignorance facing a similar distribution problem.

Nevertheless, many allocation problems in the health context provoke self-interested and biased answers. E. g., the studies by Johannsson-Stenman and Martinsson (2008) or Álvarez and Rodríguez-Míguez (2011) show how difficult it might be to implement impartiality. Hence, corresponding empirical work should apply state-of-the-art statistical tools to control for influences of individual characteristics. Furthermore, the requirement of abstract hypothetical situations is a serious claim.

4.4 Quantitative or Qualitative Studies?

In the introduction to this section, the importance of thorough, informed, and thoughtful judgements has already been explained. Also, the importance of empirical work on the way to a reflective equilibrium via considered judgements – but also its limitations – have been considered in subsections 3.2 and 3.3. According to Miller (1994), the central role for empirical input concerns the justification of beliefs rather than the acceptance of theories. This would allow for an interdependence between empirical and normative research. Nevertheless, Yaari and Bar-Hillel (1984) focus almost entirely on quantitative rather than qualitative studies to evaluate the tenability of axioms and distribution mechanisms. Similarly, Gaertner and Schokkaert (2012) do not explicitly discuss advantages and disadvantages of qualitative work. However, qualitative studies may complement quantitative work if detailed justifications of beliefs are seen as being helpful (as they are, I suppose). Furthermore, regarding other roles for empirical studies, reasons for potential biases or any incompleteness of a theoretical concept may certainly benefit from thoroughly and carefully conducted qualitative work.

In the health economic literature corresponding qualitative techniques have gained momentum. They have proven to be a relevant additional tool to investigate distributive preferences regarding health care resources (Cookson and Dolan 1999, Dolan and Cookson 2000, Baker, Robinson, and Smith 2008, Shah et al. 2012). In the field of ESC, Ahlert and Schwettmann (2017) identified distribution mechanisms with a combination of quantitative and qualitative instruments. Remarkably, some of these rules have not been characterised axiomatically before, so that such findings may be regarded in the model-building process in the future.

Based on the elaborations in section 3, I have focussed on selected methodological consequences for empirical studies on distributive justice in the context of scarce health care resources. In general, the choice of appropriate empirical tools is not trivial, but we know their potential effects on the results. They should be justified and depend on the role one is willing to ascribe to empirical findings for theories of distributive justice.

5 Summary and Conclusion

Fairness is a central principle for the allocation of scarce health care resources. Against this background, the chapter has focussed on the general question of how empirical work can be brought to bear on normative issues, and, vice versa, how normative research can induce fruitful empirical studies. Relevant aspects have been discussed with respect to an approach designated as empirical social choice (ESC).

So, what kind of contribution can the ESC approach generally make, i.e. which role should be played by judgements about justice collected in adequate studies? Initially, it has been argued that questionnaire studies may not only test the acceptance of a normative concept before its application, but can be used to detect potential biases and discover new puzzles. However, the claim of ESC is more ambitious. If a thoroughly conducted questionnaire study reflects tradeoffs between axioms, advocates of the ESC approach assert that their approach reveals ethical judgements and, moreover, offers reasons for them, which can be used as input to an axiomatic model-building process. Surprising empirical results of theory-based questionnaire experiments could stimulate normative thinking and lead to richer models which may then induce even richer questionnaires. This interdependence between empirical and normative research can be interpreted as a dialogue between a theorist and the public, which may finally bring us closer to an interpersonal reflective equilibrium.

However, this essential role ascribed to empirical work also determines what is meant by "thoroughly conducted". I have discussed four major methodological issues. First, studies utilising hypothetical rather than real distribution problems should be preferred. This is especially due to the problem of creating real decision problems in the context of health care. Second, if the aim is to come closer to an interpersonal reflective equilibrium, samples being representative for the general public should be the ultimate choice. Nevertheless, focussing on specific groups might be a reasonable alternative at earlier stages of the process. Third, impartiality is of major importance to receive unbiased ethical judgements. Hence, participants in corresponding studies should be brought into the position of detached outside observers. Fourth, qualitative studies may serve as a complement to quantitative work due to the importance of justification of beliefs.

Hopefully, the approach described leads to more tenable and sustainable allocative decisions. This should be particularly warranted in the health-policy environment initially presented, which is characterised by a strong pressure to make hard choices with respect to the allocation of increasingly scarce resources and in a political setting with highly involved stakeholders. Clearly, the focus of ESC is on justification rather than acceptance of theoretical concepts. Although both the importance of considering what people want from their health system and the necessity to survey and respect individual preferences for health states is acknowledged, researchers in the field of ESC emphasise that empirical work on preferences is unable to finally determine an ethically acceptable distribution mechanism. Philosophical reflection is also necessary. However, in the end, the interdependence between empirical and normative may help normative scholars make themselves heard (better) by health-politicians.

Acknowledgements

An earlier version of this chapter was titled "The (Difficult) Interdependence Between Empirical and Normative Research – Empirical Social Choice and the Fair Distribution of Health Care Resources" and appeared in *Discussion Papers in Economics* 78, Martin Luther University Halle-Wittenberg, June 2015. I have benefited from comments by Marlies Ahlert, Katharina Fischer, Hartmut Kliemt, Julian Klinger, Erik Schokkaert, and Mark Schweda. Helpful suggestions made by participants at the symposium "Empirie und Normativität" 2015 in Halle (Saale), at the 13th Meeting of the Society for Social Choice and Welfare 2016 in Lund, at the Deutsche Gesellschaft für Gesundheitsökonomie (dggö) 2017 meeting in Konstanz, and at the Summer School "Empirical Research and Normative Theory"

2017 in Oldenburg are also gratefully acknowledged. The usual disclaimer applies.

Bibliography

Ahlert, Marlies; Funke, Katja, and Schwettmann, Lars (2013): "Thresholds, Productivity, and Context. An Experimental Study on Determinants of Distributive Behaviour". In: *Social Choice and Welfare* 40 (4), pp. 957–984.

Ahlert, Marlies and Schwettmann, Lars (2017): "Allocating Health Care Resources. A Questionnaire Experiment on the Predictive Success of Rules". In: *International Journal for Equity in Health* 16 (112).

Álvarez, Begoña and Rodríguez-Míguez, Eva (2011): "Patients' Self-Interested Preferences. Empirical Evidence from a Priority Setting Experiment". In: *Social Science & Medicine* 72 (8), pp. 1317–1324.

Asaria, Miqdad; Griffin, Susan; Cookson, Richard; Whyte, Sophie, and Tappenden, Paul (2015): "Distributional Cost-Effectiveness Analysis of Health Care Programmes. A Methodological Case Study of the UK Bowl Cancer Screening Programme". In: *Health Economics* 24 (6), pp. 742–754.

Baker, Rachel; Robinson, Angela, and Smith, Richard (2008): "How Do Respondents Explain WTP Responses? A Review of Qualitative Evidence". In: *The Journal of Socio-Economics* 37 (4), pp. 1427–1442.

Bar-Hillel, Maya and Yaari, Menahem (1993): "Judgments of Distributive Justice". In: Mellers, Barbara and Baron, Jonathan (eds.): *Psychological Perspectives on Justice. Theory and Applications.* Cambridge: Cambridge University Press, pp. 55–84.

Bikhchandani, Sushil; Hirshleifer, David, and Welch, Ivo (1992): "A Theory of Fads, Fashion, Custom, and Cultural Change as Informational Cascades". In: *Journal of Political Economy* 100 (5), pp. 992–1026.

Bleichrodt, Han; Rohde, Kirsten, and van Ourti, Tom (2012): "An Experimental Test of the Concentration Index". In: *Journal of Health Economics* 31 (1), pp. 86–98.

Borry, Pascal; Schotsmans, Paul, and Dierickx, Kris (2004): "What Is the Role of Empirical Research in Bioethical Reflection and Decision-Making? An Ethical Analysis". In: *Medicine, Health Care and Philosophy* 7 (1), pp. 41–53.

Bosmans, Kristof and Schokkaert, Erik (2004): "Social Welfare, the Veil of Ignorance and Purely Individual Risk. An Empirical Examination". In: *Research in Economic Inequality* 11, pp. 85–114.

Bossert, Walter (1998): "Comments on 'the Empirical Acceptance of Compensation Axioms'". In: Laslier, Jean-François; Fleurbaey, Marc; Gravel, Nicolas, and Trannoy, Alain (eds.): *Freedom in Economics.* London: Routledge, pp. 282–284.

Breyer, Friedrich (2013): "Implicit Versus Explicit Rationing of Health Services". In: *CESifo DICE Report* 1, pp. 7–15.

Cookson, Richard and Dolan, Paul (1999): Public Views on Health Care Rationing. A Group Discussion Study". In: *Health Policy* 49 (1–2), pp. 63–74.

Cookson, Richard and Dolan, Paul (2000): "Principles of Justice in Health Care Rationing". In: *Journal of Medical Ethics* 26 (5), pp. 323–329.

Cookson, Richard; Mirelman, Andrew; Grifin, Susan; Asaria, Miqdad; Dawkins, Bryony; Norheim, Ole Frithjof; Verguet, Stéphane, and Culyer, Anthony (2017): "Using Cost-Effectiveness Analysis to Address Health Equity Concerns". In: *Value in Health* 20 (2), pp. 206–212.

Daniels, Norman (1979): "Wide Reflective Equilibrium and Theory Acceptance in Ethics". In: *Journal of Philosophy* 76 (5), pp. 256–282.

Daniels, Norman (1993): "Rationing Fairly. Programmatic Considerations". In: *Bioethics* 7 (2–3), pp. 224–233.

Daniels, Norman (2008): *Just Health*. Cambridge: Cambridge University Press.

Diederich, Adele; Schwettmann, Lars, and Winkelhage, Jeannette (2014): "Does Lifestyle Matter When Deciding on Co-Payment for Health Care? A Survey of the General Public". In: *Journal of Public Health* 22 (5), pp. 443–453.

Doctor, Jason; Miyamoto, John, and Bleichrodt, Han (2009): "When Are Person Tradeoffs Valid?". In: *Journal of Health Economics* 28 (5), pp. 1018–1027.

Dolan, Paul (1998): "The Measurement of Individual Utility and Social Welfare". In: *Journal of Health Economics* 17 (1), pp. 39–52.

Dolan, Paul and Cookson, Richard (2000): "A Qualitative Study of the Extent to Which Health Gain Matters When Choosing Between Groups of Patients". In: *Health Policy* 51 (1), pp. 19–30.

Dolan, Paul; Olsen, Jan; Menzel, Paul, and Richardson, Jeff (2003): "An Inquiry into the Different Perspectives That Can Be Used When Eliciting Preferences in Health". In: *Health Economics* 12 (7), pp. 545–551.

Elster, Jon (1995): "The Empirical Study of Justice". In: Miller, David and Walzer, Michael (eds.): *Pluralism, Justice and Equality*. Oxford: Oxford University Press, pp. 81–98.

Frohlich, Norman and Oppenheimer, Joe (1992): *Choosing Justice. An Experimental Approach to Ethical Theory*. Berkeley: University of California Press.

Gaertner, Wulf (2009): *A Primer in Social Choice Theory*. Oxford: Oxford University Press.

Gaertner, Wulf and Schokkaert, Erik (2012): *Empirical Social Choice. Questionnaire-Experimental Studies on Distributive Justice*. Cambridge: Cambridge University Press.

Gerber-Grote, Andreas; Sandmann, Frank Gerd; Zhou, Min; ten Thoren, Corinna; Schwalm, Anja; Weigel, Carolin; Balg, Christiane; Mensch, Alexander; Mostardt, Sarah; Seidl, Astrid, and Lhachimi, Stefan (2014): "Decision Making in Germany. Is Health Economic Evaluation as a Supporting Tool a Sleeping Beauty?". In: *Zeitschrift für Evidenz, Fortbildung und Qualität im Gesundheitswesen* 108 (7), pp. 390–396.

Godager, Geir and Wiesen, Daniel (2013): "Profit or Patients' Health Benefit? Exploring the Heteroneity in Physician Altruism". In: *Journal of Health Economics* 32 (6), pp. 1105–1116.

Goodin, Robert (1986): "Laundering Preferences". In: Elster, Jon and Hylland, Anund (eds.): *Foundations of Social Choice Theory*. Cambridge: Cambridge University Press, pp. 75–102.

Güth, Werner and Kliemt, Hartmut (2010): "What Ethics Can Learn From Experimental Economics – If Anything". In: *European Journal of Political Economy* 26 (3), pp. 302–310.

Harsanyi, John (1953): "Cardinal Utility in Welfare Economics and the Theory of Risk-Taking". In: *Journal of Political Economy* 61 (5), pp. 434–435.

Harsanyi, John (1955): "Cardinal Welfare, Individualistic Ethics, and Interpersonal Comparisons of Utility". In: *Journal of Political Economy* 63 (4), pp. 309–321.
Hausman, Daniel (2000): "Why Not Just Ask? Preferences, 'Empirical Ethics' and the Role of Ethical Reflection". In: *Department of Philosophy, University of Wisconsin-Madison*. https://hausman.philosophy.wisc.edu/papers/, retrieved on November 14, 2018.
Hausman, Daniel (2002): "The Limits of Empirical Ethics". In: Murray, Christopher; Salomon, Joshua; Mathers, Colin, and Lopez, Alan (eds.): *Summary Measures of Population Health. Concepts, Ethics, Measurement and Applications*. Geneva: World Health Organization, pp. 663–668.
Hausman, Daniel (2015): *Valuing Health. Well-Being, Freedom, and Suffering*. Oxford: Oxford University Press.
Hennig-Schmidt, Heike; Selten, Reinhard, and Wiesen, Daniel (2011): "How Payment Systems Affect Physicians' Provision Behaviour. An Experimental Investigation". In: *Journal of Health Economics* 30 (4), pp. 637–646.
Hennig-Schmidt, Heike and Wiesen, Daniel (2014): "Other-Regarding Behavior and Motivation in Health Care Provision. An Experiment with Medical and Non-Medical Students". In: *Social Science & Medicine* 108 (C), pp. 156–165.
Johannesson, Magnus (1999): "On Aggregating QALYs. A Comment on Dolan". In: *Journal of Health Economics* 18 (3), pp. 381–386.
Johansson-Stenman, Olof and Martinsson, Peter (2008): "Are Some Lives More Valuable? An Ethical Preferences Approach". In: *Journal of Health Economics* 27 (3), pp. 739–752.
Klingler, Corinna; Shah, Sara; Barron, Anthony, and Wright, John (2013): "Regulatory Space and Contextual Mediation of Common Functional Pressures. Analyzing the Factors That Led to the German Efficiency Frontier Approach". In: *Health Policy* 109 (3), pp. 270–280.
Klonschinski, Andrea (2016): *The Economics of Resource Allocation in Health Care. Cost-Utility, Social Value, and Fairness*. London and New York: Routledge.
Konow, James (2003): "Which Is the Fairest One of All? A Positive Analysis of Justice Theories". In: *Journal of Economic Literature* 41 (4), pp. 1188–1239.
Konow, James (2012): "Adam Smith and the Modern Science of Ethics". In: *Economics and Philosophy* 28 (3), pp. 333–362.
Konow, James and Schwettmann, Lars (2016): "The Economics of Justice". In: Sabbagh, Clara and Schmitt, Manfred (eds.): *Handbook of Social Justice Theory and Research*. New York: Springer, pp. 83–106.
Luce, Robert Duncan and Raiffa, Howard (1957): *Games and Decisions*. New York: Wiley.
Miller, David (1992): "Distributive Justice. What the People Think". In: *Ethics* 102 (3), pp. 555–593.
Miller, David (1994): "Review of Scherer, Klaus R. (ed.): Justice. Interdisciplinary Perspectives". In: *Social Justice Research* 7, pp. 167–188.
Nord, Erik (1995): "The Person-Trade-off Approach to Valuing Health Care Programs". In: *Medical Decision Making* 15 (3), pp. 201–208.
Nord, Erik; Pinto, Jose; Richardson, Jeff; Menzel, Paul, and Ubel, Peter (1999): "Incorporating Societal Concern for Fairness in Numerical Valuations of Health Programmes". In: *Health Economics* 8 (1), pp. 25–39.
Pinto-Prades, José-Luis and Abellán-Perpiñán, José-María (2005): "Measuring the Health of Populations. The Veil of Ignorance Approach". In: *Health Economics* 14 (1), pp. 69–82.
Rawls, John (1971): *A Theory of Justice*. Cambridge: Harvard University Press.

Rawls, John (1974): "The Independence of Moral Theory". In: *Proceedings and Addresses of the American Philosophical Association* 48, pp. 4–22.
Rawls, John (1993): *Political Liberalism*. New York: Columbia University Press.
Regenwetter, Michel; Grofman, Bernard; Marley, Anthony, and Tsetlin, Ilia (2007): *Behavioral Social Choice. Probabilistic Models, Statistical Inference, and Applications*. Cambridge: Cambridge University Press.
Richardson, Jeff (2002): "The Poverty of Ethical Analysis in Economics and the Unwarranted Disregard of Evidence". In: Murray, Christopher; Salomon, Joshua; Mathers, Colin, and Lopez, Alan (eds.): *Summary Measures of Population Health. Concepts, Ethics, Measurement and Applications*. Geneva: World Health Organization, pp. 627–640.
Richardson, Jeff and McKie, John (2005): "Empiricism, Ethics and Orthodox Economic Theory. What Is the Appropriate Basis for Decision-Making in the Health Sector?". In: *Social Science & Medicine* 60 (2), pp. 265–275.
Roemer, John (1993): "A Pragmatic Theory of Responsibility for the Egalitarian Planner". In: *Philosophy & Public Affairs* 22 (2), pp. 146–166.
Roemer, John (1996): *Theories of Distributive Justice*. Cambridge: Harvard University Press.
Roemer, John (1998): *Equality of Opportunity*. Cambridge: Harvard University Press.
Schokkaert, Erik and Devooght, Kurt (2003): "Responsibility-Fair Compensation in Different Cultures". In: *Social Choice and Welfare* 21 (2), pp. 207–242.
Schwettmann, Lars (2009): *Trading off Competing Allocation Principles. Theoretical Approaches and Empirical Investigations*. Frankfurt am Main: Peter Lang.
Schwettmann, Lars (2016): "Let's Talk About Health Economic Evaluation? Relevant Contextual Factors for the German 'Sonderweg'". In: Nagel, Eckhard and Lauerer, Michael (eds.): *Prioritization in Medicine. An International Dialog*. Berlin: Springer, pp. 273–281.
Sen, Amartya (1970): *Collective Choice and Social Welfare*. San Francisco: Holden-Day.
Shah, Koonal; Praet, Cecile; Devlin, Nancy; Sussex, Jonathan; Appleby, John, and Parkin, David (2012): "Is the Aim of the English Health Care System to Maximize QALYs?". In: *Journal of Health Services Research & Policy* 17 (3), pp. 157–163.
Smith, Adam (1759): *The Theory of Moral Sentiments*. London and Edinburgh: A. Strahan, T. Cadell, T. Creech, and J. Bell.
Tarroux, Benoît (2015): "Comparing Two-Dimensional Distributions. A Questionnaire-Experimental Approach". In: *Social Choice and Welfare* 44 (1), pp. 87–108.
Thomson, William (2001): "On the Axiomatic Method and Its Recent Applications to Game Theory and Resource Allocation". In: *Social Choice and Welfare* 18 (2), pp. 327–386.
Tsuchiya, Aki and Dolan, Paul (2009): "Equality of What in Health? Distinguishing Between Outcome Egalitarianism and Gain Egalitarianism". In: *Health Economics* 18 (2), pp. 147–159.
Tsuchiya, Aki and Watson, Verity (2017): "Re-Thinking 'the Different Perspectives That Can Be Used When Eliciting Preferences in Health'". In: *Health Economics* 26 (12), 103–107.
Yaari, Menahem and Bar-Hillel, Maya (1984): "On Dividing Justly". In: *Social Choice and Welfare* 1 (1), pp. 1–24.

Peter Wiersbinski
Conceiving the Anthropological Difference as a Categorical Divide

Is There Any Room Left for Empirical Research?

Abstract: Reviving the ancient doctrine that human beings are set apart from other animals by a categorical divide rather than a difference of degree, contemporary accounts of the anthropological difference appear to conflict with the fact that human rationality is investigated in empirical psychology. According to these accounts, the idea of human rationality is part of a conceptual nexus that is known a priori and can be investigated through philosophical reflection. Thus, it might seem that empirical methods cannot have any say in the matter. Against this, the author makes room for the idea that the investigation of a priori concepts is dependent on experience by exploiting an analogy between a priori concepts and thick moral concepts, which appear to be subject to moral experience and continual learning.

1 Introduction

A time-honoured tradition – spanning from Aristotle through Christian scholasticism to German idealism – conceives of the difference between humans and other animals as a basic, *categorical* difference.[1] According to this tradition, human beings on the one hand and mere animals on the other fall under different *forms of being*, where the specific difference setting apart the two domains is generally taken to be *reason*, the capacity for language, thought, and action.[2]

---

[1] Among the most prominent figures in this tradition are Aristotle (2011), Thomas Aquinas (1989), Kant (1999), and Hegel (2010).
[2] In the context of this volume it is fitting to point out that the tradition in question has a much more comprehensive understanding of rationality than some contemporary disciplines within philosophy and empirical sciences of cognition, such as, e.g., rational choice theory and cognitive science in general. "Reason" and "rational" are used to designate the capacity to act on reasons and to reflect on reasons in individual and social deliberation, where "a reason" is understood as a consideration that speaks in favour of a belief or an action. Very often, rational beings in this sense are not conscious of the reasons they have for their beliefs and actions, but they are able in principle to find out about their reasons in reflection and to assess the rationality of their behaviour in retrospection. This conception of rationality is not only more inclusive than, for in-

Ever since the advent and triumph of evolutionary biology, this tradition has lost much if not most of its appeal and authority. Given that the human species has evolved gradually from other species by natural processes such as selection and mutation, it seems utterly implausible that it constitutes an autonomous and sharply separated domain of being. From the perspective of evolutionary theory, there is no categorical difference between the "mind[s]" of human beings and other higher animals, no difference "of kind", as Darwin said, but only a "difference of degree" (Darwin 1871, p. 106); i.e., human beings stand out only with regard to the degree of *markedness* or with regard to the *combination* of abilities and properties which will be found in other parts of the animal kingdom as well. In the past years, John McDowell, Michael Thompson, Andrea Kern, Sebastian Rödl, Matthew Boyle, Matthias Haase and others have sought to revive the Aristotelian tradition in the spirit of analytic philosophy by expounding the conceptual framework through which the rather obscure and somewhat metaphysical notion of a categorical difference and its cognates becomes intelligible, and by pointing out difficulties for the Darwinian contender.[3] In this chapter, I raise the spectre of hostility towards empirical anthropology for these Neo-Aristotelians and indicate why it might really be just that, a spectre. My argument is motivated by the aim to better understand the idea of a categorical difference and how it fits into the prospering enterprise of empirical research of human life.[4]

In what follows, I am going to refer to the current views within analytic philosophy represented by these authors as the *Categorical Account*. By choosing this title, I do not mean to deny the many significant differences between their respective projects. Nor do I mean to dismiss alternative accounts of the anthropological difference as a categorical difference by excluding them from what I call the Categorical Account.[5] The main reason for focussing on the work of the aforementioned analytic authors is, as I will explain shortly, their clarity and bluntness. I will call the competing view, that there is no categorical differ-

---

stance, the consistency requirements of rational choice theory and of deductive reasoning, but it may at times deem rational a behaviour that flouts the formal norms of these narrow conceptions. Choosing contrary to one's own preference ordering can, for instance, be part of a fully rational decision in this broader sense; cf. Richardson's (1994, pp. 119 ff.) critique of the assumptions about commensurability in rational choice theory; see also my remarks in section 5, below.
3 Cf. McDowell (1994), Thompson (2004, 2008, 2013), Rödl (2003, 2007, 2012), Kern (2017), Boyle (2012, 2016), Haase (2013); for an overview cf. Kern and Kietzmann (2017).
4 As will emerge in the course of my argument, by "empirical research of human life" I am referring, among others, to disciplines such as developmental psychology, cognitive psychology, and evolutionary anthropology.
5 Here, I am mainly referring to Scheler (1961) and Plessner (2019).

ence between human beings and other animals, the *Assimilationist Account*. Two prominent advocates of this widely held position are the philosopher Markus Wild and the empirical psychologist Frans de Waal.[6]

When understood in this way, the Categorical Account provides a backdrop against which the relation between philosophical anthropology and empirical anthropology can be investigated with particular stringency. For one, adherents of the Categorical Account give a clear, head-on answer to the question what a categorical difference is at all. What is more, their answer seems to entail a problematic or possibly even outrageous thesis concerning scientific ambitions to determine the anthropological difference by means of empirical investigation. As I am going to explain in section 2, the Categorical Account assumes that the recognition and representation of categorical differences relies on *a priori* concepts. If we follow Kant, however, a priori concepts are characterised by the fact that their content can be known and understood in thinking alone and by nothing else but thinking. Thus it appears that the Categorical Account entails the claim that, in order to know the difference between human beings and mere animals, *all we have to do is think* – to reflect on the non-empirical, conceptual presuppositions of empirical knowledge. In consequence, partisans of the Categorical Account seem committed to a twofold *Thesis of Sovereignty*, namely (1) that it is the right of philosophy and of philosophy alone to investigate the questions concerning which property (or set of properties) sets human beings apart from other animals and what the nature of this property (or set of properties) is; and (2) that empirical disciplines such as evolutionary anthropology, developmental psychology, and others cannot contribute in any way to the understanding and settling of these questions.

To my knowledge, the aforementioned advocates of the Categorical Account do not explicitly affirm the Thesis of Sovereignty (henceforth "the Thesis") in their publications. Nevertheless, it is not just an optional or even far-fetched elaboration of their view. Still, in section 2 I will show that it flows naturally from the notion of a categorical concept when applied to the anthropological difference. There is no reason to discount the Thesis as a philosophical fantasy.[7]

From the point of view of the empirical sciences concerned with human life, the Thesis must appear at least wrong, if not absurd. What, one may ask, are the scientists who are working in these disciplines *doing* all day long if the road to understanding humankind admits of no vehicle other than pure conceptual

---

6 Cf. Wild (2012), de Waal and Ferrari (2010). The term "assimilationism" is used by Wild.
7 I actually did encounter the Thesis of Sovereignty in personal communication with partisans of the Categorical Account.

analysis? Moreover, there are philosophically well-versed proponents of a categorical difference *within* empirical anthropology and psychology, e. g., Michael Tomasello and Henrike Moll.[8] If the Thesis were true, then the professional self-understanding of these researchers would have to be thoroughly confused, to say the least. And if the Thesis really were to follow from the Categorical Account, this fact would dialectically augment the attractiveness of the Assimilationist Account which integrates the claims of empirical research without difficulty. Advocates of the Categorical Account should therefore be interested in learning how to cut loose the Thesis from their position. Finding out how to circumvent the Thesis might also be of interest to proponents of other accounts of the anthropological difference as a categorical difference, for instance, accounts deriving from Plessner or Scheler.[9] They might be looking for a more definite formulation of their discomfort with the Categorical Account or for a clearer understanding of the wanted or unwanted implications and dialectical prospects of their own positions. In what follows, I am therefore going to pursue the question whether the Thesis is a necessary consequence of the Categorical Account. After having explained in section 2 why this does indeed appear to be the case, I will argue in sections 3 and 4 by means of an analogy between categorical and moral concepts that it is more likely not the case. Section 5 briefly discusses a second supposedly problematic consequence of the Categorical Account, namely, that experimental research has to rely on fundamentally different methods when investigating human beings and other animals.

2 Justifying the Thesis of Sovereignty

How do you get from the Categorical Account to the Thesis? Key to this transition are these three intertwined characterisations of categorical concepts: that they are *basic*, that they *necessarily reside in thought*, and that they are *constitutive*. It follows from these characterisations that categorical concepts have to be *discerned in reflection or in thought alone*. From this, it appears to follow that *nothing but reflection* or *nothing but thinking* can contribute to the determination of these concepts.

Proponents of the Categorical Account conceive of categorical differences as differences between highest forms of being. Differences of this kind are picked out by concepts which are predicated "without combination", as Aristotle puts

---

[8] Cf. Tomasello (1999), Moll and Tomasello (2007), Moll (2013).
[9] Cf. note 5.

it in the *Categories* (Aristotle 1963, p. 3); i.e., they are not combinations, conjunctions, or associations of other concepts; they are not composed of other concepts, but are instead fundamental or *basic*.[10] This does not mean that categorical concepts cannot be articulated by using other concepts. If they could not be articulated, categorical concepts would be like colour concepts, the contents of which can only be taught by pointing to an object of the respective colour. Yet, the authors which I bracket together under the label "Categorical Account" do believe that it is possible to articulate basic, categorical concepts through other concepts. They can only be articulated, however, through concepts which *contain* the categorical concept in question – i.e., only through concepts which logically depend on the concept they articulate and on each other.[11]

If a definition of a concept aims to be more than a mere rendering of the meaning of the associated *word* or collocation of words, it tells us about necessary, specific or essential properties of what the concept refers to; i.e., the concepts used in the definition designate properties which do not merely happen to come together in the object – which are not accidental properties –, but rather the object depends on these properties for its very identity. There are different types of essential dependence and therefore different types of explanations of concepts. First, a property of an object may be related to another property of that object by being its cause, or two properties occur together in an object only because both are caused by a third property of that object. I will call dependence of this kind *existential dependence*. Pointing out a form of existential dependence is a way of explaining a concept. Second, properties might essentially belong together because the *concepts* which designate these properties depend on each other. The fact that they occur together is then due to another kind of dependence, *logical* or *conceptual dependence*. Categorical concepts are articulated by concepts which depend on each other in the conceptual way and they are explained by elucidating this conceptual dependence. Note that conceptual dependence entails existential dependence, but not vice versa.

---

10 For the notion of a "basic" concept, which may alternatively be termed a "fundamental" or an "unanalysable" concept, cf. Andrea Kern's (2017, e.g., pp. 129ff.) explanation regarding the basic concept "knowledge".

11 A quick note on terminology: I speak of the *articulation* of a concept when the conditions of application of that concept, the conditions which constitute the content of the concept, are consciously thought of or made explicit verbally or in writing. A *definition* of a concept is an articulation of that concept. By contrast, a concept is *explained* by answering the question concerning why *these specific* concepts and not any other concepts have to be used in its articulation. Finally, *knowledge* or *recognition* of a concept consists in possession both of its articulation and explanation.

Let's consider two examples. A definition of the biological genus *homo* as given by a paleoanthropologist might look like this: "Human beings are distinguished from their evolutionary ancestors by bipedalism, a bigger brain, and prolonged ontogenesis". It is easy to see that this definition does not articulate a categorical concept. "Homo" is a scientific concept in the sense that it is not a mere accident but rather due to a common cause that bipedalism and prolonged ontogenesis occur together with a bigger brain. Yet "homo" is a combination of concepts which can and do characterise not only members of this genus but also other forms of being. Birds, for instance, are bipeds as well. The concept "homo" is therefore not a basic concept and does not refer to a highest form of being. The concepts through which it is articulated and explained do not depend on each other logically or conceptually.

By contrast, the concept "life" as investigated in the first chapter of Michael Thompson's (2008) book *Life and Action* is a basic concept in the relevant sense. At first glance this might seem rather implausible. After all, "life" appears to be definable in the ordinary, garden-variety fashion. Biology textbooks often present a definition of life the structure of which strongly resembles the definition just cited of "homo". They list a set of features pertaining to living beings: a high degree of internal organisation, growth, self-preservation, reproduction, intake and transformation of energy, responsiveness to stimuli, and so on. And at first glance, these features certainly appear to be independent of living beings and of each other. Galaxies, atoms, and crystals display internal organisation, meteorological cycles preserve themselves, the desert grows, and many physical systems take in and change energy from one form to another. Thompson argues, however, that the assumption that characteristic features of living things are logically independent properties is based on a fundamental misunderstanding. This is evident, e.g., in that the manner in which living beings are organised cannot be equated with the internal organisation of crystals or galaxies. Rather, the kind of organisation in question is a specifically *vital* kind of organisation – namely, the kind of organisation that belongs to a being that has *organs*. The concept "organ" *contains*, however, the concept of life, for it is not merely *wrong* to claim of a non-living thing that it has organs – it is quite simply *unintelligible*. The concept of organisation that is definitive of life cannot be understood independently of the very concept of life. As Thompson puts it, "the relevant conception is simply equivalent to the idea of life: to be alive is to be *organ*-ized" (Thompson 2008, p. 38). The same is true of every other concept enumerated in textbook definitions of life. Thompson concludes that "these concepts [...] together form a sort of solid block, and we run into a kind of circle in attempting to elucidate any of them" (Thompson 2008, p. 47). Their relation is not like the one that holds between "homo" and its paleoanthropological definientia, since one does not run in a circle in trying to explain "homo" by "bipedal". Yet the "circle" that Thompson is talking about is not a pure circle, because the concepts of life, vital organisation, growth, and reproduction are not mere synonyms. They mutually elucidate and explain one another without being independent of each other.

The Categorical Account takes "reason" to be a concept like the one Thompson investigates in "life". The specific difference of humankind, the ability to think and judge, must accordingly be articulated and explained by means of logically dependent concepts. The Assimilationist Account, by contrast, analyses that which is specific for human beings in the same way in which paleoanthropology analyses the genus *homo:* by means of logically independent concepts.

If Thompson's approach is on the right track, categorical concepts are not only basic; rather, they also *necessarily reside in thought*, which implies that they can be articulated, explained and recognised only *in thought*. They reside in thought in a first sense insofar as they are *a priori* concepts, i.e., concepts which every thinking subject possesses just by being a thinking subject. And they reside in thought in a second sense, which is implied by the first sense but does not itself include it: Categorical concepts, and the concepts through which they are articulated, necessarily hang together not in the world alone, but in thought. It is this second sense which will be relevant to my argument in sections 3 and 4. The dependence between the concepts articulating a categorical concept can be compared to the kind of dependence at work in formal logic, i.e., to the dependence between the truth of "p and q" and the truth of "p". The fact that "p" must inevitably be true when "p and q" is true, and why this is so, can be made out only in thought. This is because the dependence in question is a *necessity of thought*. It is much the same with all elements of a definition of life. They depend on each other conceptually because their dependence is a *necessity of thought*. This is not, however, a general law of thought, as it applies to the case of formal logic. Thinking does not necessarily lead to thinking about organs, growth, and reproduction, since it is possible to think without thinking of living beings at all while it is impossible to think without following the laws of logic.[12]

---

12 The last claim assumes a certain conception of the relation between thinking and logic, namely, a conception which treats the laws of logic both as part of the *essence* of thinking and as a *norm* for thinking. The mental activity of a subject does not immediately cease to be thinking when it occasionally flouts the laws of logic. However, it gradually loses its character as thinking when the violations of logic become more frequent and ceases to count as thinking altogether when it is not informed by logic at all. According to the proponents of the Categorical Account, all categorical concepts exhibit this trait: On the one hand, they function as concepts which designate the essence of the object to which they apply, and on the other, they designate a

Thinking about organs, growth, and reproduction is nonetheless an inescapable feature of thinking specifically about the living and is in this regard a necessity of thought that can therefore be recognised in thought alone.

These remarks provide the key to understanding the transition from the Categorical Account to the Thesis of Sovereignty. The main idea is that it is impossible to *find out* that a nexus of logically dependent concepts necessarily belong together, because this knowledge is already available by representing reality through these concepts. Merely apprehending and representing a property designated by a logically dependent concept means that one necessarily already possesses the whole net of interrelated concepts. *Nothing but thinking* is needed in order to bring it out and to describe it. Unlike the case of "homo", where it is certainly possible that knowledge of bipedalism preceded knowledge of brain size and also preceded an explanation of why these features occur together, a nexus of logically dependent concepts is obtained in one dash, if it is obtained at all. Or at least this seems to follow from the notions that categorical concepts are basic and that they necessarily reside in thought. In the next section, I will argue that it does not follow.

Lastly, we should note that basic concepts which reside in thought are *constitutive* for the things represented through them. What is accurately represented through concepts of this kind in general can be represented solely through them and not through any other concepts. There is no equivalent way of representing highest forms of being via concepts which are not of the categorical kind. That is why Matt Boyle, speaking of the anthropological difference, explains that "rational specifies the sort of frame that undergirds any concrete description of what it is to be a human being" (Boyle 2012, p. 410). Whatever can be found out about human beings by empirical means therefore presupposes the non-empirical identification of human beings as rational.[13]

---

norm for these objects. Reproduction is, for instance, an essential aspect of the living, and yet there are living beings which do not reproduce, either because they lack the capacity altogether or because they do not actualise it. From the point of view of the Categorical Account, these living beings are, in this respect, living beings to a lesser degree. (Accordingly, the relevant conception of normativity is not moral and does not even necessarily presuppose a mental representation of the norm.) The same is true with regard to the concept "rational" as it applies to human beings: It designates an aspect of the essence of human beings, and yet it is possible that human beings occasionally fail to believe or to act for good reasons, or even completely lack the capacity to do so. A very irrational person is still, in this sense, a rational being by essence and by the norms applying to it. On the notion of concepts which are essential and normative at the same time cf. Rödl (2003).

13 This point corresponds to the remarks made in note 12, above.

3 Thick Moral Concepts and Moral Experience

As we saw, the notion that empirical research has nothing to say on the matter of human distinctiveness flows naturally from the Categorical Account. And yet if I am right, it does not follow in any strict sense; i.e., the thesis that a nexus of logically dependent concepts can only be articulated and explained *in thought* does not necessarily entail the thesis that *nothing but thinking is needed* in order to articulate and explain such concepts. Experience might be a necessary precondition for acquiring knowledge of such a nexus.

Indeed, I believe that we are aware of cases in which the acquisition of knowledge of basic, constitutive concepts which reside in thought (in the second sense) is reliant on experience and empirical acquaintance. I will draw on the example of *thick moral concepts* in order to bring this out. Thick moral concepts do of course differ in many respects from categorical concepts as portrayed in the previous section. They are normative and have their point in representing reasons for action.[14] They are not *a priori* concepts and do not necessarily reside in thought in the first sense distinguished above.[15] And yet it is helpful to compare them to categorical concepts because they are basic, they reside in thought in the second sense, and they are constitutive. Despite these features, it seems intuitively plausible that thick moral concepts can only be articulated against a backdrop of experience – namely, moral experience. That is the lever for my argument from analogy.

Thick moral concepts such as "courageous", "hypocritical", "generous", and "prudent" are characterised by two semantic aspects: a morally normative aspect and a descriptive aspect. *Thin* moral concepts such as "ought", "wrong", and "good", on the other hand, do not possess a descriptive but only a normative or evaluative and possibly prescriptive sense.[16] By means of their descriptive sense, thick concepts represent features of moral reality, i.e., past or proposed moral actions and certain morally relevant character traits. They even seem to be constitutive for moral reality, and that is because they are basic, which means not articulable by logically independent concepts. This can be seen by

---

[14] Categorical concepts are normative as well (cf. Thompson 2008, pp. 80ff., Rödl 2003), but not in the moral sense. Where I speak of thick concepts being "normative" I mean normative in the sense of moral evaluation or moral deliberation.
[15] It is at least controversial whether thick moral concepts necessarily reside in thought in the first sense. Relativists such as Williams (1985) and Sreenivasan (2001) clearly deny it; Rödl (2007, chapters 2 and 6), by contrast, appears to be committed to the view. As my argument from analogy does not in any way depend on the answer to this question, I will not take a stand on it.
[16] Cf. McDowell (1998, essays 3 and 4), Williams (1985, chapter 8).

considering how thick concepts *supervene* on non-normative, purely descriptive concepts. There is a strong and a weak option regarding this relation of supervenience. According to the strong option, there is for every thick moral concept another, non-normative concept or description which picks out the very same kind of action or character trait and which can stand in for the thick concept in moral judgements without altering their truth value. If thick concepts supervene on purely descriptive concepts in this sense, they are not basic; rather, they can be split up into a normative and a logically independent descriptive part. According to the weak option, by contrast, it is possible to find a purely descriptive difference in the designated action or character trait for every difference on the level of the thick concept, yet there is no logically independent description of these designated properties.[17] What a "courageous" action is, e.g., cannot be expressed without using or implicitly drawing on the concept "courageous" itself if the weak option is true.

There is some willingness among moral philosophers to accept that thick concepts supervene only in the weak and not in the strong sense on purely descriptive concepts, although there is no consensus on the significance and implications of this finding.[18] For the purposes of my argument from analogy, it will not be necessary to argue for the metaethical position that thick moral concepts supervene on purely descriptive concepts only in the weak sense. It is sufficient to make this option available as intelligible and maybe even plausible. As in the case of "life", this might seem unlikely at first glance. It is, after all, possible to define a concept like "courageous". It picks out somebody who "is prone to persevere in the face of danger". This surely appears to be a purely descriptive articulation of "courageous", but upon a closer look, we can see that it is not, for the applicability of the description "is prone to persevere in the face of danger" does not imply the applicability of "courageous". Depending on how great the danger is, it might be imprudent rather than courageous to persevere in its face. If the danger is too small, on the other hand, your perseverance risks being laughable instead of courageous. Yet *some* are courageous in braving a small or even inexistent danger, namely those who fear it for the special reason of being psychologically traumatised. (I will come back to these differentiations shortly.) The examples appear to support the conclusion that what is needed for courage cannot simply be danger, fear, and perseverance added together as stand-alone components, but rather *the right amount* of danger, *the right reason* for fear, and *the*

---

[17] For the two conceptions of supervenience, cf. McDowell (1998, p. 202), Sreenivasan (2001, pp. 14–19).
[18] McDowell (1998) and Williams (1985), e.g., think so, Hare (1963) does not.

right motivation for perseverance. These qualifying formulas indicate that "perseverance in the face of danger" is not a purely descriptive, conceptually independent definition. The meaning of "the right amount of danger", e.g., seems to be: "so much danger that *courage* is needed to persevere in its face", pointing back to the concept that it was meant to elucidate. Although we certainly do learn something about courage by being told that it is perseverance in danger's face, the definiens is not independent of the definiendum.

Just like categorical concepts, thick moral concepts necessarily reside in thought in the second sense outlined above: The concepts through which they are articulated hang together in thought and their nexus must be recognised through thinking. It is certainly possible that moral concepts are not universal, if moral universality is the thesis that every moral subject possesses and employs the same moral concepts. While the moral concepts that moral subjects employ are articulated through a nexus of logically interdependent concepts, they do not necessarily reside in thought in the first sense. And it would be utterly implausible to maintain that thinking *is the only thing we have to do* in order to articulate the content of thick moral concepts. Rather, being acquainted with courageous, hypocritical, generous, and prudent persons and their emotional and behavioural reactions to certain situations seems to be an indispensable prerequisite for the capacity to give the content of these concepts. Or, to put it differently, some kind of experience, namely *moral experience*, is a condition of being able to articulate moral concepts. This can be illustrated with the differentiations at hand: The term "courageous" is not appropriate if the danger which stands to be confronted is insignificant or inexistent. And yet somebody who fears an insignificant or inexistent danger as a result of being traumatised, and who dares nonetheless to persevere in its face, will rightly count as courageous. Qualifications of this kind apply to all thick concepts. It is implausible that a moral subject possesses the ability to articulate them out of the blue, lacking any acquaintance with situations, reactions, and behaviours which require to make the moral difference in question.

To be sure, this is still nothing more than a phenomenological finding concerning the acquisition of moral concepts. Nonetheless, it is to be taken seriously even if we still do not know why the articulation of thick concepts is dependent on experience in this way. Two observations appear to support this finding: For one, it is implausible that the relevant differentiations and qualifications can be articulated without experience because thick concepts seem to contain a potentially infinite number of such qualifications. Our example could easily be narrowed down further by adding, e.g., that "fear of danger due to psychological trauma normally implies courage but not if the trauma in question has been treated extensively and professionally", and so on. Secondly, and more fundamentally, independence of experience is implausible because the concepts which figure in these qualifications can be, like "psychological trauma", *empirical* concepts. This means that, unless a moral subject has learned what being traumatised implies and what effects it has on a human being, the subject is not able to appreciate the relevance of this mental condition for the application of "courageous". But no moral subject possesses the concept of psychological traumatisation in an a priori fashion, simply in virtue of being able to employ competently the concept of courage.[19] The infinitely many qualifications relevant to the content of a thick concept will be articulable only after having become acquainted with these partly empirical qualifications – i.e., only through moral experience. And this is the case even if the moral concepts qualified by reference to these empirical concepts are themselves understood as a priori concepts.

It should be noted that the qualifications in question really do articulate the *content*, the *conditions of application* of thick moral concepts. It would be inappropriate to regard them as accidental provisions which factually pertain to the actions, reactions, or character traits picked out by thick concepts, but which do not contribute to the content of these concepts. It is not an external and dispensable feature of the correct application of "courageous" in the case of a traumatised person who overcomes her fears that she is in a certain mental condition. Therefore, it is not a valid objection to the analogy that the real content of thick concepts is articulable without moral experience while only knowledge of non-essential ancillary properties of moral actions and traits are dependent on experience.

From these points, the following picture emerges. Empirical concepts, concepts which are picked up through experience, are relevant for differences and qualifications pertaining to the application of thick moral concepts, according to the weak sense of supervenience. These concepts are fundamental, constitutive, and they necessarily reside in thought. Thick concepts are applied spontaneously in moral judgements. And yet only the spontaneous act of applying these concepts to conditions which are known through experience allows their content to be articulated by thinking and reflecting. Thus, while thick moral concepts can be articulated only in thought and by thinking, this does not entail that nothing but thinking is needed in order to be able to articulate them. Experience,

---

19 The history of the psychiatric condition in question provides some confirmation of these remarks. Before "shell-shocked" soldiers turned up by the thousands during the First World War and their condition was investigated and gradually made known by military physicians, soldiers who showed symptoms of a post-traumatic stress disorder were often being shot for cowardice; cf. Solomon et al. (2000, pp. 126f.), Joseph (2015, pp. 26f.).

acquaintance with moral agents and their ways of acting, and responding to the affordances of situations is a necessary condition of such articulation.

I am well aware that this picture raises a lot of questions and calls for further explanations. With a view to the purpose which the picture is designed to serve within my argument – the purpose of lending plausibility to the claim that the inference leading from the Categorical Account to the Thesis of Sovereignty is not unavoidable – it should nevertheless suffice that the picture is supported by appeal to the phenomenology of thick moral concepts.

4 Two Examples from Psychology – Memory and Development

Notwithstanding the aforementioned disanalogies, the example of thick concepts introduces the possibility that the truth of the Categorical Account is compatible with the falsity of the Thesis – either in the weak sense that empirical research need not, but can, meaningfully contribute to the articulation of the anthropological difference or even in the strong sense that this articulation essentially depends on empirical research. Further support for the notion that this possibility is to be taken seriously not only within moral philosophy but also in anthropology can, I think, be gained from considering two examples from the psychology of memory and the psychology of development.

According to the Categorical Account, human *memory* is to be regarded as an integral element of the distinctively human faculty of reason. Finite rational beings necessarily possess memory in the sense that it is impossible to think through what it means to be a finite rational being without thinking of it as a being endowed with memory. That human beings possess memory is thus not simply one more empirical fact about us, nor is it a fact that could be explained by appeal to neuro-physiological, psychological, or sociological regularities.[20] What is more, human memory is a specifically *rational* kind of capacity – very much in the way the growth of plants and animals is, as Thompson explains, a specifically vital kind of process. It is not a separable module, instances of which could in principle turn up in other higher animals not endowed with reason.[21] It is therefore part of the categorical concept "reason" that the beings to

---

[20] For the claim that rational memory belongs to human beings essentially, cf. Rödl (2012, pp. 66 ff.).
[21] Boyle (2016) argues an analogous point for two other human faculties, desire and perception.

which this concept applies possess a specifically rational kind of memory. And this means that "memory" is itself a non-empirical concept, a concept to be articulated in thought alone. Yet at the same time it is hard to see how the opinion could be upheld that it is possible to articulate this concept without investigating the various functions of memory by empirical methods. Even the most general subdivisions which psychologists recognise, such as the distinctions between sensory memory, short-term and long-term memory, and the idea of working memory are not likely to be discoverable by pure conceptual analysis undertaken from the philosopher's armchair. It takes systematic empirical research to figure out the exact shape of the many functions which constitute this faculty of the mind. And therefore, the articulation of the content of "rational memory" depends on empirical efforts.

A second example is provided by developmental psychology, which, following ideas of Jean Piaget and others, can be seen as investigating *stages of the unfolding of the rational faculty in the individual* in all its facets. Developmental psychology, on the one hand, discovers relations of precondition or interdependence which hold between the development of different rational capacities and abilities and, on the other, it describes these capacities and abilities in greater detail. It would, again, be presumptuous to think that the order of this unfolding and the conditional relations which correspond to it could be extrapolated without engaging in empirical scientific research. And yet, developmental psychology in particular presents the prospect that philosophers might use its findings in their endeavour to get clear about *conceptual* relations of dependence between different rational capacities.[22] Reason is not simply to be identified with language and is, contrary to what is often assumed, not present in one stroke when linguistic abilities are. Rather, reason informs and shapes every expression and competence of children, from pre-linguistic object permanence, the representation of the most basic causal transactions, and attachment over joint attention, joint action, and the imputation of mental states up to the formation of moral judgement.[23] From the perspective of the Categorical Account, it is fitting to interpret the chronological order of this development as an indication of conceptual relations of dependence between different rational capacities. If this is correct, empirical psychology and philosophical psychology, conceived as analysis of categorical concepts, can be seen to be engaged in one and the same scientific enterprise.

---

[22] Henrike Moll (2013) is a developmental psychologist who tends to understand her work in this way.

[23] E.g., Moll (2013) rejects Brandt's view that reason is to be identified with language and provides empirical justification for this rejection.

I do not intend to claim that *every* result of psychological research concerning memory or human development contributes to the philosophical articulation of the concept of a rational memory or to the explication of conceptual relations between rational capacities. Some empirical findings might well concern accidental facts, necessary in neither the conceptual or the existential sense, and some might be necessary only in the causal, existential sense. Genuine contributions to the articulation of "rational memory" or to the interrelations of rational capacities are those findings which can be worked up into conceptual explanations.

In contrast to the case of thick moral concepts, I do not mean to claim that it is a phenomenal datum or a basic intuition about the categorical concept of reason that it can only be articulated with the help of scientific experience. For this reason, my argument from analogy starts with moral concepts and proceeds to categorical concepts: It is with regard to moral concepts that the dependence on experience can be grasped more easily. But as in the case of thick moral concepts, there are two considerations which support dependence on experience for categorical concepts. The first is, as with thick concepts, quantitative in nature. Human beings possess a multitude of interdependent and interacting rational capacities: consciousness, attention, imagination, memory, emotion, practical and theoretical deliberation, capacities for perception and intentional action, and so on. It seems, in light of the sheer number that has to be taken into account, hopeless to try to figure out the exact shape of every one of these capacities by pure reflection, let alone the forms of their dependencies and interactions. However, the second analogous point is even more important: It is possible for the content of categorical concepts to be articulated through concepts which refer to entities and states of affairs that can only be known empirically. I do not have an example at hand which uncontroversially illustrates this possibility for "reason". With regard to the categorical concept of life, which is in many respects comparable, the empirical differentiations within the concept of reproduction appear to undergird the point convincingly. "Life" is articulated through "reproduction" yet the content of "reproduction" itself is specified by "asexual", "sexual", "autogamous", and "allogamous". *These* forms of propagation are vital reproduction; *other* forms of propagation are not. But the description of these forms unavoidably makes reference to empirical concepts, e. g., the concept "cell". Thus, it seems, the second point might apply to the realm of the categorical just as well as to morality.

In this section, I have tried to make room for the notion that psychological research on human capacities might play an enabling role in the articulation of categorical concepts which describe these faculties – much like moral experience plays a role in the articulation of moral concepts. If this is plausible, acceptance of the Categorical Account would not by itself include a commitment to the Thesis of Sovereignty.

5 The Categorical Difference of Method

The Categorical Account is committed to the claim that the empirical methods employed to study human beings *cannot be the same* as those used in the study of non-human animals, for what belongs to different spheres of being is not accessible by means of the same ways of understanding. The Assimilationist Account, on the other hand, is not committed to any such thesis. If the cognitive abilities of higher animals and the human mind are set apart only by a "difference of degree", it is easy to explain how the characteristics of human beings can be studied by observation and experimentation: in the very same ways that apply to other animals. Besides the Ockhamist advantage of being unsophisticated, at first glance this view appears simply to mirror the practice in comparative experiments, for instance in evolutionary anthropology. But the impression is misleading. The disparity of methods which is demanded by the Categorical Account not only corresponds to the complexity of the object but is in fact already respected by empirical researchers.

Why is the Categorical Account committed to postulate a disparity of methods? The canon of methods that is used by an empirical discipline in order to investigate a phenomenal domain is based on the kind of regularities and forms of explanation which govern this phenomenal domain. Not all kinds of phenomena are determined by the same kinds of laws and regularities. Methods suited to investigate the laws and regularities of one categorical kind are inappropriate when applied to another categorical kind. This might, again, be illustrated with reference to the categorical difference "life". The point becomes obvious if we skip the categorical tier of vegetal life and compare the inanimate with animal life. For it is evident that in the study of animal behaviour, methods need to be employed that are very different from those used to investigate the movement of particles in fields. In comparative psychology, primates are confronted with tasks and are rewarded with a treat if they manage to solve them. Tasks and rewards are integral parts of the empirical method. Accordingly, the experimental set-up and the interpretation of observed behaviour everywhere refer to the forms of explanation which are pertinent for intelligent animals. It is said that the ape does this or that *because* she is perceiving her environment, *because* she gets at the intentions of other apes, *because* she sees some treat as an incentive and so on. No movement of particles in an electric field is open to explanation by any of these forms. No particle moves in this way or that way because it perceives, sees something as an incentive, or expects something. This is why in the physical experimental set-up there is nothing that has the function of being perceivable or of being an incentive. The methods are thus different in kind because the laws and the corresponding forms of explanation which govern the two domains are fundamentally different in kind.

If the Categorical Account is correct, an analogous relation must hold between mere animals and human beings: The forms of explanation which apply to each of these phenomenal domains respectively cannot be the same. Explanations applicable to human beings make reference to *reasons*, which speak in favour of some action or mental attitude. Human beings are capable of acting and deliberating *from* reasons or *because of* the reasons they have which means that they have the capacity to orient their behaviour and thought according to their insight into reasons. These reasons are often non-conscious, but they normally can, in principle, be made conscious by reflection.[24] The behaviour of brutes is susceptible to explanation by reasons, to be sure, but these explanations cite reasons *with* which animals act, not reasons *from* which they act. For a chimp, the prospect of a grape is a reason to act, but she is in principle unable to gain conscious access to that which explains her behaviour in this case and therefore does not orient her actions according to any insight into reasons.[25]

This difference in the form of explanation should manifest itself in different empirical methods. And it does indeed. Tasks which are used in evolutionary anthropology in order to compare adult primates and human children might easily convey the impression that identical methods are employed on both sides. In the "floating peanut task", apes and children are supposed to get hold of a peanut which floats at the bottom of a long and narrow transparent receptacle.[26] The solution is of course to fill up the receptacle with whatever liquid is at hand until the floating peanut has mounted high enough that it can be picked out. Upon closer examination it becomes apparent, however, that the task set for children and the task set for apes is not at all the same. As developmental psychologist Henrike Moll (2012) has pointed out, to the human children the task has to be explained by another human before any interesting behaviour can be observed; a typically human kind of motivation needs to be generated, e. g., by ex-

---

24 Cf. notes 2 and 12 above.
25 These remarks about the repercussions of the categorical difference between human beings and mere animals with regard to the meaning of "reason" follow McDowell (1994, chapter 8) and others, e.g., Marcus (2012, chapter 3). Korsgaard (2008, chapter 7) puts forward a very similar view, yet without a metaphysically ambitious understanding of categorical differences in the background.
26 Cf. Hanus et al. (2011).

plaining that it is a game; social restrictions concerning the handling of water as a toy and as an instrument have to be eliminated, and so on. In the case of orang-utans and chimpanzees it would not only be futile to try to explain any task to them, but also unnecessary: To them, it is immediately clear what has to be done because of the natural motivation to get hold of the peanut. Also, apes do not have any inhibitions to "make a mess" with water. In short, the methods by which problem-solving behaviour in this task is studied are fundamentally different in kind. They directly mirror the forms of explanation which apply to higher animals on the one hand and to human beings on the other. Human children are already responsive to reasons and the way in which they approach the floating peanut task is due to this responsiveness, just like the difficulties they confront in solving it. It does not normally cross the mind of a child that water could be freely used as an instrument, because water is already functionally fixed within the human social practices of drinking and cleaning. The operation of instrumental intelligence on the part of the apes is, by contrast, directly explained by a natural instinct and this shows in the manner the task is tailored to them.

To sum up, it appears that the implication of different methods is by and large innocuous. It only reveals what empirical researchers already knew and respected explicitly or implicitly. However, if the Categorical Account is right, ignorance or denial of the difference of methods – due to, e.g., adherence to the Assimilationist Account – may limit or even distort the acquisition of knowledge.

Bibliography

Aquinas, Thomas (1989): *Summa Theologiae*. London: Eyre and Spottiswoode.
Aristotle (1963): *Categories and De Interpretatione*. Oxford: Clarendon Press.
Aristotle (2011): *De Anima. On the Soul*. Newburyport: Focus.
Boyle, Matthew (2012): "Essentially Rational Animals". In: Abel, Günther and Conant, James (eds.): *Rethinking Epistemology*. Vol. 2. Berlin: Walter de Gruyter, pp. 395–427.
Boyle, Matthew (2016): "Additive Theories of Rationality. A Critique". In: *European Journal of Philosophy* 4 (23), pp. 1–44.
Darwin, Charles (1871): *The Decent of Man and Selection in Relation to Sex*. London: John Murray.
de Waal, Frans and Ferrari, Pier (2010): "Towards a Bottom-Up Perspective on Animal and Human Cognition". In: *Trends in Cognitive Sciences* 14 (5), pp. 201–207.
Haase, Matthias (2013): "Life and Mind". In: Khurana, Thomas (ed.): *The Freedom of Life. Hegelian Perspectives. Freiheit und Gesetz III*. Berlin: August, pp. 69–110.
Hanus, Daniel; Mendes, Natacha; Tennie, Claudio, and Call, Joseph (2011): "Comparing the Performances of Apes (Gorilla gorilla, Pan troglodytes, Pongo pygmaeus) and Human Children (Homo sapiens) in the Floating Peanut Task". In: *PLoS ONE* 6 (6), e19555.

Hare, Richard (1963): *Freedom and Reason*. Oxford: Clarendon Press.
Hegel, Georg (2010): *Science of Logic*. Cambridge: Cambridge University Press.
Joseph, Stephen (2011): *What Doesn't Kill Us. The New Psychology of Post-Traumatic Growth*. New York: Basic Books.
Kant, Immanuel (1999): *Critique of Pure Reason*. Cambridge: Cambridge University Press.
Kern, Andrea (2017): *Sources of Knowledge. On the Concept of a Rational Capacity for Knowledge*. Cambridge: Harvard University Press.
Kern, Andrea and Kietzmann, Christian (eds.) (2017): *Selbstbewusstes Leben. Texte zu einer transformativen Theorie der menschlichen Subjektivität*. Berlin: Suhrkamp.
Korsgaard, Christine (2008): *The Constitution of Agency. Essays on Practical Reason and Moral Psychology*. Oxford: Oxford University Press.
Marcus, Eric (2012): *Rational Causation*. Cambridge: Harvard University Press.
McDowell, John (1994): *Mind and World*. Cambridge: Harvard University Press.
McDowell, John (1998): *Mind, Value, and Reality*. Cambridge: Harvard University Press.
Moll, Henrike (2012): "Comparing Tasks Used in Comparative Psychology". Talk given at a conference on "The Human Animal" at the University of Leipzig on Thursday, December 20, 2012.
Moll, Henrike (2013): "Ontogenetic Precursors of Assertion and Denial". In: Rödl, Sebastian and Tegtmeyer, Henning (eds.): *Sinnkritisches Philosophieren*. Berlin: Walter de Gruyter, pp. 337–345.
Moll, Henrike and Tomasello, Michael (2007): "Cooperation and Human Cognition. The Vygotskian Intelligence Hypothesis". In: *Philosophical Transactions of the Royal Society B* 362 (1480), pp. 639–648.
Plessner, Helmuth (2019): *Levels of Organic Life and the Human. An Introduction to Philosophical Anthropology*. New York: Fordham University Press.
Richardson, Henry (1994): *Practical Reasoning About Final Ends*. Cambridge: Cambridge University Press.
Rödl, Sebastian (2003): "Norm und Natur". In: *Deutsche Zeitschrift für Philosophie* 51 (1), pp. 99–114.
Rödl, Sebastian (2007): *Self-Consciousness*. Cambridge: Harvard University Press.
Rödl, Sebastian (2012): *Categories of the Temporal. An Inquiry into the Forms of the Finite Intellect*. Cambridge: Harvard University Press.
Scheler, Max (1961): *Man's Place in Nature*. Boston: Beacon Press.
Solomon, Zahava; Laror, Nathaniel, and McFarlane, Alexander (2000): "Posttraumatische Akutreaktionen bei Soldaten und Zivilisten". In: van der Kolk, Bessel; McFarlane, Alexander, and Weisaeth, Lars (eds.): *Traumatic Stress. Grundlagen und Behandlungsansätze. Theorie, Praxis und Forschung zu posttraumatischem Streß sowie Traumatherapie*. Paderborn: Junfermann, pp. 117–127.
Sreenivasan, Gopal (2001): "Understanding Alien Morals". In: *Philosophy and Phenomenological Research* 62 (1), pp. 1–32.
Thompson, Michael (2004): "Apprehending Human Form". In: O'Hear, Anthony (ed.): *Modern Moral Philosophy*. Cambridge: Cambridge University Press, pp. 47–74.
Thompson, Michael (2008): *Life and Action. Elementary Structures of Practice and Practical Thought*. Cambridge: Harvard University Press.

Thompson, Michael (2013): "Forms of Nature". In: Hindrichs, Gunnar and Honneth, Axel (eds.): *Freiheit. Stuttgarter Hegel-Kongress 2011*. Frankfurt am Main: Vittorio Klostermann, pp. 701–735.
Tomasello, Michael (1999): *The Cultural Origins of Human Cognition*. Cambridge: Harvard University Press.
Wild, Markus (2012): "Tierphilosophie". In: *Erwägen – Wissen – Ethik* 1 (1), pp. 21–33.
Williams, Bernard (1985): *Ethics and the Limits of Philosophy*. Cambridge: Harvard University Press.

Alexander Max Bauer and Malte Ingo Meyerhuber
Epilogue[1]

On Doxa and Aletheia

One might think that the concluding chapter of a volume on the relationship between empirical research and normative theory ought to provide some sort of a robust, conclusive, and unambiguous answer on how these two domains are and should be related. The perspectives on the relation between the two spheres illustrated throughout the chapters are manifold, especially due to the inter- or transdisciplinary nature of the chapters within this volume. Nonetheless, the interested reader may still expect an integration of these different angles into one larger comprehensive framework of how to relate empirical research and normative theory.

We may, however, need to somewhat dampen such expectations. Different fields seem to require different levels of integration between the two. Most authors in this volume appear to have an affirmative perspective on the matter at hand. Others, however, problematise certain relations of those spheres.

Several chapters discuss the relation of empirical research and normative theory for the social sciences. First, Sylke Meyerhuber (chapter 2) reflects how normative theories and value-systems can be used to guide empirical (qualitative) research. She argues for these normative theories as a valuable guiding compass for scientific professionalism and identity, concerning issues such as keeping a humanistic outlook and acting in ethical and sustainable ways. Next, Jannis Kreienkamp, Max Agostini, Malte Ingo Meyerhuber, Marvin Kunz, and Carlos A. de Matos Fernandes (chapter 3) critically reflect on the unintentional impact of normative assumptions throughout the (quantitative) empirical research process and demonstrate how this may distort the search for scientific "truth". They, thereby, demonstrate some of the dangers of unreflected intertwinement between normative assumptions and empirical research, while also offering several potential solutions to this problem. Thereafter, Guillermina Jasso (chapter 4) shows the interweaving of empirical work and normative considerations from the perspective of social sciences, providing several illustrations tracing the path from ideas to theory to empirics. Her work introduces is-about-ought questions, which represent the scientific search for knowledge about the normative views to which persons subscribe. Also at the intersection

---

[1] The considerations concerning Hannah Arendt's Socrates have been published in German as Bauer and Meyerhuber (2019).

of psychological research and philosophical considerations, Albert W. Musschenga (chapter 5) elaborates on the role of empirical research for moral intuitions, both from a philosophical and a psychological perspective. He discusses the sense and feasibility of an empirically informed moral intuitionism and demonstrates that competence and experience matter for the reliability of moral intuitions, thereby empirically arguing for the value of expert's moral judgements. However, he calls for further empirical work on the reliability of psychological moral intuitions in order to corroborate these claims, thereby seeing a clear value for empirical research in the domain of moral intuitions.

A number of chapters deal explicitly with questions of ethics. Here, Norbert Paulo (chapter 6) argues that one has to make sure when constructing a moral epistemic decision procedure that the character and decision processing prescribed are possible, or are perceived to be possible, for creatures like us. Subsequently, Stephen J. Sullivan (chapter 7) shifts the focus to the question of whether normative ethical theories can be justified in a similar fashion as scientific ones. He argues that ethical theories can, in fact, be subjected to observational testing in much the same way as their scientific counterparts. However, he also notes the limits of the approach and considers some objections to his thesis. Next, Marcel Mertz (chapter 8) establishes a number of dimensions of the validity of moral norms that correspond to specific elements of their structure, while also discussing how these dimensions may be influenced by empirical information. He concludes with a critical consideration of the significance of these dimensions of validity and the empirical influences on them for different ways of "doing ethics".

Thereafter, James Konow (chapter 9) proposes an approach for measuring impartial views, considering both normative justice theories and empirical literature, and puts this approach to an empirical test. Also dealing with questions of justice, but shifting away from impartiality, David Miller (chapter 10) then reflects on need as a principle of distributive justice, observing that surveys show evidence that people treat need claims as special and arguing that justice must give these claims a central role. Also dealing with questions of distribution, Lars Schwettmann (chapter 11) argues that theory-based questionnaire experiments can stimulate normative thinking, thus leading to improved normative models, which then again influence experiments; this interplay can be interpreted as a dialogue between theorists and the public, ideally leading to an interpersonal reflective equilibrium.

Lastly, focussed on the field of anthropology, Peter Wiersbinski (chapter 12) makes room for the idea that the investigation of a priori concepts is dependent on experience. He uses an analogy between a priori concepts and thick moral concepts, which appear to be subject to moral experience and continual learning. Therefore, e.g., some results of psychological research concerning memory or human development contribute to the philosophical articulation of the concept of a rational memory or to the explication of conceptual relations between rational capacities.

This short overview already demonstrates the difficulty of making general and universal claims about how empirical research and normative theory are or should be related. Bringing the two closer together seems, based on the chapters in this volume, highly promising for some areas. To provide some perspective on this spectrum, it may be useful to once more reflect on the historical development of especially the Platonic view according to which the two domains should be kept strictly separated, at least for the case of ethics.

In classical philosophy, a predominant paradigm is that knowledge can only be acquired through a special method of thinking. Classical philosophy, as shown both in the introduction and also reflected in some of the chapters throughout this book, has a long tradition of relying on intuition and reflection of (philosophical) experts as a primary – or sole – mean to investigating the truth of normative questions. Such a perspective is typically accompanied by a clear devaluation of mere opinion, such as when arguing that a majority of people supporting certain, e.g., discriminatory, policies does not make these policies morally right. Here the fundamental assumption is that beliefs of laypeople can (and mostly will) be wrong, confused, or imprecise, since their carriers do not operate with the appropriate means of reflection. Against this background, justification is sought to mark a theory or assumption as independent of mere opinion.

One may ask oneself – maybe in the tradition of Nietzsche, the self-declared anti-platonist – where this rejection of mere opinion in favour of a truth actually has its origin. A plausible thesis for this can be found in Hannah Arendt's work. In the spring semester of 1954 she gave a series of lectures entitled "Philosophy and Politics – The Problem of Action and Thought after the French Revolution" at the University of Notre Dame. In her third lecture, she investigated the relationship between Socrates and Plato.[2] Against this background, she pays special attention to plurality, which she identifies in her diary of thought as a central moment of the human condition, and which, according to her, cannot be avoided, even when not being together with other people:

---

[2] And as Whitehead (1979, p. 39) famously noted that the "safest general characterization of the European philosophical tradition is that it consists of a series of footnotes to Plato" it might thus be worthwhile taking a look at Plato to discover where this strand of thought might have its origins.

> Even if I were to live entirely by myself I would, as long as I am alive, live in the condition of plurality. I have to put up with myself, and nowhere does this I-with-myself show more clearly than in pure thought, always a dialogue between the two who I am. The philosopher who, trying to escape the human condition of plurality, takes his flight into absolute solitude, is more radically delivered to this plurality inherent in every human being than anybody else, because it is the companionship with others which, calling me out of the dialogue of thought, makes me one again (Arendt 1990, p. 86).

She thus refers to Plato, for whom "thought" is "the dialogue of the two-in-one, the *eme emautô*" (Arendt 1990, p. 93, see also p. 101). But "the truth", she writes to Karl Jaspers referring to Nietzsche, "begins in twos" (as cited by Bormuth 2017, p. 10; own translation).[3] By this she already hints at the meaning of the discourse, which can be identified as a central moment of life in Athens: "To persuade, *peithein*, was the specifically political form of speech and since the Athenians were proud that they, in distinction to the barbarians, conducted their political affairs in the form of speech and without compulsion, they considered rhetoric, the art of persuasion, the highest, the truly political art" (Arendt 1990, p. 73 f.). Against this background, Arendt's lecture also examines the relationship between Socrates and Plato in their time of a politically decaying society (Arendt 1990, p. 91).

Socrates is characterised as a person who seeks publicity and conversation. With Xenophon one can say accordingly: "[...] Socrates lived ever in the open; for early in the morning he went to the public promenades and training-grounds; in the forenoon he was seen in the market; and the rest of the day he passed just where most people were to be met: he was generally talking, and anyone might listen" (Xenophon 1997, p. 7). Doing so, Socrates focussed on dialogue, but "did not claim to be wise" (Arendt 1990, p. 78). In these dialogues the opinions of the others were not to be destroyed and replaced by a premise objectively regarded as true; according to Arendt it was rather a matter of making the opinions in question more truthful (Arendt 1990, p. 84 f.).

When Socrates was accused in Athens of corrupting the youth and being godless, he also entered into dialogue before a people's court. He failed in conceiving the tribunal and was punished with death. According to Arendt, this experience must have been an incisive experience for his pupil Plato, as Bormuth (2017, p. 20; own translation) states:

> In essence, Arendt shows great understanding of the deep crisis into which Plato was plunged by the process of Socrates. The fact that his teacher's apology was not listened to by the Athenians, but that they reacted to his irritating questions and self-confident

---

3 Original wording: "Die Wahrheit beginnt zu zweit".

thinking with incomprehension and a death sentence, seems to her to be a dramatic turning point in Plato's consciousness.[4]

In this crisis, Plato is said to have concluded that there is an irreconcilable "opposition of truth and opinion" (Arendt 1990, p. 75). No longer should man be the measure of all things, but something divine (Arendt 1990, p. 77):

> Closely connected with his doubt about the validity of persuasion is Plato's furious denunciation of *doxa*, opinion, which not only ran like a red thread through his political works but became one of the cornerstones of his concept of truth. Platonic truth, even when *doxa* is not mentioned, is always understood as the very opposite of opinion. The spectacle of Socrates submitting his own *doxa* to the irresponsible opinions of the Athenians, and being outvoted by a majority, made Plato despise opinions and yearn for absolute standards. Such standards, which by human deeds could be judged and human thought could achieve some measure of reliability, from then became the primary impulse of his political philosophy, and influenced decisively even the purely philosophical doctrine of ideas (Arendt 1990, p. 74).

This perspective, which opposes doxa with episteme or aletheia, is vividly expressed in the cave parable that Plato formulates in the seventh book of his *Politeia*.

Arendt (1990, p. 78) speaks in this regard of Plato's "tyranny of truth", since "Plato himself was the first to use the ideas for political purposes, that is, to introduce absolute standards into the realm of human affairs, where, without such transcending standards, everything remains relative" (Arendt 1990, p. 74f.).

It is said – spoken with Marcus Tullius Cicero (1886, p. 257) against the background of the Socratic Revolution – that Socrates brought philosophy (in terms of content) from heaven to earth. With Hannah Arendt it might be added: Plato, on the other hand, has (methodically) lifted philosophy from earth to heaven.

Bibliography

Arendt, Hannah (1990): "Philosophy and Politics". In: *Social Research* 57 (1), pp. 73–103.
Bauer, Alexander Max and Meyerhuber, Malte Ingo (2019): "Epilog. Zwischen doxa und aletheia". In: id. (eds.): *Philosophie zwischen Sein und Sollen. Normative Theorie und*

---

[4] Original wording: "Im Kern zeigt sie [Arendt] großes Verständnis für die tiefe Krise, in die Platon durch den Prozess des Sokrates gestürzt wurde. Dass sein Lehrer mit seiner Apologie kein Gehör bei den Athenern fand, sondern diese auf sein irritierendes Fragen und selbstgewisses Denken mit Unverständnis und Todesurteil reagierten, erscheint ihr als dramatischer Wendepunkt in Platons Bewusstsein".

empirische Forschung im Spannungsfeld. Berlin and Boston: Walter de Gruyter, pp. 219–223.

Bormuth, Matthias (2017): "Einleitung". In: Arendt, Hannah: *Sokrates. Apologie der Pluralität*. Berlin: Matthes & Seitz, pp. 7–33.

Cicero, Marcus Tullius (1886): *Tusculan Disputations*. Boston: Little, Brown, and Company.

Whitehead, Alfred (1979): *Process and Reality*. New York: Free Press.

Xenophon (1997): "Memorabilia". In: id.: *Memorabilia, Oeconomicus, Symposium, Apology*. Cambridge and London: Harvard University Press, pp. 1–359.

List of Contributors

Maximilian Agostini, M.Sc., is a doctoral researcher at the University of Groningen, with a specialisation in social and organisational psychology. His research background is motivational psychology; more specifically whether prosocial behaviour is a common response to goal failure. He is a founding member of the Centre for Psychological Gun Research (CPGR) and an enthusiastic climber. You can reach him via: University of Groningen, Department Social Psychology, Grote Kruisstraat 2/1, 9712 TS Groningen, The Netherlands, m.agostini@rug.nl

Alexander Max Bauer, M.A., is teaching associate and doctoral researcher at the Carl von Ossietzky University of Oldenburg as well as a research associate in the research group "Need-Based Justice and Distribution Procedures" of the German Research Foundation (DFG), where he engages with fundamental questions of distributive justice between normative theory, formal modelling, and empirical social research. His research interest is, amongst others, in experimental philosophy, justice, theory of science, and the work of Friedrich Nietzsche. You can reach him via: Carl von Ossietzky University of Oldenburg, Department of Philosophy, Ammerländer Heerstraße 114-118, 26129 Oldenburg, Germany, alexander.max.bauer@uni-oldenburg.de

Carlos A. de Matos Fernandes, M.Sc., is a doctoral researcher at the University of Groningen. His research interest is, amongst others, in cooperation problems with a focus on agent-based modelling, theoretical and analytical sociology, as well as studying upcoming and innovative statistical methods in the field of social network analysis. You can reach him via: University of Groningen, Department of Sociology, Grote Kruisstraat 2/1, 9712 TS Groningen, The Netherlands, c.a.de.matos.fernandes@rug.nl

Prof. Dr. **Guillermina Jasso** is professor of sociology and Silver professor of arts and science at the New York University. She is a fellow of the Johns Hopkins Society of Scholars, the Sociological Research Association, the New York University's Society of Fellows, and the American Association for the Advancement of Science. Her research interest is, amongst others, in basic sociobehavioural theory, distributive justice, status, international migration, inequality and stratification, probability distributions, mathematical methods for theoretical analysis, and factorial survey methods for empirical analysis. Her Erdős number is 3. You can reach her via: New York University, 295 Lafayette Street, New York, NY 10012, United States, gj1@nyu.edu

Prof. Dr. **Joshua Knobe** is professor of cognitive science and philosophy at Yale University. His research interest is, amongst others, in the field of moral cognition. He examines the ways in which people's moral judgments can influence their use of concepts that might initially seem entirely scientific or non-moral, such as intention, causation, happiness, or knowledge. You can reach him via: Yale University, Department of Psychology, 2 Hillhouse Ave, Box 208205, New Haven, Connecticut, CT 06520–8205, United States, joshua.knobe@yale.edu

List of Contributors

Prof. Dr. James Konow is chair of economics and ethics at the University of Kiel and professor of economics at Loyola Marymount University. He is a former editor of *Economics and Philosophy* and associate editor of *Social Justice Research*. His research interest is, amongst others, in economics and ethics, behavioural economics, experimental economics, public economics, and the economics of happiness. You can reach him via: Loyola Marymount University, 1 LMU Drive, Suite 4200, Los Angeles, California, CA 90045–2659, United States, jkonow@lmu.edu

Jannis Kreienkamp, M.Sc., is a doctoral researcher at the University of Groningen. His research interest is, amongst others, in the motivational basis of intergroup contact and intergroup conflict. In his research, he puts a particular focus on the function of psychological needs and goals in social contexts. As part of his doctoral research, he applies this perspective to the cultural adaptation process of refugees in the Netherlands and, as a founding member of the Center for Psychological Gun Research, he also works on an understanding of needs and motivation in more violent intergroup contexts. With his research, he is committed to robust research methods that are embedded within societal challenges and give agency to vulnerable and excluded participant groups. You can reach him via: University of Groningen, Heymans Institute for Psychological Research, Grote Kruisstraat 2/1, 9712 TS Groningen, The Netherlands, j.kreienkamp@rug.nl

Marvin Kunz, M.Sc., is a researcher at the Wageningen Economic Research Institute in The Hague. There, he works in interdisciplinary research teams on international research projects. He was a research master student at the University of Groningen and was a junior researcher of the Junior Researcher Programme, a programme supported and co-organised by the Corpus Christi College, Cambridge. Furthermore, he worked at the University of Cambridge as a visiting researcher. You can reach him via: marvin.c.kunz@gmail.com

Dr. Marcel Mertz is head of the working group "Research/Public Health Ethics & Methodology" at the Institute for History, Ethics, and Philosophy of Medicine of Hannover Medical School. His research interest is, amongst others, the methodology and inter-/transdisciplinarity of medical and research ethics, with a particular focus on empirical ethics. He is currently the coordinator of the working group "Ethics and Empirics" of the German Academy for Ethics in Medicine (AEM). You can reach him via: Hannover Medical School, Institute for History, Ethics, and Philosophy of Medicine, Carl-Neuberg-Straße 1, 30625 Hannover, Germany, mertz.marcel@mh-hannover.de

Malte Ingo Meyerhuber, M.Sc., was research master student of behavioural and social sciences at the University of Groningen, with a focus on social and organisational psychology. Both within his studies as well as during his work as a research assistant he focused on creativity and innovation research. Since 2019, he is working as a consultant. You can reach him via: m.meyerhuber@gmx.de

Dr. Sylke Meyerhuber is senior researcher associated at the University of Bremen's artec Sustainability Research Centre. Her research as an organisational psychologist is concerned with social sustainability in organisations, with special consideration of leadership. You can reach her via: University of Bremen, artec Sustainability Research Centre, Enrique-Schmidt-Straße 7, 28359 Bremen, Germany, meyerhuber@uni-bremen.de

List of Contributors

Prof. Dr. **David Miller** is professor of political theory at the University of Oxford and senior research fellow in social and political theory at Nuffield College, Oxford. His research interest is, amongst others, in justice, nationality, citizenship, and immigration. You can reach him via: Nuffield College, New Road, Oxford, OX1 1NF, United Kingdom, david.miller@nuffield.ox.ac.uk

Prof. Dr. **Albert W. Musschenga** is professor emeritus of philosophical ethics at the Vrije Universiteit Amsterdam. His research interest is, amongst others, in the universality of morality, quality of life, integrity, (moral) identity, and empirically informed ethics. You can reach him via: Vrije Universiteit Amsterdam, Department of Philosophy, De Boelelaan 1105, 1081 HV Amsterdam, The Netherlands, a.w.musschenga@vu.nl

Dr. **Norbert Paulo** is research associate at the University of Graz and at the University of Salzburg, he also is fellow at the Centre for Interdisciplinary Research at the University of Bielefeld. His main research interest is, amongst others, in empirically informed ethics, moral psychology, and experimental philosophy. You can reach him via: University of Graz, Attemsgasse 25, 8010 Graz, Austria, norbert.paulo@uni-graz.at

PD Dr. **Lars Schwettmann** is deputy director of the Institute of Health Economics and Health Care Management at the Helmholtz Zentrum München, German Research Center for Environmental Health (a member of the Helmholtz Association of German Research Centres). His research interest is, amongst others, in empirical social choice, economic inequality, behavioural economics and health behaviour, as well as normative health economics. You can reach him via: Helmholtz Zentrum München, German Research Center for Environmental Health, Institute of Health Economics and Health Care Management, Ingolstädter Landstraße 1, 85764 Neuherberg, Germany, lars.schwettmann@helmholtz-muenchen.de

Stephen J. Sullivan, Ph.D., is associate professor at Edinboro University. His research interest is, amongst others, in ethics and philosophy of religion, especially in their intersection in the issue of the relationship between morality and religion. You can reach him via: Edinboro University, 219 Meadville Street, Edinboro, Pennsylvania, PA 16444, United States, ssullivan@edinboro.edu Dr.

Dr. **Peter Wiersbinski** is research fellow at the University of Regensburg. His research interest is, amongst others, in metaethics, ethics, action theory, anthropology, and the philosophy of sex. You can reach him via: University of Regensburg, Universitätsstraße 31, 93053 Regensburg, Germany, peter.wiersbinski@psk.uni-regensburg.de

Index of Names

Adorno, Theodor 14f.
Akerlof, George 88
Albert, Hans 6, 14, 22
Amiel, Yoram 241
Antonovsky, Aaron 42
Apel, Karl-Otto 13
Aquinas, Thomas 317
Arendt, Hannah 9, 16, 337, 339–341
Aristotle 14, 17, 105–107, 116f., 169, 182, 252, 317, 320f.
Ayer, Alfred 3, 22

Badura, Albert 38
Bar-Hillel, Maya 18, 246, 250, 280, 296, 298f., 301–305, 307–310
Brock, Gillian 276

Carnap, Rudolf 3, 171
Cartwright, Nancy 83
Cassiodorus, Flavius 14
Cicero, Marcus 341
Cohn, Ruth 41, 56

Dahrendorf, Ralf 15
Darwin, Charles 12, 318
Davidson, Donald 4
Dawkins, Richard 76
Descartes, René 14, 136
Deutsch, Morton 19, 282
Dilthey, Wilhelm 14
Dworkin, Ronald 165, 277–279

Einstein, Albert 1, 24

Firth, Roderick 106
Flanagan, Owen 6, 151f., 154f., 157, 164
Foot, Philippa 4
Freud, Anna 60
Freud, Sigmund 39f., 60
Friedman, Milton 237
Frohlich, Norman 19, 238, 243, 307

Gadamer, Hans-Georg 56f.
Galilei, Galileo 11
Goldman, Alvin 138f.
Goldscheid, Rudolf 14
Goldwater, Barry 2, 25

Habermas, Jürgen 13, 15, 19, 165
Haeckel, Ernst 19
Haidt, John 129, 133–135, 137
Hare, Richard 13, 106, 174, 326
Harsanyi, John 18, 241f., 309
Hegel, Georg 317
Heisenberg, Werner 24f.
Hume, David 2f., 16, 76, 136, 169, 174, 182, 241, 282

Jaspers, Karl 26, 340
Joubert, Joseph 35, 41, 49, 65, 67

Kahneman, Daniel 19, 85, 133, 162, 246
Kant, Immanuel 13, 50, 76, 152, 175, 317, 319
Keynes, John 11
Kripke, Saul 173, 179
Kuhn, Thomas 24, 81

Leithäuser, Thomas 39, 43, 51f., 54, 56, 59, 61, 63
Locke, John 76, 94, 120

McIntyre, Alisdair 184
Mackie, John 20, 152, 170, 182f.
Mankiw, Gregory 11
Marx, Karl 273, 279, 283
McDowell, John 4, 318, 325f., 333
Mead, Georg 50, 95
Mill, John 174f., 180
Moore, George 16
Murdoch, Iris 4

Newton, Isaac 108
Nietzsche, Friedrich 23, 339f.

Oppenheimer, Joe   19, 238, 243, 307
Oppenheimer, Robert   24

Pareto, Vilfredo   117, 121, 287
Parsons, Talcott   66
Piaget, Jean   330
Plato   9, 16, 50, 106f., 116–119, 122, 339–341
Plessner, Helmuth   318, 320
Popper, Karl   14, 77, 108, 112
Putnam, Hilary   4, 17, 172f., 181
Putnam, Ruth   4

Quine, Willard   171, 177

Rawls, John   19, 120, 151f., 155–165, 170, 174, 239–243, 266, 276–278, 290, 297, 302f., 309
Robinson and Friday   246
Roemer, John   298, 301
Rogers, Carl   41, 43, 55
Roosevelt, Franklin   1, 24
Rorty, Richard   4
Russell, Bertrand   3, 105

Satir, Virginia   42

Scheler, Max   318, 320
Schmoller, Gustav   14
Sen, Amartya   277, 279, 298
Singer, Peter   21, 175, 183, 209, 229
Slote, Michael   178, 184
Smith, Adam   106, 120, 136, 197, 238–242, 266, 309
Socrates   9, 116, 337, 339–341
Sombart, Werner   14
Stevenson, Charles   3, 22

Tolstoy, Leo   3

Volmerg, Birgit   51, 54, 56f., 59–64
von Weizsäcker, Carl Friedrich   24

Weber, Max   3, 14, 16, 51
Whitehead, Alfred   9, 16, 339
Williams, Bernard   17, 20, 153, 184, 325f.
Wilson, Thomas   50–53, 56, 133
Wittgenstein, Ludwig   57

Xenophon   340

Yaari, Menahem   18, 246, 250, 280, 296, 298f., 301–305, 307–310

Index of Subjects

Academia 36, 41, 76, 80, 88, 90, 92f., 109, 229f., 238, 274, 301
Acceptance 18, 20, 24, 44, 57, 88, 155, 170, 172, 205, 207–209, 219f., 226–228, 297, 299, 302, 304f., 308–312, 331
Accountability 45, 248, 250–252, 256f., 266f.
Additivity 112
Agency 95, 154, 217f., 251
Aletheia 9, 337, 341
Allocation 8, 80, 83, 238–240, 242, 246, 249–252, 255, 273, 277, 280–282, 284, 286, 288, 295–301, 303–307, 310–312
Analysis 3, 5, 12, 15, 48f., 51–54, 56, 58f., 62–67, 75–78, 80f., 84–87, 107, 120–122, 139f., 189, 191f., 194, 197f., 205, 211, 221, 226, 229, 237–241, 243–245, 247, 249, 253, 255f., 258, 266f., 273, 283, 297, 307, 321, 323, 330
– Conceptual Analysis 16, 20, 24, 319f., 330
– Data Analysis 5, 75, 78, 81, 85–87, 96
– Discourse Analysis 214
– Document Analysis 223
– Regression Analysis 256, 260, 263f.
– Text Analysis 54f., 59, 63
– Welfare Analysis 7, 237f., 267
Anthropology 3, 66, 77, 176, 209, 318–320, 329, 338
– Anthropological Difference 8, 317–320, 322f., 329
– Evolutionary Anthropology 319, 332f.
– Philosophical Anthropology 319
Applicability 7, 11, 121, 189, 195, 200, 205f., 215f., 226, 229, 326, 333
A Priori 8, 16, 76, 86, 173, 245, 248, 266, 317, 319, 323, 325, 328, 338
Aristotelian 15, 17f., 318
Armchair Traditionalism 16
Artefact 37, 56, 61, 65, 179
Assumption 5, 7, 11f., 16, 19f., 22–25, 37, 40, 44, 53, 56f., 75, 78, 81f., 85, 91, 109, 132, 146, 171, 177–179, 189, 193, 206, 209f., 222, 229, 239, 244f., 318, 322, 337, 339
Astronomy 183
Authority 198, 200f., 209f., 212f., 220, 229, 318
Automaticity 134–136, 141, 146
Autonomy 67, 197, 209, 218
– Patient Autonomy 191, 197, 230
Aversion 16, 190
– Deficiency Aversion 111
– Loss Aversion 111, 114

Belief 3, 15f., 35–39, 42f., 65, 95f., 106, 119, 129–132, 136–140, 144, 156, 158–161, 169f., 172, 175f., 179, 183–185, 189, 238, 244, 246, 262, 274, 290, 297, 302–304, 310, 312, 317, 339
– Belief Revision 151, 160, 162, 165
Bias 18, 78, 83–85, 87, 91f., 95, 139f., 159–162, 218, 237–240, 242–245, 247, 249, 252, 256, 261, 266f., 274, 301, 303, 308–312
– Bias Avoidance 7, 151, 160, 162, 165
– Cultural Bias 37
– Experimenter's Bias 83
– Researcher's Bias 18, 95
– Selection Bias 250
– Self-Serving Bias 7, 237, 242, 245, 247, 266, 298, 301
– Social Desirability Bias 309
Biology 12, 17, 19, 318, 322

Categorical Imperative 152, 197
Characteristic 1, 49, 107, 109f., 113, 117–119, 133, 141, 171f., 190, 196f., 239f., 249, 261f., 265–267, 297, 301, 303, 306, 308, 310, 322, 332
Chemistry 79, 180, 183
Coherence 4, 21, 89, 105, 156, 158f., 206, 274
Common Sense 16–18, 138, 160, 171, 173–175, 177–181, 183f., 245
Competence 113, 132f., 146, 160, 330, 338

Index of Subjects

Complexity 53f., 59, 92, 94, 140–142, 332
Conception of Man 19, 37, 41, 43
Consciousness 5f., 21, 24, 38, 41f., 60f., 63–65, 81, 83, 117, 129f., 133–137, 140–146, 157, 163, 193, 248, 286, 317, 321, 331, 333, 341
Consensus 3, 7, 14, 46, 204, 214, 220, 237, 241, 244f., 247, 249, 258, 260, 266f., 305, 326
Consent 198–202, 207f., 230
Consequentialism 151, 153–157, 159, 164, 193, 207–209, 225, 230
Controversy 2, 4, 12, 14, 19, 25, 78, 136, 145, 159, 198, 210, 230, 325, 331
Core-Sentence Method 5, 35, 54–56
Correlation 146, 171–177, 223, 262, 265
Counselling 36, 41, 43, 55
Culture 18, 35, 37, 39, 44–48, 60f., 63f., 66f., 75, 77, 82f., 90, 92, 117, 121, 176f., 180f., 210, 301, 308

Data 75f., 81–87, 91, 93f., 116, 119, 189, 216, 265f., 275
– Data Collection 5, 75, 78, 82, 84–86, 96, 192
– Empirical Data 12, 16f., 19, 77, 82, 138f., 145, 189f., 192, 209f., 218
Deduction 2, 36, 47f., 51, 86, 105, 107–109, 112–115, 123, 140, 206, 318
Deliberation 19, 22, 135, 139, 141f., 151, 153, 159, 162f., 165, 302, 317, 325, 331
Deontology 155, 174, 193, 207, 230
Descriptivity 1f., 13, 15, 94, 106, 108, 129, 132, 135, 143, 154, 174, 189, 191–193, 229, 239, 246, 250, 297–300, 307, 309, 324–327, 331
Determinism 20, 275
Discourse 4, 13, 35, 37, 46, 49, 62, 165, 169, 191, 194, 204, 207, 209, 212, 229, 240, 340
Dispute 14, 239, 244
– Dispute About Value Judgements (*Werturteilsstreit*) 14
– Positivism Dispute (*Positivismusstreit*) 14
Distribution 6, 8, 25, 44, 46, 91, 94, 105, 115, 117f., 121, 123, 237–240, 243f., 246–248, 252f., 256, 265, 273, 275–278, 280–286, 288, 290f., 295, 298, 301, 303–312, 338
– Redistribution 80, 118, 243, 252, 261, 278
Diversity 9, 13, 15, 18, 78, 108, 132, 172, 176, 181, 197
Doctrine 8, 11, 93, 317, 341
Doxa 8f., 16, 18, 130f., 337, 341

Economics 3, 11, 15, 18f., 37, 44, 46f., 88, 114, 118f., 237–241, 246f., 250, 267, 277, 296–298, 301, 303, 307, 309–312
– Health Economics 296, 301, 304, 307, 309–311
– Normative Economics 15, 237, 297, 299
– Positive Economics 15, 297
– Welfare Economics 106, 298, 301
Efficiency 196, 239, 248, 250–252, 256f., 263f., 266f., 280f., 285, 287, 296
Egalitarianism 153, 278–280
Enlightenment 59, 76
Epistemology 3, 18, 50, 84, 95, 129f., 136–138, 145, 155, 158, 172, 182, 185, 197
– Moral Epistemology 151, 155–157, 161f., 164f., 169
Equality 47, 238, 249, 262, 277, 279, 282, 301, 304
– Inequality 105, 108, 113–115, 118–120, 123, 285, 287, 289, 296
Equilibrium 170, 303
– Reflective Equilibrium 8, 152, 156–158, 161f., 164f., 170, 174, 195, 295, 297, 300, 302–306, 308, 310–312, 338
Equity 109, 121, 135, 239, 252, 286, 296
Ethics 1–4, 6–8, 11, 13, 15, 19–21, 25, 35, 44–46, 49, 77, 80, 105, 120, 130, 144f., 152, 156, 159, 169–185, 189–197, 212, 216, 220, 223, 226, 229–231, 239, 241f., 252, 256, 295, 297–299, 302–306, 308f., 311f., 337–339
– Applied Ethics 190, 197, 230, 239, 251, 253–255, 257, 266
– Bioethics 189–191, 197, 211, 229f., 239, 251, 257, 266
– Business Ethics 251, 257, 266
– Descriptive Ethics 191
– Discourse Ethics 195, 203, 208

- Empirical Ethics 3f., 16, 20f., 77, 130, 191f., 195, 242, 296, 299, 302, 304f.
- Environmental Ethics 251, 257, 266
- Experimental Ethics 190
- Media Ethics 239, 251, 257, 266
- Medical Ethics 25, 144f., 190f., 209
- Metaethics 14, 152, 169–171, 174, 177, 182, 184, 190f., 203f., 208, 324
- Pragmatist Ethics 190
- Virtue Ethics 130, 152, 155, 184, 193, 195

Evidence 7f., 20, 36, 77, 81, 83, 114, 119, 121, 129, 131, 133, 137f., 140, 144f., 156, 160, 191f., 216, 226, 229, 237f., 240, 243–245, 248, 252, 255, 259, 265, 267, 273–275, 279–281, 283, 288, 290f., 295, 303, 338

Evolution 12, 129, 179, 305, 318, 322

Experience 4, 8, 11, 14, 36, 38, 43, 50, 55, 58f., 62, 75, 77–79, 88, 95, 114, 132, 136, 141, 143f., 146, 177, 189, 211, 217, 239, 242f., 301, 317, 325, 327f., 331, 338, 340

Experiment 8, 15, 20f., 36, 49, 77, 83f., 142–144, 209, 241, 244–248, 252, 273–275, 280–283, 290, 297, 299, 301, 305–309, 311, 320, 332f., 338
- Thought Experiment 200, 240f., 243

Expert 17f., 20, 25, 35, 52, 54, 57, 60, 85, 91, 116, 135f., 140f., 143–146, 183, 209, 254, 339
- Moral Expert 143–146, 182, 274, 295, 338

Explication 13, 21, 36, 156, 163, 171, 240, 331, 339

Fact 1, 4, 8, 11, 13, 19, 21f., 38, 48, 50f., 53f., 58, 61, 63f., 67, 84, 105, 112, 138, 153, 155f., 159f., 170, 172f., 176–178, 182, 190, 193f., 197, 199, 202–204, 207–210, 212–215, 219, 221, 225, 229, 231, 242f., 246–248, 253, 258f., 261, 266, 277, 289, 298, 301f., 307f., 317, 319–321, 323, 329, 331f., 338, 340

Fairness 7, 15, 47, 121, 237f., 246, 250, 252, 255, 266, 289f., 295, 297–299, 311

Fallacy 16, 190, 212
- Ad Populum Fallacy 212
- Naturalistic Fallacy 16, 190

Falsification 19, 178

File Drawer Problem 81

Framework 5, 13f., 35, 40f., 46, 48f., 52, 54, 56, 65, 67, 76, 78, 96, 200, 253, 318, 337

Frankfurt School 14

Free Will 20, 209, 275

Functionality 205, 224, 228

Funding 5, 75, 78–81, 88, 90–92, 96, 198, 254, 256, 295

Game 36, 65, 116, 225, 298, 334
- Dictator Game 19, 249
- Trust Game 249
- Ultimatum Game 249

Generalisation 67, 82, 111, 170–172, 177, 193, 201, 205, 207, 210f., 226

Gini Coefficient 119

Goldwater Rule 2, 25

Goodhart's Law 80, 89

Guideline 2, 12, 44, 52f., 55, 65, 86, 223, 231

Health Care 8, 216, 251, 267, 277f., 286, 295–298, 300f., 304, 306–308, 310–312

Hermeneutics 56–59, 62, 64, 192, 195

Heuristic 80, 85, 248

History 3–5, 11–14, 20, 23f., 60, 82f., 105, 129, 162, 173, 190, 194, 226, 301, 309, 328, 339

Human Condition 37, 339f.

Humanism 37, 41, 42–45, 49, 52, 55, 337

Hypothesis 8, 51, 86f., 89, 108f., 112f., 115, 136, 141f., 163–165, 171, 180, 194–196, 221, 225, 238–241, 243, 247, 250, 257–259, 278, 295, 299, 305–310, 312
- Null Hypothesis 86, 245, 258, 262

Ideal 5, 35, 40, 56, 61, 85, 92, 106, 151f., 154, 157f., 161, 164f., 175, 192, 208f., 221–223, 229, 239, 242f., 249, 261, 297

Ideology 3, 11, 16, 87, 181

Impartiality 7, 19, 105, 108, 120f., 123, 237–245, 261, 266f., 298, 303, 307, 309f., 312, 338

Index of Subjects

Incentive 15, 80, 90, 92f., 96, 226, 297, 307f., 332f.
Induction 86, 160, 170–172, 176f.
Inference 76, 85, 90, 131f., 134, 136f., 145f., 329
Institution 46, 88f., 91, 156, 198, 200, 209f., 212–214, 216, 219f., 221–223, 241–243, 247, 250f., 288, 290
Institutionalisation 143f., 146, 191, 194, 196, 203, 205, 207, 213f., 219, 222, 224, 226
Integration 5, 13, 15–17, 41, 65f., 79, 93, 107, 111f., 114, 130, 145, 225, 320, 337
Interactionism 5, 35, 38, 43, 50–54, 56f., 64f.
Interdependency 5, 8, 11, 13, 21, 23, 25, 45, 295f., 300, 310–312, 327, 330f.
Interdisciplinarity 20, 66, 79, 113, 115, 190f., 208, 229f.
Interpretation 36–38, 50f., 53–60, 62–64, 85f., 94f., 115, 151, 241, 255, 258, 260, 262, 275, 286, 303, 305f., 308, 332
Interview 37, 42–44, 52, 54–56, 58, 60, 62, 211, 213, 221
Introspection 18, 24, 131, 136, 138, 299
Intuition 3f., 6, 16–18, 20f., 24, 42, 64, 89, 129–134, 136–143, 142f., 145f., 156–159, 163, 170f., 173–178, 180, 182, 207, 220, 239, 274f., 286f., 289, 299, 302f., 306f., 325, 331, 339
– Ethical Intuition 131, 136, 306
– Moral Intuition 6, 129–133, 135–140, 145f., 159, 174, 242, 303, 338
– Psychological Intuition 6, 129, 133

Journal 82, 84, 86, 88, 90–92, 96
Judgement 1, 6, 15, 19, 22f., 25, 55, 80, 85, 88f., 92, 105f., 123, 129, 133–137, 139–146, 151, 157–160, 162–165, 170, 173f., 177f., 182, 190, 194, 239, 241–245, 247, 249f., 253, 256, 261f., 266f., 275, 280f., 297, 301f., 304f., 310f., 326, 328, 330, 338
– Considered Judgement 151, 158f., 162–164, 274, 302–304, 306, 310
– Ethical Judgement 8, 144, 182, 190, 192–194, 295, 303f., 306, 308f., 311f.
– Intuitive Judgement 134, 136, 139, 141–143, 157, 173
Justice 5, 7f., 15, 19, 105, 107–117, 120f., 123, 143f., 146, 158, 164f., 170, 174f., 179, 183, 191, 196, 237–241, 246–253, 256f., 261, 266f., 273–291, 300, 302–304, 307, 311, 338
– Distributive Justice 3, 7, 19, 21, 237, 248, 251, 253, 256, 267, 273, 275–279, 281, 284, 286, 297–300, 303f., 307, 311, 338
– Needs-Based Justice 8, 273–275, 279, 280, 284f., 288–291
– Social Justice 277, 280
Justification 6f., 16, 24, 49, 53, 76, 129–133, 137–139, 144–146, 153, 156–158, 169–174, 178 183f., 189, 192–196, 200f., 203–210, 213, 218–220, 222, 224–226, 229f., 240, 287–290, 288, 300, 302, 305, 308, 310–312, 330, 338f.

Kantianism 50, 175, 193, 195
Knowledge 4, 6, 13, 16, 21, 25, 36, 44f., 51, 57, 62, 77, 85, 105f., 118f., 124, 144, 160, 162, 169f., 172, 182, 190–192, 207, 218, 238f., 243, 249, 270, 304, 319, 321, 324f., 328, 334, 337, 339

Language 3, 13, 56f., 62, 64, 106, 170, 317, 330
Law 2, 48, 51, 65, 67, 77, 108, 118, 121, 142, 144, 173–175, 177, 195, 203, 208, 225, 239, 243, 251, 323, 332f.
Layperson 16–20, 146, 275, 297, 299, 306, 309, 339
Legitimacy 7, 48, 184, 189, 194f., 201, 205, 208, 212f., 217, 229
Locus of Control 38
Logic 2f., 20, 36, 40, 42, 52, 56–59, 62f., 85, 153, 160, 186, 190, 214, 226, 299, 303, 321–327
– Logical Fallacy 2

Mathematics   12, 36, 57, 85, 105–107, 141, 280, 299, 303
Medicine   19, 36, 77, 80, 94, 139, 141, 190 f., 198–201, 207, 209, 211, 213, 215, 222, 253, 277 f., 283–285, 295, 301
Metaphysics   3 f., 14, 18, 84, 183, 275, 318, 333
Method   3, 5–8, 11, 13, 16, 19 f., 24, 35, 43, 52–56, 60, 64 f., 76–80, 83–85, 87, 89 f., 93–95, 153, 156–159, 161 f., 164, 169–171, 174, 184, 189, 198, 214, 237 f., 240, 243–247, 249, 258 f., 266 f., 296–299, 305, 310, 317, 320, 330, 332–334, 339
Methodology   3, 6, 8, 13 f., 17, 20 f., 24, 44, 49, 53 f., 56, 60, 62, 64 f., 76 f., 83 f., 169–171, 175 f., 178, 180–184, 191 f., 195, 204, 230, 295, 297, 302, 305–307, 311 f.
Model   6, 16, 36, 39 f., 60, 66, 79, 93, 112, 118, 124, 129, 133, 142, 156, 158, 230 f., 238, 240–243, 245, 249, 255, 266, 298, 302 f., 306, 311, 338
Moral   1–4, 6–8, 13, 15–23, 35, 40, 45, 66 f., 107, 129–133, 135–140, 142–146, 151–165, 169–185, 189–200, 202–220, 222–231, 236, 239, 241 f., 244–246, 249 f., 255, 258 f., 261 f., 265–267, 274–276, 279, 295, 297–299, 302, 305, 308, 317, 320, 324–331, 338
– Thick Moral Concept   8, 132, 317, 325–329, 331, 338
– Thin Moral Concept   325
Motivation   60, 67, 107, 140, 153, 160, 172, 190, 201, 208 f., 219 f., 222, 240, 249, 251, 258, 282, 298, 304, 308 f., 318, 327, 333 f.

Natural Kind   6, 21, 169 f., 172 f., 176, 179, 181, 183 f.
Naturalism   6, 13, 169 f., 175, 178, 180–184
Need   7 f., 23, 25, 41 f., 91, 159, 196, 207, 221, 239, 246, 248, 250–253, 255–257, 262–264, 266 f., 273–291, 295 f., 308, 338
Nihilism   183

Norm   2, 4–8, 11 f., 14–16, 18, 20–25, 35–37, 39 f., 44–46, 49 f., 52, 54 f., 75–91, 93–96, 105 f., 124, 129, 142, 145, 154, 155, 160, 169–171, 174, 178, 180–182, 189–231, 237, 239–241, 244, 266 f., 274–276, 279, 284, 295–301, 303 f., 307 f., 311 f., 318, 323–326, 337–339

Objectivity   1, 3, 5, 7, 20, 36, 42 f., 46, 50, 53, 67, 75–78, 82–85, 89 f., 95, 170 f., 181, 196, 201, 203, 207, 222, 224, 237, 241 f., 279, 281, 340
Observation   2, 7, 13, 64, 76, 81, 139, 169–172, 176–178, 182, 205, 209–221, 223, 227 f., 247, 250, 256, 258, 261, 264 f., 327, 332, 338
Ockham's Razor   12, 332
Ought   1 f., 4–6, 9, 13, 15 f., 21–25, 46, 48, 60, 66, 77, 92, 105–107, 115 f., 118 f., 121–124, 138, 152–155, 183 f., 190 f., 202, 215, 219, 274, 298, 325, 337
– Ought Implies Can   151–154, 161 f., 192, 220 f.

Paradigm   5, 16, 24, 35, 38, 41, 46, 50–55, 81, 88, 182, 191, 339
Parsimony   12
Peer Review   80, 88, 90
Personality   5, 35, 37–39, 41, 44 f., 60 f., 117, 151, 161
Philanthropy   45
Philosophy   2–4, 6–9, 14, 16–18, 20, 23, 25, 35–37, 56 f., 61, 65 f., 76–78, 84, 92, 96, 105–107, 116, 120, 129–131, 133, 136 f., 139, 145, 153, 160–163, 165, 169–171, 174, 177, 180, 182, 189, 191–195, 200, 203 f., 208, 210, 212, 219 f., 229 f., 240, 267, 273–276, 278–281, 285, 290 f., 298–300, 304, 309, 312, 317–320, 326, 329–331, 338–341
– Experimental Philosophy   3, 20, 190, 267, 299
Physics   1, 12, 14, 17, 24, 105 f., 141, 181, 183, 322, 333
Platonic   15, 18, 339, 341
Pluralism   174, 275, 287, 290 f.

Policy 7, 11, 46f., 144, 216, 237–241, 246, 248, 250f., 267, 276, 287, 290, 295–297, 299f., 312, 339
Politics 14f., 19f., 42, 46–49, 77f., 83, 87f., 116, 153, 210, 212, 239, 241, 273–275, 283, 295, 297, 300, 308, 312, 339–341
Positivism 14, 50, 76f., 84, 304
Postulate 5, 89, 96, 105, 107f., 111, 115, 123, 141, 178, 245, 266, 332
Power 5, 39, 44, 46, 59, 67, 105, 107, 109f., 112, 114, 116f., 121, 123, 132f., 174–176, 201, 204, 219, 248, 250f., 277
Practitioner 45, 64, 77, 84, 90, 92, 96, 230
Prediction 5, 40, 51, 86, 94, 105, 107f., 112–116, 122f., 177–179, 225, 244f., 256, 258f., 265, 275, 304, 308
Preference 3, 7f., 15, 19, 83, 110, 121, 212, 220, 237–243, 245, 247–250, 253, 262, 265, 273, 280, 282, 297–299, 307–312, 318
Prejudice 160–162
Priming 135f.
Principle 6, 12, 19, 25, 37, 41, 44–46, 49, 56, 66, 91, 143, 145, 151–159, 161, 163–165, 175, 177–179, 181, 190–193, 197, 200f., 207, 210–212, 220–222, 230, 238–241, 245f., 249, 251f., 256f., 266f., 273–275, 277–279, 282–291, 302–304, 306, 311, 317, 329, 333, 338
Probability 6, 85f., 105, 108, 120, 123, 140, 214, 217, 223, 240, 309
Proof 12, 115, 183
Proposition 2, 20, 63, 106f., 109, 114–116, 129, 131f., 136–138, 145, 158, 203
Psychology 1, 3f., 6, 8, 17, 20, 23, 25, 35–45, 48–50, 52, 55f., 60, 63–66, 75, 77, 79, 82f., 94, 129–133, 136f., 139, 141, 145, 154, 160f., 170, 178, 184, 193, 196, 200, 202, 209, 217, 220–222, 224, 229, 244, 250, 317, 319f., 326–331, 338f.
– Cognitive Psychology 141, 182, 318
– Comparative Psychology 332
– Developmental Psychology 318f., 330, 333
– Humanistic Psychology 37, 41–44, 49, 55
– Moral Psychology 135, 299
– Social Psychology 5, 35, 37–39, 41f., 49f., 56, 60, 65f., 78f.

Quasi-Experiment 306
Quasi-Spectator 7, 237, 240, 243–246, 249, 255, 258f., 261, 265f., 307

Randomised Controlled Trial 77, 82–84
Rationality 1, 3, 8, 14, 37, 52, 60, 133, 136, 156–158, 160–163, 171, 174, 193, 196, 204, 207f., 210, 242, 286, 303, 309f., 317f., 324, 329–331, 339
Realism 170, 247
– Moral Realism 18, 170f.
– Psychological Realism 6, 151f., 154f., 157, 164
Reason 1f., 6, 13, 19, 35–38, 40, 49–51, 65, 76, 81, 83, 87, 112, 123, 129–131, 133, 136–141, 143, 146, 152, 155, 157, 159–164, 175f., 181–183, 190, 194, 196, 201, 204–206, 208, 211f., 218–220, 223f., 229, 238, 242f., 245, 247, 249, 258, 261, 265–267, 274–277, 281, 289–291, 297f., 301, 302–306, 308–312, 317–319, 323–326, 329–331, 333f.
Reflection 4, 7f., 13, 16, 20, 39, 43, 52, 57, 60–62, 75, 95f., 137, 145f., 162, 171, 189f., 193f., 196, 210, 229, 249, 258, 275, 288, 297, 299, 304, 312, 317, 320, 331, 333, 339
Relativism 66, 84, 175–178, 181, 325
Relevance 16–18, 21, 52, 85, 129, 132, 135, 138, 145, 152, 177, 192, 205, 215–217, 226, 229, 238, 248f., 255f., 259, 276, 298f., 301, 328
Reliability 6, 52, 129f., 137–139, 141–146, 174, 178, 205, 225, 338, 341
Religion 3, 16, 66, 109, 115, 175, 181, 183
Replication 24, 75f., 93
Research 3–5, 7f., 12, 16–20, 23–25, 35, 37f., 40–44, 46–67, 75–96, 119, 129, 141–146, 161f., 184, 189, 191f., 195, 198–201, 206–208, 211–213, 220, 222f., 226, 229, 237f., 241f., 246f., 249, 274f., 280, 291, 295–297, 299–

302, 304f., 307–312, 320, 330f., 337–339
– Empirical Research   1, 3–5, 8, 11, 13–25, 35, 40, 49, 65, 67, 75–78, 80, 82, 90f., 93, 95f., 115, 145f., 189–193, 209, 214, 217, 220–222, 224, 226, 230f., 237, 244, 273, 275, 296f., 312, 317f., 320, 325, 329f., 332, 334, 337–339
– Qualitative Research   4f., 8, 35f., 43, 49f., 52–55, 58, 60, 62, 64, 77, 83f., 86, 88, 94f., 109, 113, 117, 191, 210, 247, 260, 295, 310–312, 337
– Quantitative Research   4, 8, 40, 43, 50, 80f., 83f., 86, 88, 95, 109f., 113, 117, 191, 210, 295, 310–312, 331, 337
Resource   8, 12, 41f., 91, 134f., 141, 216, 224, 238, 246, 248, 251, 254, 267, 273, 275–290, 295–298, 300f., 304–306, 310–312
Responsibility   8, 25, 38, 42–47, 92, 134, 246, 254, 267, 273, 275, 278f., 282f., 291, 295, 301, 341
Revolution   114, 175, 179, 339, 341
Rightfulness   205f., 226, 229
Rokeach Value Survey   66f.

Salience   132, 244, 251, 255, 291
Sample   18, 67, 82–86, 120f., 171–173, 176, 179, 250, 281f., 308f., 312
Scholasticism   12, 317
Schwartz Value Survey   67
Science   1–7, 11f., 14–17, 19, 21, 24, 35–38, 40, 44, 46, 49, 51–54, 60–62, 65, 75–81, 83–93, 96, 105f., 108, 119, 124, 153, 169–173, 176f., 180, 182f., 185, 261–263, 267, 270, 296, 317, 319
– Advent of Modern Sciences   4, 11, 14, 36, 318
– Cognitive Science   317
– Political Science   19
– Scientific Misconduct   76
– Scientific Practice   12f., 80
– Scientific Theory   6, 15, 107f., 169f., 173, 179, 184, 189
– Social Science   3–5, 7, 11, 14, 37, 50, 66, 75–78, 82–84, 86, 91, 95, 105f., 116,

118–120, 123, 170, 184, 189, 191, 211f., 226, 240, 337
Semantics   13, 169, 173, 182, 197, 325
Sentimentalism   136
Social Choice Theory   7, 237–239, 267, 298, 300, 302, 306
– Empirical Social Choice   8, 238, 246, 250, 267, 295–300, 302–309, 311f.
Socialisation   12, 38, 176, 178
Sociology   5, 14, 50f., 53, 56, 66, 75, 95, 110, 175f., 179, 193, 209, 213, 221, 224, 229, 329
Sovereignty   176, 319f., 324, 329, 332
Spectator   7, 106, 120, 237–246, 249, 255, 258f., 261, 265–267, 307, 309
Standard   7, 40, 45f., 49, 52, 58, 76, 83–85, 91, 93, 95, 108, 120, 153–159, 161, 164, 170, 175f., 198, 231, 237f., 247, 260f., 264f., 277, 298, 341
Statement   13, 15f., 40, 45–47, 86, 131, 139, 141, 143, 145, 172, 189, 195–200, 203, 226, 300, 304
Statistics   49, 64, 76, 84–87, 93, 118, 244, 249, 257, 310
– Statistical Power   94
– Statistical Significance   81, 84–86, 89, 93, 245, 247f., 251, 256, 258f., 261f., 265–267
Status   5, 88, 105, 107, 109f., 112–118, 123, 137, 145, 180, 183, 185, 209, 274
Structure   7, 16, 23, 39f., 43, 45, 47–49, 54, 59–62, 66, 80f., 87, 90, 108, 121, 133, 189, 194f., 197f., 203–206, 209–211, 213–215, 217–220, 222–225, 229, 240, 267, 297, 300f., 305, 322, 338
– Deep Structure   194, 197–199, 203, 205f.
– Surface Structure   197–199, 202
Subjectivity   1, 7, 37–39, 43, 47, 51, 55, 60, 65f., 77, 82f., 87, 89, 94f., 135, 181, 189, 195, 199, 208, 237, 241f., 299
Survey   6, 13, 17, 53, 55, 62, 95, 105, 110, 113, 119f., 123, 211f., 214, 220f., 223, 226, 238, 240, 246–250, 252, 255, 275, 280, 288, 290, 296–298, 301, 307f., 312, 338
Sustainability   41, 46–49
– Social Sustainability   5, 35, 47–49

Theory 3–8, 11–13, 15–21, 23–25, 35–39, 47, 50, 52, 56, 60, 64, 65f., 75–79, 82, 86f., 89–93, 105–109, 111–118, 120–123, 129–132, 138f., 144f., 153f., 156–158, 163, 165, 169–184, 189, 191–193, 197, 203f., 207–209, 213, 218f., 226, 229, 236, 238–246, 251, 253, 266f., 273–304, 308–312, 317f., 331, 337–339
– Deductive Theory 51, 86, 105, 107–109, 112–115, 123
– Deep Theory 171, 173, 178–180, 183
– Evolutionary Theory 12, 129, 179, 305, 318, 322
– Folk Theory 17, 171–174, 176f., 179–181, 183
– Moral Theory 6, 16, 151–157, 159, 163f., 190–193, 212
– Normative Theory 1, 3, 5, 7, 11, 13–15, 17–25, 35–41, 44–46, 49f., 52–55, 65, 67, 189–195, 207, 209, 225f., 229f., 239, 244, 249, 267, 273f., 291, 298, 312, 337, 339
– Theory Building 12, 15f., 21, 77, 190
– Theory Justification 6, 169, 171, 173, 178
– Theory of Justice 19, 105, 109, 123, 164f., 239f., 247, 275–277, 290f., 300, 302f., 308f.
– Theory of Science 3, 12, 14
Therapy 36, 39f., 41–43, 55, 161
Transparency 5, 56, 75, 90f., 121, 197, 296, 333

Truth 4, 9, 11, 13, 16, 18f., 49, 59, 76f., 95, 106, 131, 135, 138f., 142f., 145, 170, 181f., 203f., 290, 323, 326, 329, 337, 339–341

Universalism 14, 67, 121, 181
– Moral Universalism 66f., 181, 210, 327
Utilitarianism 152f., 174f., 177–180, 193, 195, 241, 276, 307
– Act Utilitarianism 174–177, 179
– Rule Utilitarianism 175

Vagueness 57, 62, 87
Validity 7, 19, 24, 52, 78, 82, 134, 189, 194–196, 199f., 203–215, 217–231, 267, 302, 328, 338, 341
Value 1, 3f., 11, 13, 15, 19, 22, 35–40, 42f., 60, 65–67, 77f., 82, 84, 86, 88–90, 92, 94–96, 110, 113, 117, 135, 137, 143f., 154f., 163, 170, 176f., 181, 191–193, 200f., 203, 207, 209f., 224, 229, 237, 242, 244, 247, 249, 251f., 254f., 258f., 262, 264f., 280f., 290, 298, 305f., 310, 326, 337f.
Veil of Ignorance 19, 120, 164, 239–243, 303, 309f.
Verification 53, 178
Vienna Circle 77
Vote 87, 118, 213, 239, 243, 295, 297–299, 341

Zeitgeist 12, 24

www.ingramcontent.com/pod-product-compliance
Lightning Source LLC
Chambersburg PA
CBHW032101230426
43662CB00034B/128